Ancient Language Processing Workshop (RANLP-ALP 2023)

Varna, Bulgaria
8 September 2023

ISBN: 978-1-7138-9044-7

Printed from e-media with permission by:

Curran Associates, Inc.
57 Morehouse Lane
Red Hook, NY 12571

Some format issues inherent in the e-media version may also appear in this print version.

Association for Computational Linguistics
209 N. Eighth Street
Stroudsburg, Pennsylvania 18360

Phone: 1-570-476-8006
Fax: 1-570-476-0860

acl@aclweb.org

Additional copies of this publication are available from:

Curran Associates, Inc.
57 Morehouse Lane
Red Hook, NY 12571 USA
Phone: 845-758-0400
Fax: 845-758-2633
Email: curran@proceedings.com
Web: www.proceedings.com

RANLP-ALP 2023

Proceedings of the Ancient Language Processing Workshop

associated with

The 14th International Conference on Recent Advances in Natural Language Processing RANLP 2023

8 September, 2023
Varna, Bulgaria

ANCIENT LANGUAGE PROCESSING WORKSHOP
ASSOCIATED WITH THE 14TH INTERNATIONAL CONFERENCE
RECENT ADVANCES IN
NATURAL LANGUAGE PROCESSING (RANLP 2023)

PROCEEDINGS

8 September 2023
Varna, Bulgaria

Designed by INCOMA Ltd.
Shoumen, BULGARIA

Preface

The First Workshop on Ancient Language Processing (ALP-2023) is co-located with the fourteenth edition of Recent Advance in Natural Language Processing (RANLP) in Varna, Bulgaria on 8 September, 2023.

Ancient languages function as stores of the historical and cultural legacy of humanity. In recent years, significant advancements have been made through the utilization of language technologies in the analysis and interpretation of archaic languages. The purpose of the workshop is to establish a reputable platform for both scholars and practitioners, facilitating the exchange of their most recent research findings and fostering meaningful discussions.

The workshop has received thirty-six submissions covering a wide variety of ancient languages, including Ancient Chinese, Ancient Tibetan, Ancient Greek, Latin, Etruscan, Akkadian, Sumerian, Ancient Syriac, Ancient Hebrew, Basquenglish, Classical Arabic, Meroitic, Middle High German, Pali, and Sanskrit. Among these, Latin, Greek, ancient Chinese, and Sumerian are prominently featured. Within the realm of natural language processing, this collection of papers employs techniques that encompass a diverse range of methodologies, spanning from qualitative analyses and corpus construction strategies to sophisticated machine learning algorithms.

We have accepted sixteen papers for oral presentations and nine for poster presentations. The topics of the accepted submissions include: morphological analysis, POS-tagging and lemmatization, parsing, evaluation of LLMs, text annotation, corpus construction, distributional semantic models, emotion recognition, machine translation, corrupted text correction, hand-written text recognition, intertextual identification, stylistic analysis, named entity recognition, input method, and NLP pipeline systems. The quality resonating through these submissions is genuinely commendable, highlighting the excellence that characterizes the content of this workshop.

The field of ancient language processing is witnessing an expanding research community, driven by the increasing availability of ancient language resources and the growing interest of scholars with machine learning expertise in this domain. The strong turnout in the inaugural year of the ALP workshop serves as a testament to this trend. Hence, we are confident that this event will continue to thrive, fostering an environment for dynamic discussions and interdisciplinary collaborations in both the research and applications of this domain.

We extend our gratitude to the members of the Program Committee for their exhaustive reviews, including the acceptance of additional reviews. We are also appreciative of the RANLP conference chairs, whose tremendous and timely assistance proved invaluable. Last but not the least, we would like to extend our thanks to the student voluteers: Bolin Chang, Zhixiao Zhao, Yutong Zhang, Yixuan Zhang, Kaixin Yin, Feng Xie, and Zhixing Xu.

The ALP-2023 Organizers

Adam Anderson, UC Berkeley, USA
Shai Gordin, Ariel University, Israel
Stav Klein, Tel Aviv University, Israel
Bin Li, Nanjing Normal University, China
Yudong Liu, Western Washington University, USA
Marco C. Passarotti, Università Cattolica del Sacro Cuore, Italy

Organizers:

Adam Anderson (UC Berkeley, USA)
Shai Gordin (Ariel University, Israel)
Stav Klein (Tel Aviv University, Israel)
Bin Li (Nanjing Normal University, China)
Yudong Liu (Western Washington University, USA)
Marco C. Passarotti (Università Cattolica del Sacro Cuore, Italy)

Programme Committee:

Alaa Mamdouh Akef (Beking University, China)
Masayuki Asahara (National Institute for Japanese Language and Linguistics, Japan)
Jonathan Berant (Tel Aviv University, Israel)
Monica Berti (Leipzig University, Germany)
Gregory Crane (Tufts University, USA)
Sanhong Deng (Nanjing University, China)
Minxuan Feng (Nanjing Normal University, China)
Toon Van Hal (University of Leuven, Belgium)
Renfen Hu (Beijing Normal University, China)
Heidi Jauhiainen (University of Helsinki, Finland)
Kyle P. Johnson (Berlin-Brandenburg Academy of Sciences, Germany)
Orly Lewis (Hebrew University of Jerusalem, Israel)
Johann-Mattis List (Max Planck Institute for Evolutionary Anthropology, Germany)
Chao-Lin Liu (National Chengchi University, Taiwan)
Liu Liu (Nanjing Agricultural University, China)
Congjun Long (Chinese Academy of Social Sciences, China))
Longlong Ma (University of Chinese Academy of Sciences, China)
Francesco Mambrini (Università Cattolica del Sacro Cuore, Milan, Italy)
Martijn Naaijer (University of Copenhagen, Denmark)
Christian M. Prager (University of Bonn, Germany)
Luis Sáenz (Ariel University/Heidelberg University, Israel/Germany)
Si Shen (Nanjing University of Science and Technology, China)
Thea Sommerschield (Ca' Foscari University of Venice, Italy)
Rachele Sprugnoli (Università degli Studi di Parma, Italy)
Qi Su (Peking University, China)
Xurui Tang (Huazhong University of Science and Technology China)
Niek Veldhuis (University of California, Berkeley, USA)
Dongbo Wang (Nanjing Agricultural University, China)

Invited Speakers:

Dr. Chu-ren Huang (The HongKong Polytechnic University, China)
Dr. Thea Sommerschield (Ca' Foscari University of Venice, Italy)
Dr. Gabriel Stanovsky (Hebrew University of Jerusalem, Israel)

Table of Contents

Program

Friday, Sept 8, 2023

9:00–9:10 ***Opening Remarks***

9:10–9:40 **Invited Talk** by Chu-Ren Huang: *Processing of a 'living' ancient language: Issues and Insights from Chinese*

9:40–10:55 **Oral Session 1:**

9:40–9:55 *Training and Evaluation of Named Entity Recognition Models for Classical Latin*
Marijke Beersmans, Evelien de Graaf, Tim Van de Cruys and Margherita Fantoli

9:55–10:10 *Sentence Embedding Models for Ancient Greek Using Multilingual Knowledge Distillation*
Kevin Krahn, Derrick Tate and Andrew C. Lamicela

10:10–10:25 *A Transformer-based parser for Syriac morphology*
Martijn Naaijer, Constantijn Sikkel, Mathias Coeckelbergs, Jisk Attema and Willem Th. Van Peursen

10:25–10:40 *Graecia capta ferum victorem cepit. Detecting Latin Allusions to Ancient Greek Literature*
Frederick Riemenschneider and Anette Frank

10:40–10:55 *Larth: Dataset and Machine Translation for Etruscan*
Gianluca Vico and Gerasimos Spanakis

Friday, Sept 8, 2023 (continued)

10:55–11:15 Coffee break

11:15–12:00 Oral Session 2:

11:15–11:30 *Evaluation of Distributional Semantic Models of Ancient Greek: Preliminary Results and a Road Map for Future Work*
Silvia Stopponi, Nilo Pedrazzini, Saskia Peels, Barbara McGillivray and Malvina Nissim

11:30–11:45 *Latin Morphology through the Centuries: Ensuring Consistency for Better Language Processing*
Federica Gamba and Daniel Zeman

11:45–12:00 *Cross-Lingual Constituency Parsing for Middle High German: A Delexicalized Approach*
Ercong Nie, Helmut Schmid and Hinrich Schütze

12:00–13:00 Poster Session

Can Large Langauge Model Comprehend Ancient Chinese? A Preliminary Test on ACLUE
Yixuan Zhang and Haonan Li

Unveiling Emotional Landscapes in Plautus and Terentius Comedies: A Computational Approach for Qualitative Analysis
Davide Picca and Caroline Richard

Morphological and Semantic Evaluation of Ancient Chinese Machine Translation
Kai Jin, Dan Zhao and Wuying Liu

A tailored Handwritten-Text-Recognition System for Medieval Latin
Philipp Koch, Gilary Vera Nuñez, Esteban Garces Arias, Christian Heumann, Matthias Schöffel, Alexander Häberlin and Matthias Assenmacher

Evaluating Existing Lemmatisers on Unedited Byzantine Greek Poetry
Colin Swaelens, Ilse De Vos and Els Lefever

Vector Based Stylistic Analysis on Ancient Chinese Books: Take the Three Commentaries on the Spring and Autumn Annals as an Example
Yue Qi, Liu Liu, Bin Li and Dongbo Wang

Friday, Sept 8, 2023 (continued)

	A Joint Model of Automatic Word Segmentation and Part-Of-Speech Tagging for Ancient Classical Texts Based on Radicals Bolin Chang, Yiguo Yuan, Bin Li, Zhixing Xu, Minxuan Feng and Dongbo Wang
	Introducing an Open Source Library for Sumerian Text Analysis Hansel Guzman-Soto and Yudong Liu
	Coding Design of Oracle Bone Inscriptions Input Method Based on "ZhongHuaZiKu" Database Dongxin Hu
13:00–14:30	**Lunch break**
14:30–15:00	**Invited Talk** by Thea Sommerschield: *When the past meets the future at Odessus*
15:00–16:00	**Oral Session 3:**
15:00–15:15	*Word Sense Disambiguation for Ancient Greek: Sourcing a training corpus through translation alignment* Alek Keersmaekers, Wouter Mercelis and Toon Van Hal
15:15–15:30	*Enhancing State-of-the-Art NLP Models for Classical Arabic* Tariq Yousef, Lisa Mischer, Hamid Reza Hakimi and Maxim Romanov
15:30–15:45	*Logion: Machine-Learning Based Detection and Correction of Textual Errors in Greek Philology* Charlie Cowen-Breen, Creston Brooks, Barbara Graziosi and Johannes Haubold
15:45–16:00	*Classical Philology in the Time of AI: Exploring the Potential of Parallel Corpora in Ancient Languages* Tariq Yousef, Chiara Palladino and Farnoosh Shamsian

Friday, Sept 8, 2023 (continued)

Training and Evaluation of Named Entity Recognition Models for Classical Latin

Marijke Beersmans and **Evelien de Graaf** and **Tim Van de Cruys** and **Margherita Fantoli**
KU Leuven, Faculty of Arts
Blijde Inkomststraat 21, 3000 Leuven, Belgium
marijke.beersmans@kuleuven.be
evelien.degraaf@kuleuven.be
tim.vandecruys@kuleuven.be
margherita.fantoli@kuleuven.be

Abstract

We evaluate the performance of various models on the task of named entity recognition (NER) for classical Latin. Using an existing dataset, we train two transformer-based LatinBERT models and one shallow conditional random field (CRF) model. The performance is assessed using both standard metrics and a detailed manual error analysis, and compared to the results obtained by different already released Latin NER tools. Both analyses demonstrate that the BERT models achieve a better f1-score than the other models. Furthermore, we annotate new, unseen data for further evaluation of the models, and we discuss the impact of annotation choices on the results.

1 Introduction

Commonly an important precursor to information extraction, text summarisation and the creation of knowledge bases, Named Entity Recognition (NER) has become a ubiquitous task in Natural Language Processing (NLP). For modern high-resource languages, generic NER off-the-shelf solutions, focusing mainly on identifying locations, organizations and people, can produce highly accurate annotations. For historical languages, even prolific ones like Latin, the task remains a challenge, in part due to a lack of annotated corpora and tools (Ehrmann et al., 2021).

We pursue three main objectives with this paper:

- We compare the performance of three different models for Latin NER using pre-existing, openly available data. The comparison is both quantitative and qualitative.
- Based on the analysis of existing annotations and the results of automatic annotation, we publish a new set of **gold data**, providing documentation of the most critical choices.
- By using the newly annotated data to assess the results of NER, we publish the **automatic annotation** by the best-performing model of a large corpus of literary classical Latin texts and documenting the strengths and weaknesses of the resulting annotation.

The paper contributes to the application of NLP to Latin on a methodological level, since we propose a thorough analysis of the results of NER on Latin and identify the most critical points. In addition, the paper is associated with the publication of NER models and datasets, and documents the choices that have been implemented. The paper is structured as follows: after introducing existing work and datasets related to NER for Classical Languages (Section 2), we describe the data used, and the training of the models and their performance on in-domain and out-of-domain test sets (Section 3). Section 4 provides a qualitative error analysis of the best performing model based on F1 metrics. In section 5, we introduce the annotation of new data from the LASLA corpus, and analyse the results of the automatic annotation by the best-performing model. The data and code related to this paper are made available on a Github repository.[1]

2 Related work

Previous work has highlighted the challenges linked to NER for Latin. Ehrmann et al. (2021) identified among others the following relevant challenges concerning NER on historical documents: variable and sparse feature space (generalizing over different genres and domains, cf. Erdmann et al. (2016)), dynamics of language such as spelling variations and change in naming conventions, general lack of resources (e.g. typologies from modern languages not fitting for historical documents). In addition, Burns (2023) underlined another difficulty of the already scarce resources: differences in orthographic conventions and annotation

[1] https://github.com/NER-AncientLanguages/Ner-Latin-RANLP.

Proceedings of the Ancient Language Processing Workshop associated with RANLP-2023, pages 1–12,
held in Varna Bulgaria, Sept 8, 2023.
https://doi.org/10.26615/978-954-452-087-8_001

schemes. Lastly, both Chastang et al. (2021) and Torres Aguilar (2022) consider the frequency of overlapped and nested entities in Latin as a challenge.

When it comes to existing models, Chastang et al. (2021) trained a CRF-based model on Latin medieval charters from Burgundy. Later Torres Aguilar (2022) tested two approaches for creating a multilingual pipeline for medieval charters (French, Spanish and Latin): the first uses contextual and static embeddings coupled to a BiLSTM-CRF (Bidirectional Long-Short Term Memory) classifier, and the second employs a fine-tuning method using the pre-trained multilingual BERT and RoBERTa models. For both of these efforts, custom charter corpora were annotated. In the context of the Herodotos project — which aims to catalogue ancient ethno-political groups and their interactions — Erdmann et al. (2016, 2019) created a neural, BiLSTM-CRF based entity recognizer (Lample et al., 2016) trained on classical Latin texts. In addition, NER is included in text analysis pipelines for Latin, such as the Classical Language Toolkit (CLTK; Johnson et al., 2021) and LatinCy (Burns, 2023).

In recent years, transformer-based models (with the BERT architecture as one of the prime instantiations) have become the norm for various NLP applications (Ehrmann et al., 2022; Sprugnoli et al., 2022; Sommerschield et al., 2023). These models have been leveraged, *inter alia*, for Latin morphosyntactic tagging (Wróbel and Nowak, 2022; Mercelis and Keersmaekers, 2022; Nehrdich, 2022) and translation alignment for ancient languages (Yousef et al., 2022b), which could also be leveraged for named entity projection from modern languages given a parallel corpus (Yousef et al., 2023). For Greek NER, a BERT-based approach equally proved to be effective (Yousef et al., 2022a). There already exists a transformer-based model for Latin (LatinBERT; Bamman and Burns, 2020) but to the best of our knowledge, it has not yet been fine-tuned on the task of named entity recognition.

Regarding datasets, the Herodotos dataset (at the time of training) is the only available NER dataset for classical Latin (Erdmann et al., 2019, 2023). Additionally, the authors of the LatinCy pipeline are planning to make their custom dataset publicly available (Burns, 2023). Lastly, the multilingual Medieval charter dataset, which includes non-classical Latin (Torres Aguilar, 2022), is available online.[2] We decided to annotate new material to augment the availability of data for classical Latin.

text	# tokens
BGall.	58,621
NH	35,672
Ep.	18,571
Ars am.	17,102
BCiv.	4,819

Table 1: Number of tokens per text in the Herodotos dataset

3 Data and methods

3.1 Data

The Herodotos dataset contains two full texts, Caesar's *Bellum Gallicum* (*BGall.*) and Ovid's *Ars Amatoria* (*Ars am.*), and excerpts from three other texts: a part of the first book of Caesar's *Bellum Civile* (*BCiv.*); book 1, book 2 and a part of book 3 of Pliny the Younger's *Epistulae* (*Ep.*); the preface, first and a part of the second book of Pliny the Elder's *Naturalis Historia* (*NH*). The editions were taken from the Latin Library (Carey, s.d.) and the Perseus Project (Smith et al., 2000). Table 1 contains an overview of the dataset sizes.

The texts are manually annotated for location ('LOC'), person ('PERS') and (socio-ethnic) group ('GRP') entities (Erdmann et al., 2016). The annotations are encoded in BIO-format, where each token is mapped to an 'O' (for 'outside', not an entity) or an entity type with either a B- or an I-prefix. The B-prefix, for 'beginning', indicates the first or only word of an entity whereas the I-prefix, for 'inside', specifies a continuation of a multi-word entity. Nested entities were not considered.

On the whole dataset, minimal preprocessing was performed to iron out formatting mistakes. Afterwards, the five works were divided into two parts: in-domain, used for training and in-domain testing, and out-domain, used exclusively for out-domain testing. The latter should assess the model's generalizing capabilities to texts that are significantly different from the data it was trained on. In this experiment, the in-domain part consisted of the prose texts, (*BGall.*, *Bciv.*, *Ep.* and *NH.*) The out-domain part consisted of the one poetry text, *Ars. Am.*.

[2] https://gitlab.com/magistermilitum/ner_medieval_multilingual/

type	frequency	
	Train	Validation
O	82,696	13,846
B-PERS	2,706	473
I-PERS	618	125
B-LOC	839	169
I-LOC	31	10
B-GRP	1,271	207
I-GRP	4	2

Table 2: Frequency of entity types in train (left) and validation set (right)

The in-domain texts were then split into three sets: a training set (75%), a validation set (12.5%) and an in-domain test set (12.5%). As the BERT-model processes input on the sentence level, the sentence order was randomized. The sentences containing rare multi-word locations and groups were identified and split separately. Each of those splits was later appended to one of the three sets to ensure that each contained entities of every type. The frequencies of the entity types can be found in Table 2 (train and validation split) and in the 'support' column of Table 5 (test split).

To ensure representative testing, the data was augmented with manually annotated test sets from the LASLA corpus in the second part of this paper (see Section 5), both for in-domain prose and out-domain poetry.

3.2 Model training and evaluation

We created two models on the Herodotos dataset and compared the results of these models to those obtained using the recently released LatinCy toolkit. The models we trained (finetuned) ourselves are:

- A conditional random field (CRF) model. Erdmann et al. (2016) use a CRF-based baseline in a similar context. This model is fairly simple and will serve as a starting point for comparison.
- LatinBERT (Bamman and Burns, 2020), a specialized BERT model for Latin, trained using the Masked Language Modeling objective on a corpus of 642.7M words, ranging from classical Latin (from 200 BCE onwards) to Neolatin from Wikipedia. We made use of the pre-trained model, and finetuned it on the NER dataset.

The results of these models are compared to LatinCy, a SpaCy pipeline for Latin, and for the LASLA test set (see below) to the Herodotos entity recognizer (Erdmann et al., 2016) as well. In order to train several SpaCy pipelines (Honnibal and Montani, 2017) for Latin (viz. a *small*, *medium* and *large* model), Burns (2023) leveraged the five Latin Universal Dependencies treebanks and several large Latin corpora. LatinCy's named entity recognizers were trained separately from the rest of their respective pipelines, on a custom-made dataset based on the UD treebanks and the dataset of the Herodotos project. For this paper, we tested the *large* ('la_core_web_lg') pipeline, as well as the 'la_core_web_trf' pipeline, which is backed by the multilingual BERT transformer architecture (Devlin et al., 2018).

The next two subsections describe the training setup for our models; section 3.3 discusses the results of the models we trained, as well as a comparison to LatinCy's performance.

3.2.1 CRF

For the CRF model, we made use of an implementation based on CRFsuite (Okazaki, 2007). We specified the optimization method as *l-bfgs*, set the maximum number of iterations to 100 and considered all possible transitions, The following hand-crafted features are incorporated: whether the word is a digit, capitalised or fully upper-cased; whether the word is the first or last word of a sentence; the last three letters; the last two letters; a context window of two left words and two right words. Following Palladino et al. (2020), the whole word itself was not included, because this might aid generalization to other contexts.

Hyperparameter optimization was performed using a 50-fold random search, to optimize the two regularisation coefficients $c1$ (search space exponentially distributed on scale 0.5) and $c2$ (search space exponentially distributed on scale 0.05). The best hyperparameters were 0.183 and 0.086 for $c1$ and $c2$ respectively.

3.2.2 LatinBERT

Prior to the finetuning of LatinBERT, we incorporated the original subword tokenizer into our own, custom tokenizer to ensure the model was fully compatible with the *transformers* library (Wolf et al., 2020). All words were lowercased during tokenization. We proceeded to utilize the *transformers* trainer API both with and without hyperpa-

Hyperpar.	Initial	Optimized
Learning rate	2.00e-5	7.89e-5
Weight decay	0.01	0.10
Number of train epochs	3	3

Table 3: initial hyperparameters (LatinBERT1) vs. optimised hyperparameters (LatinBERT2)

rameter optimization (results reported under LatinBERT2 and LatinBERT1 respectively). During the experiments with hyperparameter optimization, we specified the optimization method as *random*. The metric for evaluation is the *validation loss*, and the goal is to minimize it based on a ten-fold search. Table 3 provides a comparison of the hyperparameters used. In both cases the per-device train batch size is 16 and the warmup ratio is 0.1.

3.3 Results

In Table 4 we report the micro-averaged f1 (or accuracy) based on the token labeling. The micro-averaged f1 computes the proportion of correctly classified observations out of all observations. In Table 5, for every entity type ('PERS', 'LOC', 'GRP'), we report the f1 score (harmonic mean of precision and recall) on the entity level, where the full entity is only considered correct if the annotations for all its comprising tokens match the gold standard exactly, and the macro f1, where the results for each model are averaged across the various labels without taking class size into account. In Appendix A, more detailed counts per label are provided (Table 10).

The overall results in Table 4 show that there is a drop in performance going from in- to out-of-domain, signaling a difficulty to generalize from prose to poetry. Both LatinBERTs outperform the other models in- and out-of-domain. However, it is important to note that optimizing the hyperparameters causes a slight increase in macro-f1 on the in-domain dataset, but a symmetrical, decrease on the out-of-domain dataset. Looking at the entity level metrics in Table 5, 'PERS' is the class that is the easiest to predict for every model. For the models exclusively trained on the Herodotos data (the CRF and LatinBERTs), single word groups are a relatively well-understood category in-domain, but cause problems out-of-domain. Unfortunately, no multi-token 'GRP' were correctly detected, which can be explained by their rarity. Multi-token 'LOC' are also rarely detected, with only the BERT models being able to recognize some in-domain (See again Table 10).

4 Error analysis

4.1 Ambiguous annotations in the training data

Although guidelines for named entities in classical scholarship exist (Romanello and Najem-Meyer, 2022), for classical Latin texts, they are still lacking (see Section 5). This is reflected in our dataset. We can hypothesize that this impacts the overall performance of the models. In particular, some tokens are annotated as different entities throughout the dataset. In some cases, this is due to the inherent ambiguity of the token, as in the following examples:

- **Homonyms**: *Galli* (genitive singular of 'Gallus', name of a man) as 'PERS' in *Ars am.* 3.334 or 'GRP' in *BGall.* 1.1 ('the Gauls');
- Tokens that occur both as **entity and non-entity** in the dataset: e.g. *Liber* (a divinity, but also 'book'), forms of *Sol* (divinity 'Sun' and the sun), and *Gratia* ('grace', but also the divinity 'Grace') appear both as entities (personifications, usually capitalized) and non-entities (regular use);
- **Patronyms** such as *Atrides* ('descendant of Atreus'): sometimes forms of these refer to one specific person, sometimes to a group.

In other cases, the differences seem to stem from inconsistent annotation choices:

- Multi-token entities that contain a toponym: e.g. the entity *Amphilocho Athenaeo* ('Amphilochus of Athens') in *NH* is annotated both as 'B-PERS B-GRP' and as 'B-PERS I-PERS'; or a building with a name *aedem Larum* ('the temple of the Lares', *NH* 2.5) is annotated as 'O B-GRP', while *aedem Feroniae* ('the temple of Feronia', *NH* 2.56) is annotated as 'B-LOC I-LOC';
- Persons referred to with only a toponym: e.g. *Cressa* ('the Cretan woman', *Ars am.* 1.327) is annotated as 'B-GRP', while *Cynthius* ('the Cynthian', *Ars am.* 2.239) is annotated as 'LOC';
- Unnamed entities annotated in some cases and not in others: e.g. some of the occurrences of

micro f1		CRF	LB1	LB2	LatinCy lg	LatinCy trf	support
Caesar/Pliny's (IN)	BIO-labels	0.98	**0.99**	0.99	0.96	0.95	14,686
	BI-labels	0.79	0.90	**0.92**	0.60	0.58	1,048
***Ars am.* (OUT)**	BIO-labels	0.97	**0.98**	**0.98**	0.96	0.95	17,102
	BI-labels	0.39	**0.65**	0.60	0.39	0.31	570

Table 4: micro f1 on the Herodotos selected test-set; **LB** stands for LatinBERT

		CRF	LB1	LB2	LatinCy lg	LatinCy trf	support
Caesar/Pliny's (IN)	PERS	0.80	0.91	**0.92**	0.64	0.64	474
	LOC	0.66	0.85	**0.87**	0.61	0.54	218
	GRP	0.74	0.89	**0.91**	0.02	0.06	247
	macro f1	0.74	0.88	**0.90**	0.43	0.44	939
***Ars Am.* (OUT)**	PERS	0.44	**0.76**	0.72	0.47	0.36	375
	LOC	0.30	**0.43**	0.38	0.28	0.18	87
	GRP	0.25	**0.45**	0.40	0.00	0.05	107
	macro f1	0.33	**0.54**	0.50	0.25	0.20	569

Table 5: f1-score per entity type on the Herodotos selected test-set

prouincia ('province') and *terra* ('region') are annotated as 'LOC', and some of the occurrences of *equestri* and *praetori* as 'GRP'.

In addition, entire parts of text are not annotated in *Ars am.* and *NH*. The scarcity of data also appears to be a problem: out of the 180 unique tokens that were not correctly identified by any model, 132 do not occur in the training data.

4.2 Qualitative analysis LatinBERT

In this section, we perform a qualitative error analysis of the performance of the two best-performing models, LatinBERT1 and 2, on both the in-domain and out-of-domain sets, in order to better understand the origin of the errors. First, LatinBERT1 and LatinBERT2 share common issues, that are generally not encountered by at least one of the other two models:

- **Boundary detection** proves particularly difficult with lists of names: *Lysiae Demosthenen Aeschinen Hyperiden multosque praeterea, Gracchis et Catoni Pollionem Caesarem Caelium [...]* (*Ep.* 1.20.4). Both models correctly identify 4 separate entities in the first part (*Lysiae .. Hyperiden*) but label '*Pollionem Caesarem Caelium*' as one entity. In addition, we find I-labels predicted for entities not occurring after B-label: for instance, both LatinBERTs predict 'I-LOC' for *Memphitidos* ('of Memphis', *Ars am.* 3.393) ('B-GRP' is the gold data) without assigning 'B-LOC' to a previous token.
- Entities with **foreign names** are often predicted as non-entity: e.g. *Adadu*, *Calymne*, *Therapnaeus*, and *Andromeda*.
- Complete sentences with clear entities predicted as non-entities in out-of-domain data (entities in bold): e.g. *Dextra* ***Lebinthos*** *erat siluisque umbrosa* ***Calymne*** *| Cinctaque piscosis* ***Astypalaea*** *uadis* (*Ars am.* 2.81-2) - non-entity predictions for all entities by LatinBERT2; LatinBERT1 only for *Astypalaea*.

LatinBERT1 and LatinBERT2 differ only in the optimization of the hyperparameters, which seems nonetheless to have a relevant impact on the performance. In a total of 223 cases, the prediction of LatinBERT2 differs from LatinBERT1. Table 8 in Appendix A shows that LatinBERT1 slightly outperforms LatinBERT2 on the label 'B-PERS'. However, in several cases, the prediction of LatinBERT2 classifies the category correctly but with wrong segmentation, predicting 'I-PERS' instead of 'B-PERS', whereas LatinBERT1 also classifies incorrectly. In 46 of the cases where only LatinBERT1 is correct, LatinBERT2 predicts a non-entity. 42 of these tokens did not appear in the train or validation set and the others were either annotated both as entities and 'O' or appeared only once in the training data. Besides this, many differences can be explained by the difficulties in 'GRP'/'LOC' distinction identified in Section 4.1.

5 Annotation of the LASLA corpus

In what follows, we discuss the performance of the same NER models on the LASLA Latin corpus.[3] As the LASLA corpus includes a diverse range of classical Latin texts, it represents an interesting test set to investigate the generalisability of the models. With this procedure, we also establish criteria for the annotation of the most problematic classes. In addition, we augment the test set by including both **prose** and **poetry** works (resp. in-domain and out-of-domain) which do not appear in the training data and that belong to different genres with respect to the training data. Overall, this process allows us to reach conclusions on the urgency of guidelines, of data generation, and the generalisability of existing models across different projects.

The portion of the LASLA corpus used for this experiment is composed of 1,738,435 tokens, belonging to 130 Latin literary texts by 21 authors ranging from the 2nd century BCE to the 2nd century CE. It is linked to the LiLa Knowledge Base, an open-ended Knowledge Base of linguistic Linked Data (Passarotti et al., 2020). The URIs for lemmas and tokens provided by the linking are published to ensure interoperability and reusability of the data.[4]

5.1 Texts annotated

To evaluate the performance of the models on the LASLA corpus, we annotated texts from three different authors. As in-domain data, we chose to annotate Tacitus' *Historiae* (*Hist.*) book 1 and the first of Cicero's *Orationes Philippicae* (*Phil.*) and for out-of-domain the first three of Juvenal's *Saturae* (*Juv.*). Tacitus and Cicero were selected as 'in-domain' data since they belong to non-fictional prose. Moreover, the *Phil.* are a different genre (oratory) than the Herodotos training data and Tacitus (Historiography and Epistolography). Juvenal's poetry, with its mentions of historical people, was selected to challenge the model, since the out-of-domain testing of Ovid's *Ars am.*, on the contrary, primarily mentions mythical persons. Good performance on these texts would indicate the models' generalisability.

5.2 Annotation process and choices

The texts were annotated by two Latin experts using the BIO-format for the entities location, person, and group (see Section 3.1). The Herodotos project annotation was taken as a reference, and the challenging points were discussed in order to address the shortcomings identified in Section 4.1. Cohesion between the annotations of the two experts was guaranteed by joint annotation of 4,463 tokens of the *Saturae* (Juv. 1-3). The Inter-Annotator Agreement (IAA) was calculated using Cohen's Kappa score (Cohen, 1960). The IAA is calculated both including and excluding the label 'O'. The resulting values are 0.87 (incl. 'O') and 0.74 (excl. 'O'). The confusion matrix (excl. 'O') is shown in Figure 1 of the Appendix A. The biggest disagreement concerns the label 'B-GRP'. The difficulties with the annotation of 'GRP' can be divided into two categories: annotation of adjectives derived from toponyms (*Tuscus* - 'Tuscan', *Aegyptius* - 'Egyptian', *Graecus* - 'Greek') and groups of individuals that do not fit the definition of political/ethnic groups as defined by the Herodotos project. Examples of this last category are names of families (e.g *Gracchos* (2.24) - 'The Gracchii'), names used as a generic category (e.g. *Proculas et Pollittas* (2.68) - 'women like Procula and Pollitta'), gods (*Asianorum ... deorum* (3.218) - 'Asian gods'), and other groups such as *Socraticos ... cinaedos* (2.10 - 'Socratic catamites') and *Manes* (2.149 - 'Shades'). For adjectives derived from toponyms, the annotators agreed to use 'GRP' to align with the Herodotos project. For the other categories, 'GRP' is used following the definition of the subcategory 'PER.Group' from the Automatic Content Extraction Guidelines (Consortium, 2008) for any Person entity referring to more than one person. Finally, we chose **not** to annotate nicknames as 'PERS' entities (e.g. *Uenusina ... lucerna* (1.51) - 'The Venusinian light', Horace, was only annotated as 'B-LOC ... O'). Following the first round of joint annotation, an agreement was reached on problematic points to enhance the consistency of the remaining annotation.

[3] https://www.lasla.uliege.be

[4] https://github.com/NER-AncientLanguages/Ner-Latin-RANLP

micro f1		CRF	LB1	LB2	LatinCy lg	Herodotos	support
Tac. and Cic. (IN)	BIO-labels	0.96	0.97	**0.98**	0.96	0.97	15,737
	BI-labels	0.61	0.78	**0.79**	0.66	0.72	1,320
Juv. (OUT)	BIO-labels	0.96	0.96	0.96	0.96	0.96	4,399
	BI-labels	0.45	0.48	0.50	**0.51**	0.48	284

Table 6: micro f1 on the LASLA corpus; **LB** stands for LatinBERT

		CRF	LB1	LB2	LatinCy lg	Herodotos	support
Tac. and Cic. (IN)	PERS	0.65	0.83	**0.85**	0.66	0.74	711
	LOC	0.31	0.51	**0.55**	0.53	0.49	222
	GRP	0.43	0.61	**0.64**	0.02	0.60	154
	macro f1	0.46	0.65	**0.68**	0.40	0.61	1,087
Juvenal (OUT)	PERS	0.48	0.53	**0.64**	0.64	0.59	143
	LOC	0.32	**0.46**	0.36	0.44	0.27	83
	GRP	0.47	0.40	**0.52**	0.00	0.23	36
	macro f1	0.43	0.46	**0.51**	0.36	0.37	262

Table 7: f1-score per entity type & macro f1 on the LASLA corpus

5.3 Results of running the model

Table 6 shows that when labelling single tokens LatinBERT2 outperforms the other models on in-domain data, whereas the models score very close on out-of-domain data, with LatinCY scoring slightly higher than LatinBERT2.[5] Table 7 shows that LatinBERT2 predicts entire entities better than the other models, except for the category 'LOC' on out-of-domain data, where LatinBERT1 performs better. These results confirm LatinBERT2's general good performance, but also its again somewhat unexpected behavior on poetry.

5.4 Error Analysis

5.4.1 Challenging aspects of NER prediction

Similarly as to the Herodotos data, many errors can again be related to the inherent ambiguity of Latin and/or the choices made in annotation (cf. Section 4.1). Both on the in- and out-of-domain LASLA data, errors were made that are related to ambiguous tokens that occur both as entity and non-entity, albeit slightly more present in out-of-domain, e.g. *Pax atque Fides, Uictoria, Uirtus* ('The Goddesses Peace, Faith, Victory and Virtue', Juv. 1.115). Also for the LASLA test-set, tokens annotated differently across the Herodotos training data result in multiple errors. For instance, non-capitalized forms of *prouincia* and *urbs* are annotated as 'LOC' in the training data only when they refer to a precise location. Likewise, *princeps* and *imperator* are annotated as 'PERS' only where they refer to specific emperors. Lastly, words like *domus* and *aedes* are sometimes annotated when they indicate a specific location: for example, *aede Apollinis* - 'the temple of Apollo' and *Tiberianam domum* - 'the palace of Tiberius'. Even though the Herodotos training data are not fully consistent in these annotations, the LASLA annotation did strictly follow these guidelines, which highlighted the inconsistent behavior of models with respect to these points.

5.4.2 Qualitative analysis LatinBERT on the LASLA dataset

In Section 4.2 we observed that LatinBERT1 and LatinBERT2 share common issues, that are generally not encountered by at least one of the other two models. On the LASLA corpus, similar and additional observations can be made. **Boundary**

[5] The major increase in performance of LatinCy on the LASLA data can be explained by two reasons: first, 38% of total errors of LatinCy concern the GRP-entities, of which there are relatively less in the LASLA test data (23.5% of the total entities are 'GRP's in Herodotos, whereas in the LASLA 14.1%); second, many other errors are caused by the tendency of LatinCy to predict entities for any and all capitalized words. In the Herodotos data, all sentences start with a capital, creating many errors for LatinCy; in the LASLA, capitalization is absent, hence such errors do not occur.

detection issues occur in comparable instances on the LASLA corpus, such as predicting separate entities in lists and predicting I-labels for entities not occurring after B-label. However, an additional boundary complication occurs in poetry in difficult nested cases such as the entity *Cecropiam ... Cotyton* (Juv. 1.7-9) separated by the entity *Baptae* occurring in between (this created the annotation 'B-PERS B-GRP I-PERS'). Both LatinBERTs predict a non-entity for *Baptae* and *Cotyton*. As in the Herodotos test set, **foreign names** again proved particularly difficult, in the LASLA out-of-domain especially those with a Greek accusative ending in 'n' (e.g. *Euphraten* (Juv. 1.104). Of the 10 tokens with this ending only Deucalion (1.81) is predicted correctly as an entity by LatinBERT1.[6] Lastly, in the out-of-domain data we again find **complete sentences** that contain multiple entities for which non-entities are predicted.

A close analysis of the performance on tokens where the manual annotation differed shows some additional challenging categories. Of the 69 tokens where the manual annotation differed, LatinBERT1 got 39 wrong (accounting for 20.5% of its total errors), and LatinBERT2 got 41 wrong (accounting for 22.5% of its total errors). For instance, both LatinBERTs predict 'O' for most **groups of individuals** that did not fit the political/ethnical 'GRP' category, except for some family names (e.g. *Catuli, Fabii*). For **Literary works** identified by a personal name, another category where the annotators disagreed but were eventually not annotated, LatinBERT2 predicts an entity but LatinBERT1 'O' (e.g. *Theseide* (1.2); *Heracleas | aut Diomedeas* (1.52-3)). Lastly, for the category of persons referred to with only a toponym, also identified as an issue in Section 4.1, we annotated 'LOC' but the LatinBERTs predicted 'GRP': e.g. *non Maurus erat neque Sarmata nec Thrax* ('it was not a Moroccan nor a Sarmatian nor a Thracian', 3.79).

The comparison between the two LatinBERTs shows that on the in-domain LASLA data, LatinBERT2 outperforms LatinBERT1, especially on I-labels (cf. Appendix A, Table 9). When considering I-label errors, both LatinBERTs classify the category correctly for more than half of these errors (40 out of 78 for LatinBERT1; 32 out of 62 for LatinBERT2), but wrongly assign the 'B-' label: the problem thus lies again with the **boundary detection**. On the out-of-domain data, LatinBERT2 outperforms LatinBERT1 in the 'B-PERS' category. As on the Herodotos project test data, in the majority cases where only LatinBERT1 is correct, LatinBERT2 predicts a non-entity: for the in-domain set 22 out of 27 total cases concern words absent from the train/validation set, for out-of-domain 16 out of 18.

This analysis confirmed that the categories identified in Section 4.2 are difficult for NER. It also emphasised the differences between in- and out-of-domain data: models only trained on prose perform worse on poetry due to stylistic and thematic differences.

6 Conclusions and future work

The process of training two new models on existing data, comparing their results on previously and newly annotated data, and comparing their performance to existing models allows us to draw several conclusions. First, the good performance of LatinBERT1 and 2 demonstrates the interest of applying **transformer-based models** for the NER task on Latin. Especially for the category 'PERS' the two models yield satisfactory results. However, the analysis of the annotations and the errors has shown that the **development of guidelines** is crucial to ensure the consistent annotation of datasets that can be reused as training- and test-sets across different projects and for different models. In addition, the significantly worse performance of the models on poetry indicates the need for training data for this specific type of texts. Future work should also consider improving the preprocessing and normalization of training data (e.g. harmonizing the use of the 'v/u' 'i/j' pairs), and testing the use of multilingual BERT models that include Latin (mBERT, XLM-Roberta) (Sprugnoli et al., 2022; Nehrdich, 2022). Likewise, additional linguistic information available in the LASLA corpus (e.g. lemmatization and PoS tagging) might improve the results of the NER. Finally, after we establish a system for Named Entity Disambiguation employing information from existing extensive resources, we will explore the potential of mutual reinforcement, i.e. we will consider whether results from one system can improve the other and vice-versa as argued by Kolitsas et al. (2018).

[6]This is particularly surprising since in the Herodotos test-set LatinBERT1 correctly predicted 29 out of 40 of such forms, and LatinBERT2 22.

References

David Bamman and Patrick J. Burns. 2020. Latin bert: A contextual language model for classical philology. (arXiv:2009.10053). ArXiv:2009.10053 [cs].

Patrick J. Burns. 2023. Latincy: Synthetic trained pipelines for latin nlp. (arXiv:2305.04365). ArXiv:2305.04365 [cs].

William L. Carey. s.d. The latin library. Accessed: July 1st, 2023.

Pierre Chastang, Sergio Torres Aguilar, and Xavier Tannier. 2021. A Named Entity Recognition Model for Medieval Latin Charters. *Digital Humanities Quarterly*, 015(4).

Jacob Cohen. 1960. A Coefficient of Agreement for Nominal Scales. *Educational and Psychological Measurement*, 20(1):37–46.

Linguistic Data Consortium. 2008. ACE (Automatic Content Extraction) English: Annotation Guidelines for Entities.

Jacob Devlin, Ming-Wei Chang, Kenton Lee, and Kristina Toutanova. 2018. BERT: pre-training of deep bidirectional transformers for language understanding. *CoRR*, abs/1810.04805.

Maud Ehrmann, Ahmed Hamdi, Elvys Linhares Pontes, Matteo Romanello, and Antoine Doucet. 2021. Named entity recognition and classification on historical documents: A survey. (arXiv:2109.11406). ArXiv:2109.11406 [cs].

Maud Ehrmann, Matteo Romanello, Sven Najem-Meyer, Antoine Doucet, and Simon Clematide. 2022. Overview of hipe-2022: Named entity recognition and linking in multilingual historical documents. In *Experimental IR Meets Multilinguality, Multimodality, and Interaction*, Lecture Notes in Computer Science, page 423–446, Cham. Springer International Publishing.

Alexander Erdmann, Christopher Brown, Brian Joseph, Mark Janse, Petra Ajaka, Micha Elsner, and Marie-Catherine de Marneffe. 2016. Challenges and solutions for Latin named entity recognition. In *Proceedings of the Workshop on Language Technology Resources and Tools for Digital Humanities (LT4DH)*, pages 85–93, Osaka, Japan. The COLING 2016 Organizing Committee.

Alexander Erdmann, David Joseph Wrisley, Benjamin Allen, Christopher Brown, Sophie Cohen-Bodénès, Micha Elsner, Yukun Feng, Brian Joseph, Béatrice Joyeux-Prunel, and Marie-Catherine de Marneffe. 2019. Practical, efficient, and customizable active learning for named entity recognition in the digital humanities. In *Proceedings of the 2019 Conference of the North American Chapter of the Association for Computational Linguistics: Human Language Technologies, Volume 1 (Long and Short Papers)*, page 2223–2234, Minneapolis, Minnesota. Association for Computational Linguistics.

Alexander Erdmann, David Joseph Wrisley, Benjamin Allen, Christopher Brown, Sophie Cohen-Bodénès, Micha Elsner, Yukun Feng, Brian Joseph, Béatrice Joyeux-Prunel, and Marie-Catherine de Marneffe. 2023. Herodotos-project-latin-ner-tagger-annotation.

Matthew Honnibal and Ines Montani. 2017. spaCy 2: Natural language understanding with Bloom embeddings, convolutional neural networks and incremental parsing. To appear.

Kyle P. Johnson, Patrick J. Burns, John Stewart, Todd Cook, Clément Besnier, and William J. B. Mattingly. 2021. The classical language toolkit: An nlp framework for pre-modern languages. In *Proceedings of the 59th Annual Meeting of the Association for Computational Linguistics and the 11th International Joint Conference on Natural Language Processing: System Demonstrations*, page 20–29, Online. Association for Computational Linguistics.

Nikolaos Kolitsas, Octavian-Eugen Ganea, and Thomas Hofmann. 2018. End-to-End Neural Entity Linking. In *Computational Natural Language Learning*, pages 519–529. Association for Computational Linguistics.

Guillaume Lample, Miguel Ballesteros, Sandeep Subramanian, Kazuya Kawakami, and Chris Dyer. 2016. Neural architectures for named entity recognition. In *Proceedings of the 2016 Conference of the North American Chapter of the Association for Computational Linguistics: Human Language Technologies*, pages 260–270, San Diego, California. Association for Computational Linguistics.

Wouter Mercelis and Alek Keersmaekers. 2022. An ELECTRA model for Latin token tagging tasks. In *Proceedings of the Second Workshop on Language Technologies for Historical and Ancient Languages*, pages 189–192, Marseille, France. European Language Resources Association.

Sebastian Nehrdich. 2022. SansTib, a Sanskrit - Tibetan parallel corpus and bilingual sentence embedding model. In *Proceedings of the Thirteenth Language Resources and Evaluation Conference*, pages 6728–6734, Marseille, France. European Language Resources Association.

Naoaki Okazaki. 2007. Crfsuite: a fast implementation of conditional random fields (crfs).

Chiara Palladino, Farimah Karimi, and Brigitte Mathiak. 2020. Ner on ancient greek with minimal annotation. *https://dh2020.adho.org/*.

Marco Passarotti, Francesco Mambrini, Greta Franzini, Flavio Massimiliano Cecchini, Eleonora Litta, Giovanni Moretti, Paolo Ruffolo, and Rachele Sprugnoli. 2020. Interlinking through lemmas. the lexical collection of the lila knowledge base of linguistic resources for latin. *Studi e Saggi Linguistici*, 58(1):177–212.

Matteo Romanello and Sven Najem-Meyer. 2022. Guidelines for the annotation of named entities in the domain of classics.

David A. Smith, Jeffrey A. Rydberg-Cox, and G. Crane. 2000. The perseus project: a digital library for the humanities. *Literary and Linguistic Computing*.

Thea Sommerschield, Yannis Assael, John Pavlopoulos, Vanessa Stefanak, Andrew Senior, Chris Dyer, John Bodel, Jonathan Prag, Ion Androutsopoulos, and Nando de Freitas. 2023. Machine learning for ancient languages: A survey. *Computational Linguistics*, page 1–44.

Rachele Sprugnoli, Marco Passarotti, Flavio Massimiliano Cecchini, Margherita Fantoli, and Giovanni Moretti. 2022. Overview of the EvaLatin 2022 evaluation campaign. In *Proceedings of the Second Workshop on Language Technologies for Historical and Ancient Languages*, pages 183–188, Marseille, France. European Language Resources Association.

Sergio Torres Aguilar. 2022. Multilingual named entity recognition for medieval charters using stacked embeddings and bert-based models. In *Proceedings of the Second Workshop on Language Technologies for Historical and Ancient Languages*, page 119–128, Marseille, France. European Language Resources Association.

Thomas Wolf, Lysandre Debut, Victor Sanh, Julien Chaumond, Clement Delangue, Anthony Moi, Pierric Cistac, Tim Rault, Remi Louf, Morgan Funtowicz, Joe Davison, Sam Shleifer, Patrick von Platen, Clara Ma, Yacine Jernite, Julien Plu, Canwen Xu, Teven Le Scao, Sylvain Gugger, Mariama Drame, Quentin Lhoest, and Alexander Rush. 2020. Transformers: State-of-the-art natural language processing. In *Proceedings of the 2020 Conference on Empirical Methods in Natural Language Processing: System Demonstrations*, pages 38–45, Online. Association for Computational Linguistics.

Krzysztof Wróbel and Krzysztof Nowak. 2022. Transformer-based part-of-speech tagging and lemmatization for Latin. In *Proceedings of the Second Workshop on Language Technologies for Historical and Ancient Languages*, pages 193–197, Marseille, France. European Language Resources Association.

Tariq Yousef, Chiara Palladino, Gerhard Heyer, and Stefan Jänicke. 2023. Named entity annotation projection applied to classical languages. In *Proceedings of the 7th Joint SIGHUM Workshop on Computational Linguistics for Cultural Heritage, Social Sciences, Humanities and Literature*, page 175–182, Dubrovnik, Croatia. Association for Computational Linguistics.

Tariq Yousef, Chiara Palladino, and Stefan Jänicke. 2022a. *Transformer-Based Named Entity Recognition for Ancient Greek*.

Tariq Yousef, Chiara Palladino, David J. Wright, and Monica Berti. 2022b. Automatic translation alignment for Ancient Greek and Latin. In *Proceedings of the Second Workshop on Language Technologies for Historical and Ancient Languages*, pages 101–107, Marseille, France. European Language Resources Association.

A Appendix

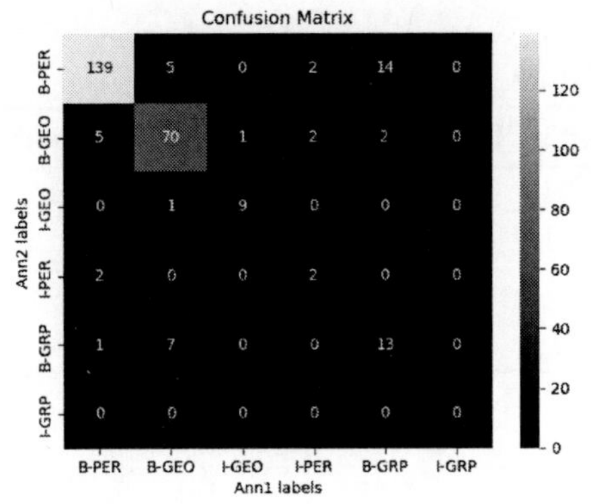

Figure 1: IAA on Juv. *Saturae* 1-3, label 'O' excluded

Gold label	1 & 2 wrong	1 correct	2 correct
O	0	11	25
B-PERS	13	47	24
I-PERS	2	1	1
B-LOC	14	12	14
I-LOC	0	0	2
B-GRP	18	16	12
I-GRP	1	0	0
Total	58	87	78

Table 8: Comparison of differences in prediction between LatinBERT1 (1) and LatinBERT2 (2) on the Herodotos data.

Gold label	1 & 2 wrong		1 correct		2 correct	
	IN	OUT	IN	OUT	IN	OUT
O	0	0	7	5	7	7
B-PERS	1	6	14	8	20	22
I-PERS	2	3	4	0	14	0
B-LOC	2	7	6	15	11	9
I-LOC	3	3	0	0	5	0
B-GRP	14	3	6	4	10	5
I-GRP	1	0	0	0	0	
Total	23	22	37	32	67	43

Table 9: Comparison of differences in prediction between LatinBERT1 (1) and LatinBERT2 (2) on in and out-of-domain LASLA data.

		CRF	LB1	LB2	LatinCy lg	LatinCy trf	support
Caesar/Pliny's (IN)	B-PERS	0.83	0.93	0.94	0.75	0.73	474
	I-PERS	0.86	0.89	0.91	0.43	0.52	98
	B-LOC	0.70	0.87	0.90	0.64	0.56	218
	I-LOC	0.00	0.33	0.50	0.00	0.00	8
	B-GRP	0.77	0.90	0.92	0.02	0.06	247
	I-GRP	0.00	0.00	0.00	0.00	0.00	3
***Ars Am.* (OUT)**	B-PERS	0.48	0.76	0.72	0.47	0.36	375
	I-PERS	0.06	0.00	0.00	0.00	0.00	1
	B-LOC	0.30	0.43	0.38	0.28	0.18	87
	B-GRP	0.25	0.45	0.40	0.00	0.05	107

Table 10: f1-score per entity type on the Herodotos dataset; **LB** stands for LatinBERT

		CRF	LB1	LB2	LatinCy lg	Herodotos	support
Tac. and Cic. (IN)	B-PERS	0.71	0.88	0.89	0.84	0.81	711
	I-PERS	0.78	0.81	0.85	0.24	0.79	188
	B-LOC	0.33	0.58	0.60	0.57	0.52	222
	I-LOC	0.00	0.00	0.18	0.00	0.13	42
	B-GRP	0.43	0.61	0.62	0.03	0.60	154
	I-GRP	0.00	0.00	0.00	0.00	0.00	3
Juv. (OUT)	B-PERS	0.55	0.55	0.65	0.66	0.64	143
	I-PERS	0.23	0.00	0.00	0.00	0.19	7
	B-LOC	0.35	0.50	0.39	0.44	0.27	83
	I-LOC	0.00	0.00	0.00	0.00	0.00	14
	B-GRP	0.47	0.40	0.52	0.00	0.23	36
	I-GRP	0.00	0.00	0.00	0.00	0.00	1

Table 11: f1-score per entity type on the LASLA corpus

Sentence Embedding Models for Ancient Greek Using Multilingual Knowledge Distillation

Kevin Krahn and **Derrick Tate** and **Andrew C. Lamicela**
Sattler College, Boston, MA
{kevin.krahn24, dtate, alamicela}@sattler.edu

Abstract

Contextual language models have been trained on Classical languages, including Ancient Greek and Latin, for tasks such as lemmatization, morphological tagging, part of speech tagging, authorship attribution, and detection of scribal errors. However, high-quality sentence embedding models for these historical languages are significantly more difficult to achieve due to the lack of training data. In this work, we use a multilingual knowledge distillation approach to train BERT models to produce sentence embeddings for Ancient Greek text. The state-of-the-art sentence embedding approaches for high-resource languages use massive datasets, but our distillation approach allows our Ancient Greek models to inherit the properties of these models while using a relatively small amount of translated sentence data. We build a parallel sentence dataset using a sentence-embedding alignment method to align Ancient Greek documents with English translations, and use this dataset to train our models. We evaluate our models on translation search, semantic similarity, and semantic retrieval tasks and investigate translation bias. We make our training and evaluation datasets freely available at this url.

1 Introduction

Sentence embedding models, which map sentences or other sequences of text to a dense vector space, such that semantically similar sentences are close together in the vector space, have many applications in NLP. Current state-of-the-art sentence embedding models, however, are trained on modern, high-resource languages such as English and use massive datasets consisting of billions of sentence pairs (Ni et al., 2022). A different approach is needed for historical languages, which have much less data available.

In this work, we train several sentence embedding models for Ancient Greek. Many more Ancient Greek texts have survived compared to texts from most other ancient languages, which makes sentence embedding models both more feasible and useful.

Several previous works have trained language models for Ancient Greek. Johnson et al. (2021) introduced the Classical Language Toolkit (CLTK) which includes several tools for Ancient Greek processing, including static word embeddings. Singh et al. (2021) fine-tuned a Modern Greek BERT model (Koutsikakis et al., 2020) on Ancient Greek text for PoS tagging, morphological tagging, and lemmatization tasks. Yamshchikov et al. (2022) trained a BERT model for authorship classification of Pseudo-Plutarch texts. Cowen-Breen et al. (2023) trained another BERT model for the purpose of identifying errors in scribal transmission. Riemenschneider and Frank (2023) produced the most comprehensive work on Classical language models to date, training multiple models on a large multilingual corpus of Ancient Greek, Latin, and English texts and comprehensively evaluating and comparing their new models to previous models on a variety of tasks. None of these works, however, produce sentence embedding models for Ancient Greek.

Although there are many digitized Ancient Greek texts available, there is a lack of suitable training data for training sentence embedding models from scratch. The best approaches for high-resource languages involve large human-annotated datasets, such as the natural language inference (NLI) datasets used by Sentence-BERT (Reimers and Gurevych, 2019). Needless to say, such datasets are not available for Ancient Greek.

Following Reimers and Gurevych (2020), we use *multilingual knowledge distillation* to train sentence embedding models with an aligned vector space for Ancient Greek and English. Given a teacher model M for a language s, and a dataset of translated sentences $((s_1, t_1)..(s_n, t_n))$ where s_i and t_i are parallel sentences, we train a new stu-

Proceedings of the Ancient Language Processing Workshop associated with RANLP-2023, pages 13–22,
held in Varna Bulgaria, Sept 8, 2023.
https://doi.org/10.26615/978-954-452-087-8_002

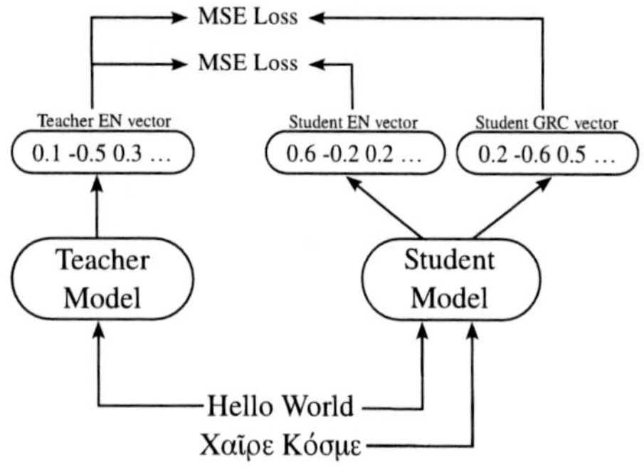

Figure 1: Multilingual knowledge distillation for English to Ancient Greek sentence pairs.

dent model $\hat{M}$ to mimic the sentence embeddings of the teacher M using mean squared loss, such that $\hat{M}(s_i) \approx M(t_i)$ and $\hat{M}(t_i) \approx M(s_i)$. In our case, the teacher model is English and the student model learns both Greek[1] and English embeddings.

This approach has numerous advantages: 1) it requires a relatively small amount of training data, 2) the student model inherits the vector space properties of a state-of-the-art English sentence embedding model, 3) the student model is multilingual, and 4) the vector spaces are aligned across languages.

The cross-lingual nature of this approach is especially useful for Ancient Greek semantic retrieval, since it is much easier to formulate search queries in English than in Ancient Greek. Although it is possible to operate on the English translations of Greek texts, translations are not readily available for all Greek texts, and the available translations are usually not aligned at the sentence level, making it difficult to quickly find the corresponding Greek text. Furthermore, English translations can suffer from various kinds of translator bias, whereas a language model that operates directly on the Greek text can offer an "average" of multiple translators' interpretations of the text (See Section 4.4).

We produce a training dataset of parallel sentences using a two-step translation alignment process: an initial, smaller dataset was produced using a sentence-length heuristic and dictionary-based alignment technique (Halácsy et al., 2007), and this initial dataset was used to train an intermediate multilingual sentence embedding model, which was used to align a larger dataset using the approach introduced by Liu and Zhu (2023), which uses sentence embeddings for state-of-the-art alignment quality.

We create new evaluation datasets for Ancient Greek translation search, semantic textual similarity (STS), and semantic retrieval (SR) and we evaluate our models on these datasets.

In summary, our contributions are as follows:

1. We use a multilingual knowledge distillation approach to train several Ancient Greek sentence embedding models.

2. We use translation alignment to produce a dataset of Ancient Greek sentences and their English translations.

3. We develop evaluation datasets for translation search, semantic retrieval, and semantic textual similarity, and we evaluate our sentence embedding models on these tasks.

2 Training

2.1 Base Models

To train a sentence embedding model, we first need a base language model trained on Ancient Greek text. The existing Ancient Greek language models were unsuitable for our purposes; most of them are monolingual, but we are training a multilingual model. The models trained by Riemenschneider and Frank (2023) would be the best candidates because they include English, but one of their goals was to avoid contamination from modern languages, such as modern concepts and technology like cellphones which were unknown in antiquity. However, for us this is not a concern, since one of our goals is to train a model to facilitate semantic search with modern language and terminology.

Instead, we fine-tune multilingual BERT-base (mBERT) (Devlin et al., 2019) and XLM-RoBERTa-base (XLM-R) (Conneau et al., 2020) for our base models. Pires et al. (2019) shows that low-resource languages can benefit from multilingual pre-training. We use masked language modeling (MLM) to fine-tune mBERT, (denoted as $_{\text{GRC}}$mBERT) and XLM-R (denoted as $_{\text{GRC}}$XLM-R) with Ancient Greek text, and we use these as base models. See Appendix A for training details.

Both mBERT and XLM-R were trained on Modern Greek, among many other languages, but not on Ancient Greek, and hence one disadvantage of these models is that their tokenizers are not optimized for Ancient Greek morphology, which could

[1]When we refer to "Greek" in an unqualified way in this paper we are referring to Ancient Greek.

Model	Symbols/token	Words/token
mBERT	2.29	0.37
XLM-R	2.66	0.43

Table 1: The XLM-R tokenizer produces longer tokens and a higher number of words per token on Ancient Greek text compared to the mBERT tokenizer.

negatively impact performance (Park et al., 2021; Hofmann et al., 2021).

We use a similar approach to Yamshchikov et al. (2022) to compare the mBERT and XLM-R tokenizers. We take a random sample of 20k Ancient Greek sentences from the pre-training corpus and compute the average token length and average words per token for a rough estimation of tokenization quality (See Table 1). The XLM-R tokenizer scores higher on both metrics compared to the mBERT tokenizer. However, a higher score for either metric does not guarantee superior performance in downstream tasks, since it does not measure how well the sub-word tokens capture Ancient Greek morphology.

2.2 Knowledge Distillation

To train multilingual sentence embedding models on English and Ancient Greek with an aligned vector space we use *multilingual knowledge distillation* (Reimers and Gurevych, 2020). This process requires a teacher model M for a source language s, and a dataset of translated sentences $((s_1, t_1)..(s_n, t_n))$ where s_i and t_i are parallel sentences. We train a student model $\hat{M}$ to mimic the sentence embeddings of the teacher M such that $\hat{M}(s_i) \approx M(t_i)$ and $\hat{M}(t_i) \approx M(s_i)$. The following mean squared loss function is minimized for each mini-batch β:

$$\frac{1}{|\beta|} \sum_{j \in \beta} \left[((M(s_j) - \hat{M}(s_j))^2 + (M(s_j) - \hat{M}(t_j))^2 \right]$$

Thus, the student $\hat{M}$ learns to map each target and source sentence to the same location in vector space.

For the teacher M we compare two models:

1. `all-mpnet-base-v2`,[2] a model tuned for semantic search, trained on a large and diverse training set of 1B+ pairs (Denoted as `mpnet`).
2. `sentence-t5-large`,[3] a T5 model tuned for sentence similarity tasks, trained on 2B pairs (Ni et al., 2022) (Denoted as `st5`).

Both above models have a final normalization layer which we remove prior to training to allow student model to learn the original vector space properties of the teacher model.

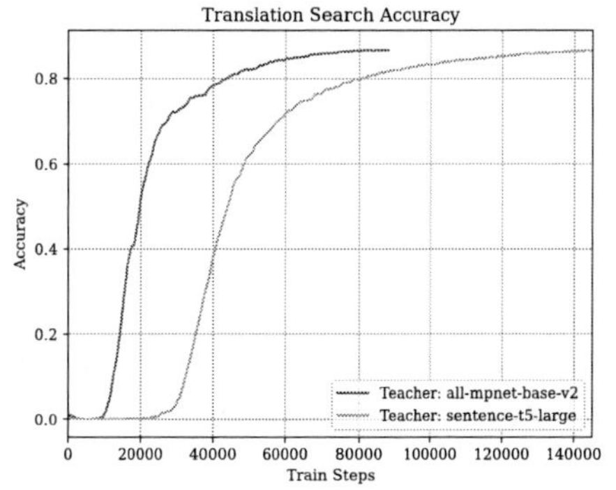

Figure 2: Translation search accuracy over training steps with $_{\text{grc}}$XLM-R student model.

We compare $_{\text{GRC}}$mBERT and $_{\text{GRC}}$XLM-R as the student model $\hat{M}$. We add a mean pooling layer and pair both student models with both teacher models (4 configurations) and train all the student parameters. With `mpnet` as the teacher, we train for 15 epochs, but with `st5` the student model took twice as long to converge (See Figure 2), so we train for 30 epochs. We use a batch size of 128, a max sequence length of 128 tokens, 2000 warmup steps, and a learning rate of 2e-5. Every 500 training steps we measure STS performance as well as MSE loss and translation search accuracy on 5k hold-out pairs, keeping the model with best average performance across these tasks. Regardless of teacher model, $_{\text{GRC}}$XLM-R took many more training steps to converge than $_{\text{GRC}}$mBERT and was prone to catestrophic forgetting, which was alleviated by increasing the number of warmup steps.

We also experiment with training on parallel Modern Greek data from Wikipedia for 3 epochs and then on Ancient Greek data for 15 epochs if `mpnet` is the teacher and 6 and 30 epochs if `st5` is the teacher. Although Modern Greek differs in many significant ways from Ancient Greek, training on this data gives the model additional exposure

[2] `https://huggingface.co/sentence-transformers/all-mpnet-base-v2`

[3] `https://huggingface.co/sentence-transformers/sentence-t5-large`

to aspects of Greek that have remained unchanged since antiquity, such as historical proper nouns. All evaluations are reported with and without training on this additional data.

2.3 Contrastive Learning

As a baseline against which to compare the models trained via the distillation method, we also train sentence embedding models using *Simple Contrastive Learning of Sentence Embeddings* (SimCSE), the contrastive learning method introduced by Gao et al. (2021). Contrastive learning pulls semantically-close neighbors together and pushes apart non-neighbors, and has been shown to be effective for training multilingual sentence embeddings (Gao et al., 2021; Tan et al., 2023). In addition to using dropout as noise, we use each Greek sentence and its English translation as positive pairs and other pairs in the same batch as negatives.

We use the CLS token representation and train for a maximum of 10 epochs with a batch size of 82, a max sequence length of 128 tokens, 2000 warmup steps, and a learning rate of 2e-5. Every 500 training steps we measure performance on the STS evaluation and translation search accuracy on the 5k hold-out pairs, keeping the highest performing model. As above, we also experiment with training on Modern Greek data for 3 epochs, and then Ancient Greek data for 10 epochs.

3 Training Data

3.1 Pre-training

Our pre-training dataset consists of the Ancient Greek text from the Perseus Digital Library[4] and First1KGreek,[5] which are part of the Open Greek and Latin project.[6] Different documents containing the same Greek work were removed. These sources contain approximately 32 million words of Ancient Greek text. Although Riemenschneider and Frank (2023) produced a much larger corpus of Greek text (100+ million words) using additional sources, at the time of writing their data is not publicly available. Our smaller dataset is sufficient for our purposes, as Reimers and Gurevych (2020) show that even languages with little pre-training in a multilingual student model can be effective targets for knowledge distillation.

This dataset consist of Greek texts spanning a thousand years, covering different dialects and time periods of the language. We do not filter out any texts based on their dialect or time period.

In addition to the Greek text, we also collect all the English translations in the Open Greek and Latin project to finetune our models with an additional 10 million words of historical English text.

3.2 Preprocessing

Following Yamshchikov et al. (2022) and Singh et al. (2021), we lowercase all the Greek text and strip diacritics, but keep punctuation. Although diacritics contain important information for disambiguating between words that only differ by breathing marks or accent marks, the correct word can usually be inferred from context. The contextual nature of BERT models allows them to learn to use context to disambiguate.

3.3 Parallel Data

Human Aligned A portion of our parallel sentence dataset is taken from human aligned sources:

1. Verses of the Greek New Testament with English translations (15k pairs),
2. Verses of the Greek Septuagint with English translations (29k pairs),
3. Verses of the Greek works of Flavius Josephus with English translations (15k pairs),
4. Other minor sources: OPUS (Tiedemann and Nygaard, 2004), Greek Learner Texts[7], manually aligned passages from Perseus and First1KGreek (total 23k pairs).

Translation Alignment The bulk of the parallel data is produced using translation alignment. We take all the texts from our pre-training corpus that have English translations and split them into sentences or sub-sentence segments (see Appendix B). We then use a two-step process to align Greek sentences with their English translations. First, we use Hunalign (Halácsy et al., 2007), a sentence-length heuristic and dictionary-based alignment technique on the translated texts. This produced an initial dataset of approximately 150k parallel sentences (including the human-aligned sources listed above).

Using this initial dataset, we trained a sentence embedding model with an aligned vector space for

[4] https://github.com/PerseusDL/canonical-greekLit

[5] https://github.com/OpenGreekAndLatin/First1KGreek

[6] https://opengreekandlatin.org

[7] https://greek-learner-texts.org

English and Ancient Greek using SimCSE (See Section 2.3). Next, we use this model to align all the texts again, using a better alignment method introduced by Liu and Zhu (2023), dubbed Bertalign, which uses multilingual sentence embeddings to achieve state-of-the-art alignment quality. If the Greek and English documents are already aligned by sections, we align the sentences in each section individually. This increases alignment accuracy and makes it possible to keep the parts of the document that have good alignments and to discard the rest. Otherwise, if no section alignments exist, we run the aligner on the entire text.

We do not filter out multiple translations of the same Greek texts, since different translations can have different nuances and word choices, with the hope that the resulting sentence embeddings will be more robust to translation differences.

Finally, we remove all duplicate sentence pairs from the dataset and all pairs with very short sentences (<5 characters). We also ensure that no sentence pairs from the STS dataset (See Section 4.2) are included in the training data. This results in approximately 380k sentence pairs after holding out 5k pairs for evaluation purposes.

Modern Greek The Modern Greek (EL) sentence pairs from Wikipedia are taken from the OPUS project (Tiedemann and Nygaard, 2004). We remove all duplicate pairs and pairs with very short sentences (<10 characters), resulting in approximately 800k sentence pairs. This dataset contains a rich and diverse set of topics, including historical topics which will hopefully transfer to the Ancient Greek models. We compare all the models with and without training on this data.

4 Evaluations

4.1 Translation Similarity Search

The first measure of the quality of the sentence embeddings is each model's accuracy at choosing the correct English translation for each Ancient Greek sentence from the 5k hold-out pairs. The score is computed as the percentage of sentence pairs for which the embedding of source sentence s_i has the closest cosine similarity to the embedding of translated sentence t_i out of all the target sentences. The accuracy is computed in both directions and averaged. The results are reported in Table 2.

Model	Accuracy
SimCSE	
GRC mBERT (GRC)	95.92
GRC mBERT (EL,GRC)	96.09
GRC XLM-R (GRC)	95.86
GRC XLM-R (EL,GRC)	**96.64**
Teacher: `sentence-t5-large`	
GRC mBERT (GRC)	87.78
GRC mBERT (EL,GRC)	90.80
GRC XLM-R (GRC)	87.02
GRC XLM-R (EL,GRC)	91.60
Teacher: `all-mpnet-base-v2`	
GRC mBERT (GRC)	87.77
GRC mBERT (EL,GRC)	89.15
GRC XLM-R (GRC)	86.48
GRC XLM-R (EL,GRC)	90.12

Table 2: Translation similarity search accuracy. Best result is bolded.

The SimCSE models perform on this task better than the distillation models, which is not surprising since they specifically trained to maximize the cosine similarity between translation pairs and minimize similarity between non-pairs. There is no significant difference in the performance between the two base models. All the models performed better when first trained on Modern Greek before Ancient Greek.

4.2 Semantic Textual Similarity

Sentence Pair	Score
Στωικοὶ ἀποφαίνονται σφαιροειδῆ τὸν κόσμον. Stoics declare the world to be spherical. Στωικός νομίζει ὅτι ἡ γῆ σφαίρα ἐστιν. A Stoic thinks that the earth is a sphere.	0.9
ἐπὶ δὲ τοῦ ὄρους τῇ ἄκρᾳ Διός ἐστιν ναός. On the top of the mountain is a temple of Zeus. ὁ Ζεὺς οἰκεῖ ἐπὶ τὰ ὄρη ἐν Ὀλύμπῳ. Zeus dwells on the mountains in Olympus.	0.8
Τὰ παιδία παίζουσιν ἐν τῇ ἀμμουδιᾷ. The children are playing in the sand. Τὰ παιδία ἀναπαύονται ἐν τῷ κήπῳ. The children rest in the garden.	0.5
Σωκράτης εἶδεν ἓξ βόας. Socrates saw six cows. Ῥώμουλος εἶδεν ἓξ οἰωνοὺς ὄρνιθας. Romulus saw six birds of omen.	0.1

Table 3: Example pairs from STS evaluation dataset. Scores are examples and not actual scores.

We compiled a dataset of Ancient Greek sentence pairs with gold scores to measure semantic textual similarity in the range [0,1], with 0 representing completely unrelated meaning, and 1 representing full semantic equivalence. Each sentence was given a corresponding English translation to

Model	GRC↔GRC	EN↔EN	GRC↔EN	Average
SimCSE				
$_{GRC}$mBERT (GRC)	75.68	77.58	76.30	76.52
$_{GRC}$mBERT (EL,GRC)	74.85	78.30	76.40	76.52
$_{GRC}$XLM-R (GRC)	77.83	78.82	77.21	77.95
$_{GRC}$XLM-R (EL,GRC)	78.27	79.11	77.76	78.38
Teacher: `sentence-t5-large`				
$_{GRC}$mBERT (GRC)	82.17	87.54	84.02	84.58
$_{GRC}$mBERT (EL,GRC)	84.84	**89.33**	**86.37**	**86.84**
$_{GRC}$XLM-R (GRC)	82.37	85.37	82.56	83.43
$_{GRC}$XLM-R (EL,GRC)	84.88	88.37	85.45	86.24
Teacher: `all-mpnet-base-v2`				
$_{GRC}$mBERT (GRC)	82.30	87.60	84.68	84.86
$_{GRC}$mBERT (EL,GRC)	84.84	88.77	86.28	86.63
$_{GRC}$XLM-R (GRC)	83.80	87.07	84.53	85.13
$_{GRC}$XLM-R (EL,GRC)	**85.18**	88.24	85.92	86.45

Table 4: Spearman rank correlation ρ between the cosine similarity of sentence embeddings and gold labels for STS dataset. Scores are reported as $\rho \times 100$. Best results are bolded. There are twice as many *GRC-EN* pairs as *GRC-GRC* pairs so their scores are not directly comparable.

allow for cross-lingual evaluation (See Table 3).

The gold scores for STS datasets are typically produced by averaging the scores from many human annotators. However, for Ancient Greek it is difficult to find enough annotators to produce high quality gold scores. Our solution is to use a Cross-Encoder[8] to produce the gold scores based on the English translations of each pair. A Cross-Encoder takes two sentences as input and produces a similarity score in the range $[0, 1]$ without the need to encode the semantic properties of each sentence into a vector, and therefore performs better than cosine similarity between embeddings (See Figure 3). With this setup, we measure how closely each model can match the performance of the English Cross-Encoder. The accuracy of this method depends on how closely the English translations match the meaning of the Greek sentences. Therefore the English translations are reviewed by an expert to ensure that they are literal and accurate translations of the Greek text.

Due to the need to manually verify the translations for each pair, the STS dataset is relatively small. The dataset consists of 165 Ancient Greek sentences pairs, each having an English translation: $((a_{GRC}, a_{EN}), (b_{GRC}, b_{EN}))$. The GRC↔EN comparison can be performed two ways: $a_{GRC} \leftrightarrow b_{EN}$ and $a_{EN} \leftrightarrow b_{GRC}$ for a total of 330 GRC↔EN comparisons, 165 GRC↔GRC comparisons, and 165 EN↔EN comparisons.

[8] `https://huggingface.co/cross-encoder/stsb-roberta-base`

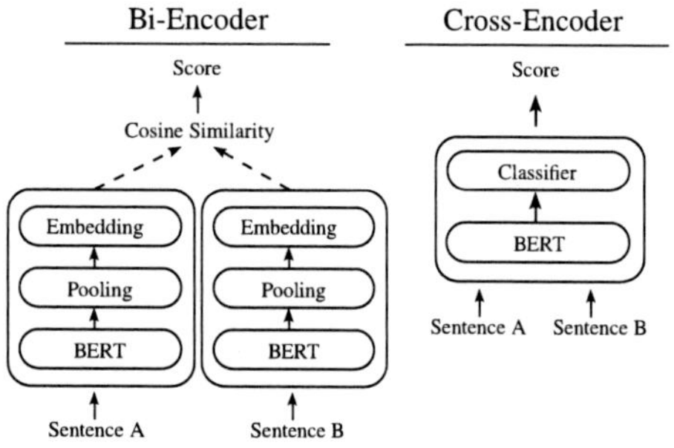

Figure 3: We use a Cross-Encoder (right) to produce STS gold scores which are used to evaluate our sentence embedding models, which are Bi-Encoders (left).

The score for each model is computed as Spearman correlation between gold scores and the cosine similarities between the sentence embeddings. The results are reported in Table 4.

The models trained via knowledge distillation significantly outperform the SimCSE models, showing that they have inherited the properties of the teacher models for STS tasks. The models with the `st5` teacher have a small lead, which is expected since `st5` was trained for STS tasks. All the models improve slightly when first trained on Modern Greek before Ancient Greek.

4.3 Semantic Retrieval

Sentence embeddings can be used for semantic retrieval tasks by ranking a set of passage embeddings by cosine similarity with a query embedding. Performing this process with our models on the Greek sentences in the Perseus and First1KGreek corpora yields promising results. For example, the following query is correctly answered by several passages in the top 10 highest ranked passages:

Query: "Was Aristotle a student of Plato?"

- Ἀριστοτέλης Πλάτωνος μαθητής· οὗτος τὴν διαλεκτικὴν συνεστήσατο. - Hyppolytus of Rome
  Aristotle, a disciple of Plato — He established dialectics.
- ἀλλὰ καὶ τοῖς Πλάτωνος ἐγκαλέσαι ἄν τις δόγμασι δι᾽ Ἀριστοτέλην, ἀποφοιτήσαντα τῆς διατριβῆς αὐτοῦ ἐν καινοτομίαις. - Origen
  But someone could also challenge certain doctrines of Plato through Aristotle, who, upon completing his studies, departed from his teachings with innovations.
- παρὰ Πλάτωνι Ἀριστοτέλης φιλοσοφήσας μετελθὼν εἰς τὸ Λύκειον κτίζει τὴν Περιπατητικὴν αἵρεσιν. - Clement of Alexandria
  After studying philosophy under Plato, Aristotle, having come to the Lyceum, founded the Peripatetic school.

To quantify the performance of each model for semantic retrieval, we compile a dataset of 40k Greek passages from the Perseus and First1KGreek corpora. We then produce 100 English queries (in the form of both phrases and questions) and associate them with relevant passages. We measure recall and mean average precision (mAP) for each model. The scores are reported in Table 5.

The SimCSE models perform poorly, which is expected since they were not trained for retrieval tasks. The models with the `mpnet` teacher, which was trained for semantic search, score highest by a large margin. The models with the `st5` teacher, which was trained for semantic textual similarity tasks, perform better than the SimCSE models but worse than the `mpnet` models. The models generally perform much better when trained on Modern Greek. Perhaps this is because many of the queries involve proper nouns for which Modern Greek data gave additional training examples, or perhaps the student models benefited from the additional English examples to learn the vector space properties of the teacher. The GRCmBERT models consistently perform better than GRCXLM-R models.

Overall performance on this task was rather poor even for the best models. An analysis of the top ranked passages for each query revealed that passages about related topics often ranked above the desired passages. In particular, it often confused proper names, e.g. preferring passages about other philosophers for queries about Plato.

4.4 Translation Bias

To determine whether the models are biased towards certain translation styles, especially those

Model	Recall@10	mAP@20
SimCSE		
GRCmBERT (GRC)	26.61	15.33
GRCmBERT (EL,GRC)	18.08	10.84
GRCXLM-R (GRC)	21.50	9.86
GRCXLM-R (EL,GRC)	29.56	15.08
Teacher: `sentence-t5-large`		
GRCmBERT (GRC)	41.34	25.37
GRCmBERT (EL,GRC)	49.63	36.17
GRCXLM-R (GRC)	34.88	20.07
GRCXLM-R (EL,GRC)	47.07	31.31
Teacher: `all-mpnet-base-v2`		
GRCmBERT (GRC)	63.60	44.97
GRCmBERT (EL,GRC)	**69.87**	**53.00**
GRCXLM-R (GRC)	53.84	36.42
GRCXLM-R (EL,GRC)	60.13	44.36

Table 5: Recall@10 and mAP@20 scores for English search queries and Ancient Greek passages. Best results are bolded.

included in the training set, a text with many different translations is needed. The New Testament is a good candidate for this, since many translations exist in different styles and eras of the English language. We take nine New Testament translations, ranging from literal (NASB), archaic (KJV), and paraphrase (MSG), all fully aligned at the verse level (7654 verses). There are no other Greek texts that we are aware of that have this many translations available for comparison. We generate embeddings for each verse from the Greek text and the translations. We also generate an "average" translation for each verse by averaging the embeddings of all the English translations. We take the cosine similarity between the Greek embedding and each translation and use it to compute the Mean Reciprocal Rank (MRR) across all verses, for each model:

$$MRR = \frac{1}{|T|} \sum_{v \in T} \frac{1}{rank_v}$$

where T is a set of verses in a translation and $rank_v$ is the rank of the translation for verse v. The results are reported in Table 6.

The literal translations score highest, and the score decreases the more non-literal the translations become, with the MSG translation having the lowest score. Surprisingly, the archaic KJV translation ranks highly, which is likely due to a high quantity of archaic English text in the training data. This suggests that the models are slightly biased to this older English translation style. Verses from two of the translations (NKJV and NET) were included in the training data. Despite being in the training data,

Model	KJV	NKJV*	NASB	ESV	RSV	NET*	NIV	NLT	MSG	Avg. Emb.
SimCSE										
GRCmBERT (GRC)	32.59	36.56	**39.97**	32.17	29.28	25.91	20.32	12.92	11.14	52.04
GRCmBERT (EL,GRC)	33.27	36.05	**40.79**	31.97	28.74	26.17	20.15	12.79	11.21	51.75
GRCXLM-R (GRC)	35.78	37.85	**38.17**	32.15	29.76	26.03	20.58	13.14	11.32	48.11
GRCXLM-R (EL,GRC)	35.34	36.74	**38.02**	32.96	30.06	25.76	20.75	13.09	11.25	48.93
Teacher: `sentence-t5-large`										
GRCmBERT (GRC)	29.63	**30.70**	30.13	27.81	25.90	23.05	20.09	14.43	12.49	78.66
GRCmBERT (EL,GRC)	28.73	**30.66**	29.98	28.02	25.82	23.39	19.70	13.93	12.24	80.42
GRCXLM-R (GRC)	**31.82**	29.70	29.14	28.10	26.39	23.82	20.38	14.24	12.90	76.40
GRCXLM-R (EL,GRC)	**30.41**	30.01	29.08	28.35	26.82	23.61	19.75	13.68	12.36	78.82
Teacher: `all-mpnet-base-v2`										
GRCmBERT (GRC)	**31.76**	31.15	29.93	30.04	28.94	23.33	19.52	13.93	11.98	72.32
GRCmBERT (EL,GRC)	30.42	**31.20**	30.37	30.35	28.68	23.51	19.53	13.76	11.81	73.26
GRCXLM-R (GRC)	**37.25**	31.31	29.91	30.00	29.42	23.32	19.67	13.97	12.32	65.74
GRCXLM-R (EL,GRC)	**33.08**	31.21	29.64	30.25	29.59	23.55	19.32	13.61	11.89	70.76

* Verses from the NET and NKJV were included in parallel training data.

Table 6: Mean Reciprocal Rank (MRR) $\times 100$ of cosine similarity between Greek verses of the New Testament and English translations, as well as MRR of per-verse averaged embedding of all the translations. Highest translation MRR for each model is bolded. MRR of averaged embedding is underlined if it is higher than any of the translations.

there does not appear to be bias to the NET since it consistently ranks lower than other translations. The NKJV ranks highly, but does not consistently outrank other literal translations. Interestingly, the average embedding of all the translations ranked highest by a significant margin.

5 Discussion and Future Work

Overall, the base models mBERT and XLM-R performed similarly except for the semantic retrieval task where the mBERT-derived models have a sizeable lead. The reason for this is unclear, since these models have different tokenizers, parameter counts, and vocabularies. It is also unclear how much the pre-training process affects the results. An area of future research would be to investigate the effect of student model architecture, tokenizer, and pre-training on the ability of the student model to learn from the teacher model.

The main limitation of using multilingual knowledge distillation to train sentence embedding models is that the embeddings produced are almost entirely derived from English translations, which could be undesirable if the goal is to study Ancient Greek text without any prior translator's interpretation. Furthermore, the student model can never fully replicate the performance of the teacher model when transfering to another language, since translated sentences are often not entirely semantically equivalent to their source sentences, especially when removed from the original context via translation alignment.

Although contamination from modern languages is not a big concern for the tasks in this paper, there could be issues of anachronisms when searching Ancient Greek texts with English. Furthermore, using texts from such a long chronological period of the Greek language could introduce additional lexical polysemy as Greek words changed in meaning over time. This could explain why the averaged embedding of many translations had a higher MRR than any individual translation source in Table 6, since the combination of many translations represents a higher degree of polysemy. In future work, such historical polysemy could be measured by sampling translations of words from texts of different historical periods. This could help to determine whether the high MRR of the averaged embedding is a useful result or simply an artifact of a potentially high amount of polysemy in the training data.

6 Conclusion

In this paper, we have shown that multilingual knowledge distillation is an effective approach for training sentence embedding models for Ancient Greek, in spite of the lack of available training data compared to modern, high-resource languages. In addition, we have produced a new dataset of parallel Ancient Greek and English sentences as well as evaluation datasets for translation search, semantic textual similarity, and semantic retrieval, which we make publicly available.

References

Steven Bird, Ewan Klein, and Edward Loper. 2009. *Natural Language Processing with Python*, 1st ed edition. O'Reilly, Beijing ; Cambridge [Mass.].

Alexis Conneau, Kartikay Khandelwal, Naman Goyal, Vishrav Chaudhary, Guillaume Wenzek, Francisco Guzmán, Edouard Grave, Myle Ott, Luke Zettlemoyer, and Veselin Stoyanov. 2020. Unsupervised cross-lingual representation learning at scale. In *Proceedings of the 58th Annual Meeting of the Association for Computational Linguistics*, pages 8440–8451, Online. Association for Computational Linguistics.

Charlie Cowen-Breen, Creston Brooks, Johannes Haubold, and Barbara Graziosi. 2023. Logion: Machine Learning for Greek Philology.

Jacob Devlin, Ming-Wei Chang, Kenton Lee, and Kristina Toutanova. 2019. BERT: Pre-training of deep bidirectional transformers for language understanding. In *Proceedings of the 2019 Conference of the North American Chapter of the Association for Computational Linguistics: Human Language Technologies, Volume 1 (Long and Short Papers)*, pages 4171–4186, Minneapolis, Minnesota. Association for Computational Linguistics.

Tianyu Gao, Xingcheng Yao, and Danqi Chen. 2021. SimCSE: Simple contrastive learning of sentence embeddings. In *Proceedings of the 2021 Conference on Empirical Methods in Natural Language Processing*, pages 6894–6910, Online and Punta Cana, Dominican Republic. Association for Computational Linguistics.

Péter Halácsy, Andras Kornai, Viktor Nagy, László Németh, and Viktor Trón. 2007. Parallel corpora for medium density languages. In *Recent Advances in Natural Language Processing IV*, pages 247–258.

Valentin Hofmann, Janet Pierrehumbert, and Hinrich Schütze. 2021. Superbizarre is not superb: Derivational morphology improves BERT's interpretation of complex words. In *Proceedings of the 59th Annual Meeting of the Association for Computational Linguistics and the 11th International Joint Conference on Natural Language Processing (Volume 1: Long Papers)*, pages 3594–3608, Online. Association for Computational Linguistics.

Kyle P. Johnson, Patrick J. Burns, John Stewart, Todd Cook, Clément Besnier, and William J. B. Mattingly. 2021. The Classical Language Toolkit: An NLP framework for pre-modern languages. In *Proceedings of the 59th Annual Meeting of the Association for Computational Linguistics and the 11th International Joint Conference on Natural Language Processing: System Demonstrations*, pages 20–29, Online. Association for Computational Linguistics.

John Koutsikakis, Ilias Chalkidis, Prodromos Malakasiotis, and Ion Androutsopoulos. 2020. GREEK-BERT: The Greeks visiting Sesame Street. https://arxiv.org/abs/2008.12014v2.

Lei Liu and Min Zhu. 2023. Bertalign: Improved word embedding-based sentence alignment for Chinese–English parallel corpora of literary texts. *Digital Scholarship in the Humanities*, 38(2):621–634.

Jianmo Ni, Gustavo Hernandez Abrego, Noah Constant, Ji Ma, Keith Hall, Daniel Cer, and Yinfei Yang. 2022. Sentence-t5: Scalable sentence encoders from pretrained text-to-text models. In *Findings of the Association for Computational Linguistics: ACL 2022*, pages 1864–1874, Dublin, Ireland. Association for Computational Linguistics.

Hyunji Hayley Park, Katherine J. Zhang, Coleman Haley, Kenneth Steimel, Han Liu, and Lane Schwartz. 2021. Morphology matters: A multilingual language modeling analysis. *Transactions of the Association for Computational Linguistics*, 9:261–276.

Telmo Pires, Eva Schlinger, and Dan Garrette. 2019. How multilingual is multilingual BERT? In *Proceedings of the 57th Annual Meeting of the Association for Computational Linguistics*, pages 4996–5001, Florence, Italy. Association for Computational Linguistics.

Nils Reimers and Iryna Gurevych. 2019. Sentence-BERT: Sentence embeddings using Siamese BERT-networks. In *Proceedings of the 2019 Conference on Empirical Methods in Natural Language Processing and the 9th International Joint Conference on Natural Language Processing (EMNLP-IJCNLP)*, pages 3982–3992, Hong Kong, China. Association for Computational Linguistics.

Nils Reimers and Iryna Gurevych. 2020. Making monolingual sentence embeddings multilingual using knowledge distillation. In *Proceedings of the 2020 Conference on Empirical Methods in Natural Language Processing (EMNLP)*, pages 4512–4525, Online. Association for Computational Linguistics.

Frederick Riemenschneider and Anette Frank. 2023. Exploring Large Language Models for Classical Philology.

Pranaydeep Singh, Gorik Rutten, and Els Lefever. 2021. A pilot study for BERT language modelling and morphological analysis for ancient and medieval Greek. In *Proceedings of the 5th Joint SIGHUM Workshop on Computational Linguistics for Cultural Heritage, Social Sciences, Humanities and Literature*, pages 128–137, Punta Cana, Dominican Republic (online). Association for Computational Linguistics.

Weiting Tan, Kevin Heffernan, Holger Schwenk, and Philipp Koehn. 2023. Multilingual representation distillation with contrastive learning. In *Proceedings of the 17th Conference of the European Chapter of the Association for Computational Linguistics*, pages 1477–1490, Dubrovnik, Croatia. Association for Computational Linguistics.

Jörg Tiedemann and Lars Nygaard. 2004. The OPUS corpus - parallel and free: `http://logos.uio.no/opus`. In *Proceedings of the Fourth International Conference on Language Resources and Evaluation (LREC'04)*, Lisbon, Portugal. European Language Resources Association (ELRA).

Ivan Yamshchikov, Alexey Tikhonov, Yorgos Pantis, Charlotte Schubert, and Jürgen Jost. 2022. BERT in plutarch's shadows. In *Proceedings of the 2022 Conference on Empirical Methods in Natural Language Processing*, pages 6071–6080, Abu Dhabi, United Arab Emirates. Association for Computational Linguistics.

A Appendix: Training Details

Parameter	GRCmBERT	GRCXLM-R
Batch Size	140	128
Learning Rate	2e-5	2e-5
LR Scheduler	linear	linear
Epochs	10	10
Warmup Steps	2000	2000
Mask Percentage	15%	15%

Table 7: Pre-training hyperparameters

Parameter	GRCmBERT	GRCXLM-R
Batch Size	128	128
Learning Rate	2e-5	2e-5
LR Scheduler	linear	linear
Max Seq. Length	128	128
Pooling	mean	mean
Embedding Dim.	768	768
Teacher: `all-mpnet-base-v2`		
Epochs (GRC)	15	15
Epochs (EL)	3	3
GRC Warmup Steps	2000	2000
EL Warmup Steps	2000	8000
Teacher: `sentence-t5-large`		
Epochs (GRC)	30	30
Epochs (EL)	6	6
GRC Warmup Steps	2000	2000
EL Warmup Steps	2000	2000

Table 8: Knowledge distillation hyperparameters

Parameter	GRCmBERT	GRCXLM-R
Batch Size	82	82
Learning Rate	2e-5	2e-5
LR Scheduler	linear	linear
Warmup Steps	2000	2000
Max Seq. Length	128	128
Epochs (GRC)	10	10
Epochs (EL)	3	3
Pooling	CLS	CLS
Embedding Dim.	768	768

Table 9: SimCSE hyperparameters

B Appendix: Sentence Segmentation

For translation alignment, it is not necessary that each segment be a sentence, since the alignment process can handle 1-many, many-1 or many-to-many relations. The Greek texts in our corpus contain punctuation, so we segment them by period (.), question mark (;), and raised dot (·). Some of the Greek texts use a colon instead of a raised dot, and in these cases we treat colons as raised dots. For the English texts we first segment using the NLTK sentence tokenizer (Bird et al., 2009) then further subdivide these segments by semicolon (;) and colon (:).

A Transformer-based Parser for Syriac Morphology

Martijn Naaijer♡[1] Constantijn Sikkel♠ Mathias Coeckelbergs♣
Jisk Attema◇ Willem Th. Van Peursen♠
♡University of Copenhagen, Denmark ♠Vrije Universiteit Amsterdam, The Netherlands
♣Katholieke Universiteit Leuven, Belgium ◇Netherlands eScience Center, The Netherlands

Abstract

In this project we train a Transformer-based model from scratch, with the goal of parsing the morphology of Ancient Syriac texts as accurately as possible. Syriac is a low-resource language, only a relatively small training set was available. Therefore, the training set was expanded by adding Biblical Hebrew data to it. Five different experiments were done: the model was trained on Syriac data only, it was trained with mixed Syriac and (un)vocalized Hebrew data, and it was trained first on (un)vocalized Hebrew data and then trained further on Syriac data. The models trained on Hebrew and Syriac data consistently outperform the models trained on Syriac data only. This shows that the differences between Syriac and Hebrew are small enough that it is worth adding Hebrew data to train the model for parsing Syriac morphology. Training models with data from multiple languages is an important trend in NLP, we show that this works well for relatively small datasets of Syriac and Hebrew.

1 Introduction

In this paper we develop a morphological parser for the Syriac language. The trained model is able to segment graphical units into distinct words, it segments the morphemes within a word, and disambiguates morphemes and lexemes, all at the same time.

Syriac is a Semitic language with a rich morphology. Therefore, to add linguistic annotations to a text, it is better to encode the smaller parts of a word (morphemes) rather than the complete words. A complication is that the Syriac language is written without vowels, which leads to the problem that a word can be parsed in different ways. Furthermore, we only have a small Syriac training set. Therefore, we try to improve the model's prediction accuracy by adding Biblical Hebrew data to the training process. Biblical Hebrew is a Semitic language that is closely related to Syriac, and the training set that we have for this language is substantially bigger.

Since the late 1970s, the Eep Talstra Center for Bible and Computer (ETCBC) of the Vrije Universiteit Amsterdam has developed and maintained a richly annotated dataset of the Masoretic Text of the Hebrew Bible. This dataset contains a wealth of linguistic features on the levels of words, phrases, clauses and larger text units. More recently, ancient texts in Syriac have been prepared in a similar way. However, a vast corpus of Syriac texts is available, and we hope to develop a faster approach to annotate these texts, because annotating them manually is a labor-intensive task.

We have trained the Transformer model in five different ways, to see which approach gives the highest accuracy on the Syriac test set: a model trained on Syriac data only, a model trained on a mix of (vocalized or unvocalized) Hebrew and Syriac data, and a model which is trained on (vocalized or unvocalized) Hebrew data first and trained further on Syriac data.

A trained model can make predictions on "new" Syriac texts, resulting in morphologically segmented texts. These results need to be corrected manually, and these corrected results can be processed further in a rule-driven way to produce the linguistic annotations. Therefore, training the models is the first step in a longer pipeline.

2 State of the art

Between 2000 and 2020 a number of studies were published in which Natural Language Processing (NLP) tasks for Semitic languages are described, often dealing with part of speech tagging (e.g.,

[1] Corresponding author: mna@teol.ku.dk.

Proceedings of the Ancient Language Processing Workshop associated with RANLP-2023, pages 23–29,
held in Varna Bulgaria, Sept 8, 2023.
https://doi.org/10.26615/978-954-452-087-8_003

Modern Hebrew: Bar Haim et al. 2008; Amharic: Tachbelle et al. 2011; Arabic: Kübler, and Mohamed 2012; Mishnaic Hebrew: Giovanetti et al. 2018). Other studies deal with morphological analysis (Daya et al. 2004, Lembersky et al. 2014) and segmentation (Zeldes 2018).

With the larger availability of digital (annotated) Semitic texts and the advent of large, Transformer-based language models, there is an acceleration in the development of models and tools for NLP tasks for Semitic languages. A Large Language Model which focuses on Modern Hebrew, is AlephBERT (Seker et al. 2021), which can be used for a number of tasks, including segmentation, part of speech tagging, full morphological tagging, named-entity recognition and sentiment analysis. A similar model for Arabic, AraBERT, was developed by Antoun, Bali and Hajj (2021).

Relatively close to our research is a paper on adding diacritics to consonantal Hebrew texts (Shmidman et al. 2020). It uses a combination of a machine learning ("several bi-LSTM based modules") and a rule-driven approach ("comprehensive inflection tables and lexicons"). Koppel and Shmidman (2020) give an overview of developments in Machine Learning in relation to the Hebrew language and its texts.

A list of NLP resources for Hebrew can be found here: `https://github.com/NNLP-IL/Resources`.

An important trend in NLP is the development of multilingual models. These are models that can be used for a number of NLP tasks in various languages. Some of these models are trained on one language, like English, and they can be trained further on other languages, but there are also models that are trained from scratch on a number of languages (Ruder 2020).

3 Data

Our dataset consists of five files[2], which are based on the ETCBC database. The Hebrew files that can serve as the input data for the model, contain vocalized or unvocalized text of the Masoretic Text (MT) of the Hebrew Bible. The Hebrew output file contains the morphologically parsed MT. The text of these datasets is based on the fifth edition of the Biblica Hebraica Stuttgartensia[3]. The Syriac input file contains some books from the Peshitta, a translation of the Hebrew Bible in Syriac[4] (Ter Haar Romeny and Van Peursen, 1966–) and some non-biblical texts[5]. The Syriac input texts are unvocalized, but they contain some diacritics, which can be found in the Syriac manuscripts.

Each line in a data file contains one verse, and the text is represented in the ETCBC transcription. The first line of the vocalized Hebrew dataset, which is the first sentence of the Hebrew Bible, looks as follows:

```
Gen 1 1 B.:R;>CIJT B.@R@> >:ELOHIJM
>;T HAC.@MAJIM W:>;T H@>@REY
```

This line contains four tab-separated fields, with the following data: book, chapter, verse, and text.

In Hebrew script, the text, which means "In the beginning God created the heaven and the earth", looks as follows:

בְּרֵאשִׁית בָּרָא אֱלֹהִים אֵת הַשָּׁמַיִם וְאֵת הָאָרֶץ

All consonants, vowel signs and diacritics have a value in the transcription, e.g., ב is transcribed with B, א with >, qametz is transcribed with @, shewa with ":", and dagesh with ".". The transcription is read from left to right, unlike the text in Hebrew script.

The same line, but taken from the unvocalized dataset looks as follows:

```
Gen 1 1 BR>CJT BR> >LHJM >T HCMJM
W>T H>RY
```

This text contains the same consonants as the vocalized text, but it misses the vowel signs.

Finally, the corresponding verse in the morphologically parsed output file looks as follows:

[2] The files can be found in the data folder of our GitHub repository: `https://github.com/etcbc/ssi_morphology`. The raw input files are s2-in (Syriac), t-in_voc (vocalized Hebrew), t-in_con (unvocalized Hebrew), the corresponding parsed output files are s2-out (Syriac) and t-out (Hebrew). In this repository one can also find the code.

[3] For an electronic edition of the MT with all the annotations, see: `https://github.com/ETCBC/bhsa`.

[4] A digitized version of the whole Peshitta can be found here: `https://github.com/ETCBC/peshitta`.

[5] For the texts, see also: `https://github.com/ETCBC/linksyr/tree/master/data`.

```
Gen 1 1 B-R>CJT/ BR>[ >LH(J(M/JM >T
H-CMJ(M/(JM W->T H->RY/:a
```

The output dataset contains the same consonantal text as the input data, with a number of extra signs which indicate the morphological structure of the words:
The dash (-) separates different words within a graphical unit.
A word can have different morphemes, which are marked with special signs:
After "[" follow verbal endings, and after "/" follow nominal endings.
"+" initializes a pronominal suffix.
Between exclamation marks, one finds the verbal preformative, e.g., !J! in a 3rd person masculine singular yiqtol, !T! in a 2nd person masculine singular yiqtol or !! in a qal infinitive or imperative.
Between closing square brackets one finds the prefix that is characteristic for a verbal stem, e.g.]HT] for hitpael,]N] for niphal, etc.
"~" initializes a univalent final, for example, a ~H is a locative he.

The ETCBC approach of encoding morphology distinguishes between a paradigmatic form and a realized form of the morphemes. E.g., the paradigmatic form of the masculine plural marker is JM (ים- in Hebrew script). In several places in the MT, it is spelled as M (ם). Here the J (י), which is part of the paradigmatic form, is not written. This is indicated in the encoding with an opening parenthesis. E.g., in Genesis 17:20, one finds נשיאם ("princes"), which has the morphological encoding NFJ>/(JM, indicating that the J occurs in the paradigmatic plural form, but it is not realized. The opposite can also occur. If a character occurs in the text, but not in the paradigmatic form, it is preceded by "&".

In the morphological encoding, there are some Latin letters preceded by a colon:
:a marks that a word is in absolute state.
:c marks that a word is in construct state.
:n marks the narrative vocalization of the waw.
:d marks the D-stem.
:u marks the u-a pattern of the passive.

The "=" sign is used to disambiguate consonantal homographs, e.g., one distinguishes between KBD/ (כָּבֵד, "heavy"), KBD=/ (כָּבֵד, "liver"), and KBD==/ (כֹּבֶד, "heaviness").

The alphabets of Syriac and Hebrew are identical, also in the ETCBC transcription, except that the *sin* (שׂ) is lacking in Syriac. The Syriac dataset contains three different Syriac diacritics: dots below and above the text, and seyame.

A limitation of the present dataset is that for every word in the input, there is only one correct parsing in the output. In some cases, the text is ambiguous, and a word could be parsed correctly in different ways. A possible improvement of the dataset is to include alternative parsing options.

4 Data preparation

We start with texts that do not have any parsing, which means that a text has not been segmented in phrases, clauses, or sentences. All verses of a book in the dataset are concatenated and split separately in shorter sequences of n graphical units. n is one of the required hyperparameters for training a model. These shorter sequences are partly overlapping and form a moving window. E.g., if the text is:

```
BR>CJT BR> >LHJM >T HCMJM W>T H>RY
```

and n is 5, the text will be split in the following three training inputs:

```
BR>CJT BR> >LHJM >T HCMJM
BR> >LHJM >T HCMJM W>T
>LHJM >T HCMJM W>T H>RY
```

When all the texts are split in partly overlapping sequences and a subset is selected randomly as Syriac test set, a problem is that part of the sequences in the test set can also be found in the training set, which means that training and test set are not independent of each other. A possible solution is to select a few complete books as test set, but that leads to the problem that the language of these books may not be representative of Syriac in general. Therefore, we have used a different solution. If n is 5, the texts of 5 consecutive verses are grouped, and from all these groups of 5 verses, the validation and test set are selected. With this approach, it is guaranteed that the texts are long enough to extract at least one sequence of 5 graphical units, and they are short enough to split a book in many sequences, with the result that parts of the book can be found in the training, validation and test set, without overlap between these datasets. After this split, each sequence of 5 verses is split further in the partly overlapping shorter sequences of 5 graphical units. All short sequences that contain a case of ketiv/qere in the Hebrew datasets are removed, because the consonantal text that is written (the ketiv) and the morphological analysis generally do not match. These words are indicated with a "*" in the data files.

5 The model

The morphological analysis is approached here as a sequence to sequence (seq2seq) problem, for which we use a Transformer model [6]. The Transformer is the state-of-the-art model for numerous NLP tasks (Vaswani et al. 2017) and is also the basis of Large Language Models like ChatGPT and GPT4. The Transformer seq2seq model has an encoder/decoder architecture. The encoder consists of a stack of encoder layers, in which the output of one layer serves as the input of the next one. Each layer consists of two components: multi-head attention and a feedforward network. Fundamental for the transformer model is the concept of self-attention, with which a word is related to all other words in a text sequence. In the self-attention mechanism, the embedding matrix of a sentence is multiplied with three randomly initialized matrices W^Q, W^K, and W^V, thus forming three new matrices Q (Query), K (Key) and V (Value). From these matrices, the attention matrix Z_1 is calculated as follows:

$$Z_1 = softmax\left(\frac{QK^T}{\sqrt{(d^k)}}\right)V_1$$

Z_1 has the index 1, because this is the first attention head. There can be an arbitrary number of heads that are concatenated:

$$Multihead\ attention = Concatenate(Z_1, Z_2, Z_3, \dots)W_0$$

in which W_0 is a new weight matrix.

After that, information of the word order in a sentence is added using positional encoding. The resulting matrix is fed to a feedforward network consisting of two dense layers with ReLU activation.

Just like the encoder, the decoder consists of a number of layers, one layer giving its output to the next one.

The decoder of the transformer model starts with a start symbol and the representation of the sentence produced by the encoder, and from that the first word of the output after the start symbol is generated. Then, the representation, the start symbol and the first word together are fed to the encoder, after which the second word is generated. This is done until a stop symbol is generated.

In the present implementation, various hyperparameters can be tweaked, which can be found in the README of the GitHub repo. The only thing that we vary in the experiments described here are the number of epochs and the training datasets.

The model is trained from scratch, which makes it possible to get a good impression of what the difference is between a model trained on Syriac data alone, and a model that is trained on Hebrew and Syriac data.

In all our experiments, the number of heads in the encoder is 8, and the number of encoder layers and decoder layers is 3. The feedforward hidden dimension is 512. During decoding we used beam search, with a beam size of 3. The length of the partly overlapping text sequences is 7 graphical units.

6 Results

The model was trained with five different training strategies:

1. The model was trained on Syriac data.
2. The model was trained on a mix of unvocalized Hebrew and Syriac data.
3. The model was trained on a mix of vocalized Hebrew and Syriac data.
4. The model was trained first on unvocalized Hebrew data (10 epochs), and after that trained further on Syriac data.
5. The model was trained first on vocalized Hebrew data (10 epochs), and trained further on Syriac data.

The approach of two experiments is called transfer learning. In transfer learning, a model is

[6] The code for the model can be found in the file model_transformer.py in the scr folder in the GitHub repository.

trained first on a large dataset, after which the model is trained further on a smaller dataset for a specialized task. This is generally beneficial if there is only a small training dataset available for the specialized task, like in our case.

In all the experiments, we varied the number of epochs in the main training loop (20, 25, 30, 35, and 40 epochs).

We checked the accuracy of the predictions on the Syriac test set, which is identical for each experiment. The accuracy is defined as the percentage of graphical units that is predicted fully correctly at a specific index of the test sequences. These test sequences are partly overlapping, just like the training sequences. Therefore, for most words in the test set multiple predictions are made.

The results can be found in figure 1, which shows the results of the index with the highest accuracy.

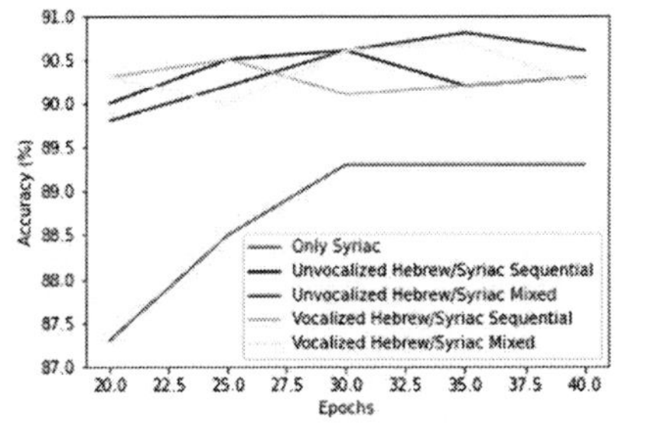

Figure 1. The accuracy of predictions on the Syriac test set with five different training strategies.

The accuracy of the model trained on Syriac data increases with the number of epochs from 87.3% for 20 epochs to 89.3% for 30 or more epochs. The accuracy of the predictions of the models trained on Hebrew and Syriac data vary somewhat between 89.8% (20 epochs) and 90.8% (35 epochs), both achieved by the model trained simultaneously on unvocalized Hebrew and Syriac data.

The models trained on Hebrew and Syriac data perform consistently better than the models trained on Syriac data only. Even though the accuracy of the latter models is only 1-2% higher, this is quite substantial, and it is hard to achieve this result by tuning hyperparameters.

The Hebrew datasets consisting of 22946 verses are substantially bigger than the Syriac datasets (5596 verses) we used. Therefore, training a model with Hebrew data takes substantially longer, which may be a disadvantage for including this dataset, especially if one wants to optimize the model further by tuning the hyperparameters. So, as is often the case, there is a tradeoff between speed and performance.

7 Error analysis

In the predictions on the test set, the model can make different kinds of mistakes. We provide a notebook in the GitHub repository[7], with which each mistaken prediction is classified as one of six error categories, with the goal of further improving the model. The following kinds of mistakes are distinguished:

0. Parse errors in the encoding. In this case, the prediction is ungrammatical according to the parsing conventions.
1. The consonantal form of the prediction and the true surface form differ.
2. Ungrammatical morpheme type combinations. This is the case if there is, e.g., a combination of verbal and nominal morphemes that do not match.
3. Unparadigmatic morphemes. In this case the model predicts a morpheme that falls outside of the ETCBC inventory of paradigmatic Syriac morphemes.
4. Difference in number of analytical words with the true form. In this case, the number of "-" signs in the graphical unit is incorrect.
5. Difference in morphemes with the true form. In this case, the analysis of the word is grammatically correct, but not within the given context, there could for instance be an incorrect number of "=" signs at the end of the lexeme.

[7] This is the file evaluation_syriac.ipynb in the folder badness_analysis.

The results are shown in figure 2. It shows the results for the number of epochs with the highest accuracy.

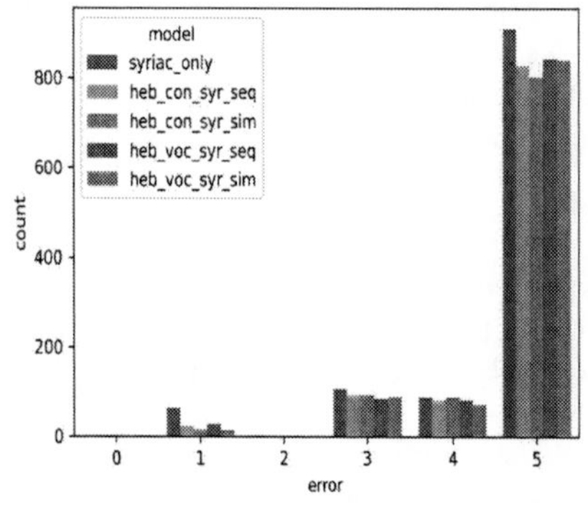

Figure 2. Frequencies of different types of errors made by the five models.

In general, the models show similar patterns. For every model, the most frequent type of error is 5, which means that the parsing is grammatically correct, but not in the given context. The error types 0 and 2 hardly occur.

In most error categories, the model which was trained on Syriac only has more errors than the other models. An important difference between this model and the other models is found in error type 1, indicating errors in the surface text, where the model trained on Syriac has 2-3 times more errors than the models trained on both Hebrew and Syriac data. The consonantal text of the input and output should be identical, and this is language independent. This is a clear sign that adding the Hebrew data helps here, simply because the volume increases. The same may be true for the error categories 3, 4, and 5. Here and there, the Hebrew may help because a morpheme is the same as in Syriac, but it is likely that it helps mostly because it adds volume to the dataset, which helps to make the model more consistent in analyzing morphemes.

8 Conclusions

In this paper we trained a Transformer model from scratch with the goal of analyzing Syriac morphology. An important part of the research was to see if adding Hebrew to the training set would improve the accuracy of the predictions on the Syriac test set. We compared results of the models that were trained on Syriac data alone, models that were trained on (un)vocalized Hebrew and then trained on Syriac, and models that were trained on (un)vocalized Hebrew and Syriac simultaneously. The highest accuracy of the model trained on Syriac data was 89.3%. The best model overall was trained on unvocalized Hebrew and Syriac simultaneously with an accuracy of 90.8%, which outperforms the best "Syriac only" model with 1.5%.

Further improvements can possibly be achieved by optimizing the hyperparameters of the models, but it is clear that adding Hebrew data to the training set helps with improving the performance on the Syriac test set. The same effect may be expected with a larger Syriac dataset, but as long as that dataset is relatively small, adding Hebrew data is a good solution. Another way to expand the dataset is to use data augmentation, which we are considering for future experiments.

It has been shown in other tasks that a model trained on a variety of data can be very useful to be trained further for specialized tasks. In our project we see the same phenomenon. The experiment could be broadened in various ways. One could for instance use one of our models and train it further on data from other languages than Hebrew and Syriac, such as Akkadian or Arabic, or train models to parse Syriac texts syntactically.

Acknowledgments

We thank Martin Ehrensvärd for proofreading the manuscript and the Netherlands eScience Center for their support in this project.

References

Shihadeh Alqrainy and Muhammed Alawairdhi. 2020. Towards Developing a Comprehensive Tag Set for the Arabic Language. *Journal of Intelligent Systems* 30:287–296. https://doi.org/10.1515/jisys-2019-0256.

Wissam Antoun, Fady Baly, and Hazem Hajj. 2021. AraBERT: Transformer-based Model for Arabic Language Understanding. *Proceedings of the 4th Workshop on Open-Source Arabic Corpora and Processing Tools, with a Shared Task on Offensive Language Detection*, 9–15. https://aclanthology.org/2020.osact-1.2.

Roy Bar-Haim, Khalil Sima'an, and Yoad Winter. 2008. Part-of-speech tagging of Modern Hebrew text. *Natural Language Engineering* 14(2):223–251. https://doi.org/10.1017/S135132490700455X.

Ezra Daya, Dan Roth, and Shuly Wintner. 2004. Learning Hebrew Roots: Machine Learnng with Linguistic Constraints. *Proceedings of the 2004 Conference on Empirical Methods in Natural Language Processing*, 357–364.

Emiliano Giovannetti, Davide Albanesi, Andrea Bellandi, Simone Marchi, and Alessandra Pecchioli. 2018. Constructing an Annotated Resource for Part-Of-Speech Tagging of Mishnaic Hebrew. *Proceedings of the Fifth Italian Conference on Computational Linguistics CLiC-it 2018: 10–12 December 2018, Torino*. Torino: Accademia University. https://doi.org/10.4000/books.aaccademia.3394.

Moshe Koppel and Avi Shmidman. 2020. Torah Study and the Digital Revolution, a Glimpse of the Future. https://thelehrhaus.com/commentary/torah-study-and-the-digital-revolution-a-glimpse-of-the-future.

Sandra Kübler and Emad Mohamed. 2012. Part of speech tagging for Arabic. *Natural Language Engineering* 18(4):521–548. https://doi.org/10.1017/S1351324911000325.

Gennadi Lembersky, Danny Shacham, and Shuly Wintner. 2012. Morphological disambiguation of Hebrew: A case study in classifier combination, *Natural Language Engineering* 20(1):69–97. https://doi.org/10.1017/S1351324912000216.

Amit Seker, Elron Bandel, Dan Bareket, Idan Brusilovsky, Refael Shaked Greenfeld, and Reut Tsarfaty. 2021. AlephBERT: A Hebrew Large Pre-Trained Language Model to Start-off your Hebrew NLP Application. https://arxiv.org/abs/2104.04052.

Avi Shmidman, Shaltiel Shmidman, Moshe Koppel, and Yoav Goldberg. 2020. Nakdan: Professional Hebrew Diacritizer. *Proceedings of the 58th Annual Meeting of the Association for Computational Linguistics: System Demonstrations*, Association for Computational Linguistics 197–203. https://doi.org/10.18653/v1/2020.acl-demos.23.

Martha Y. Tachbelie, Solomon T. Abate, and Laurent Besacier. 2011. Part-of-Speech Tagging for Under-Resourced and Morphologically Rich Languages–The Case of Amharic. *Conference on Human Language Technology for Development, Alexandria, Egypt, 2–5 May 2011.* https://www.cle.org.pk/hltd/pdf/HLTD201109.pdf.

Bas Ter Haar Romeny and Willem Th. Van Peursen (eds.). 1966–. *The Old Testament in Syriac according to the Peshiṭta Version.* Leiden: Brill.

Sebastian Ruder. 2022. The State of Multilingual AI. https://www.ruder.io/state-of-multilingual-ai.

Ashish Vaswani, Noam Shazeer, Niki Parmar, Jakob Uszkoreit, Llion Jones, Aidan N Gomez, Łukasz Kaiser, and Illia Polosukhin. 2017. Attention is all you need. *Advances in Neural Information Processing Systems*, 6000–6010. https://arxiv.org/pdf/1706.03762.pdf.

Amir Zeldes. 2018. A Characterwise Windowed Approach to Hebrew Morphological Segmentation. *Proceedings of the 15th SIGMORPHON Workshop on Computational Research in Phonetics, Phonology, and* Morphology, 101–110. http://dx.doi.org/10.18653/v1/W18-5811.

Graecia capta ferum victorem cepit
Detecting Latin Allusions to Ancient Greek Literature

Frederick Riemenschneider **Anette Frank**
Department of Computational Linguistic
Heidelberg University
69120 Heidelberg, Germany
{riemenschneider|frank}@cl.uni-heidelberg.de

Abstract

Intertextual allusions hold a pivotal role in Classical Philology, with Latin authors frequently referencing Ancient Greek texts. Until now, the automatic identification of these intertextual references has been constrained to monolingual approaches, seeking parallels solely within Latin or Greek texts. In this study, we introduce SPHILBERTA, a trilingual Sentence-ROBERTA model tailored for Classical Philology, which excels at cross-lingual semantic comprehension and identification of identical sentences across Ancient Greek, Latin, and English. We generate new training data by automatically translating English texts into Ancient Greek. Further, we present a case study, demonstrating SPHILBERTA's capability to facilitate automated detection of intertextual parallels. Our models and resources are available at https://github.com/Heidelberg-NLP/ancient-language-models.

1 Introduction

The study of intertextuality and allusions to literary sources has a longstanding tradition in Classical Philology, highlighting complex interconnections between different literary works. During the 1960s, the concept of intertextuality was shaped by a comprehensive theoretical framework developed by scholars such as Julia Kristeva, Ferdinand de Saussure, and Michail Bakhtin. The term "intertextuality" itself was introduced by Kristeva during this pivotal era (Alfaro, 1996; Bendlin, 2006; Kristeva, 1986; Orr, 2003).

Intertextuality proves particularly crucial when examining Roman literature's relationship with Ancient Greek texts. Many Latin authors consciously mirrored elements of Greek classics, making intertextuality an essential concept for understanding this cultural literary exchange.[1]

The importance of intertextuality, especially given the considerable attention it has received, is beyond dispute. While there exists a plethora of theoretical work exploring specific forms of intertextuality, our focus in this work is on the general occurrence of textual resemblances, specifically within Latin and Greek texts.

Traditionally, the identification of such parallels has largely relied on scholars' close reading. However, recent years have seen the development of statistical NLP tools – driven especially by the Tesserae project (Coffee et al., 2012; Forstall et al., 2014) at the forefront of this movement – that are able to automatically uncover a considerable number of textual parallels. These approaches, however, typically rely on string-level parallels and are grounded in carefully designed rules and scoring functions. Notably, these systems are generally restricted to detecting parallels in the same language, as they rely on identifying identical tokens or stems.

Recently, the breakthrough in self-supervised training of powerful pre-trained language models (PLMs) has also led to a surge of diverse PLMs for Classical Philology (Bamman and Burns, 2020; Yamshchikov et al., 2022; Mercelis and Keersmaekers, 2022; Singh et al., 2021; Riemenschneider and Frank, 2023). In fact, two recent case studies in Bamman and Burns (2020) and Burns (2023) have shown that contextualized embeddings produced by such models can indeed identify texts bearing similar content. While a rigorous quantitative evaluation of these findings still remains to be conducted, the perceived potential of using these models for finding intertextual relations is clearly sparking widespread interest.

However, research into modern language analysis tasks has demonstrated that sentence embeddings derived solely from standalone BERT- or ROBERTA-based models generate suboptimal and inefficient embeddings. This insight led to

[1] Cf. Hutchinson (2013): "How Latin literature relates to Greek literature is one of the most fundamental questions for Latin literature, and for the reception of Greek."

Proceedings of the Ancient Language Processing Workshop associated with RANLP-2023, pages 30–38,
held in Varna Bulgaria, Sept 8, 2023.
https://doi.org/10.26615/978-954-452-087-8_004

the creation of Sentence-BERT (SBERT) models (Reimers and Gurevych, 2019).

Among the latest language models introduced in the field of Classical Philology is PHILBERTA (Riemenschneider and Frank, 2023), a ROBERTA-based model pre-trained on Ancient Greek, Latin, and English language data. Building upon this model, we present SPHILBERTA, a model tailored to the discovery of intertextual parallels across Latin, Ancient Greek, and English texts.

In this work, our goal is to move away from systems relying on hand-crafted rules, and instead to employ state-of-the-art tools for identifying intertextual relations that are easy to adapt to a wide variety of languages from Classical Philology and beyond. Most importantly, we probe the feasibility of uncovering intertextual parallels *across languages*, an area that has been largely neglected in the automatic identification of intertextual allusions until this point. This novel capability will considerably enlargen the space for new findings, by being able to compare texts directly across languages.

We show that SPHILBERTA is proficient in recognizing direct translations of sentences in Ancient Greek, Latin, and English, thereby demonstrating comprehensive cross-lingual competence. Applying our model directly to texts of philological significance not only underlines its practical applicability but also highlights areas for improvement, suggesting promising avenues for future exploration.

In summary, our contributions are as follows:

i) We introduce SPHILBERTA, a multilingual sentence transformer for Latin, Ancient Greek, and English. To our knowledge, we are the first to apply this type of model to automatically detect passages of potential *cross-lingual* allusions in Latin texts.
ii) To alleviate the scarcity of parallel sentence pairs for training SPHILBERTA, we augment the available resources by automatically translating English texts to Ancient Greek using an existing multilingual T5 model pre-trained on Ancient Greek, Latin, and English data.
iii) We conduct experiments on retrieving translations or similar sentences from textual passages in foreign-language texts, using cross-lingual SPHILBERTA sentence embeddings.
iv) Our experiments demonstrate that SPHILBERTA is able to detect translations with high accuracy and that data augmentation significantly enhances the performance of the system for Ancient Greek. While finding textual allusions still requires philological expertise, we present cases where the model identifies passages linked to known allusive texts.

2 Related Work

Detecting Intertextual Allusions. Initiated in 2008, the Tesserae project (Coffee et al., 2012; Forstall et al., 2014) has been instrumental in advancing the automatic detection of intertextuality in Latin and Greek texts. Their open-source tools have seen numerous enhancements and refinements over the years.[2]

Existing research has explored matching words or stems (Coffee et al., 2012) as well as methods that focus on semantics (Scheirer et al., 2014). Additionally, techniques that combine both lexical and semantic elements have been examined, where semantic understanding is established through word embeddings (Manjavacas et al., 2019) or via the (Ancient Greek) WordNet (Bizzoni et al., 2014). While the majority of preceding studies have concentrated on detecting text reuse in the Bible and various religious texts, Burns et al. (2021) focus on Classical Latin literature.

However, to our knowledge, no efforts have been undertaken to automatically detect intertextual similarities across languages, specifically between Greek, Latin, and English texts. This lack is likely due to the inherent complications of inducing cross-language mappings, a difficulty that arises both with surface form-based strategies and with techniques utilizing word embeddings. Notwithstanding, this gap is of significant importance, as it overlooks the frequent appearance of such allusions, especially from Latin to Greek literature.

Language Models for Classical Philology. Bamman and Burns (2020) and Mercelis and Keersmaekers (2022) introduced Latin BERT and ELECTRA models, respectively. For Ancient Greek, Singh et al. (2021) and Yamshchikov et al. (2022) provided BERT models, initialized from Modern Greek BERT and subsequently trained on Ancient Greek data. Similarly, the UGARIT project has successfully explored the usage of the XLM-R model (Conneau et al., 2020) for Ancient Greek and Latin texts (Yousef et al., 2022a,b), even

[2] https://tesserae.caset.buffalo.edu/blog/about-tesserae/.

though XLM-R has not been pre-trained on Ancient Greek texts. Recently, Riemenschneider and Frank (2023) have complemented the encoder-only landscape with encoder-decoder models and developed trilingual models using Ancient Greek, Latin, and English texts. Moreover, Kostkan et al. (2023) and Burns (2023) have developed odyCy and latinCy, respectively, as dedicated spaCy pipelines[3] for Ancient Greek and Latin.

SBERT Embeddings. Reimers and Gurevych (2019) have shown that vanilla BERT embeddings are not suitable for creating sentence embeddings, and instead proposed the S(entence)-BERT models, which are based on Siamese and triplet network structures. Building on their work, Reimers and Gurevych (2020) introduced a method to learn multilingual sentence embeddings via multilingual knowledge distillation. This method realizes knowledge transfer from a monolingual teacher model to a student model, by training the student model to align the original sentence and its translation to the same location in the embedding space.

3 Methodology

We closely follow Reimers and Gurevych's (2020) multilingual knowledge distillation recipe. Their method requires a monolingual teacher model M and parallel sentences in the given source language and the target language(s) $((s_1, t_1), ..., (s_n, t_n))$.

The teacher trains a student model $\hat{M}$ such that $\hat{M}(s_i) \approx M(s_i)$ and $\hat{M}(t_i) \approx M(s_i)$. For a given mini-batch $\mathcal{B}$, the mean-squared loss is minimized:

$$\frac{1}{|\mathcal{B}|} \sum_{j \in \mathcal{B}} \left[(M(s_j) - \hat{M}(s_j))^2 + (M(s_j) - \hat{M}(t_j))^2 \right].$$

In other words, the student model is trained to map a given sentence to the same vector across languages, i.e., the translation of a given sentence should be mapped to the same vector as the source sentence. Notably, this method is not restricted to a bilingual setup. Instead, the student can be trained to map sentence vectors stemming from multiple languages to the same vector, namely the one provided by the teacher model.

In our work, the teacher and student SBERT models to be used for cross-lingual knowledge transfer will be initialized from strong transformer language models for the respective languages. For the English teacher model, we build on the MPNET model of Song et al. (2020), an encoder-only model that has been pre-trained using a combination of masked language modeling and permuted language modeling. Specifically, we use different sentence transformer variants induced from MPNET, as provided by the SBERT library (Reimers and Gurevych, 2019). For the student model, we experiment with initializing it from different multilingual models: XLM-R (Conneau et al., 2020), a multilingual model based on RoBERTa that covers 100 languages, including Modern Greek and Latin, in contrast to PHILBERTA (Riemenschneider and Frank, 2023), a recent trilingual model that has been pre-trained on Ancient Greek, Latin, and English texts.

More detail about our models and the specific experimental setup is provided in Section 5.

4 Parallel Data

As outlined in Section 3, the knowledge distillation method of Reimers and Gurevych (2020) crucially depends on the availability of parallel sentences between the relevant source and target languages – here, the source language English for the teacher model, and English, Ancient Greek, and Latin for our student model.

We collect this data from various sources: from the Perseus Digital Library,[4] from parallel Bible data,[5] parallel English-to-Greek sentences from the OPUS corpus (Tiedemann, 2012), and an extensive collection of parallel English and Latin sentences available on the Huggingface Hub.[6] We refer to the latter dataset as "Rosenthal", named after its associated account.

The Perseus project features a large collection of Ancient Greek and Latin texts, many of them with corresponding translations. However, the alignment of the provided data is not always fine-grained enough for our purpose. Therefore, we align individual lines with their corresponding translation, and discard lines that we cannot align successfully.

To generate additional parallel data for enhanced knowledge transfer, we experiment with translating the English portions of the Rosenthal dataset,

[3] https://spacy.io/.

[4] https://github.com/PerseusDL/canonical-greekLit and https://github.com/PerseusDL/canonical-latinLit.

[5] https://github.com/npedrazzini/parallelbibles/tree/main.

[6] https://huggingface.co/datasets/grosenthal/latin_english_parallel.

	English	Greek	Latin
Perseus	3 743K	2 120K	384K
Bible	897K	128K	520K
Opus	5K	4K	—
Rosenthal	3 428K	2 370K†	2 095K

Table 1: Dataset statistics (in number of words) of available parallel sentences across languages. The Greek Rosenthal data marked with a dagger (†) has been translated using PHILTA$_{\text{En}\rightarrow\text{Grc}}$.[7]

which consists solely of English and Latin parallel data, into Ancient Greek. This required first fine-tuning the multilingual PHILTA model[7] on the Perseus data to enable translation from English to Ancient Greek. Subsequently, we used the trained PHILTA$_{\text{En}\rightarrow\text{Grc}}$ model to translate the Rosenthal dataset into Ancient Greek, thereby expanding it to a trilingual parallel dataset.

Table 1 provides the data statistics. Since parts of the corpora overlap, we deduplicate the data.

5 Experiments

Our first aim is to compare different model configurations. We test the following configurations:

- **Teacher Model.** We use the `all-mpnet-base-v2`[8] and the `multi-qa-mpnet-base-dot-v1`[9] model from the SBERT library (Reimers and Gurevych, 2019) as teacher models. While the former is fine-tuned on a variety of tasks, the latter is optimized for semantic search.

- **Student Model.** We compare the performance of XLM-R (Conneau et al., 2020) to that of PHILBERTA (Riemenschneider and Frank, 2023) when used as student models. XLM-R serves as a well-established multilingual baseline.

- **Data Augmentation.** We evaluate whether the automatic English-to-Greek translations produced by PHILTA$_{\text{En}\rightarrow\text{Grc}}$ to extend the Rosenthal dataset improve task performance.

In order to transparently evaluate our models, we first measure their ability to correctly detect translations of a sentence. For each parallel dataset, we hold out 1 000 sentences as test sets. Given a query, i.e., the embedding of a specific sentence in the source language, we compute the cosine similarity to the embeddings of all 1 000 sentences in the target language.

Following Reimers and Gurevych (2020), we measure the success of our models by determining *translation accuracy*: we count a translation to be correctly identified if the model computes the highest cosine similarity between the query and its correct translation, and vice versa. This evaluates the student model's ability to align a source language sentence with an equivalent target language sentence.

However, our primary interest is whether the model can effectively link Ancient Greek and Latin texts. Regrettably, the volume of parallel data available in Ancient Greek and Latin is severely constrained. Consequently, we utilize Bible data, which is accessible in Ancient Greek, Latin, and English. Again, we examine the model's performance on 1 000 test sentences, given in Ancient Greek or Latin. We ensure that the model has not encountered any of these sentences in its training data, either in English or Latin, or in Ancient Greek. In addition, we use the PHILTA$_{\text{En}\rightarrow\text{Grc}}$-generated Ancient Greek test set translations of the Rosenthal corpus and compare them to their Latin originals.

We are aware that the task of identifying intertextual allusions poses a much greater challenge than merely recognizing translations, as allusions typically exhibit more subtlety and may extend beyond sentence or verse boundaries. However, we consider this evaluation a transparent method for comparing the effectiveness of different model configurations and an approximate measure to evaluate the potential success of our models in identifying intertextual allusions across languages.

Experiment Details. We train all models with the exact same configurations. We fine-tune all models for 30 epochs, using a batch size of 32, the AdamW optimizer with a learning rate of 2e−5, and 10 000 warmup-steps. The best-performing model is selected based on the translation accuracy derived from a total of 2 000 held-out validation examples, comprised of 1 000 English-Greek and 1 000 English-Latin sentence pairs.

[7] PHILTA (Riemenschneider and Frank, 2023) is a trilingual encoder-decoder model based on T5 (Raffel et al., 2020) that was pre-trained on Ancient Greek, Latin, and English data.

[8] https://huggingface.co/sentence-transformers/all-mpnet-base-v2.

[9] https://huggingface.co/sentence-transformers/multi-qa-mpnet-base-dot-v1.

Teacher	Student	PhilTa-translations	Bible		Perseus		Rosenthal	
			En→La	La→En	En→La	La→En	En→La	La→En
`all-mpnet-base-v2`	XLM-R	✗	0.10	0.10	0.30	0.60	0.50	0.60
`all-mpnet-base-v2`	PhilBERTa	✗	96.10	95.60	90.10	88.40	95.90	95.20
`multi-qa-mpnet`	PhilBERTa	✗	**96.90**	**96.00**	91.60	**91.30**	**97.90**	**96.90**
`multi-qa-mpnet`	PhilBERTa	✓	96.40	95.90	**91.90**	90.90	97.80	96.60

Table 2: Translation accuracy for various *English-Latin* test sets. Utilizing XLM-R as a student model leads to catastrophic results. It is crucial to substitute PhilBERTa as the student model for successful model training. Switching to the semantically-oriented `multi-qa-mpnet` from the broader `all-mpnet-base-v2` provides further enhancements.

Teacher	Student	PhilTa-translations	Bible		Perseus		Rosenthal	
			En→Grc	Grc→En	En→Grc	Grc→En	En→Grc†	Grc†→En
`all-mpnet-base-v2`	XLM-R	✗	0.20	0.20	0.30	0.10	0.30	0.10
`all-mpnet-base-v2`	PhilBERTa	✗	96.50	96.50	89.50	87.40	93.39	92.49
`multi-qa-mpnet`	PhilBERTa	✗	97.80	97.70	89.80	88.80	92.29	86.99
`multi-qa-mpnet`	PhilBERTa	✓	**98.30**	**98.00**	**91.10**	**90.50**	**96.80**	**94.29**

Table 3: Translation accuracy for various *English-Greek* test sets. The Greek Rosenthal data has been translated by PhilTa. We see the same trends as in Table 2. The enrichment of the training corpus with additional PhilTa-translated content notably increases the performance for Ancient Greek.

Teacher	Student	PhilTa-translations	Bible		Rosenthal	
			La→Grc	Grc→La	La→Grc†	Grc†→La
`all-mpnet-base-v2`	XLM-R	✗	0.10	0.10	0.20	0.20
`all-mpnet-base-v2`	PhilBERTa	✗	96.10	95.60	83.97	83.67
`multi-qa-mpnet`	PhilBERTa	✗	96.50	96.69	84.97	82.57
`multi-qa-mpnet`	PhilBERTa	✓	**96.70**	**96.90**	**92.08**	**91.68**

Table 4: Translation accuracy for various *Latin-Greek* test sets. The Greek Rosenthal data has been translated by PhilTa. We see similar trends as described in Tables 2 and 3.

6 Results

We present our results for the different configurations in Tables 2 to 4. Specifically, we evaluate: i) the performance of different *teacher models* (the more general `all-mpnet-base-v2` SBERT model in comparison to the `multi-qa-mpnet` SBERT fine-tuned for semantic search), ii) different *student models* (XLM-R versus the PHILBERTA model), and iii) *augmenting the parallel data* for training SPHILBERTA using $\text{PHILTA}_{\text{En}\rightarrow\text{Grc}}$-translated texts.

Employing XLM-R as the student model leads to catastrophic performance. Specifically, the model never surpasses the 1% mark in test set performance. We observed this trend consistently, regardless of the model configuration or the random seed employed. This outcome is, to some degree, to be expected, as XLM-R is not pre-trained on Ancient Greek data. Still, it is surprising that XLM-R performs so badly also on Latin data, as its pre-training corpus contained a Latin portion. Moreover, the UGARIT project (Yousef et al., 2022a,b) has successfully adapted XLM-R to Ancient Greek. We hypothesize that the effectiveness of a broadly multilingual but unspecialized model may be task-dependent, and continuing self-supervised pre-training on Ancient Greek texts may be required for XLM-R to adapt adequately. These findings highlight the importance of initializing the student model with a model that is proficient in the target languages.

Initializing the student model with PHILBERTA yields strong performance, often surpassing 95% translation accuracy. Generally, employing `multi-qa-mpnet` as a teacher model contributes to a slight performance improvement over `all-mpnet-base-v2`. Yet, when testing the model on the Ancient Greek Rosenthal corpus, using the `multi-qa-mpnet` teacher model results in a performance decline. Importantly, the Greek part of this dataset has been translated by $\text{PHILTA}_{\text{En}\rightarrow\text{Grc}}$, which could possibly have affected the quality of the dataset. Indeed, while we see this negative trend when *testing* on the generated data, the inclusion of the PHILTA-generated Ancient Greek Rosenthal corpus as additional *training data* leads to a notable enhancement for the Greek datasets, while the performance for Latin translation retrieval remains largely unaffected.

The results for Latin-to-Greek and Greek-to-Latin translations are shown in Table 4. Our models notably exhibit strong performance across both datasets. Again, utilizing the Greek Rosenthal data considerably improves performance. These results show that SPHILBERTA can be efficiently utilized in a scenario that solely involves Greek and Latin texts, without necessitating the involvement of English texts.

7 Case Study: The *Aeneid* and Homer's *Odyssey*

Examinations of the intertextual allusions in Virgil's *Aeneid* to both the *Iliad* and the *Odyssey* have a long history, dating back to antiquity. Structurally, the *Aeneid's* initial six books mirror the narrative of the *Odyssey*, while the concluding six books correspond more closely to the *Iliad*.

In the second book of the *Aeneid*, the protagonist Aeneas attempts to escape from the ravaged city of Troy with his family. Tragically, his wife, Creusa, is lost amidst the chaos. Creusa's ghost consoles him and bids him goodbye before receding into thin air: "*This speech uttered, while I wept and would have said many a thing, she left me and retreated into thin air. Thrice there was I fain to lay mine arms round her neck; thrice the vision I vainly clasped fled out of my hands, even as the light breezes, or most like to fluttering sleep.*"[10]

These verses mirror closely a scene in the Nekyia of the *Odyssey*, where Odysseus meets his mother Anticleia in the underworld: "*So she spoke, and I pondered in heart, and was fain to clasp the spirit of my dead mother. Thrice I sprang towards her, and my heart bade me clasp her, and thrice she flitted from my arms like a shadow or a dream, and pain grew ever sharper at my heart.*"[11]

To evaluate our model's proficiency in identifying these intertextual allusions, we employ each verse of the *Aeneid* passage (i.e., 5 verses) as a query, which we then compare to the verse embeddings (approx. 11 000 verses) of the complete *Odyssey*. Table 5 shows the three highest results for each verse, according to our best-performing model setup (teacher: `multi-qa-mpnet`; student: PHILBERTA; additional PHILTA-generated Rosenthal data).

We note that these verses do not share a direct one-to-one relationship and they are not translations of each other, the scenario in which our model

[10] Virgil, *Aeneid*, 2.790–794, translated by Mackail (1885).

[11] Homer, *Odyssey*, 11.204–208, translated by Murray (1919).

Query	**Results**
Haec ubi dicta dedit, lacrimantem et multa volentem This speech uttered, while I wept and would have said many a thing,	τῆς δ᾽ ἄρ᾽ ἀκουούσης ῥέε δάκρυα, τήκετο δὲ χρώς· and as she listened her tears flowed and her face melted ὣς φάτο, τῆς δ᾽ εὔνησε γόον, σχέθε δ᾽ ὄσσε γόοιο. So she spoke, and lulled Penelope's laments, and made her eyes to cease from weeping. ὣς φάτο, τῇ δ᾽ ἄρα θυμὸν ἐνὶ στήθεσσιν ὄρινε. So he spoke, and stirred the heart in her breast.
dicere deseruit, tenuisque recessit in auras. [...said], she left me and retreated into thin air.	ἡ μὲν ἄρ᾽ ὣς ἔρξασ᾽ ἀπεβήσετο δῖα θεάων, Now when she had done this the fair goddess departed, ἡ μὲν ἄρ᾽ ὣς εἰποῦσ᾽ ἀπέβη πρὸς δώματα καλά, So saying, she departed to the fair palace. ἡ μὲν ἄρ᾽ ἐς κρήνην κατεβήσετο καλλιρέεθρον [She] had come down to the fair-flowing spring [Artacia],
Ter conatus ibi collo dare bracchia circum: Thrice there was I fain to lay mine arms round her neck;	ὄπτ᾽ ἐν χερσὶν ἑλών, τά ῥά οἱ γέρα πάρθεσαν αὐτῷ. he took in his hands roast meat and set it before them, [...] which they had set before himself as a mess of honor. τρὶς μέν μιν πελέμιξεν ἐρύσσεσθαι μενεαίνων, Thrice he made it quiver in his eagerness to draw it, αὐτίκ᾽ ἔπειτα τρίαιναν ἑλὼν χερσὶ στιβαρῇσιν straightway took his trident in his mighty hands,
ter frustra comprensa manus effugit imago, thrice the vision I vainly clasped fled out of my hands,	τρὶς δέ μοι ἐκ χειρῶν σκιῇ εἴκελον ἢ καὶ ὀνείρῳ and thrice [she flitted] from my arms like a shadow or a dream, τρὶς μὲν ἐφωρμήθην, ἑλέειν τέ με θυμὸς ἀνώγει, Thrice I sprang towards her, and my heart bade me clasp her, χερσὶ δὲ μή τι λίην προκαλίζεο, μή με χολώσῃς, But with thy [hands] do not provoke me overmuch,
par levibus ventis volucrique simillima somno. even as the light breezes, or most like to fluttering sleep.	ἡ δ᾽ ἔθεεν Βορέῃ ἀνέμῳ ἀκραέϊ καλῷ, And she ran before the North Wind, blowing fresh and fair, ὄρσας ἀργαλέων ἀνέμων ἀμέγαρτον ἀϋτμήν, when he had roused a furious blast of cruel winds ἐς πνοιὰς ἀνέμων. ἡ δ᾽ ἐξ ὕπνου ἀνόρουσε into the breath of the winds. And [she] started up from sleep

Table 5: Top 3 predictions of our best-performing SPHILBERTA model (teacher: `multi-qa-mpnet`; student: PHILBERTA; additional PHILTA-generated Rosenthal data) when queried over the whole *Odyssey*. We mark corresponding cross-lingual concept pairs with individual colors.

was trained. Even so, we observe that verse 793 ("*thrice the vision I vainly clasped fled out of my hands*") is correctly paired with the best corresponding Greek verse ("*and thrice she flitted from my arms like a shadow or a dream*"). In the majority of cases, our model accurately captures crucial concepts, such as *weeping*, *departing*, *triplicity*, *wind*, and *sleep*, linking them reasonably to different verses. However, our verse-to-verse mapping, which precludes longer texts, results in a lack of a cohesive concept of extended intertextually alluding passages.

Still, our case study demonstrates the proficiency of our models in recognizing sentence structures and translating them to a different language (as in "*this speech uttered*" → "*so she spoke*"), and in identifying common topics or concepts across languages, even locating verses where multiple relevant concepts exist within the same verse ("*thrice*", "*the vision*", "*out of my hands*" → "*thrice*", "*a shadow or a dream*", "*from my arms*").

Despite these remarkable results, our case study also reveals the need for a more sophisticated retrieval mechanism that extends beyond verse boundaries to search for broader patterns. Yet, already in the present state, our SPHILBERTA model can serve as a useful tool for automatic first-pass exploration of potential cross-lingual intertextual allusions, and in this way can support philologists in the search for intertextual allusions.

8 Conclusion

We introduce SPHILBERTA, a multilingual PHILBERTA-derived sentence transformer model, specifically adapted to Classical Philology. Our model represents a pioneering effort in detecting intertextual allusions between Ancient Greek and Latin texts, which is characteristic of many Roman writers who used Greek literature for juxtaposition. SPHILBERTA displays impressive performance across various datasets, confidently identifying direct translations among English, Latin, and Ancient Greek. We have illustrated that SPHILBERTA holds strong potential in revealing intertextual allusions; however, additional research is needed to fully exploit the model's capabilities. Our multilingual SPHILBERTA and the similarity-driven retrieval settings built upon it offer, for the first time, the option to study intertextuality cross-lingually on a broader scale in original Classical Literature.

Acknowledgements

We thank Nina Stahl for the insightful discussions we shared on the Greek and Latin parallel passages.

References

María Jesús Martínez Alfaro. 1996. Intertextuality: Origins and development of the concept. *Atlantis*, 18(1/2):268–285.

David Bamman and Patrick J Burns. 2020. Latin bert: A contextual language model for classical philology. *arXiv preprint arXiv:2009.10053*.

Andreas Bendlin. 2006. Intertextuality. http://dx.doi.org.ubproxy.ub.uni-heidelberg.de/10.1163/1574-9347_bnp_e525570. Accessed: 28 June 2023.

Yuri Bizzoni, Federico Boschetti, Harry Diakoff, Riccardo Del Gratta, Monica Monachini, and Gregory Crane. 2014. The making of Ancient Greek WordNet. In *Proceedings of the Ninth International Conference on Language Resources and Evaluation (LREC'14)*, pages 1140–1147, Reykjavik, Iceland. European Language Resources Association (ELRA).

Patrick J Burns. 2023. Latincy: Synthetic trained pipelines for latin nlp. *arXiv preprint arXiv:2305.04365*.

Patrick J. Burns, James A. Brofos, Kyle Li, Pramit Chaudhuri, and Joseph P. Dexter. 2021. Profiling of intertextuality in Latin literature using word embeddings. In *Proceedings of the 2021 Conference of the North American Chapter of the Association for Computational Linguistics: Human Language Technologies*, pages 4900–4907, Online. Association for Computational Linguistics.

Neil Coffee, Jean-Pierre Koenig, Shakthi Poornima, Christopher W Forstall, Roelant Ossewaarde, and Sarah L Jacobson. 2012. The tesserae project: intertextual analysis of latin poetry. *Literary and linguistic computing*, 28(2):221–228.

Alexis Conneau, Kartikay Khandelwal, Naman Goyal, Vishrav Chaudhary, Guillaume Wenzek, Francisco Guzmán, Edouard Grave, Myle Ott, Luke Zettlemoyer, and Veselin Stoyanov. 2020. Unsupervised cross-lingual representation learning at scale. In *Proceedings of the 58th Annual Meeting of the Association for Computational Linguistics*, pages 8440–8451, Online. Association for Computational Linguistics.

Christopher Forstall, Neil Coffee, Thomas Buck, Katherine Roache, and Sarah Jacobson. 2014. Modeling the scholars: Detecting intertextuality through enhanced word-level n-gram matching. *Digital Scholarship in the Humanities*, 30(4):503–515.

G. O. Hutchinson. 2013. *Greek to Latin: Frameworks and Contexts for Intertextuality*. Oxford University Press.

Jan Kostkan, Márton Kardos, Jacob Palle Bliddal Mortensen, and Kristoffer Laigaard Nielbo. 2023. OdyCy – a general-purpose NLP pipeline for Ancient Greek. In *Proceedings of the 7th Joint SIGHUM Workshop on Computational Linguistics for Cultural Heritage, Social Sciences, Humanities and Literature*, pages 128–134, Dubrovnik, Croatia. Association for Computational Linguistics.

Julia Kristeva. 1986. Word, dialogue, and novel. In *The Kristeva reader*, pages 34–61. Columbia University Press.

John William Mackail. 1885. *The Aeneid of Virgil*, volume 36. Macmillan.

Enrique Manjavacas, Brian Long, and Mike Kestemont. 2019. On the feasibility of automated detection of allusive text reuse. In *Proceedings of the 3rd Joint SIGHUM Workshop on Computational Linguistics for Cultural Heritage, Social Sciences, Humanities and Literature*, pages 104–114, Minneapolis, USA. Association for Computational Linguistics.

Wouter Mercelis and Alek Keersmaekers. 2022. An ELECTRA model for Latin token tagging tasks. In *Proceedings of the Second Workshop on Language Technologies for Historical and Ancient Languages*, pages 189–192, Marseille, France. European Language Resources Association.

A. T. Murray. 1919. *Homer. The Odyssey with an English Translation*. Harvard University Press, London.

Mary Orr. 2003. Intertextuality: Debates and contexts. *Polity Press*.

Colin Raffel, Noam Shazeer, Adam Roberts, Katherine Lee, Sharan Narang, Michael Matena, Yanqi Zhou, Wei Li, and Peter J. Liu. 2020. Exploring the limits of transfer learning with a unified text-to-text transformer. *Journal of Machine Learning Research*, 21(140):1–67.

Nils Reimers and Iryna Gurevych. 2019. Sentence-BERT: Sentence embeddings using Siamese BERT-networks. In *Proceedings of the 2019 Conference on Empirical Methods in Natural Language Processing and the 9th International Joint Conference on Natural Language Processing (EMNLP-IJCNLP)*, pages 3982–3992, Hong Kong, China. Association for Computational Linguistics.

Nils Reimers and Iryna Gurevych. 2020. Making monolingual sentence embeddings multilingual using knowledge distillation. In *Proceedings of the 2020 Conference on Empirical Methods in Natural Language Processing (EMNLP)*, pages 4512–4525, Online. Association for Computational Linguistics.

Frederick Riemenschneider and Anette Frank. 2023. Exploring large language models for classical philology. In *Proceedings of the 61st Annual Meeting of the Association for Computational Linguistics (Volume 1: Long Papers)*, pages 15181–15199, Toronto, Canada. Association for Computational Linguistics.

Walter Scheirer, Christopher Forstall, and Neil Coffee. 2014. The sense of a connection: Automatic tracing of intertextuality by meaning. *Digital Scholarship in the Humanities*, 31(1):204–217.

Pranaydeep Singh, Gorik Rutten, and Els Lefever. 2021. A pilot study for BERT language modelling and morphological analysis for ancient and medieval Greek. In *Proceedings of the 5th Joint SIGHUM Workshop on Computational Linguistics for Cultural Heritage, Social Sciences, Humanities and Literature*, pages 128–137, Punta Cana, Dominican Republic (online). Association for Computational Linguistics.

Kaitao Song, Xu Tan, Tao Qin, Jianfeng Lu, and Tie-Yan Liu. 2020. Mpnet: Masked and permuted pre-training for language understanding. *arXiv preprint arXiv:2004.09297*.

Jörg Tiedemann. 2012. Parallel data, tools and interfaces in OPUS. In *Proceedings of the Eighth International Conference on Language Resources and Evaluation (LREC'12)*, pages 2214–2218, Istanbul, Turkey. European Language Resources Association (ELRA).

Ivan Yamshchikov, Alexey Tikhonov, Yorgos Pantis, Charlotte Schubert, and Jürgen Jost. 2022. BERT in plutarch's shadows. In *Proceedings of the 2022 Conference on Empirical Methods in Natural Language Processing*, pages 6071–6080, Abu Dhabi, United Arab Emirates. Association for Computational Linguistics.

Tariq Yousef, Chiara Palladino, Farnoosh Shamsian, Anise d'Orange Ferreira, and Michel Ferreira dos Reis. 2022a. An automatic model and gold standard for translation alignment of Ancient Greek. In *Proceedings of the Thirteenth Language Resources and Evaluation Conference*, pages 5894–5905, Marseille, France. European Language Resources Association.

Tariq Yousef, Chiara Palladino, David J. Wright, and Monica Berti. 2022b. Automatic translation alignment for Ancient Greek and Latin. In *Proceedings of the Second Workshop on Language Technologies for Historical and Ancient Languages*, pages 101–107, Marseille, France. European Language Resources Association.

Larth: Dataset and Machine Translation for Etruscan

Gianluca Vico and **Gerasimos Spanakis**
Department of Advanced Computing Sciences / Paul-Henri Spaaklaan 1
Maastricht University / Maastricht, The Netherlands
`g.vico@student.maastrichtuniversity.nl`
`jerry.spanakis@maastrichtuniversity.nl`

Abstract

Etruscan is an ancient language spoken in Italy from the 7th century BC to the 1st century AD. There are no native speakers of the language at the present day, and its resources are scarce, as there exist only around 12,000 known inscriptions. To the best of our knowledge, there are no publicly available Etruscan corpora for natural language processing. Therefore, we propose a dataset for machine translation from Etruscan to English, which contains 2891 translated examples from existing academic sources. Some examples are extracted manually, while others are acquired in an automatic way. Along with the dataset, we benchmark different machine translation models observing that it is possible to achieve a BLEU score of 10.1 with a small transformer model. Releasing the dataset [1] can help enable future research on this language, similar languages or other languages with scarce resources.

1 Introduction

Etruscan (ISO 639-3 code: `ett`) is a language spoken in the Etruria region (modern-day centre Italy) from the 7th century BC to the 1st century AD (Wallace, 2008). It is written right to left using the Etruscan alphabet, derived from the Greek alphabet (Wallace, 2008). The predominant word order in this language is mostly subject-object-verb (Wallace, 2008). This pattern is similar to Latin, but distinguishing it from other languages like English, where the words follows the subject-verb-object order. It has 5 cases (accusative, nominative, genitive, dative and locative), two numbers (singular and plural) and takes into consideration animacy and gender (Wallace, 2008).

Only a small number of inscriptions in this language survived up to the present day: an estimated 12,000 inscriptions have been recovered (Wallace, 2008). However, only a few of them have a significant length to be considered complete. Other ancient languages used in similar areas and periods in history, such as Latin and Ancient Greek, have more resources, thus, making natural language processing techniques and tools easier to develop for these languages.

The contribution of this paper is threefold: First, we build a corpus of Etruscan inscriptions usable for natural language processing. We use as a starting point existing academic resources for this language exist, and we try to create our corpus both by manual and automatic work. Second, we focus on the machine translation task from Etruscan to English. We evaluate whether neural models can be trained with this data and if they can outperform less data-hungry models. Finally, we investigate if it is possible to exploit any similarity between Etruscan and Latin or Ancient Greek to improve the aforementioned model.

In Section 2, we introduce state-of-the-art techniques relevant to this paper. Then, in Sections 3 and 4 we explain the methods used to work on the data and the model used. Section 5 and Section 6 illustrate the experiments and compare the different techniques. Finally, Section 7 concludes the paper.

2 Literature review

The Etruscan Texts Project (ETP) (Wallace et al., 2004) is a digital Etruscan corpus which contains 369 inscriptions. The project is based on Etruskische Texte (Rix and Meiser, 1991) and is used in the book Zihk Rasna (Wallace, 2008). Another digital Etruscan work is the Corpus Inscripionum Etruscarum Plenissimum (CIEP) (Hill, 2018), based on the Corpus Inscriptionum Etruscarum (CIE) (Pauli, 1893).

Similar works exist for Latin and Ancient Greek, like I.PHI (Sommerschield et al., 2021) and Perseus (Crane, 1985). In addition, toolkits like CLTK (Johnson et al., 2021) offer natural language pro-

[1] The data and code are available here: `https://github.com/GianlucaVico/Larth-Etruscan-NLP.git`

Proceedings of the Ancient Language Processing Workshop associated with RANLP-2023, pages 39–48,
held in Varna Bulgaria, Sept 8, 2023.
https://doi.org/10.26615/978-954-452-087-8_005

cessing for these languages. Projects that aim to increase the resources available for low-resource languages may also include ancient languages, like the Tatoeba Translation Challenge (Tiedemann, 2020). It has Latin and Ancient Greek datasets, however, it does not include Etruscan.

The machine translation task can be solved via neural machine translation (Sutskever et al., 2014a), which involves training neural networks that take texts from the source language and generate the translation in the target language. Popular architectures include Long short-term memory (LSTM) (Hochreiter and Schmidhuber, 1997) and transformers (Vaswani et al., 2017). These models are sequence-to-sequence (Sutskever et al., 2014b), meaning they take a sequence as input and generate a sequence of possibly different lengths as output. One approach is to feed word or word pieces to the model like in T5 (Raffel et al., 2020) or Bahdanau et al. (2014). Yang et al. (2016) and Ling et al. (2015) show that it is possible to work directly on characters, while other models (Shahih and Purwarianti, 2019 and Bansal and Lobiyal, 2020) use a hybrid approach by working on both the character and word sequences.

Besides neural networks, other approaches include rule-based models, such as dictionary models, which translate the text based on explicit rules, and statistical models (Koehn, 2010).

By using the transformer architecture, Ithaca (Assael et al., 2022) is able to perform textual restoration and geographical and chronological attribution of ancient Greek inscriptions. The model consists of a sparse self-attention encoder (Zaheer et al., 2021) that takes as input the characters and the words of the input text, and then three feed-forward blocks generate the output for each task. Other examples of transformer models working on ancient languages are the multi-language translation model Opus-MT (Tiedemann and Thottingal, 2020), tested on the Latin $\rightarrow$ English split of the Tatoeba dataset, or the language model Latin-BERT (Bamman and Burns, 2020).

Translation models can be evaluated by using various metrics. Papineni et al. (2002) proposes BLEU: this metric considers the average matching precision of n-grams between the reference text and the machine-translated text. Another metric is TER (Snover et al., 2006), which measures the quality of the translation based on the number of edits needed to change the system text to the reference one. TER and BLEU are based on word n-grams, while chrF (Popović, 2015) uses the F-score of matching character n-grams.

3 Data

3.1 Etruscan

First, we collect a dataset containing Etruscan texts. The main sources used are CIEP (Hill, 2018), ETP (Wallace et al., 2004), and the book "Zikh Rasna: A Manual of the Etruscan Language and Inscriptions" (Wallace, 2008), which cites "Etruskische Texte" (Rix and Meiser, 1991). It is possible to extract Etruscan inscriptions and their translations where available from ETP and Zikh Rasna. In addition, we extract the date and location of the inscriptions. Also, Zikh Rasna contains a list of Etruscan words and proper names used to make a dictionary. From CIEP, we extract only the inscriptions and the translations. However, the inscriptions are often incomplete or noisy due to the structure of CIEP itself and the limitation of the PDF extracting software (PyMuPDF, McKie and Liu, 2016). We make two datasets. The first, **ETP**, uses data from ETP and ZIkh Rasna, while the second **ETP+CIEP**, adds the data from CIEP.

After removing strings that are in the wrong language, the text is normalised. CIEP and ETP use two different transcription conventions. Also, Etruscan uses several symbols as word separators ("
", "·", ":", "⁝"), which are converted to white space (" "). Table 1 illustrates how the Etruscan alphabet is transcribed by ETP and by us (Larth). Note that the transcription is not reversible.

In the end, we obtain 7139 Etruscan texts (561 from ETP and 6578 from CIEP). Among these, a translation is available for only 2891 inscriptions (239 from ETP and 2652 from CIEP). Also, the vocabulary built from ETP contains 1122 words, of which 956 with a translation. Each word is also described by 54 binary grammatical features (e.g., plural, active, passive, ...). The type of text is not included in the dataset, however, ETP lists on their website mostly proprietary and funerary texts (Wallace et al., 2004) (137 and 104 out of 369).

Since the data is limited, we perform data augmentation. Many inscriptions contain proper nouns, so we use the dictionary we built to replace them with other proper nouns with the same grammatical features. The substitution is done simultaneously on the Etruscan and English texts in order to keep the translations correct, as shown in Figure 1. Also,

Etruscan	ETP	Larth
𐌀	a	a
𐌁	b	b
𐌂	c	c
𐌃	d	d
𐌄	e	e
𐌅	v	v
𐌆	z	z
𐌇	h	h
𐌈	θ	th
𐌉	i	i
𐌊	k	k
𐌋	l	l
𐌌	m	m
𐌍	n	n
𐌎	$\overset{+}{s}$	s
𐌏	o	o
𐌑	σ, σ́	s, sh
𐌐	p	p
𐌒	q	q
𐌓	r	r
𐌔	s, ś, ς, ς́	s, sh, s, sh
𐌕	t	t
𐌖	u	u
𐌗	š	sh
𐌘	ϕ	ph
𐌙	χ	kh
𐌚	f	f

Table 1: Texts from ETP are already transliterated, but CIEP transliteration is sometimes ambiguous. We further reduce the number of symbols by using a subset of the Latin alphabet.

inscriptions can be damaged, so parts of the words cannot be read and the translation models have to either discard those words or rely only on the remaining characters. So, we generate more training samples by damaging more words. We assume that the damage occurs at the beginning or end of the words with a set probability. Also, we assume the number of damaged characters follows a geometric distribution. In this way, for instance, the word "clan" can stay unchanged or it might become "–an", "cla-", "-l–".

3.2 Latin and Ancient Greek

Models introduced later in the paper use Latin or Ancient Greek documents. Tatoeba eng-lat (Tiedemann, 2020) is used to train the Latin model. The text is normalised and non-Latin characters are removed. For Ancient Greek, we use Perseus (Crane, 1985). In this case, we also remove all diacritical marks and transliterate the text to Latin. In this way, all the languages used share the same alphabet.

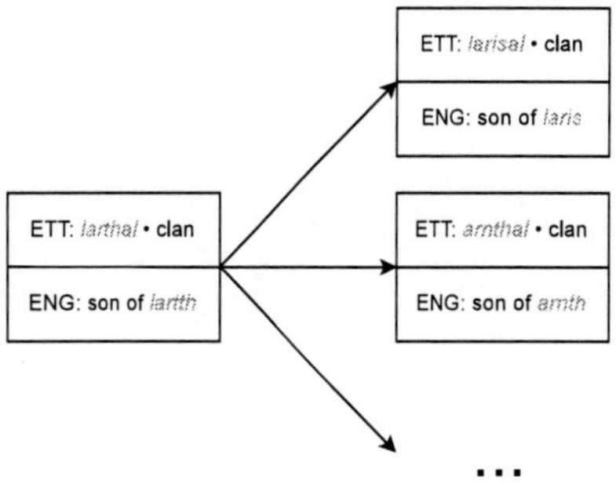

Figure 1: Example of data augmentation by replacing proper names. The name is replaced both in the Etruscan text and the English translation.

4 Machine Translation

We compare different models for machine translation on the BLEU metric but chr-F and TER metrics are also reported. The metrics are computed by SacreBLEU (Post, 2018). Higher BLEU and chr-F and lower TER indicate a better-performing model. Moreover, we evaluate the case where we use only ETP and ETP+CIEP for training and testing the models.

4.1 Random Model

The output of this model does not depend on the Etruscan inputs, but only on the training translations. It assumes that the length of the translations follows a normal distribution whose parameters are estimated from the training data. Then, it samples English tokens from the training distribution. The experiment is repeated 10 times with random splits of the dataset in training and testing data. The resulting metrics are then averaged.

4.2 Dictionary-based Model

The second model is a dictionary-based model based on the vocabulary provided in Zihk Rasna (Wallace, 2008). The model assumes that each word has one meaning and one translation. Moreover, it does not rearrange the word order and it does not consider the grammar of the source language or the target language. This model splits the input text into word tokens. Then, for each token, it searches for the exact match in the dictionary. If a

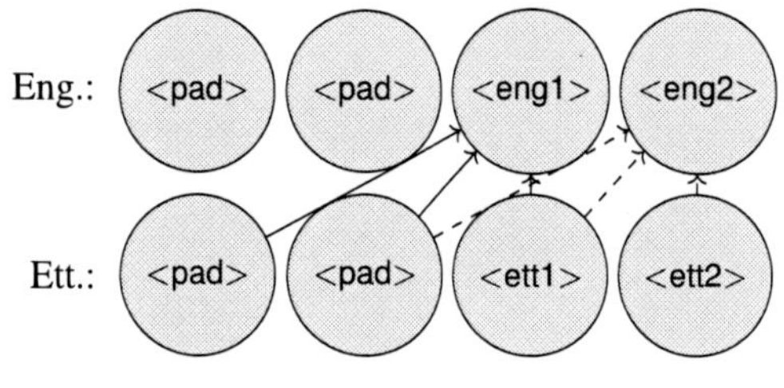

Figure 2: The first approach for the n-gram model. *<eng n>* indicates English tokens, while *<et n>* are Etruscan tokens; *<pad>* is the padding token. The example shows P(<eng1>|<pad><pad><et1>) and P(<eng2>|<pad><et1><et2>). The context is made up of Etruscan trigrams.

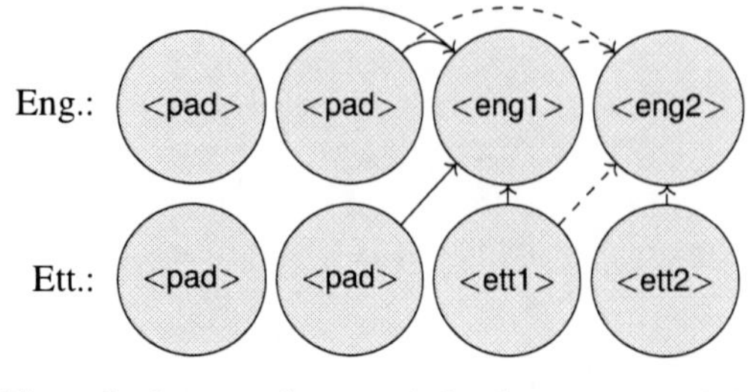

Figure 3: the second approach for the n-gram model. *<eng n>* indicates English tokens, while *<ett n>* are Etruscan tokens; *<pad>* is the padding token. The example shows P(<eng1>|<pad><ett1>, <pad><pad>) and P(<eng2>|<ett1><ett2>, <pad><eng1>). The context is made up of Etruscan and English bigrams.

match is found, it adds the translation to the output; otherwise, the token is ignored.

4.3 N-gram and Naïve Bayes Models

Then, we try to translate Etruscan taking into consideration the previous n tokens. The model estimates the probability distribution $\mathbb{P}(eng_i|ett_i, ett_{i-1}, ...ett_{i-n})$, where eng_i and ett_i are tokens at position i. This is done either directly from the training data or as a Naïve Bayes model with the following expression:

$$\mathbb{P}(eng_i|ett_i, ett_{i-1}, ...ett_{i-n}) \propto \\ \propto \mathbb{P}(eng_i) \prod_{j=0}^{n} \mathbb{P}(ett_{i-j}|eng_i) \quad (1)$$

The model assumes that one n^{th}Etruscan token is translated into the single n^{th}English token. Figure 2 shows how the sequences are aligned and which Etruscan context is used for each English token.

A second N-gram model also includes the previous English tokens in the context by computing $\mathbb{P}(eng_i|ett_i, ...ett_{i-n}, eng_{i-1}, ..., eng_{i-n-1})$ as shown in Figure 3. When the probability distribution is estimated directly, we consider the case when the word order is taken into account and when it is not. We use beam search to generate the output.

4.4 IBM Models

Next, we compare our models to existing ones. To do so, we consider the IBM models (Koehn, 2010) from the NLTK package (Bird and Loper, 2004). They are a series of 5 models with increasing complexity. These models consider the alignment between the source strings and the target strings, however, the Etruscan-English pairs we are using do not contain this information. Therefore, we test the models as if the sequences were aligned.

IBM1 does not consider the word order. IBM2 introduces the word order, while IBM3 takes also into consideration that a word can be translated into zero or more words. IBM4 and IBM5 can also reorder the output words. Moreover, IBM4 and IBM5 also need the part-of-speech (POS) tags of both the source and target sequences. POS tags are inferred from the grammatical features listed in the dictionary. For Etruscan, these are obtained by a manually annotated list of words, while the English sequences are tagged by NLTK perceptron tagger.

4.5 Transformer Models - Larth

Finally, we propose a transformer model, **Larth**. The encoder is based on Ithaca (Assael et al., 2022). It takes both the characters and the words as input and concatenates their embeddings. Then, the sequence is encoded with a BigBird attention block (Zaheer et al., 2021). The character and word sequences are aligned so that they have the same length. To do so, we test two approaches: we either extend the word sequence by repeating the word tokens or by adding space tokens as shown in Figure 4.

The decoder uses the encoded and the translated word sequences as input. First, it applies self-attention to the translated sequence, and then it computes the cross-attention between the translation and the encoded inputs. A feed-forward layer generates the output. Figure 5 illustrates this architecture.

First, we train the model from scratch on Etruscan → English. Then, the model is initially trained for Latin → English or Ancient Greek →

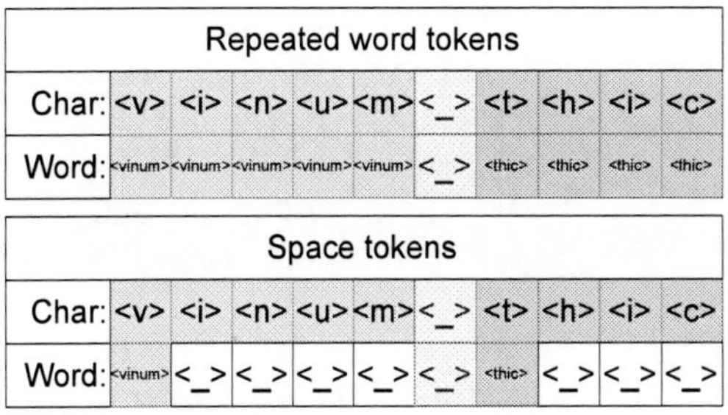

Figure 4: Example of how the character and word sequence are aligned. The string *vinum thic* means *wine and water*.

Dataset	BLEU	chr-F	TER
ETP+	0.059	9.263	194.977
CIEP	(0.0174)	(0.295)	(10.676)
ETP	0.324	13.970	133.878
	(0.064)	(1.150)	(11.877)

Table 2: Performance of the random model on the different Etruscan datasets. The table reports the mean value and the standard deviation of the metrics.

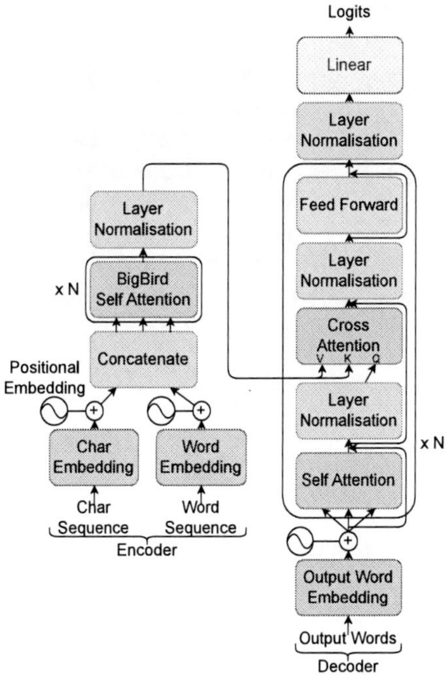

Figure 5: Transformer architecture used to translate Etruscan to English. The encoder imitates Ithaca's torso. For both the encoder and the decoder, one attention block is used.

English and later fine-tuned on the original task Etruscan $\rightarrow$ English.

Moreover, we investigate the effect of using both the character and the word sequence by training with only one of the sequences and the effect of data augmentation The model uses beam search when generating the output sequences, but we use one beam when evaluating during the training for efficiency. Sequences are truncated at 256 tokens due to memory and computational resources.

5 Experiments

In this section, we compare different machine translation models trained on Etruscan data. The models are compared on the BLEU score.

5.1 Random Model

First, we run the random model on the Etruscan-Englih data. The dataset is split into 80 % for training and 20 % for testing. Only English labels are used for the training. Each experiment is repeated 10 times with random dataset splits. Table 2 reports the mean scores and the standard deviation of the models with different combinations of the datasets.

5.2 Dictionary-based Models

From the book Zikh Rasna is possible to build a dictionary containing 821 vocables and their translations.

Dataset	BLEU	chr-F	TER
ETP+CIEP	0.167	9.120	89.799
ETP	4.505	40.771	68.135
CIEP	0.000	1.896	98.672
ETP (Suffix)	1.605	37.669	82.666

Table 3: Results of the dictionary-based model when tested on the different sets. *ETP (Suffix)* is the model tested on ETP with the suffix tokenizer.

We compare two tokenizers for Etruscan: the first uses white spaces to split the tokens, and the second also separates the suffixes from the root. The list of suffixes is also obtained from Zikh Rasna and the tokenizer recognises 178 suffixes. Table 3 shows the results of this model when translating Etruscan.

If we consider the example *"itun turuce venel atelinas tinas dlniiaras"* with the reference translation *"venel atelinas dedicated this vase to the sons of tinia"*, this model predicts *"this dedicated venel atelina tinia"*. If we use the suffix tokenizer the prediction is *"this for him dedicated three this venel laris atelina shows"*.

Context: ETT - Word order: No

N-gram	BLEU	chr-F	TER
1	**0.406** (0.163)	**7.727** (0.867)	**92.605** (0.960)
2	0.006 (0.001)	3.249 (0.752)	98.035 (0.821)
3	0.001 (0.001)	2.523 (0.753)	98.553 (0.821)

Context: ETT - Word order: Yes

N-gram	BLEU	chr-F	TER
1	**0.405** (0.163)	**7.727** (0.867)	**92.605** (0.960)
2	0.005 (0.005)	3.211 (1.004)	98.013 (1.089)
3	0.001 (0.001)	2.523 (0.748)	98.531 (0.870)

Table 4: Mean scores and their standard deviation (in parenthesis) of the n-gram models that use only the Etruscan texts.

Context: ETT-ENG - Word order: No

N-gram	BLEU	chr-F	TER
1	**0.218** (0.018)	**3.059** (0.301)	**92.902** (1.160)
2	0 (0)	0 (0)	100 (0)
3	0 (0)	0 (0)	100 (0)

Context: ETT-ENG - Word order: Yes

N-gram	BLEU	chr-F	TER
1	**0.447** (0.211)	**5.360** (0.856)	**92.105** (1.117)
2	0.000 (0.000)	0.370 (0.167)	99.705 (0.346)
3	0.000 (0.000)	0.357 (0.097)	99.690 (0.297)

Table 5: Mean scores and their standard deviation (in parenthesis) of the n-gram models that use the Etruscan texts and the English translations. When the scores are zero is because the models immediately predict the end-of-sequence (EOS) token.

5.3 N-gram and Naive Bayes models

Similarly to the random models, 80% of the data is used for training, while the remaining 20% is for testing. The dataset is ETP. Each experiment is repeated 10 times with different random splits.

With the N-gram models, we compare models with a context size of 1, 2 and 3 that use only Etruscan or both Etruscan and English as context and whether they consider the word order. Out-of-vocabulary (OOV) tokens are handled with additive smoothing. We use 8 beams when generating the output sequence, however, this is equivalent to greedy search when the context uses only Etruscan. Table 4 shows the results of the models that use only the Etruscan sequence, while Table 5 shows the models that also use the English translations.

For the Naive Bayes models, we only use a context size of 2 and 3, and the models always consider the word order. Table 6 reports the results.

N	Context	BLEU	chr-F	TER
2	Ett.	**0.160** (0.023)	12.609 (1.009)	**101.482** (1.251)
3	Ett.	0.146 (0.030)	**12.708** (0.921)	103.867 (1.220)
2	Ett.-Eng.	**0.055** (0.048)	9.547 (1.821)	**101.522** (0.851)
3	Ett.-Eng.	**0.055** (0.048)	**9.954** (2.103)	103.038 (1.005)

Table 6: Mean scores and their standard deviation (in parenthesis) of the Naïve Bayes models.

5.4 IBM models

We split 80 % of the data for training and 20 % for testing. Moreover, we use the previously built dictionary as training data. No alignment information is given to the model, but IBM4 and IBM5 receive a dictionary that maps words to POS tags. We assume that words can only have one tag.

IBM3, IBM4, and IBM5 are trained only with the dictionary data. Models trained on ETP+CIEP are tested on ETP+CIEP, while models trained on ETP are tested on ETP as shown in Tables 7 and 8.

As an example, IBM3 translates *"eca shuthic velus ezpus clensi cerine"* as *"this funerary vel etspus son constructed"*, while the reference translation is *"this funerary monument belongs to vel etspu it is constructed by his son"*.

5.5 Transformer Models - Larth

The model is trained for Etruscan $\rightarrow$ English translation with ETP+CIEP and with ETP only. The models are tested on the same split of the dataset. Due to the small size of the dataset, 95 % of the data is used for training.

The optimizer is RAdam (Liu et al., 2019), with an initial learning rate of 0.002 and 250 warmup steps. We use a reverse square root learning sched-

Model	ETP+CIEP BLEU	chr-F	TER
IBM1	**0.402**	**19.744**	**89.213**
	(0.183)	(1.178)	(0.693)
IBM2	0.392	19.450	89.551
	(0.183)	(1.383)	(0.487)
IBM3(*)	0.105	8.629	91.052
	(0.046)	(1.148)	(1.507)
IBM4(*)	0.105	8.627	91.052
	(0.046)	(1.148)	(1.507)
IBM5(*)	0.105	8.631	91.063
	(0.046)	(1.147)	(1.516)

Table 7: Performance of the IBM models on the ETP+CIEP dataset. (*): IBM3, IBM4 and IBM5 are trained only with the dictionary.

Model	ETP BLEU	chr-F	TER
IBM1	2.187	37.363	73.917
	(0.596)	(2.011)	(2.163)
IBM2	2.104	36.721	74.334
	(0.449)	(2.098)	(2.090)
IBM3(*)	**2.482**	**39.393**	**71.270**
	(0.513)	(2.229)	(2.456)
IBM4(*)	**2.482**	39.391	**71.270**
	(0.514)	(2.228)	(2.456)
IBM5(*)	2.481	39.416	71.331
	(0.513)	(2.235)	(2.415)

Table 8: Performance of the IBM models on the ETP dataset. (*): IBM3, IBM4 and IBM5 are trained only with the dictionary.

ule. The loss function is cross-entropy, and the batch size is 32. We set the label smoothing to 0.1.

We first try to train from scratch and with different alignment techniques. The BLEU, chr-F and TER scores are shown in Table 9. We use data augmentation with ETP+CIEP with the sequences aligned by repeating the word tokens, however, we do not use it on ETP due to the decrease in performance.

Next, we train the same architecture with only the word sequence or only the character sequence. The results are shown in Table 10.

When training the same model with the Latin and Greek data, it achieved, respectively, BLEU/chr-F/TER of 0.4968/5.01/151.4 and 0.12/6.186/107.3. Then, we fine-tune those models with Etruscan as shown in Table 11.

Larth trained on ETP translates *"mi aveles metienas"* as *"i am the tomb"* while the reference translation is *"i am the tomb of avele metienas"*. Note that in this example *"the tomb"* is implied and not mentioned explicitly.

When trained on ETP+CIEP, we have *"e ca shuthi anes cuclnies"* translated as *"this tomb"* but the reference is *"this is the tomb of ane cuclnies"*. In this case *"the tomb"* is mentioned, but the model misses the name of the owner, which is also mentioned.

Model	BLEU	chr-F	TER
ETP+CIEP			
repeat	**10.1**	15.11	**144.5**
space	5.201	**16.9**	274.8
repeat+unk	2.8	14.8	189.1
repeat+name	1.004	12.2	615.9
ETP			
repeat	**9.053**	**17.24**	137
space	5.784	15.88	**124.7**

Table 9: Larth trained from scratch for Etruscan → English. *Repeat* and *space* indicate how the character and the word sequence are aligned. *+name* is trained with data augmented by changing names, while *+unk* is augmented by deleting characters.

Inputs	BLEU	chr-F	TER
ETP+CIEP			
char	0.9694	14.42	254.8
word	2.776	13.49	**99.88**
char+word	**10.1**	**15.11**	144.5
ETP			
char	0.1431	11.22	528.1
word	7.679	**18.48**	**131.6**
char+word	**9.053**	17.24	137

Table 10: Larth trained from scratch for Etruscan → English with only the character or the word sequence or both as input.

6 Results & Discussion

Figure 6 and Figure 7 compare the scores of the models presented in the previous Section. Compared to the random model, the dictionary-based model shows higher BLEU and chr-F scores and lower TER scores except when tested only on CIEP. This suggests that CIEP is noisier than ETP and that the dictionary is not suited for CIEP.

The N-gram models perform better than random

Data	BLEU	chr-F	TER
Lat+ETP+CIEP	0.1965	2.195	351.6
Grc+ETP+CIEP	**1.011**	**8.148**	**215.3**
Lat+ETP	0.293	3.784	654.4
Grc+ETP	**2.037**	**6.04**	**164**

Table 11: Larth trained with Latin (Lat) or Ancient Greek (Grc) and then fine-tuned on Etruscan.

only when using unigrams as context. With longer n-grams, the performance decrease until the model only predicts the EOS token. We can make similar observations for Naïve Bayes models.

IBM models are able to perform better than random. When trained on ETP+CIEP, simpler models work better. This, again, might depend on the noise in CIEP. IBM3 works better on ETP despite being trained only with the dictionary. Adding POS information (IBM4 and IBM5) does not improve the results. However, on ETP the dictionary-based model still performs better than the IBM models.

Larth is able to achieve a better BLEU score than the previous models on both ETP and ETP+CIEP. However, it needs to use both the character and word sequences and the word tokens are repeated to align the two sequences, whereas the other models only use the word tokens. Using the space token to align the sequences decrease the performance, but the BLEU score is still higher than the dictionary-based model. A similar observation can be made for the model using only the word sequence. Using data augmentation or only the character sequences reduces the performance that is still higher than random.

Fine-tuning from Latin and Ancient Greek always performs worse than the dictionary-based model. This may depend on the small size of the model that is not able to adapt.

As for chr-F and TER, the dictionary model and IBM models perform better than Larth. These two models can only output tokens from the training set and ignore unknown tokens. Thus, they can generate longer sequences of correct characters (high chr-F) and the errors are mainly for unknown tokens or from English tokens that are not directly present in the Etruscan texts like articles (low TER). Whereas, Larth uses tokens that can be word pieces and it still generates a translation for unknown tokens.

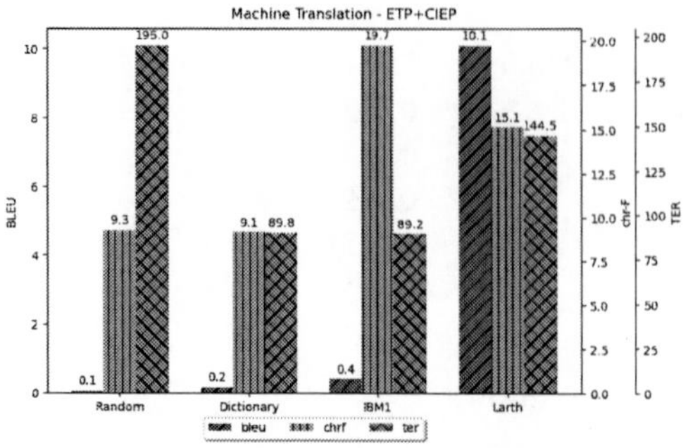

Figure 6: Comparison of the models with the best BLEU scores on ETP+CIEP. One model from each type is selected.

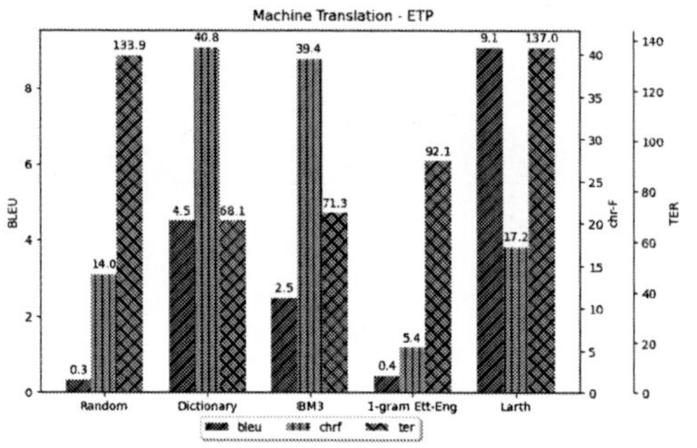

Figure 7: Comparison of the models with the best BLEU scores on ETP. One model from each type is selected.

7 Discussion

In this paper, we present a dataset for Etruscan → English machine translation. Although the dataset is not very big, we show that it is possible to train statistical and transformer models. Given the unexplored nature of Etruscan language, the fact that trained models perform better than random is an important first step for this language. Moreoever, we demonstrated that Larth performs better than the IBM models when trained on the available data.

However, our model does not provide any explanation about the generated translation neither it guarantees whether it is correct. Our model's performance also depends on the dataset itself, which does not contain any bibliographic information or the reasoning that the original authors used to translate the inscriptions. Future work includes delivering a cleaner and more complete version of the dataset and the inclusion of additional metadata, such as bibliographic information, more accurate location, or interesting graphical information (e.g. the direction of the inscription).

References

Yannis Assael, Thea Sommerschield, Brendan Shillingford, Mahyar Bordbar, John Pavlopoulos, Marita Chatzipanagiotou, Ion Androutsopoulos, Jonathan Prag, and Nando de Freitas. 2022. Restoring and attributing ancient texts using deep neural networks. *Nature*.

Dzmitry Bahdanau, Kyunghyun Cho, and Yoshua Bengio. 2014. Neural machine translation by jointly learning to align and translate. *CoRR*, abs/1409.0473.

David Bamman and Patrick J. Burns. 2020. Latin BERT: A contextual language model for classical philology. *CoRR*, abs/2009.10053.

Mani Bansal and D.K. Lobiyal. 2020. Word-character hybrid machine translation model. In *2020 8th International Conference on Reliability, Infocom Technologies and Optimization (Trends and Future Directions) (ICRITO)*, pages 270–274.

Steven Bird and Edward Loper. 2004. NLTK: The natural language toolkit. In *Proceedings of the ACL Interactive Poster and Demonstration Sessions*, pages 214–217, Barcelona, Spain. Association for Computational Linguistics.

Gregory R. Crane. 1985. Perseus digital library.

Jeff Hill. 2018. Corpus inscriptionum etruscarum plenissimum.

Sepp Hochreiter and Jürgen Schmidhuber. 1997. Long Short-Term Memory. *Neural Computation*, 9(8):1735–1780.

Kyle P. Johnson, Patrick J. Burns, John Stewart, Todd Cook, Clément Besnier, and William J. B. Mattingly. 2021. The Classical Language Toolkit: An NLP framework for pre-modern languages. In *Proceedings of the 59th Annual Meeting of the Association for Computational Linguistics and the 11th International Joint Conference on Natural Language Processing: System Demonstrations*, pages 20–29, Online. Association for Computational Linguistics.

Philipp Koehn. 2010. *Statistical Machine Translation*, 1st edition. Cambridge University Press, United States.

Wang Ling, Isabel Trancoso, Chris Dyer, and Alan W. Black. 2015. Character-based neural machine translation. *CoRR*, abs/1511.04586.

Liyuan Liu, Haoming Jiang, Pengcheng He, Weizhu Chen, Xiaodong Liu, Jianfeng Gao, and Jiawei Han. 2019. On the variance of the adaptive learning rate and beyond. *CoRR*, abs/1908.03265.

Jorj X. McKie and Ruikai Liu. 2016. PyMuPDF.

Kishore Papineni, Salim Roukos, Todd Ward, and Wei-Jing Zhu. 2002. Bleu: A method for automatic evaluation of machine translation. In *Proceedings of the 40th Annual Meeting on Association for Computational Linguistics*, ACL '02, page 311–318, USA. Association for Computational Linguistics.

Carl Pauli. 1893. *Corpus Inscriptionum Etruscarum*. J. A. Barth.

Maja Popović. 2015. chrF: character n-gram F-score for automatic MT evaluation. In *Proceedings of the Tenth Workshop on Statistical Machine Translation*, pages 392–395, Lisbon, Portugal. Association for Computational Linguistics.

Matt Post. 2018. A call for clarity in reporting BLEU scores. In *Proceedings of the Third Conference on Machine Translation: Research Papers*, pages 186–191, Belgium, Brussels. Association for Computational Linguistics.

Colin Raffel, Noam Shazeer, Adam Roberts, Katherine Lee, Sharan Narang, Michael Matena, Yanqi Zhou, Wei Li, and Peter J. Liu. 2020. Exploring the limits of transfer learning with a unified text-to-text transformer. *J. Mach. Learn. Res.*, 21(1).

Helmut Rix and Gerhard Meiser. 1991. *Etruskische Texte*. A. G. Narr.

Khaidzir Muhammad Shahih and Ayu Purwarianti. 2019. Combining word and character vector representation on neural machine translation. In *2019 Fourth International Conference on Informatics and Computing (ICIC)*, pages 1–4.

Matthew Snover, Bonnier Dorr, Richard Schwartz, Linnea Micciulla, and John Makhoul. 2006. A study of translation edit rate with targeted human annotation. In *Proceedings of Association for Machine Translation in the Americas*.

Thea Sommerschield, Yannis Assael, Brendan Shillingford, Mahyar Bordbar, John Pavlopoulos, Marita Chatzipanagiotou, Ion Androutsopoulos, Jonathan Prag, and Nando de Freitas. 2021. I.PHI dataset: ancient greek inscriptions. `https://github.com/sommerschield/iphi`.

Ilya Sutskever, Oriol Vinyals, and Quoc V. Le. 2014a. Sequence to sequence learning with neural networks. *CoRR*, abs/1409.3215.

Ilya Sutskever, Oriol Vinyals, and Quoc V. Le. 2014b. Sequence to sequence learning with neural networks. *CoRR*, abs/1409.3215.

Jörg Tiedemann. 2020. The Tatoeba Translation Challenge – Realistic data sets for low resource and multilingual MT. In *Proceedings of the Fifth Conference on Machine Translation*, pages 1174–1182, Online. Association for Computational Linguistics.

Jörg Tiedemann and Santhosh Thottingal. 2020. OPUS-MT — Building open translation services for the World. In *Proceedings of the 22nd Annual Conference of the European Association for Machine Translation (EAMT)*, Lisbon, Portugal.

Ashish Vaswani, Noam Shazeer, Niki Parmar, Jakob Uszkoreit, Llion Jones, Aidan N. Gomez, Łukasz Kaiser, and Illia Polosukhin. 2017. Attention is all you need. In *Proceedings of the 31st International Conference on Neural Information Processing Systems*, NIPS'17, page 6000–6010, Red Hook, NY, USA. Curran Associates Inc.

Rex Wallace. 2008. *Zikh Rasna: A Manual of the Etruscan Language and Inscriptions*. Beech Stave Press.

Rex Wallace, Michael Shamgochian, and James Patterson. 2004. Etruscan texts project.

Zhen Yang, Wei Chen, Feng Wang, and Bo Xu. 2016. A character-aware encoder for neural machine translation. In *Proceedings of COLING 2016, the 26th International Conference on Computational Linguistics: Technical Papers*, pages 3063–3070, Osaka, Japan. The COLING 2016 Organizing Committee.

Manzil Zaheer, Guru Guruganesh, Avinava Dubey, Joshua Ainslie, Chris Alberti, Santiago Ontanon, Philip Pham, Anirudh Ravula, Qifan Wang, Li Yang, and Amr Ahmed. 2021. Big bird: Transformers for longer sequences.

Evaluation of Distributional Semantic Models of Ancient Greek: Preliminary Results and a Road Map for Future Work

Silvia Stopponi
CLCG, University of Groningen, The Netherlands
s.stopponi@rug.nl

Nilo Pedrazzini
The Alan Turing Institute / University of Oxford
United Kingdom
npedrazzini@turing.ac.uk

Saskia Peels
CLCG, University of Groningen, The Netherlands
s.peels@rug.nl

Barbara McGillivray
King's College London
United Kindgom
barbara.mcgillivray@kcl.ac.uk

Malvina Nissim
CLCG, University of Groningen
The Netherlands
m.nissim@rug.nl

Abstract

We evaluate four count-based and predictive distributional semantic models of Ancient Greek against AGREE, a composite benchmark of human judgements, to assess their ability to retrieve semantic relatedness. On the basis of the observations deriving from the analysis of the results, we design a procedure for a larger-scale intrinsic evaluation of count-based and predictive language models, including syntactic embeddings. We also propose possible ways of exploiting the different layers of the whole AGREE benchmark (including both human- and machine-generated data) and different evaluation metrics.

1 Introduction

The application of Natural Language Processing to the study of Ancient Greek semantics is an emerging research area which has proven to be a fruitful avenue for our understanding of the Ancient Greek language and culture. Previous work has focused on the training of Distributional Semantic Models (DSMs) on Ancient Greek corpora (Boschetti, 2009; Rodda et al., 2017, 2019; McGillivray et al., 2019; Perrone et al., 2021a), a task enabled by the relatively large quantity of extant texts available for this language. DSM evaluation is a necessary step to properly assess the usefulness of applying these models to large-scale studies of Ancient Greek, but is made particularly challenging by the lack of native speakers and, compared to modern languages, a limited number of experts available.

This paper offers an evaluation of DSMs for Ancient Greek against the newly created AGREE benchmark (Stopponi et al., 2024b) and a road map for further, wider evaluation. We exploit the layered nature of AGREE to assess at different levels four DSMs, and discuss results not only in terms of model comparison, but mostly in terms of best evaluation strategies, suggesting various precision- and recall-based options. On that basis, in Section 6 we propose a road map for a more comprehensive evaluation campaign, which would involve training a wider range of models, including dependency-based embeddings (see, among others, Padó and Lapata 2007; Levy and Goldberg 2014; Lapesa and Evert 2017; Lenci et al. 2022), already preliminarily tested in Stopponi et al. (2024a), and studying their behaviour with respect to a number of metrics. Specifically, we propose to assess the difference in performance between syntactic embeddings trained on manually tagged and on automatically tagged treebanks. We plan to evaluate the DSMs, trained with different parameters, against the full version of AGREE, including both human- and machine-generated judgements. We also suggest alternative ways to use the data collected for AGREE and possible evaluation metrics.

2 Previous work

Few resources exist as gold standards for the evaluation of DSMs on Ancient Greek. Vatri and Lähteenoja (2019) contains the manual annotation of the senses of the lemmas μῦς, ἁρμονία, and κόσμος (Vatri and McGillivray, 2018) and was used in Perrone et al. (2021a) and Perrone et al. (2021b) to evaluate models for semantic change detection.

Rodda et al. (2019) evaluated count-based DSMs for Ancient Greek against benchmarks obtained

Proceedings of the Ancient Language Processing Workshop associated with RANLP-2023, pages 49–58,
held in Varna Bulgaria, Sept 8, 2023.
https://doi.org/10.26615/978-954-452-087-8_006

from an ancient lexicon, a modern dictionary of synonyms, and the computational lexicon *Ancient Greek WordNet* (Boschetti et al., 2016). The data they released represent the first benchmark for the evaluation of Ancient Greek DSMs.[1] Reusing preexisting resources, as they did, allows incorporating in the evaluation the semantic knowledge of real speakers of Ancient Greek (as in the case of the ancient lexicon) and to leverage the semantic knowledge of highly specialized experts, from resources that can be the product of years of work. This data collection seems less biased by the aims of the research, however it also has downsides. Lexical resources, compiled by humans, can suffer from idiosyncrasies, for example being biased by the interests and language taste of their author, and if the author is not alive anymore, it is not possible to get explanations about specific choices. Moreover, ancient resources can reflect ideas of semantic relationships between words (e.g. word similarity) that are different from the contemporary conceptualization, as also noticed by Rodda et al. (2019, 6–8) and discussed in Stopponi et al. (2024b).

3 Training Data for DSMs of Ancient Greek

The largest corpus of Ancient Greek, the Thesaurus Linguae Graecae (Pantelia, 2022), containing more than 110 million tokens,[2] is only accessible through the web interface. However, scholars can use a number of open-access machine-readable Ancient Greek corpora, containing different ranges of text types.[3] Some corpora are annotated, for example with lemma, POS, and syntactic information. The Diorisis Ancient Greek Corpus (Vatri and McGillivray, 2018), a portion of which was used as training data for the study presented in this paper, contains 10,206,421 automatically lemmatized and POS-tagged tokens. But many corpora with syntactic annotation also exist: an overview of the most often used treebanks for Ancient Greek is in Table 1.

As the case of GLAUx shows (see Table 1), automatic parsing allows for the creation of larger treebanks, even if the syntactic annotation is expected to be less accurate. We thus plan to train syntactic embeddings on two corpora, GLAUx and the largest possible manually-annotated treebank, created from a collation of the available corpora.

4 The AGREE Benchmark

The AGREE benchmark contains pairs of lemmas semantically related to 36 selected 'seed' lemmas (12 nouns, 12 adjectives, and 12 verbs), for a total of 638 lemma pairs.[4] The judgements were collected via questionnaires distributed to a large number (> 50) of academic scholars of Ancient Greek. The final benchmark, AGREE, incorporates a mix of expert-elicited pairs and expert-assessed, machine-generated pairs. The machine-generated items are pairs of [seed lemma - nearest neighbour], with nearest neighbours extracted from Word2Vec models (Mikolov et al., 2013) that underwent expert judgement and were assessed as highly related. For the experiments reported in this paper, we only use the human-elicited portion of the benchmark: *AGREE-task1*. This portion can be further divided into the subset of pairs that were proposed by one expert only, and the subset of pairs that were proposed by more than one annotator, under the assumptions that the latter might be cases of a stronger relatedness, and/or higher frequency.

5 Evaluation of DSMs of Ancient Greek

5.1 Procedure

For this study we evaluated two count-based and two predictive DSMs trained on a portion of the Diorisis corpus (Vatri and McGillivray, 2018), merging text from the Archaic, Classical and Hellenistic periods, since the AGREE benchmark (and especially the pairs proposed by experts) is particularly suited to the evaluation of models trained on texts from those periods (Stopponi et al., 2024b). The lemmatized version of Diorisis was used, to reduce the impact of word sparsity. Stop word filtering was performed, according to the list also used in Rodda et al. (2019)[5]. Stop word filtering reduced the size of the corpus from 5,768,916 to 2,960,459 tokens. The four models were evaluated against AGREE-task1, by comparing the top 5, 10, 15 (k) nearest neighbours of each of the 36 seed lemmas in the benchmark with the lemmas related to the same seed in AGREE-task1. The nearest neighbours extracted from the models were compared

[1] https://zenodo.org/record/3552763#.YfAItOrMKWA

[2] https://wiki.digitalclassicist.org/Thesaurus_Linguae_Graecae

[3] A review of most available open-access corpora for Ancient Greek is in Keersmaekers (2021, 40).

[4] https://zenodo.org/record/8027490.

[5] https://figshare.com/articles/dataset/Ancient_Greek_stop_words/9724613, by A. Vatri.

Treebank	N. tokens	Manual annotation	Texts
Ancient Greek Dependency Treebank (Perseus, Bamman and Crane, 2011)	ca. 550K*	yes	Literary, full list at `http://perseusdl.github.io/treebank_data/`
PROIEL Treebank (Haug and Jøhndal, 2008)	ca. 250.5K	yes	*The Greek New Testament*, *Histories* (Herodotus), *Chronicles* (Sphrantzes)
Gorman Trees (Gorman, 2020)	ca. 240K*	yes	Literary prose, full list at `https://perseids-publications.github.io/gorman-trees/`
Pedalion Trees (Keersmaekers et al., 2019)	ca. 300K	yes	Literary, full list at `https://perseids-publications.github.io/pedalion-trees/`
Harrington Treebanks (Harrington, 2018)	ca. 18K*	yes	*Nicene Creed*; *Book of Susanna* (Septuaginta), *Verae historiae* (Lucian of Samosata), *Vita Aesopi*
PapyGreek (Vierros and Henriksson, 2021)	ca. 44K	syntactic layer only	Papyri
Aphthonius (Yordanova, 2018)	ca. 7K*	yes	*Progymnasmata* (Aphtonius)
GLAUx corpus (Keersmaekers, 2021)	ca. 11,860K	no	Literary, papyrological, epigraphical. A sample was released at `https://perseids-publications.github.io/glaux-trees/`

Table 1: Some available treebanks for Ancient Greek. If the size of the treebank is followed by a *, it is taken from Keersmaekers et al. (2019, 110). The size of the PapyGreek treebanks has been calculated by summing up all the 'word' elements in the XML files.

to: all the lemmas in AGREE-task1, the lemmas in AGREE-task1 proposed by more than one expert, and the lemmas in AGREE-task1 proposed by only one expert. Precision and recall were adopted as evaluation metrics and defined as follows:

$$\text{Precision@K} = \frac{\text{overlap model's near. neighb. and benchmark}}{k}$$

$$\text{Recall@K} = \frac{\text{near. neighb. model also in benchmark}}{\text{n. related lemmas benchmark}}$$

5.2 Models

The models selected for evaluation are two Word2Vec models, one SGNS and one CBOW, and two count-based models. The matrices of the count-based models were weighted with PPMI and one one of the two dimensionality reduction was performed with Singular Value Decomposition (SVD). The two count-based models were built by using the software provided by the LSCDetection repository (Schlechtweg et al., 2019) with $window = 5$ and the following other parameters: $k = 1$ and $alpha = 0.75$ for PPMI, 300 dimensions and $gamma = 0.0$ for SVD. The two Word2Vec models were trained with the Gensim library (Řehůřek and Sojka, 2010) and the following parameters: $size = 30$, $window = 5$, $min\_count = 5$, $negative = 20$.

5.3 Results

The average precision and recall are reported in Table 2. We immediately see that recall is generally low. This can be explained by the fact that there are on average 14 neighbours per lemma[6] in AGREE-task1, so that the denominator in recall@k is generally larger than the numerator when $k = 5$ or $k = 10$. The recall consequently increases (on average) if k also increases, while the opposite happens for precision, which increases if k decreases. Taking into account recall for $k < 15$ makes thus little sense, since it is never possible to achieve full recall when the lemmas related to a certain seed in the benchmark are more than the extracted k-nearest neighbours. Conversely, it is theoretically possible to achieve 100% precision if all the extracted k-nearest neighbours are also in the benchmark. The higher precision with smaller values of k seems to confirm that the closest neighbours in the semantic space are actually more strictly related to the seed lemma, while the strength of the seed-

[6]Min. = 6, max. = 24, standard deviation = 4.43.

k	Precision	Recall
5	**0.20**	0.06
10	0.16	0.09
15	0.13	**0.11**

Table 2: Average precision and recall calculated against the whole AGREE-task1 benchmark and divided by k.

Model	Precision	Recall
SGNS	0.11	0.06
CBOW	0.15	0.08
SVD	0.16	0.09
PPMI	**0.22**	**0.12**

Table 3: Average precision and recall calculated against the whole AGREE-task1 benchmark, divided by model.

neighbour relationship declines for neighbours that are further away from the seed.

Model architecture also has an impact, with count-based performing better than predictive models. This is in line with what is observed by Lenci et al. (2022). Moreover, the model without dimensionality reduction performs better than the one to which SVD was applied, as shown in Table 3. Further, Word2Vec CBOW seems to perform better than Word2Vec SGNS. However, parameter optimization was not performed for this preliminary study, and a limited number of model architectures was tested. In future, larger evaluation will probably give a better picture of the differences between count-based and predictive models.

For example, for the seed lemma εἰρήνη, 'peace', there are 9 related lemmas in AGREE-task1: πόλεμος, 'war', σπονδή, 'drink-offering/treaty', ἥσυχος, 'quiet' (adj.), ἡσυχία, 'quiet, silence' (noun), σπένδω, 'make a drink-offering', μάχη, 'battle', γαληνός, 'calm', πολιτεία, 'citizenship', συγγραφή, 'writing', ὁμολογέω, 'agree', νίκη, 'victory', ὄλβος, 'happiness', γαλήνη, 'stillness', and φιλία, 'friendship'. Both the CBOW and the PPMI model have precision 0.2 with $k = 5$, i.e. among the first 5 nearest neighbours returned there is one that is also in AGREE-task1. The recall is 0.07 (1/14). The overlapping lemma is σπονδή, 'drink-offering/treaty' for the CBOW model, (which also returns as the other four nearest neighbours διάλυσις, 'separating/ending', συμμαχία, 'alliance', Λακεδαιμόνιος, 'Spartan', and πολεμέω, 'fight') and it is πόλεμος, 'war' for the PPMI, which also returns συμμαχία, 'alliance', Φίλιππος, 'Philip', πολεμέω, 'fight', and πρεσβεία, 'embassy'. We notice that both models return συμμαχία, 'alliance' among their first 5 neighbours. This word was not proposed by the experts in the first phase of data collection for the AGREE benchmark, but is however semantically related to εἰρήνη, 'peace'. More in general, we deem all the top 5 nearest neighbours returned by both models as acceptable results, since they all are related to εἰρήνη, 'peace'; the two models just differ in results from one other, as well as from the benchmark. Of course, there are also cases in which the overlapping lemma(s) are the same between models. One example is μέγας, 'big', for which there are 15 related lemmas in AGREE-task1.[7] Both the CBOW and the PPMI model have precision 0.2 (1/5) and recall 0.07 (1/14) with k = 5, and the lemma overlapping with the AGREE-task1 benchmark is the same for both models, μέγεθος, 'greatness'. Again, the extracted nearest neighbours that are not in the benchmark are not necessarily unrelated to the seed μέγας, 'big'. The CBOW model also returns τηλικοῦτος, 'of such an age/so large', ἄξιος, 'weighing as much/worthy', ῥοπή, 'weight', and ὑπερβάλλω, 'surpass/exceed', while the PPMI model also returns ἐλάσσων, 'smaller', ἴσος, 'equal', ἄρος, 'use/profit', and πολύς, 'many'. Except from ἄρος, 'use/profit', they all relate to μέγας, even if, intuitively,with a different strength and with different types semantic relations.

The internal layering of the benchmark AGREE-task1, which accounts for the number of experts who proposed a specific lemma, allows for other observations (Table 4). On average, the lemmas returned by only one expert (*AGREE-task1-only1* in 4) are more (13.02 per seed lemma) than those returned by several experts (*AGREE-task1-more1*, 4.69 per seed). We could hypothesize that the relatedness among the latter may be stronger or more evident, since more than one expert independently had proposed the same lemmas as related to the relevant seed word. When we evaluate against lemma pairs proposed by more than one expert higher pre-

[7]They are μικρός, 'small', ὅρκος, 'oath', βασιλεύς, 'king', θαῦμα, 'wonder', θεός, 'god', μακρός, 'long', ὀλίγος, 'little', βραχύς, 'short', μέγεθος, 'greatness', αὐξάνω, 'increase', μεγαλοψυχία, 'greatness of soul', ἥρως, 'hero', γίγας, 'giant', καλός, 'beautiful', and μεγαλοφροσύνη, 'greatness of mind'.

Benchmark subset	Prec	Rec
AGREE-task1	**0.16**	**0.09**
AGREE-task1-more1	0.09	0.05
AGREE-task1-only1	0.07	0.04

Table 4: Average precision and recall calculated against different subsets of the AGREE-task1 benchmark. The results with the three values of k were averaged.

cision and recall scores are observed, possibly suggesting that pairs proposed by more experts are more closely related to their seed lemma, and possibly more frequent. This is particularly true for the PPMI model, which achieves an average of 0.22, 0.14, and 0.09 precision, and an average of 0.12, 0.07, and 0.05 recall against, respectively, the whole AGREE-task1, the pairs proposed by more than one expert, and the pairs proposed by only one expert (the results are averaged across the three values of k). This is observed when averaging the results of all models, but it does not necessarily hold for each model. The CBOW model, for example, achieves a higher precision against the set of pairs proposed by only one expert than against those proposed by more experts. Both Word2Vec models instead achieve the same precision and recall on both subsets of AGREE-task1. The results discussed until now are summarised in Table 5.

Another dimension of the benchmark is the part-of-speech (POS) of the seed lemmas. In Table 6 we see that evaluating against pairs including an adjective seed lemma the highest precision is achieved, followed by noun seeds and verb seeds. The recall is higher when evaluated against pairs including adjective or noun seeds. However, the differences in precision and recall are very small.

Finally, dividing the results by lemma reveals a great variety in precision and recall among the different lemmas. For example, with $k = 5$ the highest precision is achieved. The average precision per lemma calculated against the whole AGREE-task1 is 0.20, with standard deviation 0.16. There is indeed a large variability between the average precision against the "best" and the "worst-performing" lemmas. Those yielding the highest precision are some nouns and adjectives: ἅρμα, 'chariot', average precision 0.6; ψευδής, 'false', 0.55; ἐλεύθερος, 'free', 0.45; πατήρ, 'father', 0.45; and ἄγριος, 'wild', 0.45. However, they are immediately followed by verbs, ἔρχομαι, 'go' and ὁράω, 'see', both with average precision 0.4. The lowest precision, 0, is achieved with the seed lemmas ἀκτή, 'headland', κλυτός, 'renowned', ναίω, 'dwell', ῥῆσις, 'speech', σῆμα, 'sign/mark', and τεύχω, 'make/build', all with average precision 0. Nevertheless, as we already observed, a low precision does not necessarily correspond to bad results (i.e. unrelated lemmas), even if it is true that some of the nearest neighbours returned by the models to these are unrelated or intuitively less strictly related to the seed lemmas. Moreover, a higher precision seems to correspond to higher-frequency words, while the lemmas yielding the lowest precision also have a low frequency in the corpus.[8] In Table 7 the average precision and recall for each lemma are reported, calculated against the whole AGREE-task1 and with $k = 15$. Note that changing the value of k the order of the seed lemmas, ranked by precision, also changes.

6 Road Map for Future Work

We plan a larger evaluation including more model architectures, different parameters and different evaluation metrics, with the aim of understanding the differences between model types, rather than finding the 'best' model (see also Lenci et al., 2022), and evaluation adequacy. More investigation is needed to understand whether the difference between count-based and predictive models trained on Ancient Greek lies in the quality of results (i.e., if some architectures actually return less relevant nearest neighbours), or only in the kind of relationships they capture. Further experiments will also concern dependency-based embeddings.

Moreover, this extended study will exploit the full dataset produced for the AGREE benchmark, including the second part of the dataset, not used for the current evaluation. Since in the second phase of the data collection the experts assigned relatedness scores to human- and machine- generated lemma pairs, these items items allows ranking the lemma pairs according to their degree of relatedness, and thus for a more nuanced evaluation.

[8]The frequency in the subcorpus of the mentioned "best performing" lemmas is: ἅρμα: 541, ψευδής: 1048, ἐλεύθερος: 940, πατήρ: 5685, ἄγριος: 348, ἔρχομαι: 5251, ὁράω: 4987, while the frequency of the mentioned "worst-performing lemmas is: ἀκτή: 177, κλυτός: 142, ναίω: 283, ῥῆσις: 48, σῆμα: 213, τεύχω: 255.

		Precision				Recall						
Bench. subset	k	PPMI	SVD	CBOW	SGNS	PPMI	SVD	CBOW	SGNS	Tot. prec.	Tot. rec.	Tot. pairs
AGREE-task1	all k	0.22	0.16	0.15	0.11	0.12	0.09	0.08	0.06	0.16	0.09	638
	k = 5	0.28	0.19	0.19	0.14	0.08	0.06	0.05	0.04	0.20	0.06	
	k = 10	0.22	0.16	0.14	0.11	0.12	0.09	0.08	0.07	0.16	0.09	
	k = 15	0.17	0.13	0.11	0.09	0.15	0.11	0.10	0.08	0.13	0.11	
AGREE-task1-more1	all k	0.14	0.09	0.07	0.06	0.07	0.05	0.04	0.03	0.09	0.05	169
	k = 5	0.19	0.11	0.08	0.07	0.06	0.03	0.02	0.02	0.11	0.03	
	k = 10	0.13	0.10	0.06	0.05	0.08	0.06	0.04	0.03	0.09	0.05	
	k = 15	0.10	0.08	0.06	0.04	0.09	0.07	0.05	0.04	0.07	0.06	
AGREE-task1-only1	all k	0.09	0.07	0.08	0.06	0.05	0.04	0.04	0.03	0.07	0.04	469
	k = 5	0.09	0.08	0.11	0.07	0.03	0.02	0.03	0.02	0.09	0.02	
	k = 10	0.09	0.07	0.08	0.06	0.05	0.04	0.04	0.03	0.07	0.04	
	k = 15	0.07	0.06	0.06	0.04	0.06	0.05	0.05	0.04	0.06	0.05	

Table 5: Average precision and recall calculated against different subsets of the AGREE-task1 benchmark, divided by model type and by k. The recall for values of k lower than 15 has been reported for completeness, but it has limited usefulness (see above). The column 'Tot. pairs' contains the total number of pairs in the relevant subsets.

POS	Precision	Recall
A	0.18	0.09
N	0.15	0.09
V	0.15	0.08

Table 6: Average precision and recall calculated against the whole AGREE-task1 benchmark and divided by POS of the seed lemmas.

6.1 Models

We will test a selection of popular DSMs belonging to the first two generations defined by Lenci et al. (2022), i.e. count-based models (PPMI and GloVe) and predictive models (Word2Vec and FastText). In particular, we will test:

1. two count-based models trained by using Positive Pointwise Mutual Information (PPMI) as association measure,[9] with and without dimensionality reduction with the Singular Value Decomposition (SVD);
2. GloVe (Pennington et al., 2014));
3. FastText (Bojanowski et al., 2017);
4. the two architectures of word2vec (Mikolov et al., 2013), the Skip-gram with Negative Sampling (SGNS) and the Continuous-Bag-of-Words (CBOW);
5. two 'syntax-filtered' models (Padó and Lapata, 2007; Lapesa and Evert, 2017; Lenci et al., 2022), a SGNS one but using direct dependency between tokens to extract co-occurrences rather than mere token windows and one trained using the SuperGraph approach described in Al-Ghezi and Kurimo (2020). The latter method consists in using dependency relations between tokens to generate graph structures for every sentence in a treebank, before merging all graphs into one SuperGraph. The SuperGraph then serves as input to Node2Vec (Grover and Leskovec, 2016), a modification of the SGNS architecture which enables the training of word representations starting from nodes in a graph.

Contextual models will not be included, instead. Even if some work exists on the training of contextual models of Ancient Greek (Singh et al., 2021; Keersmaekers and Mercelis, 2021; Yamshchikov et al., 2022; Riemenschneider and Frank, 2023) (despite the fact that contextual models require huge quantities of training data (Lenci et al., 2022, 1274)), the only existing evaluation datasets for semantic models of Ancient Greek (Rodda et al., 2019 and Stopponi et al., 2024b) were created

[9] About association measures, see Evert et al. (2008).

Lemma	Precision	Recall	Lemma	Precision	Recall
ἅρμα, 'chariot'	0.32	0.22	εἰρήνη, 'peace'	0.10	0.11
ὁράω	0.30	0.24	Ἀθηναῖος, 'Athenian'	0.08	0.08
ναῦς, 'ship'	0.27	0.25	νόστος, 'return'	0.08	0.07
χρυσός, 'gold'	0.27	0.27	παλαιός, 'old'	0.08	0.07
ἄγριος, 'wild'	0.23	0.17	ζεύγνυμι, 'yoke'	0.08	0.09
ἐλεύθερος, 'free'	0.23	0.17	μέγας, 'big'	0.08	0.08
ἔρχομαι, 'go'	0.23	0.19	μῦθος, 'word/story'	0.07	0.07
πατήρ, 'father'	0.22	0.30	ἀκτή, 'headland'	0.07	0.07
ψευδής, 'false'	0.20	0.18	μοχθέω, 'labour'	0.07	0.07
κακός, 'bad'	0.17	0.12	Σάμος, 'Samos'	0.07	0.06
οἰκέω, 'inhabit'	0.17	0.11	ἄλκιμος, 'brave'	0.05	0.04
αὐξάνω, 'increase'	0.17	0.14	ῥῆσις, 'speech'	0.05	0.04
ὀρφανός, 'orphan'	0.17	0.14	τέμνω, 'cut'	0.03	0.03
πόντος, 'sea'	0.15	0.12	κλυτός, 'renowned'	0.02	0.01
φιλέω, 'love'	0.15	0.15	λείπω, 'leave/quit'	0.02	0.01
αἴθω, 'light up'	0.13	0.10	τεύχω, 'make/build'	0.02	0.01
πρέσβυς, 'old man, elder'	0.13	0.11	ναίω, 'dwell'	0.00	0.00
ἐνδέκατος, 'eleventh'	0.13	0.11	σῆμα, 'sign/mark'	0.00	0.00

Table 7: Average precision and recall calculated against the whole AGREE-task1 benchmark and with $k = 15$, divided by seed lemma. The lemmas are ranked by average precision.

for the evaluation of static (type-based) embeddings. Although type-based embeddings can be obtained from contextualized token embeddings, e.g. by averaging the model representations of each word (see the discussion in Lenci et al., 2022, 1290–1291), their superiority over type embeddings obtained from static DSMs has been questioned (Lenci et al., 2022, 1289–1293). This evaluation will thus be limited to the evaluation of static embeddings, leaving the training and evaluation of contextual embeddings for future work.[10] All the models will be trained with two different context windows, e.g. 5 and 10. According to the large-scale evaluation of Lenci et al. (2022), model architecture and context window size are the two parameters that significantly affect model performance (especially model architecture). We thus concentrate on testing of these two.

[10]It should be noted that the training corpus of Lenci et al. (2022, 1279) are English texts from the Web. Their conclusions could thus not entirely apply to Ancient Greek, a language with a different syntax and morphology.

6.2 Dependency-based embeddings

Ancient Greek syntactic embeddings obtained with the SuperGraph method have already been compared with window-based models by Stopponi et al. (2024a), clearly suggesting that the former capture functional rather than topical similarity, as had already been shown at least since Levy and Goldberg (2014) on the basis of English models. Given this ontological difference between the two, an open question, then, is whether syntactic embeddings should be evaluated on a par with traditional count-based and word2vec models, namely whether there are arguments for using the same benchmark to judge the quality of models regardless of whether syntactic information is integrated in their training or not. Previous large-scale comparisons of dependency-based and window-based DSMs suggested that the latter, when fine-tuned, generally outperform the former in most downstream tasks (Kiela and Clark, 2014; Lapesa and Evert, 2017). Given the generally greater computational costs associated with dependency parsing and the extraction of syntactic collocates (i.e. tokens with a direct dependency relation), it has been questioned whether the training of dependency-based embeddings is justifiable after all. However, there is evidence, at least as far as high-resource languages such as English are concerned, that dependency-based embeddings outperform window-based models in a limited but coherent number of tasks. This has been shown to be consistently the case, for instance, of categorization tasks, namely grouping lexical items into semantically coherent categories (Rothenhäusler and Schütze, 2009; Lapesa and Evert, 2017; Lenci et al., 2022), as well as thematic fit estimation, namely evaluating the typicality of the argument of a verb given a thematic role (e.g., agent or patient) (Baroni and Lenci, 2010; Chersoni et al., 2017). Different tasks such as categorization and synonymity tests present, in many ways, the same ontological differences occurring between dependency- and window-based models as a whole. This alone would seem to warrant the training of different models (and, as a result, the development of different evaluation methods) depending on the task at hand. Classic distributional semantic models (i.e. window-based) are generally fined-tuned to capture attributional similarity (Turney, 2006), namely the number of attributes, or properties, shared by the referents of two given words. As pointed out by Baroni and Lenci (2010), words that share many collocates will show a high attributional similarity since common collocates can be seen as a proxy for some of the attributes that the two words denote. Pairs such as *dog-puppy* will then have a high attributional similarity but not necessarily a high relational similarity (Turney, 2006), which in turns refers to sharing similar semantic relations to their nearest neighbours. In Baroni and Lenci's 2010 example, the pair *dog-tail* will be more similar to *car-wheel* than it is to *dog-animal*, even though attributionally that is clearly not the case.

Building on the preliminary observation made in Stopponi et al. (2024a) about the relational, rather than attributional, similarity captured by Ancient Greek dependency-based models, we thus plan to test different Ancient Greek models on different tasks depending on the kind of similarity the model is trained to capture. Categorization and thematic fit task, for example, can be set up with the help of the richly annotated resources for the language (e.g. the verbal semantic annotation in the PROIEL treebank) for dependency-based models, in addition to similarity judgement tasks, which may be instead better suited to evaluate window-based DSMs.

6.3 Evaluation Metrics

We observed above how precision and recall only provide an absolute evaluation against the benchmark, capturing whether the words in the benchmark are returned by the models or not, but they do not allow us to take into account the strength of the semantic relationship between lemmas. Moreover, only the first k neighbours returned by the model are evaluated, while there is no information about how close to the seed lemma in a semantic space the related lemmas in the benchmark are which are not among the first k neighbours. Furthermore, the use of recall in this kind of evaluation can be problematic when the number of k is lower than the number of pairs in the benchmark.

To overcome these limitations, we plan to include additional evaluation strategies. One option is to use the evaluation items that were rated on a 0-100 relatedness scale (AGREE-task2), to calculate for each seed lemma the correlation between: (i) the scores assigned to pairs including that lemma in the benchmark; (ii) the cosine distances between the same word pairs in a semantic space. The scores can also be used to *rank* the items, and a correlation can be calculated between ranks and cosine distances. Taking into account degrees of relatedness may be a more adequate way to evaluate models on a phenomenon such as semantic relatedness.

Another possibility is to exploit the information about the number of raters who proposed the words collected in the first phase (AGREE-task1), for example by giving greater weight to pairs suggested by multiple raters. However, this will first require a deeper investigation on the nature of the pairs proposed by one versus several experts, and the impact this might have on evaluation. Relatedly, frequency should also be considered to verify the ways and extent to which precision and recall are impacted by high-frequency items (both the human-elicited ones and those returned by the models).

7 Conclusion

We presented and discussed the results of an evaluation of four Distributional Semantic Models of Ancient Greek, two count-based and two predictive models. The gold standard was a subset of the AGREE benchmark, AGREE-task1, including pairs of related lemmas proposed by experts of Ancient Greek. The evaluation showed that count-based models achieved higher precision and recall on AGREE-task1, and higher precision and recall were also achieved on average when evaluating against pairs of related lemmas proposed by more than one expert. Another important finding was the great difference in performance between different lemmas. We also presented a plan for a more extended evaluation, including more model architectures, parameters, and evaluation metrics. This evaluation will take into account different degrees of relatedness between lemmas and allow for a better understanding of the differences between DSMs of Ancient Greek and of the possible impact of such differences on computational studies in Ancient Greek lexical semantics.

Acknowledgements

This work was partially supported by the Young Academy Groningen through the PhD scholarship of Silvia Stopponi.

References

Ragheb Al-Ghezi and Mikko Kurimo. 2020. Graph-based syntactic word embeddings. In *Proceedings of the Graph-based Methods for Natural Language Processing (TextGraphs)*, pages 72–78, Barcelona, Spain (Online). Association for Computational Linguistics.

David Bamman and Gregory Crane. 2011. The Ancient Greek and Latin dependency treebanks. In *Language technology for cultural heritage: Selected papers from the LaTeCH Workshop Series*, pages 79–98. Springer.

Marco Baroni and Alessandro Lenci. 2010. Distributional memory: A general framework for corpus-based semantics. *Computational Linguistics*, 36(4):673–721.

Piotr Bojanowski, Edouard Grave, Armand Joulin, and Tomas Mikolov. 2017. Enriching word vectors with subword information. *Transactions of the Association for Computational Linguistics*, 5:135–146.

Federico Boschetti. 2009. *A Corpus-based Approach to Philological Issues*. University of Trento.

Federico Boschetti, Riccardo Del Gratta, and Harry Diakoff. 2016. Open Ancient Greek WordNet 0.5. ILC-CNR for CLARIN-IT repository hosted at Institute for Computational Linguistics 'A. Zampolli', National Research Council, in Pisa. http://hdl.handle.net/20.500.11752/ILC-56 (accessed 4 July 2022).

Emmanuele Chersoni, Enrico Santus, Philippe Blache, and Alessandro Lenci. 2017. Is structure necessary for modeling argument expectations in distributional semantics? In *IWCS 2017 - 12th International Conference on Computational Semantics - Long papers*.

Stefan Evert et al. 2008. Corpora and collocations. *Corpus linguistics. An international handbook*, 2:1212–1248.

Vanessa B Gorman. 2020. Dependency treebanks of Ancient Greek prose. *Journal of Open Humanities Data*, 6(1):1.

Aditya Grover and Jure Leskovec. 2016. node2vec: Scalable feature learning for networks. *CoRR*, abs/1607.00653.

Matthew Harrington. 2018. Perseids project. treebanked commentaries at Tufts University.

Dag TT Haug and Marius Jøhndal. 2008. Creating a parallel treebank of the old Indo-European Bible translations. In *Proceedings of the second workshop on language technology for cultural heritage data (LaTeCH 2008)*, pages 27–34.

Alek Keersmaekers. 2021. The GLAUx corpus: methodological issues in designing a long-term, diverse, multi-layered corpus of Ancient Greek. In *Proceedings of the 2nd International Workshop on Computational Approaches to Historical Language Change 2021*, pages 39–50, Online. Association for Computational Linguistics.

Alek Keersmaekers and Wouter Mercelis. 2021. Improving morphological analysis of Greek with transformer-based approaches: First results with ELECTRA.

Alek Keersmaekers, Wouter Mercelis, Colin Swaelens, and Toon Van Hal. 2019. Creating, enriching and valorizing treebanks of Ancient Greek. In *Proceedings of the 18th International Workshop on Treebanks and Linguistic Theories (TLT, SyntaxFest 2019)*, pages 109–117, Paris, France. Association for Computational Linguistics.

Douwe Kiela and Stephen Clark. 2014. A systematic study of semantic vector space model parameters. In *Proceedings of the 2nd Workshop on Continuous Vector Space Models and their Compositionality (CVSC)*, pages 21–30, Gothenburg, Sweden. Association for Computational Linguistics.

Gabriella Lapesa and Stefan Evert. 2017. Large-scale evaluation of dependency-based DSMs: Are they worth the effort? In *Proceedings of the 15th Conference of the European Chapter of the Association for Computational Linguistics: Volume 2, Short Papers*, pages 394–400, Valencia, Spain. Association for Computational Linguistics.

Alessandro Lenci, Magnus Sahlgren, Patrick Jeuniaux, Amaru Cuba Gyllensten, and Martina Miliani. 2022. A comparative evaluation and analysis of three generations of distributional semantic models. *Language resources and evaluation*, 56(4):1269–1313.

Omer Levy and Yoav Goldberg. 2014. Dependency-based word embeddings. In *Proceedings of the 52nd Annual Meeting of the Association for Computational Linguistics (Volume 2: Short Papers)*, pages 302–308, Baltimore, Maryland. Association for Computational Linguistics.

Barbara McGillivray, Simon Hengchen, Viivi Lähteenoja, Marco Palma, and Alessandro Vatri. 2019. A computational approach to lexical polysemy in Ancient Greek. *Digital Scholarship in the Humanities*, 34(4):893–907.

Tomas Mikolov, Kai Chen, Greg Corrado, and Jeffrey Dean. 2013. Efficient estimation of word representations in vector space. *arXiv preprint arXiv:1301.3781*.

Sebastian Padó and Mirella Lapata. 2007. Dependency-based construction of semantic space models. *Computational Linguistics*, 33(2):161–199.

Maria C Pantelia. 2022. *Thesaurus Linguae Graecae Digital Library*. University of California, Irvine.

Jeffrey Pennington, Richard Socher, and Christopher Manning. 2014. GloVe: Global vectors for word representation. In *Proceedings of the 2014 Conference on Empirical Methods in Natural Language Processing (EMNLP)*, pages 1532–1543, Doha, Qatar. Association for Computational Linguistics.

Valerio Perrone, Simon Hengchen, Marco Palma, Alessandro Vatri, Jim Q Smith, and Barbara McGillivray. 2021a. Lexical semantic change for Ancient Greek and Latin. In N. Tahmasebi, L. Borin, A. Jatowt, Y. Xu, and S. Hengchen, editors, *Computational approaches to semantic change*, pages 287–310. Language Science Press.

Valerio Perrone, Simon Hengchen, Marco Palma, Alessandro Vatri, Jim Q. Smith, and Barbara McGillivray. 2021b. Lexical semantic change for Ancient Greek and Latin: Computational approaches to semantic change. In Nina Tahmasebi, Lars Borin, Adam Jatowt, Yang Xu, and Simon Hengchen, editors, *Computational approaches to semantic change*, volume 6, chapter 9, pages 287–310. Language Science Press.

Radim Řehůřek and Petr Sojka. 2010. Software Framework for Topic Modelling with Large Corpora. In *Proceedings of the LREC 2010 Workshop on New Challenges for NLP Frameworks*, pages 45–50, Valletta, Malta. ELRA. `http://is.muni.cz/publication/884893/en`.

Frederick Riemenschneider and Anette Frank. 2023. Exploring large language models for classical philology. *arXiv preprint arXiv:2305.13698*.

Martina A Rodda, Philomen Probert, and Barbara McGillivray. 2019. Vector space models of Ancient Greek word meaning, and a case study on Homer. *Traitement Automatique Des Langues*, 60(3):63–87.

Martina A Rodda, Marco SG Senaldi, and Alessandro Lenci. 2017. Panta Rei: Tracking Semantic Change with Distributional Semantics in Ancient Greek. *IJCoL. Italian Journal of Computational Linguistics*, 3(3-1):11–24.

Klaus Rothenhäusler and Hinrich Schütze. 2009. Unsupervised classification with dependency based word spaces. In *Proceedings of the Workshop on Geometrical Models of Natural Language Semantics*, pages 17–24, Athens, Greece. Association for Computational Linguistics.

Dominik Schlechtweg, Anna Hätty, Marco Del Tredici, and Sabine Schulte im Walde. 2019. A wind of change: Detecting and evaluating lexical semantic change across times and domains. In *Proceedings of the 57th Annual Meeting of the Association for Computational Linguistics*, pages 732–746, Florence, Italy. Association for Computational Linguistics.

Pranaydeep Singh, Gorik Rutten, and Els Lefever. 2021. A pilot study for BERT language modelling and morphological analysis for ancient and medieval Greek. In *5th Joint SIGHUM Workshop on Computational Linguistics for Cultural Heritage, Social Sciences, Humanities and Literature, co-located with EMNLP 2021*, pages 128–137. Association for Computational Linguistics.

Silvia Stopponi, Nilo Pedrazzini, Saskia Peels-Matthey, Barbara McGillivray, and Malvina Nissim. 2024a. Natural language processing for Ancient Greek: Design, advantages, and challenges of language models. *Diachronica*.

Silvia Stopponi, Saskia Peels-Matthey, and Malvina Nissim. 2024b. AGREE: A new benchmark for the evaluation of distributional semantic models of Ancient Greek. *Digital Scholarship in the Humanities*.

Peter D. Turney. 2006. Similarity of semantic relations. *Computational Linguistics*, 32(3):379–416.

A. Vatri and B. McGillivray. 2018. The Diorisis Ancient Greek Corpus: Linguistics and literature. *Research Data Journal for the Humanities and Social Sciences*, 3(1):55 – 65.

Alessandro Vatri and Viivi Lähteenoja. 2019. Ancient Greek semantic annotation datasets.

Marja Vierros and Erik Henriksson. 2021. PapyGreek Treebanks: A dataset of linguistically annotated Greek documentary papyri. *Journal of open humanities data*.

Ivan Yamshchikov, Alexey Tikhonov, Yorgos Pantis, Charlotte Schubert, and Jürgen Jost. 2022. BERT in plutarch's shadows. In *Proceedings of the 2022 Conference on Empirical Methods in Natural Language Processing*, pages 6071–6080, Abu Dhabi, United Arab Emirates. Association for Computational Linguistics.

Polina Yordanova. 2018. Treebank of Aphtonius, Progymnasmata.

Latin Morphology through the Centuries: Ensuring Consistency for Better Language Processing

Federica Gamba and **Daniel Zeman**
Charles University, Faculty of Mathematics and Physics,
Institute of Formal and Applied Linguistics, Prague, Czechia
gamba,zeman@ufal.mff.cuni.cz

Abstract

This paper focuses on the process of harmonising the five Latin treebanks available in Universal Dependencies with respect to morphological annotation. We propose a workflow that allows to first spot inconsistencies and missing information, in order to detect to what extent the annotations differ, and then correct the retrieved bugs, with the goal of equalising the annotation of morphological features in the treebanks and producing more consistent linguistic data. Subsequently, we present some experiments carried out with UDPipe and Stanza in order to assess the impact of such harmonisation on parsing accuracy.

1 Introduction

In Universal Dependencies (de Marneffe et al., 2021) five treebanks are available for Latin:[1] Index Thomisticus Treebank (ITTB; Passarotti, 2019), Late Latin Charter Treebank (LLCT; Cecchini et al., 2020b), Perseus (Bamman and Crane, 2011), PROIEL (Haug and Jøhndal, 2008), UDante (Cecchini et al., 2020a). These treebanks differ on multiple levels. First, they cover different domains: a shallow distinction can be made between poetry (found in Perseus and, less, in UDante) and prose (all treebanks), but it can be further specified in terms of specific genre included. For instance, ITTB encompasses philosophical texts, while LLCT consists of charters, representing an instance of documentary genre. Additionally, the history of Latin, spoken for over two millennia, entails a substantial diachronic variation, as the language gradually evolved over time. Indeed, the five Latin treebanks include data that differ substantially in this respect. Already considering the Medieval treebanks alone, we can observe how wide the covered time range is: ITTB encompasses Medieval texts dating back to XIII century, LLCT features Early Medieval charters (VIII-IX century), while Dante Alighieri's work available in UDante belongs to XIV century. In addition to that, Perseus and PROIEL include classical texts (I BC - IV AD), as well as the *Vulgate* (IV century). A level of spatial variability can be observed too; for instance, LLCT includes texts written in Tuscany, Italy, and some features typical of the Romance languages are already emerging.

In addition to the aforementioned levels of variability, and besides variation in size, Latin treebanks also differ in terms of annotation choices, in spite of the UD work towards consistency. This issue can be doubly problematic: first with respect to UD itself, as the annotation is expected to be consistent across and within languages; secondly, in light of the fact that the quality of data may affect the results of any experiment or linguistic investigation carried out on those data. Gamba and Zeman (2023), investigating parsing performances, already observe this as regards the syntactic layer of these data. Nevertheless, what has been observed with respect to syntax does not necessarily apply to morphological features as well, and the extent to which inconsistent morphological annotation affects parsing performances thus remains unclear.

For this purpose, we first propose a harmonisation of the morphological features of the five treebanks, and thereafter assess its impact on models predicting morphology, as well as syntactic parsers. Section 2 presents some related work and the motivation behind our study. Section 3 features an overview of the harmonisation process, while in Section 4 we describe the strategy designed to spot inconsistent or missing annotations. Section 5 highlights the main harmonising interventions, whose impact on parsing accuracy is assessed in Section 6. Finally, Section 7 concludes the paper and suggests future research directions.

[1] See https://universaldependencies.org/.

Proceedings of the Ancient Language Processing Workshop associated with RANLP-2023, pages 59–67,
held in Varna Bulgaria, Sept 8, 2023.
https://doi.org/10.26615/978-954-452-087-8_007

2 Related Work and Motivation

Any NLP task is likely to show degraded performance when a model is applied to data that differ from training data. It has been observed several times that this issue is particularly prominent in (morpho-)syntactic parsing of Latin texts. The issue is strongly intertwined with Latin intra-linguistic variability, as the language has undergone a number of significant changes by spreading over a period of more than two millennia and across Europe. In order to investigate genuine linguistic diversity, first and foremost the impact of divergent annotation styles has to be ruled out. To perform any experiment that exploits data, we need those data to be consistent. Harmonising such discrepancies would allow for the isolation of the impact that annotation choices have, so that actual intra-linguistic variability can emerge and be examined.

The issue of Latin variability has been addressed in the two EvaLatin campaigns (Sprugnoli et al., 2020; Sprugnoli et al., 2022), aiming to evaluate NLP tools for Latin. In particular, EvaLatin has been focusing on lemmatisation, morphological analysis and POS tagging. However, Latin diversity has been observed several times already before, in light of the behaviour of parsing accuracy, which was far from being homogeneous. See, for instance, Passarotti and Ruffolo (2010), Ponti and Passarotti (2016), Passarotti and Dell'Orletta (2010). Several studies have also been addressing the issue of inconsistent annotations. Dickinson and Meurers (2003), Volokh and Neumann (2011), Ambati et al. (2011), de Marneffe et al. (2017), Aggarwal and Zeman (2020), and Aggarwal and Alzetta (2021) are only some of the methods that have been proposed to detect inconsistencies in treebanks. Gamba and Zeman (2023) present a harmonisation of dependency relations in Latin treebanks, yet without intervening at the level of morphological features. Their harmonisation highlighted several levels of inconsistencies and proved to lead to substantial improvements in terms of parsing accuracy. We investigate whether similar improvements can be achieved by also addressing inconsistencies in morphological annotation.

The output of the present study is two-fold:

- Producing a new version of the treebanks, harmonised at the level of morphological features, to be potentially contributed to the UD official release or to serve as an inspiration for other treebank maintainers to refine morphological annotation. Towards the latter goal, we develop a UDapi (Popel et al., 2017) block for detecting required and allowed morphological features in Latin treebanks. The Latin block was inspired by a similar block for Czech and we will contribute it to the official UDapi repository; it can be adapted to any other language by modifying the template according to language-specific features.

- Investigating the impact of harmonised morphological features in parsing, by assessing if and to what extent they affect accuracy scores. A comparison of two parsers, UDPipe (Straka et al., 2016) and Stanza (Qi et al., 2020) is proposed.

3 Overview of the Harmonisation Process

The focus of the harmonisation process is exclusively on morphological features.

We define the workflow to detect inconsistencies and missing features as follows. First, we run the UDapi block on the input data, with the goal of spotting features which are either required but missing, or not allowed. As output, the trees that feature either of these two kinds of inconsistencies are stored in a `html` file, where those bugs are prominently highlighted (see Figure 1). In light of the output `html` file, we build Python scripts that address and fix the observed bugs.

We employ the harmonised version of the five treebanks, as made available by Gamba and Zeman (2023), as input. Nevertheless, differently from what was done for syntactic harmonisation, we do not strictly follow UDante annotation. This choice is justified by the fact that we observe a considerable difference in the set of morphological features employed in UDante – predominantly – and the other treebanks (ITTB and LLCT) maintained by the same developers, i.e. the team at Università Cattolica del Sacro Cuore in Milan, Italy, as opposed to the two remaining treebanks (Perseus and PROIEL) out of the five available for Latin. We thus decide to define two levels of coherence:

- lower level (default): only information which can be considered somehow core, or more essential, is required. For instance, all pronouns must have a `PronType`, and all verbs must have `VerbForm` and `Aspect`.

- higher level: additional information, such as `InflClass`, is expected and allowed. This level of validation can be applied only to a subset of the Latin treebanks.

By default, the block operates at the lower level, but a parameter can be supplied to UDapi, which will trigger the more detailed features.

Morphologically harmonised treebanks and harmonisation scripts are available on GitHub,[2] while the block is available in UDapi GitHub repository. Moreover, we are ready to contribute the harmonised treebanks to the official UD release.

4 The `markFeatsBugs` Block

The `markFeatsBugs` block is structured as follows. For each UPOS tag, a set of *required* features is first defined. (Note that the official UD validator[3] has some limited ability to check *permitted* UPOS-feature combinations, but not to enforce required features.) Additional features that are permitted but not required are listed, and for each permitted feature the set of its permitted values is defined. Unlike in the official UD validator, the conditions for a feature-value to be permitted or required are not limited to whole UPOS categories. For example, the UD validator knows that the `Person` feature is allowed for verbs and auxiliaries; but we further restrict it to finite forms, i.e., the feature `VerbForm` must be present and its value must be `Fin`.

The set of allowed features is then expanded to include additional feature-value pairs that may be found in UDante, ITTB or LLCT (higher level of detail). Eventually, the block checks for each node whether its morphological features are permitted and if every node has all the required features. If not, invalid and missing features are explicitly marked with a transparent label allowing to easily distinguish them, and saved in the `Bug` attribute in the MISC column of the CoNLL-U file. It can be later used in filters and highlighted in the data. The code snippet in Script 1 provides an example, although not exhaustive, of the block section concerning verbs and auxiliaries, in compliance to what has been implemented in the treebanks among all the proposals illustrated in Cecchini (2021). Script 2

```
if re.match(r'^(VERB|AUX)$', node.upos):
    rf = ['VerbForm', 'Aspect']
    af = {'VerbForm': ['Inf', 'Fin',
    ↪  'Part', 'Conv'],
          'Aspect': ['Imp', 'Inch', 'Perf',
          ↪  'Prosp']}
    if node.feats['VerbForm'] not in
    ↪  ['Part', 'Conv']:
        rf.append('Tense')
        af['Tense'] = ['Past', 'Pqp',
        ↪  'Pres', 'Fut']
    if node.upos == 'VERB' or (node.upos
    ↪  == 'AUX' and node.lemma !=
    ↪  'sum'):
        rf.append('Voice')
        af['Voice'] = ['Act', 'Pass']
    if node.feats['VerbForm'] == 'Fin':
        rf.extend(['Mood', 'Person',
        ↪  'Number'])
        af['Mood'] = ['Ind', 'Sub',
        ↪  'Imp']
        af['Person'] = ['1', '2', '3']
        af['Number'] = ['Sing', 'Plur']
    elif node.feats['VerbForm'] ==
    ↪  'Part':
        rf.extend(['Gender', 'Number',
        ↪  'Case'])
        af['Number'] = ['Sing', 'Plur']
        ↪  if
        ↪  node.misc['TraditionalMood']
        ↪  != 'Gerundium' else ['Sing']
        af['Gender'] = ['Masc', 'Fem',
        ↪  'Neut'] if
        ↪  node.misc['TraditionalMood']
        ↪  != 'Gerundium' else ['Neut']
        af['Case'] = ['Nom', 'Gen',
        ↪  'Dat', 'Acc', 'Voc', 'Loc',
        ↪  'Abl']
        af['Degree'] = ['Abs', 'Cmp']
        if node.misc['TraditionalMood'].
        ↪  startswith('Gerundi'):
            af['Voice'] = ['Pass']
            af['Aspect'] = 'Prosp'
    elif node.feats['VerbForm'] ==
    ↪  'Conv':
        rf.extend(['Case', 'Gender',
        ↪  'Number'])
        af['Case'] = ['Abl', 'Acc']
        af['Gender'] = ['Masc']
        af['Number'] = ['Sing']
        af['Voice'] = ['Act']
    elif node.feats['VerbForm'] ==
    ↪  'Inf':
        af['Tense'].remove('Pqp')
```

Script 1: Portion of the block that partially exemplifies how morphological features are checked for the verbal system: `rf` stands for 'required features', `af` stands for 'allowed features'.

illustrates the expansion of the feature-value sets to the higher level, applicable to only three treebanks. UDante is used as reference to select those features.

[2] https://github.com/fjambe/Latin-variability/tree/main/morpho_harmonization (commit 2d14807).

[3] https://github.com/UniversalDependencies/tools/blob/master/validate.py.

```
if self.flavio:
    af['Compound'] = ['Yes']
    af['Variant'] = ['Greek']
    af['NameType'] = ['Ast', 'Cal',
     ↪  'Com', 'Geo', 'Giv', 'Let',
     ↪  'Lit', 'Met', 'Nat', 'Rel',
     ↪  'Sur', 'Oth']
    af['InflClass'] = ['Ind', 'IndEurA',
     ↪  'IndEurE', 'IndEurI', 'IndEurO',
     ↪  'IndEurU', 'IndEurX']
```

Script 2: Richer, more detailed morphological features as allowed by the relevant parameter if set to 1.

The most representative example is `InflClass`,[4] which reflects the original endings of the Proto-Indo-European stems. `InflClass` has not been added everywhere in UDante, therefore – when higher-level validation is turned on – it is only considered as allowed, instead of required.

5 Harmonisation Examples

Three treebanks have been harmonised to the higher level of detail (as defined in the previous sections): LLCT, ITTB and UDante. The remaining two treebanks (Perseus and PROIEL) have been harmonised to the lower level because the high-level annotation is not available for them.

The harmonisation process derives transparently from the feature constraints in the UDapi block. It would not be helpful to discuss every constraint in detail here (and if necessary, the reader can refer directly to the source code of the block); nonetheless, we want to discuss some interesting examples regarding verbs and auxiliaries. There is a more general issue raised by Cecchini (2021), who proposes a reorganisation of Latin non-finite verbal features towards a higher degree of universality. In accordance with their proposal,[5] we reannotate all gerund and gerundive forms as participles (`VerbForm=Part`) with `Aspect=Prosp`. Traditional terminology used in grammars, i.e. gerund and gerundive, is saved in the MISC field as `TraditionalMood=Gerund` and `TraditionalMood=Gerundive` to prevent loss of information and allow linguistic research based on traditional categories. Similarly, supine forms are reannotated as `VerbForm=Conv` with `Aspect=Prosp` and `TraditionalMood=Sup`. The use of `TraditionalMood` and `TraditionalTense` is extended to finite forms as well, for the purpose of consistency and in line with UDante. As far as finite forms are concerned, auxiliaries occurring in ITTB require some intervention as well. Unlike in the other treebanks, such forms (e.g. *sum* 'they are') do not present `Aspect`, `Mood`, `Person` and `Tense`. For the sake of consistency, we annotate them with respect to those features, assigning the relevant value.

Overall, the examinations of bugs highlighted by the block confirms what has been already noted in Gamba and Zeman (2023) with respect to Perseus and PROIEL status: their level of annotation detail is remarkably lower in comparison to ITTB, LLCT and UDante. An outstanding example is provided by `PronType`, which is a key feature for pronouns and determiners. Often missing in particular in Perseus, it is systematically added during the harmonisation process.

Additionally, the block can also serve as a tool to spot isolated errors. Whenever such errors are highlighted, we proceed to correct them.

Table 1 presents a quantitative overview of the major interventions applied.

6 Impact on Parsing

To evaluate the significance of the harmonisation process of morphological features, we try to investigate its impact on parsing accuracy. Therefore, we train new models for every morphologically harmonised treebank. The models are trained on the same data, but in the first case UDPipe 1.2 is used, while for the second one we choose to employ Stanza. With both Stanza and UDPipe we train the parser model on predicted lemmas and tags. Indeed, through Stanza's `prepare_depparse_treebank.py` script,[6] the trained POS tagging model is used to retag the training data before training the parser. Similarly, for UDPipe[7] we train a parsing model that relies on lemmas, UPOS tags and features as generated by the tagger. We use pretrained fastText embeddings[8] (Grave et al., 2018) and training hyperparameters as used for syntactic harmonisation in Gamba and Zeman (2023). For UDPipe, these hyperparameters correspond to the optimised ones

[4] `https://universaldependencies.org/la/feat/InflClass.html`.

[5] With the only exception of the `VNoun` feature, which has eventually not been introduced in UDante.

[6] `https://stanfordnlp.github.io/stanza/training_and_evaluation.html`.

[7] `https://ufal.mff.cuni.cz/udpipe/1/users-manual#model_training_parser`.

[8] Available at `https://fasttext.cc/docs/en/crawl-vectors.html`.

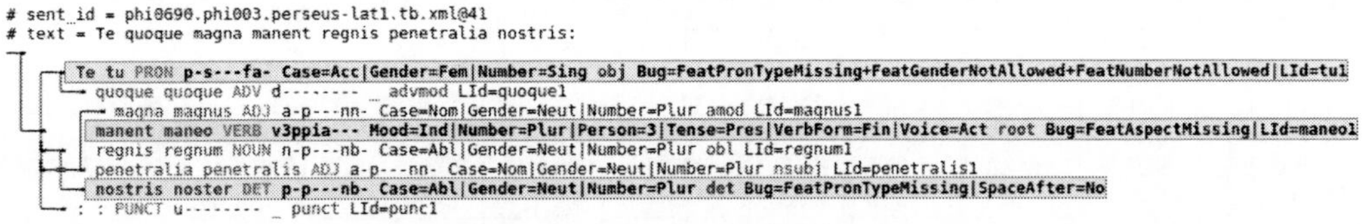

Figure 1: Example of the `html` file highlighting bugs found in the data.

	ITTB	LLCT	Perseus	PROIEL	UDante	notes
`Aspect`	26,243	4,596	4,344	35,420	-	`Aspect` is added.
`Gender_N`	2,655	9,746	1,037	11,756	-	`Gender` is added, corrected or deleted (nominal only).
`Gender_V`	1,514	1,834	30	3,899	-	`Gender` is added, corrected or deleted (verbal only).
Gerund(ive)s	2,740	1,855	91	1,046	-	Interventions on gerunds and gerundives.
`Mood`	20,269	-	-	-	-	`Mood` is added.
`Number_V`	21,783	1,834	30	322	-	`Number` is added (verbal only).
`NumForm=Word`	2,029	2,415	162	1,671	142	`NumForm=Word` is added to numerals like *viginti* 'twenty'.
`Person`	20,269	-	-	-	-	`Person` is added to verbs.
`Person_P`	-	-	1,346	15,887	-	`Person` in pronouns is either added, if missing, or deleted, if not relevant.
`PronType`	24,825	21,062	3,105	31,023	21	`PronType` is either added, if missing, or corrected.
`Tense`	51,096	10,988	1,277	9,430	-	`Tense` is either added, corrected or deleted.
`Voice`	2,591	1,855	216	1,064	-	`Voice` is added when missing.
`Voice_NO`	-	4,113	369	7,848	-	`Voice` is deleted when not relevant.

Table 1: Count of harmonising interventions.

made available for reproducible training by Straka and Straková (2019) when available (ITTB, Perseus and PROIEL), and to parameters inspired by those in the case of LLCT and UDante.[9]

We then evaluate the parsing model on morphologically harmonised test data for each treebank and compare results to the accuracy scores obtained with parsing models trained on data that underwent a harmonisation process only at syntax level.[10] Tables 2 and 3 report results obtained with UDPipe, in terms of Labeled Attachment Score (LAS) and Unlabeled Attachment Score (UAS) (Buchholz and Marsi, 2006), whereas Tables 6 and 7 presents analogous scores as obtained by the model trained with Stanza. Scores highlighted in blue denote an increase, while scores highlighted in red pinpoint decreased results. Accuracy is measured with the evaluation script[11] designed for the CoNLL 2018 Shared Task on Multilingual Parsing from Raw Text to Universal Dependencies (Zeman et al., 2018), which takes into consideration main dependency relations only and not subtypes.

First and foremost, a clarification is necessary. As explained earlier, the treebanks are not forced all to the same set of features: LLCT, ITTB and UDante have some extra features that are not found in Perseus and PROIEL. It would be possible to remove these extra features for the sake of parsing evaluation but we chose to keep them. One can thus expect somewhat worse results when applying models from one of these treebank groups to test data from the other group.

As illustrated in the tables, the results do not show any clear pattern and, overall, the improvements are neither widespread nor substantial. A closer look at the scores reveals that UDPipe shows improved accuracy scores in less than half of the cases, and in general performs worse than Stanza, with the gap being almost around 10% on average. Improvements obtained with models trained on UDPipe are never substantial and, in general, very hard to interpret. Stanza seems to allow for some additional remark. We first want to examine distinctly the two groups that correspond to the two possible values of the discussed parameter. The

[9]LLCT: learning_rate=0.02, transition_system=swap, transition_oracle=static_lazy, structured_interval=8.
UDante: learning_rate=0.01, transition_system=projective, transition_oracle=dynamic, structured_interval=8.

[10]In both cases parsing models are trained on predicted tags.

[11]`https://github.com/UniversalDependencies/tools/blob/master/eval.py`.

	ittb.udp		llct.udp		perseus.udp		proiel.udp		udante.udp	
	LAS	UAS	LAS	UAS	LAS	UAS	LAS	UAS	LAS	UAS
ITTB	**79.86%**	**83.11%**	38.62%	50.59%	44.16%	53.86%	45.19%	55.56%	53.51%	63.06%
LLCT	35.50%	45.63%	**91.84%**	**93.20%**	32.64%	42.66%	35.81%	47.55%	30.86%	41.31%
Perseus	44.14%	55.57%	32.60%	45.50%	**43.73%**	**57.28%**	40.36%	53.25%	42.13%	54.23%
PROIEL	49.37%	58.58%	36.67%	48.72%	45.23%	54.41%	**70.02%**	**75.16%**	41.85%	53.13%
UDante	46.89%	57.28%	31.85%	44.31%	34.51%	45.73%	35.50%	47.64%	**48.24%**	**57.99%**

Table 2: UDPipe LAS and UAS before morphological harmonisation. Columns correspond to trained models, rows to test data.

	ittb.udp		llct.udp		perseus.udp		proiel.udp		udante.udp	
	LAS	UAS	LAS	UAS	LAS	UAS	LAS	UAS	LAS	UAS
ITTB	**81.01%**	**84.05%**	39.31%	51.29%	45.22%	55.37%	44.42%	54.10%	53.66%	62.40%
LLCT	34.76%	44.55%	**91.57%**	**92.72%**	32.12%	41.00%	36.55%	48.25%	32.69%	42.44%
Perseus	42.89%	53.76%	31.52%	44.65%	**47.76%**	**57.33%**	39.99%	51.96%	41.49%	53.36%
PROIEL	49.96%	58.89%	36.84%	49.02%	45.16%	54.51%	**70.24%**	**75.59%**	41.80%	52.72%
UDante	46.31%	56.18%	31.20%	43.72%	34.20%	45.60%	35.76%	46.51%	**47.99%**	**57.44%**

Table 3: UDPipe LAS and UAS after morphological harmonisation. Columns correspond to trained models, rows to test data.

LLCT model obtains lower accuracy scores only on Perseus, which presents a more coarse-grained morphological annotation, but not on any of the treebanks belonging to the same class. A similar remark could be made about the ITTB model; the lower scores obtained on ITTB test data, despite being coloured in red, are probably not significant. Nevertheless, this reasoning does not hold true for the model trained on UDante, which incongruously performs best on Perseus and PROIEL. On the other hand, the PROIEL model is the only one showing improvements on all test data; despite not being substantial in most of the cases, a +3% increase can be observed when the model is used to parse LLCT data.

All the discussion so far concerns syntactic parsing, which is only indirectly affected by the consistency of morphological annotation. So the natural next question is about the impact of the harmonisation on prediction of morphology. Both UDPipe and Stanza predict morphological annotation together with syntax. Tables 4 and 8 show accuracy of feature prediction (percentage of correct words, whereas a word is correct if all its feature-value pairs have been predicted correctly). Each accuracy is computed before and after harmonisation, shown in the same table. Here we see a clear improvement in all experiments where a model is applied to data from different treebank; and for ITTB and PROIEL, the improved consistency led to improvement also in the in-domain experiment. The improvement is further confirmed in Tables 5 and 9, which show the MLAS scores (Zeman et al., 2018), combining morphology and syntax.

7 Conclusion and Future Work

The paper presents the harmonisation process that we carried out, with respect to morphology, on the five Latin UD treebanks. We first defined an UDapi block for Latin, listing which morphological features a token should possess. Such lists of features are defined based on UPOS tags. Subsequently, we corrected the retrieved inconsistencies – consisting in either missing or not allowed features – via Python scripts. As a result, we produced morphologically harmonised versions of the Latin treebanks that were previously harmonised syntactically (Gamba and Zeman, 2023). We contributed the script to investigate Latin features, possibly reusable by anyone working on Latin treebanks, and we described a workflow that can be replicated and applied to potentially any other language, provided that language-specific information is supplied within the template. In the second part of the paper, we presented some parsing experiments carried out with UDPipe and Stanza. By comparing syntactic attachment scores before and after morphological harmonisation, we observed the absence of a clear pattern that would allow to explain results; on the other hand, morphological accuracy clearly improved. The coexistence of a coarse-grained and a fine-grained level of consistency in annotation partially explains the outcome of the parsing experiments, that however must not discourage from pursuing an ever-growing harmonisation of linguistic resources in terms of annotation choices. Intra- and inter-resource consistency is a key factor to exploit data, whether it comes to

	ittb.udp		llct.udp		perseus.udp		proiel.udp		udante.udp	
	before	after	before	after	before	after	before	after	before	after
ITTB	**93.57%**	**93.91%**	55.41%	63.72%	53.76%	69.09%	54.50%	78.02%	62.67%	70.68%
LLCT	52.38%	60.39%	**95.89%**	95.86%	50.53%	60.36%	54.45%	67.45%	50.59%	58.68%
Perseus	52.54%	65.25%	46.74%	55.10%	**72.03%**	71.11%	69.45%	76.26%	45.12%	57.77%
PROIEL	46.47%	69.98%	45.12%	56.83%	61.16%	69.11%	**87.19%**	**88.87%**	40.35%	59.81%
UDante	58.30%	64.99%	47.47%	54.90%	44.60%	59.29%	48.30%	69.57%	**74.84%**	74.67%

Table 4: Comparison of UDPipe accuracy scores on morphological features. Columns correspond to trained models, rows to test data.

	ittb.udp		llct.udp		perseus.udp		proiel.udp		udante.udp	
	before	after	before	after	before	after	before	after	before	after
ITTB	**69.97%**	**71.64%**	15.10%	17.23%	15.24%	22.90%	18.68%	30.85%	25.39%	29.04%
LLCT	10.41%	13.14%	**85.76%**	85.50%	6.49%	11.38%	11.07%	17.04%	7.52%	8.93%
Perseus	15.37%	21.98%	8.68%	12.80%	**28.60%**	**28.89%**	23.59%	29.45%	10.70%	17.59%
PROIEL	16.14%	29.49%	10.81%	15.58%	19.00%	25.21%	**56.42%**	**58.07%**	11.47%	18.82%
UDante	18.87%	21.32%	8.62%	10.15%	8.94%	13.53%	11.97%	19.43%	**25.90%**	25.46%

Table 5: Comparison of UDPipe MLAS scores. Columns correspond to trained models, rows to test data.

	ittb.mdl		llct.mdl		perseus.mdl		proiel.mdl		udante.mdl	
	LAS	UAS	LAS	UAS	LAS	UAS	LAS	UAS	LAS	UAS
ITTB	**88.60%**	**90.55%**	45.63%	58.74%	50.55%	61.47%	51.16%	60.72%	63.78%	72.96%
LLCT	40.84%	52.66%	**94.61%**	**95.81%**	37.82%	47.50%	40.97%	53.24%	43.64%	56.09%
Perseus	57.68%	67.85%	40.80%	53.88%	**58.41%**	**68.22%**	47.30%	58.68%	52.98%	64.06%
PROIEL	62.34%	71.27%	46.76%	59.92%	55.03%	65.25%	**80.57%**	**84.36%**	52.61%	63.91%
UDante	56.62%	67.27%	39.67%	52.97%	39.53%	52.98%	41.27%	52.41%	**57.92%**	**67.60%**

Table 6: Stanza LAS and UAS before morphological harmonisation. Columns correspond to trained models, rows to test data.

	ittb.mdl		llct.mdl		perseus.mdl		proiel.mdl		udante.mdl	
	LAS	UAS	LAS	UAS	LAS	UAS	LAS	UAS	LAS	UAS
ITTB	88.29%	90.28%	46.93%	60.21%	50.02%	60.22%	52.86%	62.13%	64.87%	72.91%
LLCT	42.18%	54.50%	**94.91%**	**96.08%**	38.10%	48.50%	42.48%	56.08%	42.43%	54.97%
Perseus	59.00%	69.00%	39.82%	53.34%	**59.43%**	**68.97%**	47.97%	59.36%	54.26%	65.17%
PROIEL	62.33%	71.27%	48.17%	61.25%	55.56%	64.81%	**81.25%**	**84.91%**	54.37%	64.41%
UDante	58.24%	68.42%	40.39%	53.84%	39.73%	52.47%	41.41%	52.74%	57.40%	66.79%

Table 7: Stanza LAS and UAS after morphological harmonisation. Columns correspond to trained models, rows to test data.

	ittb.mdl		llct.mdl		perseus.mdl		proiel.mdl		udante.mdl	
	before	after	before	after	before	after	before	after	before	after
ITTB	**95.70%**	**96.15%**	57.07%	66.19%	55.19%	72.91%	52.14%	79.97%	66.22%	75.34%
LLCT	56.92%	63.95%	**96.89%**	96.81%	53.53%	65.33%	57.07%	71.87%	55.73%	63.47%
Perseus	57.29%	72.49%	48.66%	57.23%	**78.02%**	77.86%	70.01%	79.51%	49.75%	64.63%
PROIEL	49.88%	75.90%	48.31%	60.97%	66.57%	75.95%	**90.91%**	**92.72%**	44.53%	67.10%
UDante	62.47%	69.85%	48.56%	56.32%	45.89%	63.42%	46.22%	70.64%	**79.39%**	79.30%

Table 8: Comparison of Stanza accuracy scores on morphological features. Columns correspond to trained models, rows to test data.

	ittb.mdl		llct.mdl		perseus.mdl		proiel.mdl		udante.mdl	
	before	after	before	after	before	after	before	after	before	after
ITTB	**78.97%**	**80.74%**	16.56%	19.07%	19.45%	27.87%	22.13%	40.05%	33.14%	39.59%
LLCT	12.22%	17.67%	**89.46%**	**90.04%**	9.12%	16.63%	15.98%	24.25%	12.59%	18.02%
Perseus	22.63%	35.20%	11.57%	16.92%	**38.86%**	**40.21%**	31.33%	38.66%	16.25%	27.29%
PROIEL	22.23%	41.32%	14.86%	22.74%	27.64%	35.92%	**68.49%**	**71.23%**	17.17%	30.61%
UDante	25.06%	29.95%	12.21%	14.77%	10.64%	17.37%	13.45%	25.40%	**35.96%**	35.32%

Table 9: Comparison of Stanza MLAS scores. Columns correspond to trained models, rows to test data.

linguistic research or any other application.

In light of the slight improvement that resulted in parsing accuracy from the harmonisation process, we do not plan on further developing the harmonisation of treebanks. The higher degree of consistency in treebank annotation, i.e. the availability of more homogeneous data, allows now to investigate the actual reasons for variability in parsing. Syntactic constructions evolving over time may be inspected, as well as other factors that may affect parsing results on data that differ from training data – as already problematised several times, e.g. by Passarotti and Dell'Orletta (2010), Passarotti and Ruffolo (2010), Ponti and Passarotti (2016). Variation in time is most probably expected to be a relevant factor, and it is strongly connected to two other relevant variables, i.e. space and domain. Consider, for instance, the Late Latin Charter Treebank: while featuring early medieval Latin (VIII-IX century), not as late as ITTB (XIII century) and UDante (XIV century) Latin varieties, the treebank does not include literary texts yet charters written in Tuscany, Italy. The gradual development of Latin towards Romance languages, exemplified by evolving syntactic constructions and changes in word endings, can already be observed in the treebank (Cecchini et al., 2020c). Variation in terms of genre appears to be relevant also with respect to the distinction between poetry and prose. With Latin treebanks encompassing mostly literary data, such distinction cannot be overlooked. Indeed, Latin poetry is strongly affected by prosody and metre: the sequence of short and long syllables in words, as defined by prosodic rules, together with the specific structure of the selected metre, rigidly determine possible sequences of words. As a result, the natural word order is unsettled, and the position of a word in the verse (and, hence, in the sentence) is mostly defined by the way its short and long syllables follows one another. This whole mechanism, highly affecting word order, entails a high degree of non-projectivity, and would need to be further inspected.

Acknowledgements

This work was supported by the Grant No. 20-16819X (LUSyD) of the Czech Science Foundation (GAČR).

References

Akshay Aggarwal and Chiara Alzetta. 2021. Atypical or underrepresented? A pilot study on small treebanks. In *Proceedings of the Eighth Italian Conference on Computational Linguistics, CLiC-it 2021, Milan, Italy, January 26-28, 2022*, volume 3033 of *CEUR Workshop Proceedings*. CEUR-WS.org.

Akshay Aggarwal and Daniel Zeman. 2020. Estimating POS annotation consistency of different treebanks in a language. In *Proceedings of the 19th International Workshop on Treebanks and Linguistic Theories*, pages 93–110, Düsseldorf, Germany. Association for Computational Linguistics.

Bharat Ram Ambati, Rahul Agarwal, Mridul Gupta, Samar Husain, and Dipti Misra Sharma. 2011. Error detection for treebank validation. In *Proceedings of the 9th Workshop on Asian Language Resources*, pages 23–30, Chiang Mai, Thailand. Asian Federation of Natural Language Processing.

David Bamman and Gregory Crane. 2011. The Ancient Greek and Latin Dependency Treebanks. In *Language technology for cultural heritage*, pages 79–98. Springer.

Sabine Buchholz and Erwin Marsi. 2006. CoNLL-X shared task on multilingual dependency parsing. In *Proceedings of the Tenth Conference on Computational Natural Language Learning (CoNLL-X)*, pages 149–164, New York City. Association for Computational Linguistics.

Flavio M Cecchini, Rachele Sprugnoli, Giovanni Moretti, and Marco Passarotti. 2020a. UDante: First Steps Towards the Universal Dependencies Treebank of Dante's Latin Works. In *Seventh Italian Conference on Computational Linguistics*, pages 1–7. CEUR Workshop Proceedings.

Flavio Massimiliano Cecchini. 2021. Formae reformandae: for a reorganisation of verb form annotation in Universal Dependencies illustrated by the specific case of Latin. In *Proceedings of the Fifth Workshop on Universal Dependencies (UDW, SyntaxFest 2021)*, pages 1–15, Sofia, Bulgaria. Association for Computational Linguistics.

Flavio Massimiliano Cecchini, Timo Korkiakangas, and Marco Passarotti. 2020b. A New Latin Treebank for Universal Dependencies: Charters between Ancient Latin and Romance Languages. In *Proceedings of the 12th Language Resources and Evaluation Conference*, Marseille, France. European Language Resources Association.

Flavio Massimiliano Cecchini, Timo Korkiakangas, and Marco Passarotti. 2020c. A new Latin treebank for Universal Dependencies: Charters between Ancient Latin and Romance languages. In *Proceedings of the Twelfth Language Resources and Evaluation Conference*, pages 933–942, Marseille, France. European Language Resources Association.

Marie-Catherine de Marneffe, Matias Grioni, Jenna Kanerva, and Filip Ginter. 2017. Assessing the annotation consistency of the Universal Dependencies corpora. In *Proceedings of the Fourth International Conference on Dependency Linguistics (Depling 2017)*, pages 108–115, Pisa,Italy. Linköping University Electronic Press.

Marie-Catherine de Marneffe, Christopher Manning, Joakim Nivre, and Daniel Zeman. 2021. Universal Dependencies. *Computational Linguistics*, 47(2):255–308.

Markus Dickinson and W Detmar Meurers. 2003. Detecting inconsistencies in treebanks. In *Proceedings of TLT*, volume 3, pages 45–56.

Federica Gamba and Daniel Zeman. 2023. Universalising Latin Universal Dependencies: a harmonisation of Latin treebanks in UD. In *Proceedings of the Sixth Workshop on Universal Dependencies (UDW, GURT/SyntaxFest 2023)*, pages 7–16, Washington, D.C. Association for Computational Linguistics.

Edouard Grave, Piotr Bojanowski, Prakhar Gupta, Armand Joulin, and Tomas Mikolov. 2018. Learning word vectors for 157 languages. In *Proceedings of the Eleventh International Conference on Language Resources and Evaluation (LREC 2018)*, Miyazaki, Japan. European Language Resources Association (ELRA).

Dag TT Haug and Marius Jøhndal. 2008. Creating a Parallel Treebank of the Old Indo-European Bible Translations. In *Proceedings of the Second Workshop on Language Technology for Cultural Heritage Data (LaTeCH 2008)*, pages 27–34.

Marco Passarotti. 2019. The Project of the Index Thomisticus Treebank. *Digital Classical Philology*, 10:299–320.

Marco Passarotti and Felice Dell'Orletta. 2010. Improvements in parsing the index Thomisticus treebank. revision, combination and a feature model for medieval Latin. In *Proceedings of the Seventh International Conference on Language Resources and Evaluation (LREC'10)*, Valletta, Malta. European Language Resources Association (ELRA).

Marco Passarotti and Paolo Ruffolo. 2010. Parsing the Index Thomisticus Treebank. Some Preliminary Results. In *15th International Colloquium on Latin Linguistics*, pages 714—725. Innsbrucker Beiträge zur Sprachwissenschaft.

Edoardo Maria Ponti and Marco Passarotti. 2016. Differentia compositionem facit. a slower-paced and reliable parser for Latin. In *Proceedings of the Tenth International Conference on Language Resources and Evaluation (LREC'16)*, pages 683–688, Portorož, Slovenia. European Language Resources Association (ELRA).

Martin Popel, Zdeněk Žabokrtský, and Martin Vojtek. 2017. Udapi: Universal API for Universal Dependencies. In *Proceedings of the NoDaLiDa 2017 Workshop on Universal Dependencies (UDW 2017)*, pages 96–101, Gothenburg, Sweden. Association for Computational Linguistics.

Peng Qi, Yuhao Zhang, Yuhui Zhang, Jason Bolton, and Christopher D. Manning. 2020. Stanza: A python natural language processing toolkit for many human languages. In *Proceedings of the 58th Annual Meeting of the Association for Computational Linguistics: System Demonstrations*, pages 101–108, Online. Association for Computational Linguistics.

Rachele Sprugnoli, Marco Passarotti, Flavio Massimiliano Cecchini, Margherita Fantoli, and Giovanni Moretti. 2022. Overview of the EvaLatin 2022 evaluation campaign. In *Proceedings of the Second Workshop on Language Technologies for Historical and Ancient Languages*, pages 183–188, Marseille, France. European Language Resources Association.

Rachele Sprugnoli, Marco Passarotti, Flavio Massimiliano Cecchini, and Matteo Pellegrini. 2020. Overview of the EvaLatin 2020 evaluation campaign. In *Proceedings of LT4HALA 2020 - 1st Workshop on Language Technologies for Historical and Ancient Languages*, pages 105–110, Marseille, France. European Language Resources Association (ELRA).

Milan Straka, Jan Hajič, and Jana Straková. 2016. UDPipe: Trainable pipeline for processing CoNLL-U files performing tokenization, morphological analysis, POS tagging and parsing. In *Proceedings of the Tenth International Conference on Language Resources and Evaluation (LREC'16)*, pages 4290–4297, Portorož, Slovenia. European Language Resources Association (ELRA).

Milan Straka and Jana Straková. 2019. Universal dependencies 2.5 models for UDPipe (2019-12-06). LINDAT/CLARIAH-CZ digital library at the Institute of Formal and Applied Linguistics (ÚFAL), Faculty of Mathematics and Physics, Charles University.

Alexander Volokh and Günter Neumann. 2011. Automatic detection and correction of errors in dependency treebanks. In *Proceedings of the 49th Annual Meeting of the Association for Computational Linguistics: Human Language Technologies*, pages 346–350, Portland, Oregon, USA. Association for Computational Linguistics.

Daniel Zeman, Jan Hajič, Martin Popel, Martin Potthast, Milan Straka, Filip Ginter, Joakim Nivre, and Slav Petrov. 2018. CoNLL 2018 shared task: Multilingual parsing from raw text to Universal Dependencies. In *Proceedings of the CoNLL 2018 Shared Task: Multilingual Parsing from Raw Text to Universal Dependencies*, pages 1–21, Brussels, Belgium. Association for Computational Linguistics.

Cross-Lingual Constituency Parsing for Middle High German: A Delexicalized Approach

Ercong Nie[1,2] **Helmut Schmid**[1] **Hinrich Schütze**[1,2]
[1]Center for Information and Language Processing (CIS), LMU Munich, Germany
[2] Munich Center for Machine Learning (MCML), Germany
nie@cis.lmu.de

Abstract

Constituency parsing plays a fundamental role in advancing natural language processing (NLP) tasks. However, training an automatic syntactic analysis system for ancient languages solely relying on annotated parse data is a formidable task due to the inherent challenges in building treebanks for such languages. It demands extensive linguistic expertise, leading to a scarcity of available resources. To overcome this hurdle, cross-lingual transfer techniques which require minimal or even no annotated data for low-resource target languages offer a promising solution. In this study, we focus on building a constituency parser for **M**iddle **H**igh **G**erman (**MHG**) under realistic conditions, where no annotated MHG treebank is available for training. In our approach, we leverage the linguistic continuity and structural similarity between MHG and **M**odern **G**erman (**MG**), along with the abundance of MG treebank resources. Specifically, by employing the *delexicalization* method, we train a constituency parser on MG parse datasets and perform cross-lingual transfer to MHG parsing. Our delexicalized constituency parser demonstrates remarkable performance on the MHG test set, achieving an F1-score of 67.3%. It outperforms the best zero-shot cross-lingual [1] baseline by a margin of 28.6% points. These encouraging results underscore the practicality and potential for automatic syntactic analysis in other ancient languages that face similar challenges as MHG.

1 Introduction

Constituency parsing, which involves analyzing the grammatical structure of sentences and identifying the hierarchical relationships between words, plays a crucial role in linguistic research, especially for the analysis of ancient languages that are no longer spoken. Its significance extends beyond linguistic analysis, serving as a building block for various natural language processing (NLP) applications, such as information extraction (Jiang, 2012; Jiang and Diesner, 2019), sentiment analysis (Li et al., 2020), question answering (Hermjakob, 2001), etc. However, ancient languages lack large labeled and unlabeled corpora (Assael et al., 2022) and treebanks suitable for parser training are seldom available. This scarcity of resources can be attributed to two reasons. Firstly, ancient languages usually have a dearth of digital text resources. Secondly, the construction of a treebank for an ancient language requires substantial linguistic expertise and manual effort. Nonetheless, the continuity in the process of language evolution gives rise to linguistic similarities between ancient languages and their corresponding modern counterparts (Parravicini and Pievani, 2018). Cross-lingual transfer techniques (Ruder, 2019; Lauscher et al., 2020) are trained on high-resource languages and require little or no annotated data from low-resource target languages. They can effectively be applied to languages with similar sentence structure and word order. Hence, they can be a viable solution to this challenge.

In this work, we focus on building a constituency parser for Middle High German (MHG). MHG is a historical stage of the German language that was spoken between 1050 and 1350. It is the linguistic predecessor of Modern German (MG). Both languages have many similarities in word formation and grammatical features, e.g., similar word order patterns and inflectional systems (Salmons, 2018). The availability of MHG parse trees is extremely limited. The *Deutsche Diachrone Baumbank (German Diachronical Treebank, DDB)* (Hirschmann and Linde, 2023) comprises merely around 100 manually annotated parse trees, encompassing less than 3000 tokens. These resources are far from

[1]As is prevalent in the realm of multilingual NLP, the term "zero-shot cross-lingual" in this context pertains to a transfer learning method where we finetune the model with task-specific data in a source language and test on the target language directly (Sitaram et al., 2023).

Proceedings of the Ancient Language Processing Workshop associated with RANLP-2023, pages 68–79,
held in Varna Bulgaria, Sept 8, 2023.
https://doi.org/10.26615/978-954-452-087-8_008

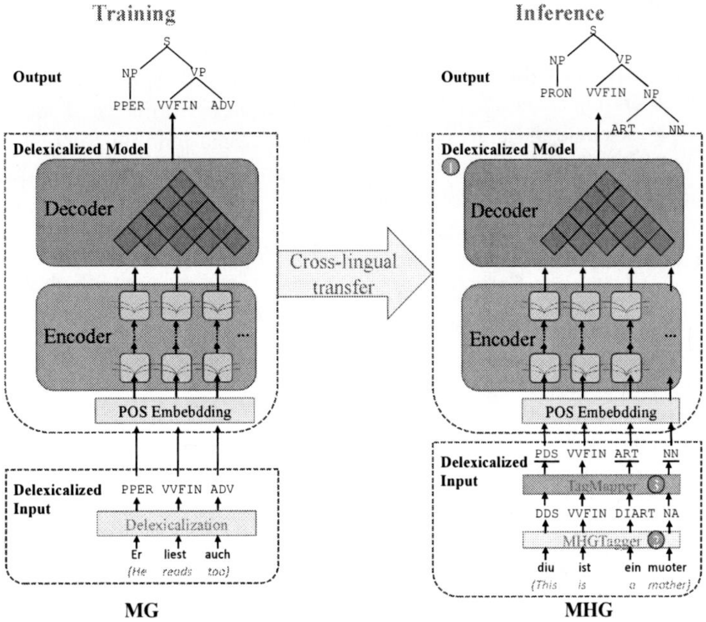

Figure 1: Overview of the cross-lingual delexicalized parsing system for MHG. In the training, the delexicalized parsing model is trained on the delexicalized MG trees. The trained parser is subsequently applied to MHG sentences. The delexicalized parsing system for MHG consists of three key modules: (1) *Delexicalized parsing model* trained on delexicalized MG trees, (2) *MHG POS tagger*, and (3) *Tag mapper*.

what is required to train an automatic syntactic analysis system, and are only suitable for use as test sets. On the other hand, there is an abundance of treebank resources available for MG, in particular the Tiger Treebank (Smith, 2003). Hence, we capitalize on the structural similarity between MHG and MG, as well as the rich MG treebank resources in order to develop a cross-lingual *delexicalized* constituency parsing model that we can directly apply to MHG sentences.

In the delexicalized approach, the parsing model operates on part-of-speech (POS) sequences rather than token sequences. We accomplish this by training a cross-lingual parser using POS sequences from high-resource source languages as input. Subsequently, we utilize this trained parser to directly parse POS sequences of low-resource target languages (McDonald et al., 2011).

In our work, we first train a delexicalized constituency parsing model on a delexicalized MG treebank. In order to parse MHG sentences with this model, we need to annotate them first with the POS tags used in the MG treebank. To this end, we train a POS tagger on an MHG corpus which has been manually annotated using a POS tag set similar, but not identical to the MG tag set. We employ a POS mapper to replace the MHG tags by the corresponding MG tags, ensuring the uniformity of the model's inputs across the two languages, which is a prerequisite of the delexicalization method. The experimental results show that our delexicalized constituency parser substantially outperforms all other zero-shot cross-lingual parsing baselines, achieving an F1-score of 67.3% on the MHG parse test set.

The delexicalization method is particularly well-suited for languages which (1) lack treebank resources, (2) possess sufficient annotated data for training POS taggers, and (3) exhibit syntactic similarities with a high-resource language. Our investigation of this realistic scenario shows the feasibility of automatic syntactic analysis for an ancient language.

The subsequent sections of this paper are organized as follows. In Sec. 2, we discuss related work. Sec. 3 gives an overview of our research languages and the available corpora. The delexicalization method employed in our approach is detailed in Sec. 4. Sec. 5 describes our experimental setup, and in Sec. 6, we analyze the results. We conclude in Sec. 7.

2 Related Work

Cross-Lingual Transfer Learning The fundamental principle underlying cross-lingual transfer is that the processing of source and target languages uses a shared input representation, which can be either discrete or continuous. The delexicalization method is based on a shared discrete input representation, i.e., POS tags. Other discrete representation types include glossed words (Zeman and Resnik, 2008) and grounding texts in multilingual knowledge bases (Lehmann et al., 2015). Continuous cross-lingual representation spaces emerged with advancements in neural networks. Typical examples are cross-lingual word embeddings (Ammar et al., 2016) and sentence embeddings (Artetxe and Schwenk, 2019).

The emergence of massively multilingual transformers (Devlin et al., 2019; Conneau et al., 2020), which are jointly pretrained on multilingual corpora, introduces a novel pattern of zero-shot cross-lingual transfer learning. In this paradigm, a pretrained multilingual model is finetuned on a downstream NLP task dataset of a source language. The finetuned multilingual model is then directly applied to target language data for the same task (K et al., 2019; Hu et al., 2020; Liu et al., 2022; Nie et al., 2023).

Neural Constituency Parsing Recent advances in constituency parsing have witnessed a growing emphasis on harnessing neural network representations, making a shift from the previously prominent role of grammars, whose relevance has gradually diminished. Cross and Huang (2016) propose a span-based constituency parsing system specifically designed to leverage the powerful representation capabilities of the bidirectional long short-term memory (LSTM) networks (Hochreiter and Schmidhuber, 1997). In this method, an input sentence is represented as a set of spans, and each span is assigned a score. The best-scoring parse tree is computed using dynamic programming techniques. They combine smaller spans into larger spans until the entire sentence is covered. Subsequently, several variations of the span-based method have been proposed, e.g. approaches replacing the inference algorithm with chart-based methods (Stern et al., 2017), using character-level representations instead of word-level representations (Gaddy et al., 2018), and replacing LSTMs with self-attention modules (Kitaev and Klein, 2018). Kitaev et al. (2019) take advantage of the newly developed pretrained language models (PLMs) and use BERT (Devlin et al., 2019) to compute the span representations, resulting in enhanced performance. Kitaev and Klein (2020) improve the runtime complexity of constituency parsing to linear time by reducing parsing to tagging.

Cross-Lingual Constituency Parsing There has been relatively limited scholarly attention dedicated to cross-lingual constituency parsing in recent studies, especially for target languages situated in low-resource settings, such as MHG. Kitaev et al. (2019) have employed the multilingual BERT model to train a single parser with parameters shared across languages. They jointly finetune the multilingual BERT on 10 languages utilizing a common BERT backbone, but the model contains distinct MLP span classifiers for each language to accommodate the different tree labels. However, their approach necessitates the availability of treebanks of all the encompassed languages as training datasets. Kaing et al. (2021) undertake a comprehensive series of experiments to validate the efficacy of delexicalization techniques for zero-shot cross-lingual constituency parsing. Additionally, their study underscores significance of typological affinity in the source language selection. We build upon these investigations and apply their findings to the zero-shot parsing of MHG within a practical contextual framework.

Constituency Parsing on Historical German There is a notable scarcity of syntactically annotated corpora for historical German. In instances where annotated treebanks are absent, approaches such as rule-based, unsupervised, or zero-shot cross-lingual methods can be employed for constituency parsing, For instance, Chiarcos et al. (2018) have created a rule-based shallow parser for MHG. Recent advancements in the construction of such corpora encompass:

- *German Diachronical Treebank (DDB)*: a small yet syntactically deeply annotated corpus, comprising three subcorpora of different stages of German, i.e., Old High German, Middle High German and Early New High German (Hirschmann and Linde, 2023). The construction of the DDB corpus is oriented towards the Tiger Corpus (Smith, 2003), one of the largest German treebanks.
- *UP Treebank of Early New High German*

(ENHG): a syntactically annotated corpus of ENHG containing 21,432 sentences consisting of 600,569 word tokens based on the Reference Corpus of ENHG (Demske, 2019).

- *Corpus of Historical Low German (CHLG)*: a Penn-style treebank of Middle Low German (Booth et al., 2020)

Contemporary work on historical German parsing based on previously mentioned corpora includes endeavors such as cross-dialectal parsing for ENHG based on CHLG (Sapp et al., 2023).

3 Languages and Corpora

The ancient language which we study in this paper is Middle High German (MHG). MHG and Modern German (MG) are stages of the same Germanic language family, representing different historical periods. MHG emerged during the Middle Ages in the German-speaking regions of Central Europe. It was primarily used in literary and administrative contexts and played an important role in medieval literature, including epic poems such as the *Nibelungenlied* and *Minnesang* (courtly love poetry) (Salmons, 2018).

Linguistic Considerations of MHG MHG has a phonetic system that included a set of vowel and consonant sounds. The pronunciation and sound patterns differ from those of MG, but some MHG words are still recognizable in MG. MHG has a more complex grammatical system, such as a more extensive case system with different noun and adjective declensions. Besides, verb conjugation has more intricate forms and patterns (Jones and Jones, 2019). In terms of orthography, the spelling and writing conventions of MHG are different from MG. For example, *ü*, the umlaut of *u*, is usually written *iu* in MHG. The transition from MHG to MG was a gradual process, occurring over several centuries. MG can be considered the linguistic descendant of MHG, with linguistic changes and developments shaping the language over time.

MHG Corpora Resources During the MHG period, the amount of textual material that survives to the present increases markedly. The *Reference Corpus of Middle High German* (*ReM*) (Klein et al., 2016) encompasses a large collection of non-literary and non-religious texts. ReM is a corpus of diplomatically transcribed and annotated texts of MHG with a size of around 2 million word forms. Texts in ReM have been digitized and richly annotated, e.g., with POS, morphological and lemma features. The morphological annotation uses the HiTS tag set (Dipper et al., 2013), a tag set for historical German, derived from the Stuttgart-Tübinger Tag Set (STTS) for modern German texts (Schiller et al., 1995). Although the ReM corpus provides rich morphologically annotated text data for MHG, the availability of syntactically annotated data for MHG is severely limited, with only approximately 100 MHG parse trees included in the DDB treebank. In contrast, the treebank resources for MG are abundant. The Tiger Treebank (Brants et al., 2002), for instance, consists of approximately 40,000 sentences of German newspaper text, taken from the Frankfurter Rundschau.

4 Methods

In our work, we focus on developing a constituency parser for MHG. In the previous section, we reviewed annotated resources available for MHG and MG. Basically, we have ample treebank resources for MG and plenty of POS-tagged texts for MHG, whereas the treebank resources for MHG are extremely limited. Given the resource availability for MG and MHG along with the linguistic connection between the two languages, employing a cross-lingual constituency parsing approach utilizing delexicalization proves to be an effective solution. As Figure 1 shows, the delexicalized model is trained on the delexicalized inputs of MG. In the inference stage, the delexicalized parser is directly applied to MHG POS sequences. The delexicalization method requires that MHG and MG share the same set of POS tags. The final constituency parser for MHG (the right side of Figure 1 comprises three modules: (1) the delexicalized parser, (2) the MHG POS tagger, and (3) the POS mapper from MHG to MG. In the next section, we describe the delexicalized parsing system in more detail.

4.1 Delexicalized Parser

Our delexicalized MHG parser is based on the Berkeley neural parser (Benepar) (Kitaev and Klein, 2018), a span-based parser using self-attention. As illustrated in Figure 1, Benepar has an encoder-decoder architecture which combines a chart decoder with a sentence encoder based on self-attention. The sentence encoder computes contextualized representations for all word positions and combines them to form span representations.

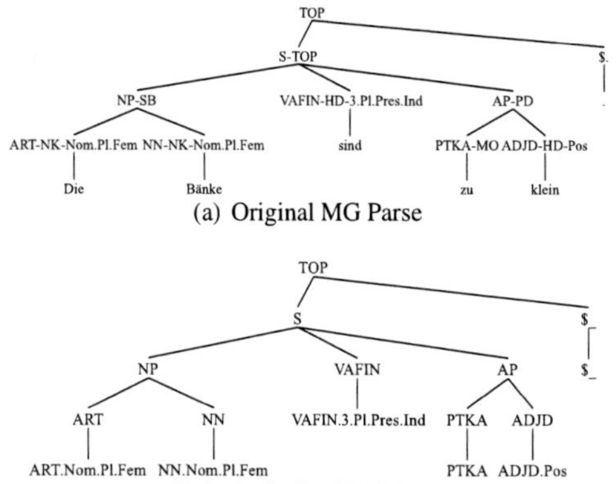

(a) Original MG Parse

(b) Delexicalized MG Parse

Figure 2: An example illustrating the delexicalization process of a MG tree.

From the span representations, the parser computes label scores, which are subsequently used to incrementally construct a tree using a chart parsing algorithm (Sakai, 1961).

According to Kaing et al. (2021), Benepar exhibits two key features which are advantageous for cross-lingual transfer. Firstly, it employs a self-attentive encoder that effectively captures global context information and exhibits less sensitivity to word order. Secondly, the parser independently scores each span without considering the label decisions of its children or parent. This means that a failure in label prediction for a certain span does not strongly impact the label prediction for other spans (Gaddy et al., 2018). Consequently, the prediction errors resulting from local syntax variations between two languages have a limited effect on the overall prediction.

While our delexicalized parser adopts the same architecture to Benepar, there exist distinctions in the inputs of the two. Specifically, Benepar is trained on parse trees with words, whereas our delexicalized parser operates on POS sequences as inputs, i.e. tree strings devoid of words. Therefore, the delexicalized version of the MG treebank is required to train the delexicalized parser. For the MHG parsing in the inference, we feed the delexicalized model with the POS sequences of MHG sentences.

4.2 Delexicalization for MG and MHG

Delexicalization for MG We use the Tiger Treebank to train the delexicalized parsing model on MG parse trees. The parse trees in the Tiger Treebank contain additional semantic information, such as edge labels, and special structures, such as coreference indices and trace nodes. We remove all of them during delexicalization.

In the Tiger treebank, the label of each preterminal node contains not only the POS tag, but also morphological features, such as case, number, gender. During delexicalization, we overwrite the word at the leaf node with this extended POS tag, but only keep the POS information in the label of the preterminal node. This means that the input of our delexicalized parser contains information about morphological features. Figure 2 shows an example of the delexicalization for a MG sentence. As shown the edge labels, e.g., "`NK`" are removed and the tokens are replaced by the POS tag combined with morphological features, e.g., "`ART.Nom.Pl.Fem`", where "`ART`" (determiner) is the POS tag, and "`Nom.Pl.Fem`" denotes the morphological information with case being nominative, number being plural, and gender being feminine.

MHG POS Tagger For the delexicalization of MHG sentences, we need a POS tagger for MHG. We use the RNNTagger of Schmid (2019) for this purpose, which annotates MHG sentences with POS tags as well as morphological features and has been trained on the ReM corpus. RNNTagger uses deep bidirectional LSTMs with character-based word representations.

4.3 Tag Set Mapping

The Tiger Treebank uses the STTS tag set, whereas the MHG version of the RNNTagger and the ReM corpus on which it was trained employ the HiTS tag set. Due to this discrepancy, we cannot directly use the POS labels from RNNTagger as input to the delexicalized parser. HiTS, for example, has separate tags for definite (`DDART`) and indefinite articles (`DIART`), whereas STTS uses the tag "`ART`" for both of them. Since the delexicalization method demands that the source and target languages share the same tag set, we have to map the MHG tags to the MG . The small MHG treebank that we use for evaluation purposes uses STTS and requires no mapping.

The mapping process involves two dimensions. Firstly, we map the morphological features of MHG to those of MG. Secondly, we map the POS tags of MHG to those of MG primarily based on a mapping dictionary. Table 2 shows a selected part

	Type	Language	Size	Usage
Tiger	Treebank	MG	50,474 trees	Parser training
DDB	Treebank	MHG	96 trees	Parser evaluation
ReM	POS-tagged corpus	MHG	2,269,738 tokens	POS tagger training

Table 1: Overview of the datasets.

MHG Tag	MG Tag
CARDD	CARD
DDA	PDAT
DDART	ART
DIA	PIAT
DIART	ART
DID	PDAT
NA	NN
VAPS	ADJD.Pos

Table 2: Representative mapping pairs in the mapping dictionary.

of the POS tag mapping dictionary. It should be noted that our mapping is not flawless due to certain challenges. For instance, the composite word in MHG "*enerde (on earth)*" is separated into "*auf*" and "*Erde*" in MG and are tagged as "APPR|NA". In the DDB treebank, such composite words are annotated with two separate tags combined with "|" in the DDB treebank. However, for simplification purposes, our mapping only retains the first part of the tag, leading to a loss of information.

5 Experiments

We begin by training Benepar on the delexicalized Tiger treebank for MG. Then we annotate the sentences of the small DDB treebank for MHG with RNNTagger and map the HiTS tags that it returns to STTS tags. Finally, we parse the POS tag sequences with the trained parser.

5.1 Datasets

In our experiments, we utilize the following three corpora (see also Table 1).

Tiger Treebank The delexicalized parser is trained on the Tiger Treebank (Smith, 2003), which comprises a total number of 50,474 parse trees for MG. We use a version of the Tiger Treebank which has been converted to the Penn Treebank format (Marcus et al., 1993). We delexicalize the Tiger corpus and divide it into a training set and a development set. The first 47,474 parse trees in the Tiger corpus comprise the training set and the last 3,000 parse trees comprise the development set.

DDB The German Diachronic Treebank (DDB) (Hirschmann and Linde, 2023) consists of a limited number of 100 parse trees for MHG. Due to the small data size, we utilize the DDB treebank solely for the cross-lingual evaluation of the delexicalized parser. To prepare the DDB treebank for evaluation, we perform preprocessing steps, including converting it to the format of the Penn Treebank and removing incomplete parse trees and parse trees with mostly Latin words. We also removed numbers and periods which formed the first token of a parse tree and corrected a few more minor problems. At the end, we had 96 sentences for evaluation purposes.

ReM The Reference Corpus for Middle High German (ReM) (Klein et al., 2016) is an extensive collection of texts written in MHG. This corpus encompasses approximately 2.3 million tokens and provides comprehensive linguistic annotations, including POS tags, morphological analysis, lemma features, and more. The ReM corpus has been used by Schmid (2019) to train the MHG version of his RNNTagger which annotates MHG texts with POS tags and morphological features.

5.2 Baselines

We evaluate the performance of our proposed delexicalized MHG parser which is based on the Benepar parser (Kitaev and Klein, 2018), and compare it with the cross-lingual transfer performance of the original Benepar without using the delexicalization method and other parsing approaches that incorporate pretrained language models, which have shown promising results in various NLP tasks.

Vanilla Benepar The vanilla Benepar model is trained directly on the original training set of the Tiger Treebank for MG without delexicalization. After training, the parser is directly used to parse the MHG sentences as token sequences. This allows us to compare the performance of the delexicalized MHG parser with the vanilla Benepar model, highlighting the impact of delexicalization on cross-lingual parsing performance.

	Recall		Precision		FScore		CM	
	MG	MHG	MG	MHG	MG	MHG	MG	MHG
Baselines								
Vanilla Benepar	84.18	34.41	87.57	44.40	85.84	38.77	45.80	0.00
Tetra-gBERT	**86.31**	23.20	**88.19**	29.53	**87.24**	25.98	**51.70**	3.12
Tetra-mBERT	60.68	19.69	65.61	23.25	63.15	21.32	21.35	0.00
Our proposed method								
Dexparser	81.39	**64.72**	84.89	**70.19**	83.10	**67.34**	39.03	**12.50**

Table 3: Main results of the cross-lingual parsing transfer performance of different parsers. **CM** refers to "complete match". gBERT refers to the pretrained German BERT and mBERT refers to the multilingual version BERT. The best value of each column is indicated in **bold**.

Tetra-Tagging with PLMs Tetra-tagging (Kitaev and Klein, 2020) is a technique for reducing constituency parsing to sequence labeling. In this approach, special parsing tags are predicted in parallel using a PLM, and then merged into a parse tree. In our experiment, we use the pretrained German BERT model (Chan et al., 2020) and the multilingual BERT model (Devlin et al., 2019) available on the HuggingFace website (Wolf et al., 2020). We start by finetuning these models on the Tiger Treebank using the Tetra-tagging technique. Subsequently, we evaluate their performance on the MHG parse test set.

5.3 Evaluation

Following Kitaev and Klein (2018), we use the the standard `evalb` measures (Sekine and Collins, 1997; Collins, 1997) for the parser quality evaluation. `evalb` is a software tool that provides metrics to assess the accuracy and similarity of parsed sentences against reference or gold standard parse trees, including precision, recall, F1 score, and complete match.

- **Precision** measures the proportion of predicted constituents in the generated parse tree which are also contained in the reference parse tree. It quantifies the accuracy of the parser in correctly identifying constituents.
- **Recall** measures the proportion of constituents in the reference parse tree which were predicted by the parser in the generated parse tree. It quantifies the parser's ability to generate all the constituents present in the reference parse tree.
- **F1 Score** is the harmonic mean of precision and recall.
- **Complete Match** measures the proportion of predicted parse trees which were exactly identical to the respective reference parse trees.

As is the standard practice, the evaluation disregards POS labels and punctuation.

5.4 Training Setup

For training the delexicalized parser, we adopt the same hyperparameter settings as described in (Kitaev and Klein, 2018). The encoder architecture consists of a character-level bidirectional LSTM neural network. We configure the encoder with a dimension of 1024, utilizing 8 layers, 8 attention heads, and a dimension of 64 for the key, query, and value. The size of the feedforward layer is set to 2048, and the character embedding dimension is 64. The batch size is set to 32, the learning rate is 5e-5, and the maximum sequence length of the encoder is 512. We use the random seed 10 for training. We conduct all our experiments using a server with 8 GPUs with 11GB RAM (NVIDIA GeForce GTX 1080 Ti).

6 Results and Analysis

6.1 Main Results

Table 3 shows the parsing performance of different cross-lingual parsers. Notably, our proposed parser attains the highest scores across all metrics for MHG, demonstrating that the delexicalized parser possesses superior cross-lingual parsing performance on MHG. Our delexicalized parser demonstrates substantial advantages in parsing MHG, achieving an impressive increase of almost 30% points in F1 score. Besides, it achieves comparable results on MG. In terms of the baselines, the Vanilla Benepar and the Tetra-gBERT parser both achieve relatively high recall and precision for MG but have noticeably lower values for MHG. The Tetra-mBERT parser exhibits lower values for both recall and precision for both MG and MHG. It is

	Recall	Precision	FScore	CM
Delexicalized parser using gold tags	**66.18**	**71.17**	**68.59**	**14.58**
- *using predicted tags*	64.72	70.19	67.34	12.50
- *without mapping*	59.16	68.82	63.63	7.29
- *without morphological information*	48.66	65.38	55.8	9.28

Table 4: The MHG parsing results with delexicalized parser in the ablation study.

worth noting that the parsing performance of the delexicalized model on the source language MG is surpassed by the two strong baselines, Vanilla Benepar and Tetra-gBERT. This outcome is expected as the delexicalization process diminishes the semantic information present in the input sequences. However, the trade-off of the performance loss in MG leads to a big leap in the cross-lingual parsing performance for MHG.

Our delexicalized constituency parser exhibits outstanding performance on the MHG test set, attaining an impressive F1-score of 67.3%. This substantial improvement outperforms the best zero-shot cross-lingual baseline by a considerable margin of 28.6%. Although there is a slight decline in the parsing performance for MG, the trade-off proves worthwhile considering the substantial gains achieved in parsing MHG. This emphasizes the effectiveness of the delexicalized approach in facilitating cross-lingual transfer and highlights its potential for parsing ancient and historical languages like MHG.

6.2 Ablation Study

We now examine how the parsing performance changes (i) as we replace predicted POS tags with goldstandard POS tags, (ii) as we use the original HiTS tags instead of mapping them to STTS tags, and (iii) as we remove the morphological features from the parser input. Table 4 presents the results of our ablation study.

Goldstandard POS Tags We observe that the f-score of the delexicalized parser increases by 1.3% points when it processes gold standard POS tag sequences instead of POS tag sequences predicted by RNNTagger. This finding underscores the quality of the POS tags predicted by RNNTagger. We loose very little performance due to POS tagging errors.

Tag Set Mapping Table 4 demonstrates a noticeable decline in parsing performance from 67.34% to 43.43% in terms of F1 score when the delexicalized MHG sequences are directly processed by the cross-lingual parser without mapping them from HiTS to STTS. This finding highlights the indispensability of mapping from MHG to MG for maintaining satisfactory parsing performance. The results underscore the significance of aligning the tag sets between MHG and MG to ensure effective cross-lingual parsing and emphasize the necessity of this mapping process in our approach.

Morphological Information The inclusion of morphological markers provides the neural model with valuable additional information for parsing MHG sentences. In our experiments, we augment the delexicalized MHG sequences with morphological information, such as case, gender, number, and more. The outcomes of the ablation study clearly indicate that removing this morphological information from the delexicalized input sequences obviously impairs parsing performance. Specifically, this exclusion leads to a noticeable decline in the F1 score, amounting to a reduction of 11.5%.

6.3 Case Study

Figure 3 shows two MHG trees generated by our delexicalized parser and the corresponding gold standard trees for comparison. This case study reveals that the delexicalized parser demonstrates relatively accurate predictions of constituents when compared to the reference trees, especially for short MHG sentences. Some prediction errors in constituents stem from the intricacy and the ambiguity of the MHG grammar, as exmplified by the case of "*her*" in Example 2. From a linguistic perspective, determining whether "*her*" functions as an adverb (`ADV`) or a separated verb prefix (`PTKVZ`) poses challenges. However, in longer and more complex sentences, e.g., the sentence in Example 1, the parser typically maintains a high level of accuracy locally while occasionally struggling to accurately determine the overall structure of the entire sentence. Besides, the presence of noise in the ancient texts is another factor that can impact the effectiveness of the cross-lingual parsing for MHG. Overall, the qualitative analysis provides further evidence of the effectiveness of the delexicalized parser for

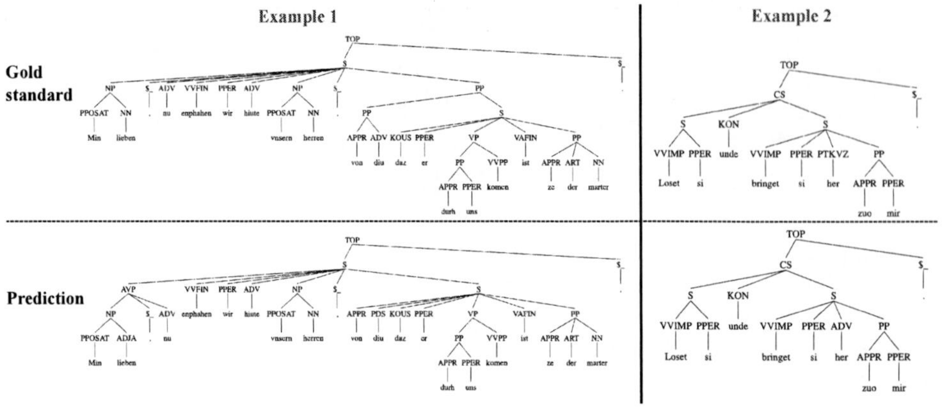

Figure 3: Two examples of the trees generated by our delexicalized parser compared to the reference parses.

MHG, emphasizing its ability to accurately predict constituents, especially in shorter sentences. While challenges may arise in handling longer and more complex sentences, the delexicalized parser showcases promising results, contributing to the advancement of MHG parsing.

7 Conclusion

In conclusion, our study presents an effective cross-lingual constituency parsing approach for ancient languages, specifically focusing on the parsing of Middle High German (MHG) sentences. Through the utilization of delexicalization and and the similarities between MHG and Modern German (MG), we have developed a delexicalized parser based on the rich treebank resources of MG, which demonstrates remarkable performance in parsing MHG sentences. Our experimental results showcase the efficacy of the delexicalized approach, outperforming existing baselines and achieving substantial improvements in parsing accuracy. These findings highlight the practicality and promise of our approach for parsing historical and ancient languages, addressing the challenges posed by limited annotated data and linguistic variations.

Limitations

One limitation of our study is the need for further improvement in the robustness of the delexicalized parsing method, particularly when applied to ancient texts. By addressing this limitation, we can further enhance the applicability of our approach to a wider range of ancient languages and ensure more reliable parsing results. Besides, our proposed method is only applicable to the scenario where a POS tagger for the target language and a related language with a treebank exist.

Acknowledgements

We extend our sincere gratitude to the anonymous reviewers for their invaluable contributions and constructive feedback that have greatly enriched the quality and scope of this paper. This work was supported by China Scholarship Council (CSC).

References

Waleed Ammar, George Mulcaire, Miguel Ballesteros, Chris Dyer, and Noah A. Smith. 2016. Many languages, one parser. *Transactions of the Association for Computational Linguistics*, 4:431–444.

Mikel Artetxe and Holger Schwenk. 2019. Massively multilingual sentence embeddings for zero-shot cross-lingual transfer and beyond. *Transactions of the Association for Computational Linguistics*, 7:597–610.

Yannis Assael, Thea Sommerschield, Brendan Shillingford, Mahyar Bordbar, John Pavlopoulos, Marita Chatzipanagiotou, Ion Androutsopoulos, Jonathan Prag, and Nando de Freitas. 2022. Restoring and attributing ancient texts using deep neural networks. *Nature*, 603(7900):280–283.

Hannah Booth, Anne Breitbarth, Aaron Ecay, and Melissa Farasyn. 2020. A Penn-style treebank of Middle Low German. In *Proceedings of the 12th Language Resources and Evaluation Conference*, pages 766–775, Marseille, France. European Language Resources Association.

Sabine Brants, Stefanie Dipper, Silvia Hansen, Wolfgang Lezius, and George Smith. 2002. The tiger treebank. In *Proceedings of the workshop on treebanks and linguistic theories*, volume 168, pages 24–41.

Branden Chan, Stefan Schweter, and Timo Möller. 2020. German's next language model. In *Proceedings of the 28th International Conference on Computational Linguistics*, pages 6788–6796, Barcelona, Spain (Online). International Committee on Computational Linguistics.

Christian Chiarcos, Benjamin Kosmehl, Christian Fäth, and Maria Sukhareva. 2018. Analyzing Middle High German syntax with RDF and SPARQL. In *Proceedings of the Eleventh International Conference on Language Resources and Evaluation (LREC 2018)*, Miyazaki, Japan. European Language Resources Association (ELRA).

Michael Collins. 1997. Three generative, lexicalised models for statistical parsing. In *35th Annual Meeting of the Association for Computational Linguistics and 8th Conference of the European Chapter of the Association for Computational Linguistics*, pages 16–23, Madrid, Spain. Association for Computational Linguistics.

Alexis Conneau, Kartikay Khandelwal, Naman Goyal, Vishrav Chaudhary, Guillaume Wenzek, Francisco Guzmán, Edouard Grave, Myle Ott, Luke Zettlemoyer, and Veselin Stoyanov. 2020. Unsupervised cross-lingual representation learning at scale. In *Proceedings of the 58th Annual Meeting of the Association for Computational Linguistics*, pages 8440–8451, Online. Association for Computational Linguistics.

James Cross and Liang Huang. 2016. Span-based constituency parsing with a structure-label system and provably optimal dynamic oracles. In *Proceedings of the 2016 Conference on Empirical Methods in Natural Language Processing*, pages 1–11, Austin, Texas. Association for Computational Linguistics.

Ulrike Demske. 2019. Referenzkorpus frühneuhochdeutsch: Baumbank. *UP. Universität Potsdam: Institut für Germanistik (https://hdl. handle. net/11022/0000-0007-EAF7-B)*.

Jacob Devlin, Ming-Wei Chang, Kenton Lee, and Kristina Toutanova. 2019. BERT: Pre-training of deep bidirectional transformers for language understanding. In *Proceedings of the 2019 Conference of the North American Chapter of the Association for Computational Linguistics: Human Language Technologies, Volume 1 (Long and Short Papers)*, pages 4171–4186, Minneapolis, Minnesota. Association for Computational Linguistics.

Stefanie Dipper, Karin Donhauser, Thomas Klein, Sonja Linde, Stefan Müller, and Klaus-Peter Wegera. 2013. Hits: ein tagset für historische sprachstufen des deutschen. *Journal for Language Technology and Computational Linguistics*, 28(1):85–137.

David Gaddy, Mitchell Stern, and Dan Klein. 2018. What's going on in neural constituency parsers? an analysis. In *Proceedings of the 2018 Conference of the North American Chapter of the Association for Computational Linguistics: Human Language Technologies, Volume 1 (Long Papers)*, pages 999–1010, New Orleans, Louisiana. Association for Computational Linguistics.

Ulf Hermjakob. 2001. Parsing and question classification for question answering. In *Proceedings of the ACL 2001 Workshop on Open-Domain Question Answering*.

Hagen Hirschmann and Sonja Linde. 2023. Deutsche diachrone baumbank (version 1.0). Humboldt-Universität zu Berlin.

Sepp Hochreiter and Jürgen Schmidhuber. 1997. Long short-term memory. *Neural computation*, 9(8):1735–1780.

Junjie Hu, Sebastian Ruder, Aditya Siddhant, Graham Neubig, Orhan Firat, and Melvin Johnson. 2020. XTREME: A massively multilingual multitask benchmark for evaluating cross-lingual generalisation. In *Proceedings of the 37th International Conference on Machine Learning*, volume 119 of *Proceedings of Machine Learning Research*, pages 4411–4421. PMLR.

Jing Jiang. 2012. Information extraction from text. *Mining text data*, pages 11–41.

Ming Jiang and Jana Diesner. 2019. A constituency parsing tree based method for relation extraction from abstracts of scholarly publications. In *Proceedings of the Thirteenth Workshop on Graph-Based Methods for Natural Language Processing (TextGraphs-13)*, pages 186–191, Hong Kong. Association for Computational Linguistics.

Howard Jones and Martin H Jones. 2019. *The Oxford Guide to Middle High German*. Oxford University Press.

Karthikeyan K, Zihan Wang, Stephen Mayhew, and Dan Roth. 2019. Cross-lingual ability of multilingual bert: An empirical study. *ArXiv*, abs/1912.07840.

Hour Kaing, Chenchen Ding, Masao Utiyama, Eiichiro Sumita, Katsuhito Sudoh, and Satoshi Nakamura. 2021. Constituency parsing by cross-lingual delexicalization. *IEEE Access*, 9:141571–141578.

Nikita Kitaev, Steven Cao, and Dan Klein. 2019. Multilingual constituency parsing with self-attention and pre-training. In *Proceedings of the 57th Annual Meeting of the Association for Computational Linguistics*, pages 3499–3505, Florence, Italy. Association for Computational Linguistics.

Nikita Kitaev and Dan Klein. 2018. Constituency parsing with a self-attentive encoder. In *Proceedings of the 56th Annual Meeting of the Association for Computational Linguistics (Volume 1: Long Papers)*, pages 2676–2686, Melbourne, Australia. Association for Computational Linguistics.

Nikita Kitaev and Dan Klein. 2020. Tetra-tagging: Word-synchronous parsing with linear-time inference. In *Proceedings of the 58th Annual Meeting of the Association for Computational Linguistics*, pages 6255–6261, Online. Association for Computational Linguistics.

Thomas Klein, Klaus-Peter Wegera, Stefanie Dipper, and Claudia Wich-Reif. 2016. Reference Corpus of Middle High German (1050–1350) (Version 1.0). Rheinische Friedrich-Wilhelms-Universität Bonn, Ruhr-Universität Bochum.

Anne Lauscher, Vinit Ravishankar, Ivan Vulić, and Goran Glavaš. 2020. From zero to hero: On the limitations of zero-shot language transfer with multilingual Transformers. In *Proceedings of the 2020 Conference on Empirical Methods in Natural Language Processing (EMNLP)*, pages 4483–4499, Online. Association for Computational Linguistics.

Jens Lehmann, Robert Isele, Max Jakob, Anja Jentzsch, Dimitris Kontokostas, Pablo N Mendes, Sebastian Hellmann, Mohamed Morsey, Patrick Van Kleef, Sören Auer, et al. 2015. Dbpedia–a large-scale, multilingual knowledge base extracted from wikipedia. *Semantic web*, 6(2):167–195.

Yuncong Li, Cunxiang Yin, and Sheng-hua Zhong. 2020. Sentence constituent-aware aspect-category sentiment analysis with graph attention networks. In *Natural Language Processing and Chinese Computing: 9th CCF International Conference, NLPCC 2020, Zhengzhou, China, October 14–18, 2020, Proceedings, Part I 9*, pages 815–827. Springer.

Yongkang Liu, Shi Feng, Daling Wang, and Yifei Zhang. 2022. MulZDG: Multilingual code-switching framework for zero-shot dialogue generation. In *Proceedings of the 29th International Conference on Computational Linguistics*, pages 648–659, Gyeongju, Republic of Korea. International Committee on Computational Linguistics.

Mitchell P. Marcus, Beatrice Santorini, and Mary Ann Marcinkiewicz. 1993. Building a large annotated corpus of English: The Penn Treebank. *Computational Linguistics*, 19(2):313–330.

Ryan McDonald, Slav Petrov, and Keith Hall. 2011. Multi-source transfer of delexicalized dependency parsers. In *Proceedings of the 2011 Conference on Empirical Methods in Natural Language Processing*, pages 62–72, Edinburgh, Scotland, UK. Association for Computational Linguistics.

Ercong Nie, Sheng Liang, Helmut Schmid, and Hinrich Schütze. 2023. Cross-lingual retrieval augmented prompt for low-resource languages. In *Findings of the Association for Computational Linguistics: ACL 2022*, Toronto, Canada. Association for Computational Linguistics.

Andrea Parravicini and Telmo Pievani. 2018. Continuity and discontinuity in human language evolution: putting an old-fashioned debate in its historical perspective. *Topoi*, 37(2):279–287.

Sebastian Ruder. 2019. *Neural Transfer Learning for Natural Language Processing*. Ph.D. thesis, National University of Ireland, Galway.

Itiroo Sakai. 1961. Syntax in universal translation. In *Proceedings of the International Conference on Machine Translation and Applied Language Analysis*, National Physical Laboratory, Teddington, UK.

Joseph Salmons. 2018. *A history of German: What the past reveals about today's language*. Oxford University Press.

Christopher Sapp, Daniel Dakota, and Elliott Evans. 2023. Parsing early New High German: Benefits and limitations of cross-dialectal training. In *Proceedings of the 21st International Workshop on Treebanks and Linguistic Theories (TLT, GURT/SyntaxFest 2023)*, pages 54–66, Washington, D.C. Association for Computational Linguistics.

Anne Schiller, Simone Teufel, and Christine Thielen. 1995. Guidelines f ur das tagging deutscher textcorpora mit stts. *Universität Stuttgart, Universität Tübingen, Germany*.

Helmut Schmid. 2019. Deep learning-based morphological taggers and lemmatizers for annotating historical texts. In *Proceedings of the 3rd international conference on digital access to textual cultural heritage*, pages 133–137.

Satoshi Sekine and Michael Collins. 1997. Evalb bracket scoring program. *URL: http://www. cs. nyu. edu/cs/projects/proteus/evalb*.

Sunayana Sitaram, Monojit Choudhury, Barun Patra, Vishrav Chaudhary, Kabir Ahuja, and Kalika Bali. 2023. Everything you need to know about multilingual LLMs: Towards fair, performant and reliable models for languages of the world. In *Proceedings of the 61st Annual Meeting of the Association for Computational Linguistics (Volume 6: Tutorial Abstracts)*, pages 21–26, Toronto, Canada. Association for Computational Linguistics.

George Smith. 2003. A brief introduction to the tiger treebank, version 1. Technical report, Universität Potsdam.

Mitchell Stern, Jacob Andreas, and Dan Klein. 2017. A minimal span-based neural constituency parser. In *Proceedings of the 55th Annual Meeting of the Association for Computational Linguistics (Volume 1: Long Papers)*, pages 818–827, Vancouver, Canada. Association for Computational Linguistics.

Thomas Wolf, Lysandre Debut, Victor Sanh, Julien Chaumond, Clement Delangue, Anthony Moi, Pierric Cistac, Tim Rault, Remi Louf, Morgan Funtowicz, Joe Davison, Sam Shleifer, Patrick von Platen, Clara Ma, Yacine Jernite, Julien Plu, Canwen Xu, Teven Le Scao, Sylvain Gugger, Mariama Drame,

Quentin Lhoest, and Alexander Rush. 2020. Transformers: State-of-the-art natural language processing. In *Proceedings of the 2020 Conference on Empirical Methods in Natural Language Processing: System Demonstrations*, pages 38–45, Online. Association for Computational Linguistics.

Daniel Zeman and Philip Resnik. 2008. Cross-language parser adaptation between related languages. In *Proceedings of the IJCNLP-08 Workshop on NLP for Less Privileged Languages*.

Can Large Language Model Comprehend Ancient Chinese? A Preliminary Test on ACLUE

Yixuan Zhang **Haonan Li**
Mohamed bin Zayed University of Artificial Intelligence, UAE
haonan.li@mbzuai.ac.ae

Abstract

Large language models (LLMs) have showcased remarkable capabilities in understanding and generating language. However, their ability in comprehending ancient languages, particularly ancient Chinese, remains largely unexplored. To bridge this gap, we present ACLUE, an evaluation benchmark designed to assess the capability of language models in comprehending ancient Chinese. ACLUE consists of 15 tasks cover a range of skills, spanning phonetic, lexical, syntactic, semantic, inference and knowledge. Through the evaluation of eight state-of-the-art LLMs, we observed a noticeable disparity in their performance between modern Chinese and ancient Chinese. Among the assessed models, ChatGLM2 demonstrates the most remarkable performance, achieving an average score of 37.4%. We have made our code and data public available.[1]

1 Introduction

The study of ancient languages provides valuable insights into the past civilizations' thoughts, languages, societies, and histories (Zhiming, 1990; Woodard, 2008; Bouchard-Côté et al., 2013). Ancient China, as one of the oldest civilizations, has left a significant impact on contemporary societies including Japan, Korea, and Vietnam. However, existing research in ancient Chinese language processing have primarily focused on specific time periods or genres (Yan et al., 2016; Xie et al., 2019; Liu et al., 2020; Hu et al., 2021; Tian et al., 2021). Typically, the previously proposed models require customized fine-tuning for particular tasks.

Recently, the significant advancements made in large language models (LLMs) underscore their remarkable proficiency across a range of tasks, showcasing their potential in performing various tasks without the need for fine-tuning (Brown et al., 2020; Scao et al., 2022; Touvron et al., 2023; Muennighoff et al., 2022; Zeng et al., 2023). These models encapsulate extensive knowledge and sophisticated reasoning capabilities. Notably, the emergence of ChatGPT (OpenAI, 2023) and Chinese-oriented LLMs such as ChatGLM (Zeng et al., 2023), has accentuated their remarkable ability in comprehending and generating modern language. However, due to the lack of ancient language benchmarks, the abilities of LLMs in handling ancient language remains largely unexplored.

We present the Ancient Chinese Language Understanding Evaluation (ACLUE), an evaluation benchmark consisting of 15 tasks. These tasks are derived from a combination of manually curated questions from publicly available resources, and automatically generated questions from classical Chinese language corpora. The range of questions span from the Xia dynasty (2070 BCE) to the Ming dynasty (1368 CE), covering a broad temporal range. Similar to the well-established LLM benchmarks such as ARC (Clark et al., 2018) and MMLU (Hendrycks et al., 2021), ACLUE adopts multiple-choice question format for all tasks. This ensures simplicity and uniformity in evaluating models, accommodating variations in different training or fine-tuning procedures and prompting methodologies.

In our preliminary experiments, we assessed the performance of 8 advanced LLMs, where the Chinese LLM ChatGLM2 demonstrates the best performance with an average accuracy of 37.4%, slightly surpassing ChatGPT. However, considering the baseline accuracy of 25% from random guessing and the average accuracy of around 50% achieved by the same models on contemporary modern Chinese benchmarks such as AGIEval (Zhong et al., 2023) and CMMLU (Li et al., 2023), we believe there is still ample room for improvement in the proficiency of existing LLMs in understanding ancient Chinese.

[1] `https://github.com/isen-zhang/ACLUE`

Proceedings of the Ancient Language Processing Workshop associated with RANLP-2023, pages 80–87,
held in Varna Bulgaria, Sept 8, 2023.
https://doi.org/10.26615/978-954-452-087-8_009

2 ACLUE Benchmark

ACLUE consists of 15 tasks that encompassing lexical, syntactic, semantic, inference, and general knowledge of ancient Chinese. The details of the tasks are provided in Appendix A, where basic statistics can be found in Table 2, and examples of each task are listed in Table 3. The questions cover a wide range of genres, including poetry, prose, classical novels, couplets, historical records, and biographies, spanning the period from 2070 BCE to 1368 CE. Among the 15 tasks, 8 were automatically generated using existing corpora or datasets, 5 were collected from freely available standard tests, and 2 were directly sourced from other work. Each task includes 100 to 500 questions, exceeding the number required for testing a human participant.

ACLUE serves as an evaluation suite for LLMs ability in understanding ancient Chinese without task-specific fine-tuning. To ensure fair comparison among different models trained with varying approaches, all tasks are formatted into multiple-choice questions with four choices, of which only one is correct. The task details and dataset construction process are elaborated in this section.

2.1 Lexical Tasks

We create three lexical tasks using the ancient Chinese corpus, which includes over 50,000 word sense annotations and 3,000 named entity annotations (Shu et al., 2021).

Polysemy resolution aims to understand the different senses or meanings of words. Two types of questions are created: one asks which character in a given sentence carries a particular meaning, while the other requires identifying the meaning of a character within the sentence.

Homographic character resolution focuses on recognizing homographic characters in ancient Chinese texts. Homographic characters, also known as "通假字" (tōng jiǎ zì) in Chinese, are substitutions of characters in ancient Chinese texts with others that have similar pronunciation or appearance.

Named entity recognition focuses on identifying named entities (e.g., names of people, places, dynasties, etc.) in ancient Chinese texts. Two types of questions are created: one type asks for the specific entity type of a given entity within a contextual sentence, while the other type asks in which context a Chinese word represents an entity.

2.2 Syntactic and Semantic Tasks

Sentence segmentation is a task that involves choosing the correct segmentation of a given sentence. Since ancient Chinese lacks punctuation marks, accurate sentence segmentation becomes crucial for analyzing syntax and semantics of a sentence. We create the task by sampling sentences from the Classical-Modern Chinese Corpus,[2] which provides labeled sentence segmentation. To create false options, we manipulate the original punctuation marks by moving, adding, or deleting them.

Couplet prediction involves predicting the most likely second line of a Chinese couplet based on a given first line. Chinese couplet, also known as "对联" (duì lián), is a traditional form of poetic expression consisting of two lines of verse. The two lines are expected to match in terms of meaning, rhyme, and other poetic elements. We construct this task using a couplet dataset.[3]

Poetry context prediction is a task constructed using the Chinese-poetry corpus.[4] The objective of this task is to select the most likely next or previous sentence given a specific sentence from a poem.

2.3 Inference

Poem quality estimation task is constructed based on dataset proposed by Yi et al. (2018), which consists of 173 Chinese quatrains, with each one being rated for fluency, coherence, and meaningfulness on a scale of 0 to 5 by human expert. We randomly select four poems and create questions asking models to identify the best or worst poem based on a specific criterion. To ensure clear distinctions, we maintain a minimum score differences of 2 between the correct option and the other options. The task aims to evaluate the ability of models to compare the quality of Chinese quatrains.

Reading comprehension is based on the AGIEval dataset (Zhong et al., 2023). It contains a subset of Chinese Gaokao questions. We select questions that contains ancient Chinese text from this subset.

Poetry sentiment analysis involves predicting the sentiment of an entire poem or parts of a poem, determining whether it is positive, neutral, or negative. We utilize a dataset proposed by Shao et al. (2021), which contains 5,000 poems. Each poem

[2] https://github.com/NiuTrans/Classical-Modern

[3] https://github.com/wb14123/couplet-dataset

[4] https://github.com/chinese-poetry

以下是关于 古代文学知识 的单项选择题，请直接给出正确答案的选项。
Here are some multiple-choice questions about Ancient Chinese literature, please provide the correct answer choice directly.

题目：下列诗句中，属于杜牧咏史诗的是：
Question: Among the following lines of poetry, the one that belongs to Du Mu's historical poem is:
A. 旧时王谢堂前燕，飞入寻常百姓家
In former times, the swallows in front of the halls of Wang and Xie flew into the homes of ordinary people
B. 长空澹澹孤岛没，万古销沉向此中
The vast sky engulfed the desolate island, and for eternity it sank into this place.
C. 千寻铁锁沉江底，一片降幡出石头
Thousands of chains sank to the bottom of the river, and a stone emerged with a descending flag
D. 三百年间同晓梦，钟山何处有龙盘
For three hundred years, the same dream awakened at dawn, where on Zhongshan Mountain can a dragon coil
答案是：(Answer:)

Figure 1: An examples from ACLUE. English translations are provided for better readability.

and its individual sentences are labeled with fine-grained sentiment categories, including negative, implicit negative, neutral, implicit positive, and positive sentiments. We merge implicit negative and implicit positive labels with their respective categories to address ambiguity.
Poetry appreciation is manually curated from openly accessible online resources.

2.4 Knowledge-intensive Tasks

Ancient Chinese knowledge tasks cover various subjects, including **ancient Chinese medical**, **ancient Chinese literature**, **traditional Chinese culture**, and **ancient Chinese phonetics**. To create these tasks, we collected relevant questions from various online open resources. Additionally, we extracted a subset of questions from the CMMLU dataset (Li et al., 2023), which consist of questions at the high-school level in current Chinese education. This selection allows us to form the tasks of **basic ancient Chinese**.

3 Experiment

To provide an overview of the language ability of existing open-sourced LLMs on ancient Chinese, we assess 8 models including 4 multilingual models: ChatGPT (OpenAI, 2023), LLaMA (Touvron et al., 2023), Falcon (Almazrouei et al., 2023), BLOOMZ (Muennighoff et al., 2022), and 4 Chinese models: ChatGLM (Du et al., 2022), Baichuan,[5] ChatGLM2 (Zeng et al., 2023), and MOSS (OpenLMLab, 2023). Details about these models are introduced in Appendix C.

For models optimized to function as chatbots, such as ChatGPT and ChatGLM, we generate output and use regular expressions to extract the answer key. For other models, we directly obtain the probability of the next tokens after the prompt and selected the one with the highest probability among the answer keys (i.e., 'A','B','C','D'). We employ both zero-shot (do not provide examples) and in-context five-shot (provide few examples) evaluation. An example of evaluation instance is shown in Figure 1.

3.1 Results

Table 1 shows the zero-shot performance of all models. The five-shot results are similar to the zero-shot results, suggesting that models can comprehend the task without additional demonstrations. Overall, the Chinese model ChatGLM2 demonstrates the best performance, with an average accuracy of 37.4%. Moreover, its performance on almost all tasks is above the random guessing (25%). The multilingual model ChatGPT achieves a slightly lower accuracy of 36.9%, compared to ChatGLM2, yet it maintains relatively consistent performance in terms of standard deviation.

Regarding specific tasks, we have several findings: (1) BLOOMZ exhibits exceptional performance in *couplet prediction* (T5), achieving an accuracy of 60.2%. This accuracy is nearly double that of most other models, possibly due to BLOOMZ's training set, xP3, having overlaps with our data source. Similar, ChatGLM2 may have been exposed to the original texts used for *sentence segmentation* (T4) and *poetry appreciation* (T9), which explains its proficient performance in these tasks. (2) All models face challenges in the *homographic character resolution* (T2), with performance close to random guessing. This issue likely arises because the auto-regressive training objective does not emphasize understanding of homographic concepts. (3) *Reading comprehension* (T8) poses a considerable challenge for all models due to the extreme long length of the question (nearly 1,000 tokens on average). Specifically, BLOOMZ, LLaMA, and Baichuan are significantly affected, exhibiting lower performance on this task compared to their average across other tasks. This observation suggests that these models may lack adequate support for processing very long input.

[5]https://github.com/baichuan-inc/baichuan-7B

Model	Lexical			Syntactic	Semantic		Inference				Knowledge					Overall
	T1	T2	T3	T4	T5	T6	T7	T8	T9	T10	T11	T12	T13	T14	T15	
ChatGLM2	**45.4**	24.4	34.8	**46.4**	39.8	24.6	28.3	29.7	**42.7**	**52.6**	28.9	**50.7**	34.6	43.8	**35.0**	**37.4**$\pm$8.9
ChatGPT	41.8	20.6	**41.2**	43.0	45.4	27.4	**39.7**	**39.6**	38.8	47.8	29.3	43.4	34.6	33.8	27.0	36.9$\pm$7.6
BLOOMZ	45.2	22.4	35.6	32.2	**60.2**	27.2	31.5	17.8	26.2	45.2	29.7	44.1	**39.3**	**44.4**	29.0	35.3$\pm$10.7
ChatGLM	39.6	19.4	39.4	36.6	37.2	23.4	30.8	32.7	30.1	43.8	29.3	36.8	30.8	40.6	27.0	33.2$\pm$6.6
Falcon	40.4	**28.8**	21.2	32.6	37.2	**31.4**	36.9	22.8	31.1	43.8	**30.5**	30.1	30.3	36.9	26.0	32.0$\pm$6.0
Baichuan	31.6	26.4	22.0	33.0	37.2	27.8	30.3	16.8	25.2	38.2	27.3	36.0	37.0	41.9	31.0	30.8$\pm$6.5
LLaMA	36.4	22.2	26.4	33.0	29.6	29.6	31.5	18.8	24.3	41.8	24.5	23.5	29.4	29.4	31.0	28.8$\pm$5.6
MOSS	30.6	27.6	25.8	24.0	30.0	25.0	29.8	27.7	21.4	30.8	26.5	22.1	24.6	22.5	26.0	26.3$\pm$3.0

Table 1: Zero-shot average accuracy of all models. The overall results are averaged (with standard deviation) over all tasks. T1: Polysemy resolution, T2: Homographic character resolution, T3: Named entity recognition, T4: Sentence segmentation, T5: Couplet prediction, T6: Poetry context prediction, T7: Poetry quality estimation, T8: Reading comprehension, T9: Poetry appreciation, T10: Poetry sentiment analysis, T11: Basic ancient Chinese, T12: Traditional Chinese culture, T13: Ancient Chinese medical, T14: Ancient Chinese literature, T15: Ancient Chinese phonetics.

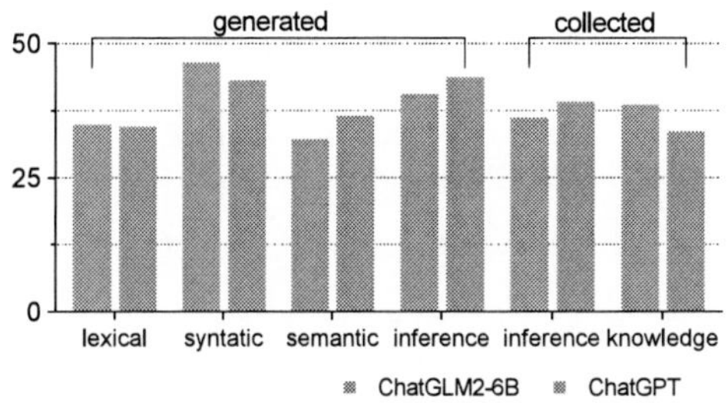

Figure 2: The performance of ChatGPT and ChatGLM2 on ACLUE of different categories.

Based on data origin, we divide the tasks into two categories: auto-generated and manually collected. In Figure 2, we compare the performance of ChatGPT and ChatGLM2, the best multilingual and Chinese models, respectively. We find that while ChatGLM2 exhibits superior overall performance on ACLUE, its dominance only observed in the auto-generated syntactic tasks and collected knowledge categories. More comparison results are provided in Appendix B.

In terms of data quality and reliability, auto-generated questions within ACLUE were slightly less intricate than collected questions, but the difference was not significant. This suggests that the auto-generated questions hold reasonable potential for effectively evaluating models' grasp of ancient Chinese language.

4 Related Work

A lot of research has been conducted on various aspects of ancient Chinese language processing, encompassing topics such as ancient Chinese to modern Chinese translation (Liu et al., 2020), Chinese couplets generation (Yan et al., 2016; Yuan et al., 2019; Qu et al., 2022), Classic Chinese poem generation (Yi et al., 2017; Yang et al., 2018; Guo et al., 2019; Xie et al., 2019; Zhao et al., 2022; Ma et al., 2023), and ancient Chinese sentence segmentation (Han et al., 2018; Hu et al., 2021), as well as general language model pre-training (Tian et al., 2021). However, many of these studies focus on specific types or literary formats that were popular during specific time periods.

Recently, large language models have demonstrated remarkable language understanding and generation capabilities (Brown et al., 2020; Scao et al., 2022; Almazrouei et al., 2023). Researchers have began to evaluate these LLMs based on their performance across a wide range of tasks (Touvron et al., 2023; Muennighoff et al., 2022; OpenAI, 2023). However, the absence of a comprehensive evaluation benchmark poses a challenge in assessing the performance of LLMs in ancient language understanding. Existing ancient Chinese evaluation datasets either have a narrow focus on specific tasks, limiting the scope of evaluation, or require model fine-tuning prior to evaluation. In contrast, ACLUE provides a natural support for evaluation under zero-shot and in-context learning settings, making it more compatible with LLMs.

5 Conclusion

We propose ACLUE, the first evaluation benchmark for ancient Chinese language understanding. Our preliminary evaluation of 8 large language models reveals that, despite their exceptional performance in modern language understanding, they struggle with even basic tasks in ancient Chinese. Through analysis, we illustrate that the auto-generated questions possess similar difficulty levels to those found in actual school tests.

References

Ebtesam Almazrouei, Hamza Alobeidli, Abdulaziz Alshamsi, Alessandro Cappelli, Ruxandra Cojocaru, Merouane Debbah, Etienne Goffinet, Daniel Heslow, Julien Launay, Quentin Malartic, Badreddine Noune, Baptiste Pannier, and Guilherme Penedo. 2023. Falcon-40B: an open large language model with state-of-the-art performance.

Alexandre Bouchard-Côté, David Hall, Thomas L. Griffiths, and Dan Klein. 2013. Automated reconstruction of ancient languages using probabilistic models of sound change. *Proc. Natl. Acad. Sci. USA*, 110(11):4224–4229.

Tom B. Brown, Benjamin Mann, Nick Ryder, et al. 2020. Language models are few-shot learners. In *Advances in Neural Information Processing Systems 33: Annual Conference on Neural Information Processing Systems 2020, NeurIPS 2020, December 6-12, 2020, virtual*.

Peter Clark, Isaac Cowhey, Oren Etzioni, Tushar Khot, Ashish Sabharwal, Carissa Schoenick, and Oyvind Tafjord. 2018. Think you have solved question answering? try arc, the AI2 reasoning challenge. *CoRR*, abs/1803.05457.

Zhengxiao Du, Yujie Qian, Xiao Liu, Ming Ding, Jiezhong Qiu, Zhilin Yang, and Jie Tang. 2022. Glm: General language model pretraining with autoregressive blank infilling. In *Proceedings of the 60th Annual Meeting of the Association for Computational Linguistics (Volume 1: Long Papers)*, pages 320–335.

Zhipeng Guo, Xiaoyuan Yi, Maosong Sun, Wenhao Li, Cheng Yang, Jiannan Liang, Huimin Chen, Yuhui Zhang, and Ruoyu Li. 2019. Jiuge: A human-machine collaborative chinese classical poetry generation system. In *Proceedings of the 57th Conference of the Association for Computational Linguistics, ACL 2019, Florence, Italy, July 28 - August 2, 2019, Volume 3: System Demonstrations*, pages 25–30. Association for Computational Linguistics.

Xu Han, Hongsu Wang, Sanqian Zhang, Qunchao Fu, and Jun S. Liu. 2018. Sentence segmentation for classical chinese based on LSTM with radical embedding. *CoRR*, abs/1810.03479.

Dan Hendrycks, Collin Burns, Steven Basart, Andy Zou, Mantas Mazeika, Dawn Song, and Jacob Steinhardt. 2021. Measuring massive multitask language understanding. In *9th International Conference on Learning Representations, ICLR 2021, Virtual Event, Austria, May 3-7, 2021*. OpenReview.net.

Renfen Hu, Shen Li, and Yuchen Zhu. 2021. Knowledge representation and sentence segmentation of ancient chinese based on deep language models. *Journal of Chinese Information Processing*, 35(4):8–15.

Haonan Li, Yixuan Zhang, Fajri Koto, Yifei Yang, Hai Zhao, Yeyun Gong, Nan Duan, and Timothy Baldwin. 2023. Cmmlu: Measuring massive multitask language understanding in chinese.

Dayiheng Liu, Kexin Yang, Qian Qu, and Jiancheng Lv. 2020. Ancient-modern chinese translation with a new large training dataset. *ACM Trans. Asian Low Resour. Lang. Inf. Process.*, 19(1):6:1–6:13.

Jingkun Ma, Runzhe Zhan, and Derek F. Wong. 2023. Yu sheng: Human-in-loop classical chinese poetry generation system. In *Proceedings of the 17th Conference of the European Chapter of the Association for Computational Linguistics. EACL 2023 - System Demonstrations, Dubrovnik, Croatia, May 2-4, 2023*, pages 57–66. Association for Computational Linguistics.

Niklas Muennighoff, Thomas Wang, Lintang Sutawika, Adam Roberts, Stella Biderman, Teven Le Scao, M. Saiful Bari, Sheng Shen, Zheng Xin Yong, Hailey Schoelkopf, Xiangru Tang, Dragomir Radev, Alham Fikri Aji, Khalid Almubarak, Samuel Albanie, Zaid Alyafeai, Albert Webson, Edward Raff, and Colin Raffel. 2022. Crosslingual generalization through multitask finetuning. *CoRR*, abs/2211.01786.

OpenAI. 2023. Gpt-4 technical report.

OpenLMLab. 2023. Moss.

Guilherme Penedo, Quentin Malartic, Daniel Hesslow, Ruxandra Cojocaru, Alessandro Cappelli, Hamza Alobeidli, Baptiste Pannier, Ebtesam Almazrouei, and Julien Launay. 2023. The RefinedWeb dataset for Falcon LLM: outperforming curated corpora with web data, and web data only. *arXiv preprint arXiv:2306.01116*.

Qian Qu, Jiancheng Lv, Dayiheng Liu, and Kexin Yang. 2022. Coupgan: Chinese couplet generation via encoder-decoder model and adversarial training under global control. *Soft Comput.*, 26(15):7423–7433.

Teven Le Scao, Angela Fan, Christopher Akiki, Ellie Pavlick, Suzana Ilic, et al. 2022. BLOOM: A 176b-parameter open-access multilingual language model. *CoRR*, abs/2211.05100.

Yizhan Shao, Tong Shao, Minghao Wang, Peng Wang, and Jie Gao. 2021. A sentiment and style controllable approach for chinese poetry generation. In *CIKM '21: The 30th ACM International Conference on Information and Knowledge Management, Virtual Event, Queensland, Australia, November 1 - 5, 2021*, pages 4784–4788. ACM.

Lei Shu, Yiluan Guo, Huiping Wang, Xuetao Zhang, and Renfen Hu. 2021. 古汉语词义标注语料库的构建及应用研究(the construction and application of Ancient Chinese corpus with word sense annotation). In *Proceedings of the 20th Chinese National Conference on Computational Linguistics*, pages 549–563, Huhhot, China. Chinese Information Processing Society of China.

Huishuang Tian, Kexin Yang, Dayiheng Liu, and Jiancheng Lv. 2021. Anchibert: A pre-trained model for ancient chinese language understanding and generation. In *International Joint Conference on Neural Networks, IJCNN 2021, Shenzhen, China, July 18-22, 2021*, pages 1–8. IEEE.

Hugo Touvron, Thibaut Lavril, Gautier Izacard, Xavier Martinet, Marie-Anne Lachaux, Timothée Lacroix, Baptiste Rozière, Naman Goyal, Eric Hambro, Faisal Azhar, Aurelien Rodriguez, Armand Joulin, Edouard Grave, and Guillaume Lample. 2023. Llama: Open and efficient foundation language models. *arXiv preprint arXiv:2302.13971*.

Roger D Woodard. 2008. *The ancient languages of Europe*. Cambridge University Press.

Zhuohan Xie, Jey Han Lau, and Trevor Cohn. 2019. From shakespeare to li-bai: Adapting a sonnet model to chinese poetry. In *Proceedings of the The 17th Annual Workshop of the Australasian Language Technology Association, ALTA 2019, Sydney, Australia, December 4-6, 2019*, pages 10–18. Australasian Language Technology Association.

Rui Yan, Cheng-Te Li, Xiaohua Hu, and Ming Zhang. 2016. Chinese couplet generation with neural network structures. In *Proceedings of the 54th Annual Meeting of the Association for Computational Linguistics, ACL 2016, August 7-12, 2016, Berlin, Germany, Volume 1: Long Papers*. The Association for Computer Linguistics.

Cheng Yang, Maosong Sun, Xiaoyuan Yi, and Wenhao Li. 2018. Stylistic chinese poetry generation via unsupervised style disentanglement. In *Proceedings of the 2018 Conference on Empirical Methods in Natural Language Processing, Brussels, Belgium, October 31 - November 4, 2018*, pages 3960–3969. Association for Computational Linguistics.

Xiaoyuan Yi, Ruoyu Li, and Maosong Sun. 2017. Generating chinese classical poems with RNN encoder-decoder. In *Chinese Computational Linguistics and Natural Language Processing Based on Naturally Annotated Big Data - 16th China National Conference, CCL 2017, - and - 5th International Symposium, NLP-NABD 2017, Nanjing, China, October 13-15, 2017, Proceedings*, volume 10565 of *Lecture Notes in Computer Science*, pages 211–223. Springer.

Xiaoyuan Yi, Maosong Sun, Ruoyu Li, and Wenhao Li. 2018. Automatic poetry generation with mutual reinforcement learning. In *Proceedings of the 2018 Conference on Empirical Methods in Natural Language Processing*, pages 3143–3153, Brussels, Belgium.

Shengqiong Yuan, Luo Zhong, Lin Li, and Rui Zhang. 2019. Automatic generation of chinese couplets with attention based encoder-decoder model. In *2nd IEEE Conference on Multimedia Information Processing and Retrieval, MIPR 2019, San Jose, CA, USA, March 28-30, 2019*, pages 65–70. IEEE.

Aohan Zeng, Xiao Liu, Zhengxiao Du, Zihan Wang, Hanyu Lai, Ming Ding, Zhuoyi Yang, Yifan Xu, Wendi Zheng, Xiao Xia, Weng Lam Tam, Zixuan Ma, Yufei Xue, Jidong Zhai, Wenguang Chen, Zhiyuan Liu, Peng Zhang, Yuxiao Dong, and Jie Tang. 2023. GLM-130b: An open bilingual pre-trained model. In *The Eleventh International Conference on Learning Representations*.

Jiaqi Zhao, Ting Bai, Yuting Wei, and Bin Wu. 2022. Poetrybert: Pre-training with sememe knowledge for classical chinese poetry. In *Data Mining and Big Data - 7th International Conference, DMBD 2022, Beijing, China, November 21-24, 2022, Proceedings, Part II*, volume 1745 of *Communications in Computer and Information Science*, pages 369–384. Springer.

Bao Zhiming. 1990. Language and world view in ancient china. *Philosophy East and West*, 40(2):195–219.

Wanjun Zhong, Ruixiang Cui, Yiduo Guo, Yaobo Liang, Shuai Lu, Yanlin Wang, Amin Saied, Weizhu Chen, and Nan Duan. 2023. Agieval: A human-centric benchmark for evaluating foundation models. *CoRR*, abs/2304.06364.

A Data details

The Table 2 listed the Chinese, category, and origin of the tasks in ACLUE, and the Table 3 provides examples for each task.

B Further analysis

The performance comparison of all LLMs on different data origins is illustrated in Figure 3. Evaluating the LLMs' performance on auto-generated questions versus manually collected questions in ACLUE, we found that while the generated questions were less intricate than the collected ones, the difference was not significant. This indicates a comparable level of difficulty between the two types of questions. Among all the models, only ChatGLM2 demonstrated better performance on collected questions compared to auto-generated questions, which may indicate exposure to the original question texts used in ACLUE.

C Models being Evaluated

BLOOMZ is derived from BLOOM through fine-tuning on a crosslingual task mixture (xP3), which is an instruction-following dataset. BLOOMZ exhibits competitive performance with models that have a larger number of parameters across various non-generation tasks.

Task	Total Q.	Avg. len	Task (zh)	Category	Origin
Named entity recognition	500	138	古汉语命名体识别	lexical	generated
Polysemy resolution	500	116	古文单字多义	lexical	generated
Homographic character resolution	500	137	通假字	lexical	generated
Sentence segmentation	500	210	古文断句	syntatic	generated
Couplet prediction	500	62	对联预测	semantic	generated
Poetry context prediction	500	77	古诗词上下句预测	semantic	generated
Poetry sentiment analysis	500	60	诗词情感分类	inference	generated
Poem quality estimation	406	118	古诗词质量评估	inference	generated
Ancient Chinese medical	211	38	医古文	knowledge	collected
Ancient Chinese literature	160	44	古代文学知识	knowledge	collected
Traditional Chinese culture	136	59	国学常识	knowledge	collected
Poetry appreciation	103	258	古诗词曲鉴赏	inference	collected
Basic ancient Chinese	249	52	基础古汉语知识	knowledge	collected
Reading comprehension	101	982	古文阅读理解	inference	collected
Ancient Chinese phonetics	101	50	古音学	knowledge	collected

Table 2: ACLUE task overview. We list the total number of questions (Total Q.), average question length counted in Chinese characters (Avg. len), task names in Chinese, task type, and data origin type.

Baichuan-7b is an open-source large-scale pre-trained model developed by Baichuan Intelligence. Built on the Transformer architecture, it adopts the same model design as LLaMA. This 7-billion-parameter model was trained on approximately 1.2 trillion tokens using proprietary Chinese-English bilingual corpora, with optimization focused on Chinese.

ChatGLM-6B is bidirectional dense model pre-trained using the General Language Model (GLM) algorithm developed by Tsinghua University. It supports bilingual (Chinese and English) language processing. ChatGLM is a version of GLM that has been supplemented with supervised fine-tuning, feedback bootstrap, and reinforcement learning with human feedback, specifically optimized for Chinese question answering (QA) and dialogue tasks.

ChatGLM2-6B is the second generation of ChatGLM. It uses the hybrid objective function of GLM, and has undergone pre-training with 1.4T bilingual tokens and human preference alignment training. It offers enhanced performance and an expanded context length of 32K. With efficient inference using Multi-Query Attention technology, it achieves efficient inference with higher speed and lower memory usage.

ChatGPT is a GPT model developed by OpenAI and fine-tuned using reinforcement learning from human feedback (RLHF). As a commercial product, specific details about its model size, training data, and training process are not disclosed.

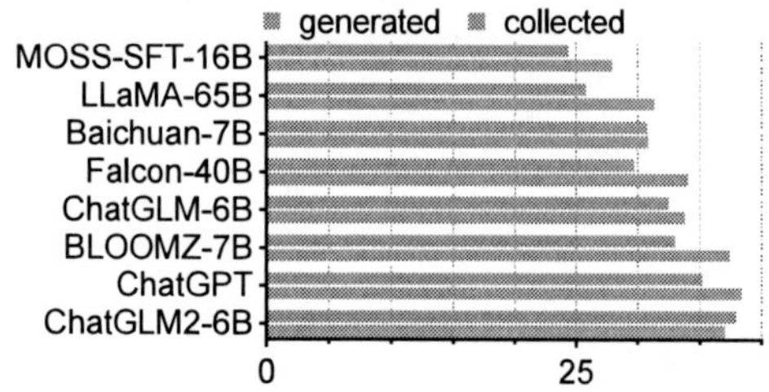

Figure 3: The performance comparison of LLMs on ACLUE across different data origins.

LLaMA-65B is an auto-regressive language model proposed by Meta. It incorporates several structural improvements over the vanilla transformer and is trained on a mixture of publicly available data sources. LLaMA has demonstrated comparable or even superior performance to models that are ten times its size.

Falcon-40B is a decoder-only model created by TII and trained on 1,000B tokens of RefinedWeb (Penedo et al., 2023) data. Due to the high quality of its training data, Falcon-40B performs competitively with LLaMA-65B on various benchmarks.

MOSS is an open-source Chinese language model proposed by Fudan University. It matches ChatGPT in terms of training scale and alignment techniques. MOSS-SFT is initialized with CodeGen and further pre-trained on 100B Chinese tokens and 20B English tokens. The SFT (supervised fine-tuned) version of MOSS-SFT enables the model to follow instructions in multi-turn dialogues.

<table>
<tr><th>ID</th><th>Task</th><th>Example</th></tr>
<tr><td>T1</td><td>单字多义
Polysemy resolution</td><td>下列选项中对“此神农之所以[长]，而尧舜之所以章也。”这句话中的“长”字理解正确的是( )
A. 首领　B.排行第一, 长子　C.长处, 专长　D. 长大，成年</td></tr>
<tr><td>T2</td><td>通假字
Homographic character resolution</td><td>列选项中[]内的“红”字是通假字的是( )
A. 吾已食禄，又夺园夫女[红]利。　B. 晓看[红]湿处，花重锦官城
C. [红] 芳满院参差折，绿醑盈杯次第衔。　D. 竹缘浦以被绿，石照涧而映[红] 。</td></tr>
<tr><td>T3</td><td>命名体识别
Named entity recognition</td><td>下列选项中[]内的“阳”字代表了地名的是( )
A. 夫人授兆丹书真文、月中玉。　B. 令飞升上造洞[阳]之宫。
C. 今朝日[阳]里，梳落数茎丝。　D. 晓发碧水[阳]，暝宿金山寺。</td></tr>
<tr><td>T4</td><td>古文断句
Sentence segmentation</td><td>以下选项断句正确的是( )
A. 史记/曰/秦使武安君白起攻赵/赵发兵拒秦/秦大破赵於长平/
B. 史记/曰秦/使武安君白起攻赵/赵发兵拒秦/秦大破赵於长平
C. 史记/曰/秦使武安君白起攻赵/赵发兵拒秦秦大/破赵於长/平
D. 史/记曰秦使武安君白起攻赵/赵发兵拒秦秦大/破赵於长平</td></tr>
<tr><td>T5</td><td>对联
Couplet prediction</td><td>“兔去龙来，交替人间春好景”的下联最可能是( )
A. 莺歌燕舞，和谐社会岁祥光。　B. 香遗书案，传家苦读育春风。
C. 赛龙夺锦，万人江岸闹端阳。　D. 情牵天下，凭谁设榻效陈蕃。</td></tr>
<tr><td>T6</td><td>古诗词上下句预测
Poetry context prediction</td><td>“何秫候明，便可一横江。”的上一句是( )
A. 江藉草作寒食，雨梨花思故。　B. 孰知文有忌，情至自生哀。
C. 樽前唱醉翁曲，歌花舞催。　D. 千村落呼客，山南北花吹香。</td></tr>
<tr><td>T7</td><td>古诗词质量评估
Poem quality estimation</td><td>下列古诗词前后文连贯性最差的是( )
A. 阴雨难侵牖|春虫足哺儿|年年秋报喜|牛女有佳期
B.富贵良非愿|林泉毕此生|酒因随量饮|诗或偶然成
C.久不闻山歌|南风五月多|牧童呼伴侣|吹笛下西坡
D.今日骐阁|当年鹦鹉洲|寄书愁不达|书达得无愁</td></tr>
<tr><td>T8</td><td>古文阅读理解
Reading comprehension</td><td>下列对原文有关内容的理解和分析，表述不正确的一项是( )
谢贞，字元正，陈郡阳夏人，晋太傅安九世孙也。父蔺，正员外郎，... ... 察因启曰：“贞有一子年六岁。”即有敕长给衣粮。（节选自《陈书·列传第二十六》，有删改）。【注】惠连：谢惠连，南朝宋文学家。
A. 谢贞天性聪慧，小时候读过不少典籍，有的读过就能背诵，有的粗通大意；他八岁时写的诗就深得长辈称赞。
B. 谢贞受府长史周确委托，为他撰写辞让都官尚书的表文。陈后主读过之后，怀疑该表文不是周确亲笔所作。
C. 谢贞非常孝顺，小时候祖母因病难以进食，他便也不进食；父亲去世他悲痛欲绝，之后，奉养母亲未曾间断。
D. 母亲去世后，谢贞一心守丧，极度悲痛，骨瘦如柴，令人叹息。他忧病而死后，后主下令长期供他儿子吃穿。</td></tr>
<tr><td>T9</td><td>古诗词曲鉴赏
Poetry appreciation</td><td>下列对这首诗的赏析，不正确的一项是( )
《幽居初夏》陆游。湖山胜处放翁家，槐柳阴中野径斜。水满有时观下鹭，草深无处不鸣蛙。箨龙已过头番笋，木笔犹开第一花。叹息老来交旧尽，睡来谁共午瓯茶。
A. 首句“湖山”二字总冒全篇，勾勒环境，笔力开张，巧妙地从山光水色中引出“幽居”。
B. 首句概言“湖山胜处”，颔联写湖，是近处宽处静景；颈联写庭院周围，是远处细处动态。
C. 诗中写放翁心中郁结与柳宗元《小石潭记》中写“以其境过清”时的心境相似。
D. 本诗前三联写景，尾联结情，景情相衬，描写与抒情紧密关联，脉络清晰。</td></tr>
<tr><td>T10</td><td>诗词情感分类
Poetry sentiment analysis</td><td>古诗词“庭前芍药妖无格|池上芙蕖净少情|唯有牡丹真国色|花开时节动京城“的整体情感是( )
A. 积极的　B. 消极的　C. 中性的　D. 无法判断</td></tr>
<tr><td>T11</td><td>国学常识
Basic ancient Chinese</td><td>"近朱者赤，近墨者黑"所蕴含的道理和下列哪句话最相似？( )
A. 青出于蓝，而胜于蓝。　B. 蓬生麻中，不扶而直。
C. 公生明，偏生暗。　D. 三天打鱼两天晒网</td></tr>
<tr><td>T12</td><td>古汉语知识
Traditional Chinese culture</td><td>下列句中，含有双宾语的一句是( )
A. 夫何之有?　B. 熏之而之。　C. 兔不可得，而身宋笑。　D. 甚矣，汝之不惠!</td></tr>
<tr><td>T13</td><td>医古文
Ancient Chinese medical</td><td>以下除（）之外，都有病愈之义。
A. 已　B. 起　C. 性　D. 差</td></tr>
<tr><td>T14</td><td>古代文学知识
Ancient Chinese literature</td><td>杜甫《春望》中的“感时花溅泪，恨别鸟惊心”所反映的是( )
A. 早年的读书和漫游生活。　B. 困居长安十年时的感受。
C. “安史之乱”时的国恨家愁。　D. 晚年漂泊西南的客旅生活。</td></tr>
<tr><td>T15</td><td>古音学
Ancient Chinese phonetics</td><td>下列字在古代的声母、调类、等和开合口标注错误的是( )
A. 温（影母平声二等开）　B. 权（群母平声三等合）
C. 空（溪母平声一等合）　D. 狂（群母平声三等合）</td></tr>
</table>

Table 3: ACLUE tasks examples.

Unveiling Emotional Landscapes in Plautus and Terentius Comedies: A Computational Approach for Qualitative Analysis

Davide Picca
University of Lausanne / Switzerland
davide.picca@unil.ch

Caroline Richard
EDITTA, Sorbonne Université / France
caroline.richard@sorbonne-universite.fr

Abstract

This ongoing study explores emotion recognition in Latin texts, specifically focusing on Latin comedies. Leveraging Natural Language Processing and classical philology insights, the project navigates the challenges of Latin's intricate grammar and nuanced emotional expression. Despite initial challenges with lexicon translation and emotional alignment, the work provides a foundation for a more comprehensive analysis of emotions in Latin literature.

1 Introduction

Emotion recognition in text, extensively applied to modern languages, has scarcely targeted classical languages like Latin, despite its rich historical and cultural data [Alswaidan and Menai, 2020, Gatley, 2023, Korolova et al., 2019]. Recognizing emotions in Latin texts could illuminate classical literature, historical documents, and the evolution of emotional expression.

Latin's intricate grammar, extensive vocabulary, and ancient emotional nuances present unique challenges, requiring sophisticated NLP techniques and cultural understanding [Buzassyova, 2016, Gruber-Miller and Mulligan, 2022]. The limited availability of large, annotated Latin corpora further complicates traditional machine learning applications [Strapparava and Mihalcea, 2008].

This paper addresses these hurdles and explores emotion recognition in Latin texts. We propose a novel method combining NLP techniques and classical philology, extending emotion recognition techniques to Latin language analysis [Pang and Lee, 2008].

2 State-of-the-Art

Remarkable strides have been made in computational linguistics and Latin language analysis, including lexicon development [Passarotti, 2016], Medieval Latin Charters annotation [Passarotti, 2019a], Lemlat enhancements [Passarotti, 2019b], and Index Thomisticus Treebank adaptation [Passarotti, 2019c]. However, emotion recognition in classical languages remains relatively untouched.

Essential contributions include Sprugnoli et al. [2020a]'s work on Latin sentiment lexicons and sentiment analysis in Latin poetry [Sprugnoli et al., 2020b]. Studies on other classical languages, like Greek, also offer valuable insights [Yeruva et al., 2020, Pavlopoulos et al., 2022].

Even with these developments, the complexity of Latin's grammar and emotion portrayal makes this a challenging, yet fertile field. A blend of advanced Natural Language Processing (NLP) techniques and a robust understanding of the language's heritage are key to unlocking this potential, promising more profound insights into emotion recognition in classical languages.

3 Methodology

3.1 Research Design

The research design for this study commences with a quantitative phase, employing NLP techniques such as tokenization and lemmatization, in conjunction with a lexicon-based approach for emotion recognition. It is worth noting that our discourse analysis deviates from conventional norms by adopting a character-based perspective, facilitating the exploration of play dynamics through emotional trajectories Vandersmissen [2019]. In alignment with this perspective, we segment and index the texts according to speaker metadata, thus facilitating an individualized character analysis.

After the quantitative phase, we integrate a qualitative analysis, studying selected Latin texts to understand language and emotion, and devising an emotion coding scheme based on study principles. We then merge quantitative and qualitative results, comparing computational and manual analyses. These findings address the research questions,

Proceedings of the Ancient Language Processing Workshop associated with RANLP-2023, pages 88–95,
held in Varna Bulgaria, Sept 8, 2023.
https://doi.org/10.26615/978-954-452-087-8_010

deepening our understanding of the issue. This approach sets the foundation for our larger project: developing an emotion lexicon for Latin studies, reducing modern language bias to ensure authentic emotional data extraction.

3.2 Data Collection

The data for this study was collected from the Perseus Digital Library[1]. Our attention centers on investigating the genre of Latin comedy, with a specific emphasis on Plautus and Terentius's works. These plays were designated for observation owing to their applicability and donations to the Latin comedy genre and to their relative completeness (indeed most comic plays have been lost or are known by fragments).

The digitization of these texts was already completed by the Perseus Digital Library [Smith et al., 2000], which has undertaken extensive efforts to digitize and preserve classical texts. The data collection process involved downloading the relevant files from the GitHub repository and processing them using a Python script. This script extracts the text content from the XML files, along with the associated metadata. The extracted data is then saved in a structured format (CSV) for further analysis.

3.3 Emotion detection on Latin comedies

This ongoing, exploratory project is centered on the investigation of Latin comedy through the application of emotion recognition theory and technology, a realm that promises significant insight into narrative structures and character developments within the genre. Comedy offers a structured medium to analyze the emotional nuances in speeches and compare them with the genre's inherent traits and expectations. Our analysis is directed towards a selected corpus of 26 extant works by the influential Roman playwrights Plautus and Terentius, utilizing advanced computational tools to discern a spectrum of emotions—specifically *anger*, *anticipation*, *disgust*, *fear*, *joy*, *sadness*, *surprise*, and *trust*—embedded in these texts.

The research methodology unfolds in three stages: (1) the integration and expansion of lexical databases, (2) the construction of a lemmatized lexicon utilizing resources from the National Research Council Canada (NRC) for Latin[2], and (3) meticulously dissecting and interpreting a Latin corpus, which has been subdivided based on speakers' speeches. We implement lemmatization to integrate and enrich the Latin lexicon, reducing word variations to their fundamental form or lemma. It is noteworthy that the lemma detection rate in both stages is approximately 15%, a figure that doubles when excluding lexicon with no emotional connotations.

After the lemmatization stage, the Latin corpus, comprising XML files each representing a Latin literary work, is extracted and parsed. Post-extraction, the speeches are evaluated for emotional content using the prepared NRCLex instance[3].

Contrary to the assumption that comedic works primarily harbor positive emotions, our preliminary findings reveal a varied emotional terrain, highlighting the complexity within comedic plays. Correlations are observed between specific emotional expressions and character archetypes. However, inherent limitations in the lexicon applied, such as automatic English to Latin translation, alignment of emotions with lemmas based on contemporary English perspectives, and authenticity of employed lemmas, warrant caution. These aspects may engender potential misinterpretations of ancient emotions [Rosenwein, 2010, Konstan, 2016], along with lexical discrepancies, hindering word recognition in the lemmatized corpus, as exemplified by the non-recognition of the verb *metuo* (to fear).

Despite these limitations, the project provides a roadmap for future exploration in this growing field. Efforts are directed towards refining the lexicon and methodology to enhance the assessment of the emotional spectrum within Latin comedy 4, and to advance the broader objective of creating a Latin-specific emotion lexicon, thus enhancing data authenticity and minimizing modern language biases.

3.4 Qualitative evaluation of emotion recognition

The computational analysis has yielded substantial insights regarding the emotional strategies employed by Plautus and Terentius to captivate their audiences. It validates the pronounced prevalence of *joy*, thereby affirming the comedic essence of the genre. Furthermore, a notable correlation exists

[1]The dataset is freely available at https://github.com/PerseusDL

[2]https://saifmohammad.com/WebPages/NRC-Emotion-Lexicon.htm

[3]GitHub repository available here: https://github.com/CarolineRichard/ENCODEM.git

between the emotion displayed and the character archetypes, suggesting that Plautus meticulously crafted character personalities and roles to evoke specific emotional responses from his audience. This endeavor has thus substantially broadened our comprehension of the intricate interplay between emotion and language within Roman New Comedy. Initial examinations reveal that comedies adhere to certain core emotional motifs, with *surprise* emerging as the most predominantly depicted and universally shared sentiment. This finding aligns with the inherent narrative logic of comedies, wherein the plot revolves around unforeseen twists, deceptive maneuvers, and mistaken identities. Emotions such as *anger* and *fear* also figure prominently in the narrative landscape. Certain characters appear to be consistently characterized by these dual emotions, such that one is seldom portrayed without the other. This pattern is discernible in characters like *Simon* from *Andria* or *Antiphon* from *Stichus*. The characters embodying these paired emotions often assume pivotal roles in the narrative, such as the *adulescens* (young man) or the *senex* (old man) as shown in Figure 4 in the Appendix.

The intricate interplay between the dual roles in the drama manifests itself through the core dynamic tension between *fear* and *anger*.

From an emotional perspective, characters can be dichotomized into two groups:

- those who experience a broad emotional spectrum.

- others who are defined by single or dual predominating emotions.

The bifurcation of emotional responses can be attributed to the alignment of specific characters with particular emotional types. For instance, as shown in Figure 3 in the Appendix, a majority of the slaves typically display a limited array of emotions, commonly *fear*, *anger*, or *joy*.

In a similar vein, the *parasitus* character is primarily associated with emotions of *anger* or *fear*, with a scant expression of other emotions. Stereotypical emotions in comedy may hint at social representation trends. A character's social status might correlate with the type and complexity of emotions they express. However, even within this framework, emotional responses exhibit significant variations within the same character archetype. For instance, within the demographic of elderly men, certain characters are solely associated with *fear* and *anger*, whereas others predominantly display *surprise*. This pattern is accentuated by the character discrepancies between the *pater lenis* (gentle father) and the *pater durus* (harsh father), as observed in the *Heautontimoroumenos* (refer to Lhostis [2019] and Figure 2 in the Appendix for further details).

Across various plays, there is a discernible consistency in the characterization: characters predominantly characterized by *anger* and *fear*; those largely exhibiting *surprise*, and others manifesting a diverse emotional range. Within this last group, *joy* tends to be the most prevalent emotion. For example, the narrative of the *Mostellaria* revolves around two young men primarily associated with *anger* and *fear*, while the characters of *Father Teuropides* and *Philematia* the freed courtesan is dominated by *surprise* (See Figure 1 in the Appendix). Other characters display a blend of emotions.

The emotional distribution among characters does not necessarily correspond to their degree of involvement in the narrative arc. For example, in *Mostellaria*, despite the central role of the character *Trianon*, his emotional display is subdued and not polarized. However, this appears more aligned with a distribution based on the characters' roles within the dramatic schema: characters in conflict tend to display polarised emotions, whereas supporting or ancillary characters exhibit a more varied, non-polarised emotional range. This pattern is discernible in plays such as *Stichus*, *Poenulus* and *Mostellaria*, among others.

Quantitative research underscores recurring patterns in the dramatic construction of comedy and stock characters, specifically in the works of Plautus and Terentius, which deftly employ complex emotion networks to enhance the dynamicity of their plays. Unexpectedly, each play exhibits a unique global emotion network thereby suggesting that each play dynamic is distinct, regardless of their stereotypical characters and plots. This emotion-centric interaction is integral in shaping audience reception. The balance struck between standard emotional archetypes, such as the *pater durus*' *anger*, and an innovative emotional dynamic indicates the nuanced comical effects.

Traditional analysis, which emphasizes plot progression and dramatic dynamics, may overlook these emotional nuances. Therefore, this study advocates an alternate perspective that emphasizes the emotional interaction between characters.

4 Future Works

This proposal seeks to build upon our initial analysis of character dialogues, with the objective of developing an enhanced lexicon, rooted in the foundational NRC-Emolex model. This process includes meticulous data sanitization and augmentation of emotional markers. After refining the model, the next step is to study two plays, comparing manual and automatic emotional annotations, to further improve emotion recognition.

The indispensable preliminary discourse analysis provides a foundational understanding, vital to the formulation of a specialized emotion lexicon for Latin textual studies. By doing so, the proposal aims to reinforce the efficiency of emotion detection and bolster the reliability and authenticity of the extracted emotional data.

The complexity of emotional semiotization necessitates that we do not solely depend on specific emotion-related lemmas, given their inherent instability and context-dependence Micheli [2014].

Utilizing emotional markers derived from a Latin corpus, along with phraseological characteristics, will enrich our lexicon via a thematic, rather than strictly lexical approach. This will enable a more precise comprehension of emotions, allowing for an accurate assessment of the emotion network and a nuanced understanding of emotional representation.

The proposed project, thus, marks a significant step towards an exhaustive tool for deep investigation of emotions within Latin literature. This innovative endeavour is set to amplify our understanding of the emotional dimensions present within these foundational texts.

References

N Alswaidan and MEB Menai. A survey of state-of-the-art approaches for emotion recognition in text. *Knowledge and Information Systems*, 2020. doi: 10.1007/s10115-020-01449-0. Query date: 2023-06-21 21:34:37.

Ludmila Buzassyova. The 'phonetic complex' in renaissance latin grammar petrus ramus's dichotomies and their reflections in two vernacular grammatical texts. *Graeco-Latina Brunensia*, 21(2):81–98, January 2016. doi: 10.5817/GLB2016-2-8.

Jane Gatley. Cultural capital, curriculum policy and teaching latin. *British Educational Research Journal*, 49:174–185, 2023.

John Gruber-Miller and Bret Mulligan. Latin vocabulary knowledge and the readability of latin texts: A preliminary study. *New England Classical Journal*, 2022. doi: 10.52284/necj.49.1.article.gruber-millerandmulligan. URL `https://dx.doi.org/10.52284/necj.49.1.article.gruber-millerandmulligan`.

Konstan. Their emotions and ours: A single history? *L'Atelier du Centre de recherches historiques*, 16, 2016. doi: https://doi.org/10.4000/acrh.6756. URL `http://journals.openedition.org/acrh/6756`. Online; accessed 27-June-2023.

Nataliia Korolova, Oksana Koshchii, and Valentyna Myronova. The latin language as a universal cultural code. *Journal of History Culture and Art Research*, 8:278–290, 2019.

Nathalie Lhostis. Le langage de la sagesse dans l'heautontimoroumenos de térence. *Vita Latina*, 199 (1):171–195, 2019. doi: 10.3406/vita.2019.1909. URL `https://www.persee.fr/doc/vita_0042-7306_2019_num_199_1_1909`.

Raphaël Micheli. *Les émotions dans les discours: modèle d'analyse, perspectives empiriques*. Champs linguistiques. de Boeck Duculot, Louvain-la-Neuve, 2014. ISBN 978-2-8011-1738-5.

B. Pang and L. Lee. Opinion mining and sentiment analysis. *Foundations and Trends in Information Retrieval*, 2(1-2), 2008.

Marco Passarotti. Building a word formation lexicon for latin. In *LREC*, 2016. URL `https://www.aclweb.org/anthology/L16-1681.pdf`.

Marco Passarotti. Annotating medieval latin charters. In *Proceedings of the NoDaLiDa 2019 Workshop on Processing Historical Language*, 2019a. URL `https://www.aclweb.org/anthology/W19-4718.pdf`.

Marco Passarotti. Enhancing the latin morphological analyser lemlat with an onomasticon. In *Proceedings of the NoDaLiDa 2019 Workshop on Processing Historical Language*, 2019b. URL `https://www.aclweb.org/anthology/W19-4719.pdf`.

Marco Passarotti. Converting the index thomisticus treebank into universal dependencies. In *Proceedings of the NoDaLiDa 2019 Workshop on Processing Historical Language*, 2019c. URL `https://www.aclweb.org/anthology/W19-4720.pdf`.

J Pavlopoulos, A Xenos, and D Picca. Sentiment analysis of homeric text: The 1st book of iliad. *Proceedings of the Thirteenth Language Resources and Evaluation Conference*, 2022. URL `https://aclanthology.org/2022.lrec-1.765/`.

Barbara Rosenwein. Problems and Methods in the History of Emotions. *Passions in Context I. International Journal for the History and Theory of Emotions*, 1, January 2010.

David A Smith, Jeffrey A Rydberg-Cox, and Gregory R Crane. The perseus project: A digital library for the humanities. *Literary and Linguistic Computing*, 15 (1):15–25, 2000.

Rachele Sprugnoli, Marco Passarotti, Daniela Corbetta, and Andrea Peverelli. Creating, evaluating and extending sentiment lexicons for latin. In *Proceedings of The 12th Language Resources and Evaluation Conference*, pages 3078–3086, 2020a.

Rachele Sprugnoli, Marco Passarotti, Daniela Corbetta, and Andrea Peverelli. Odi et amo: Creating, evaluating and extending sentiment lexicons for latin. In *Proceedings of the 12th Conference on Language Resources and Evaluation (LREC 2020)*, pages 3078–3086. European Language Resources Association (ELRA), 2020b.

C. Strapparava and R. Mihalcea. Learning to identify emotions in text. In *Proceedings of the 2008 ACM symposium on Applied computing*, 2008.

Marc Vandersmissen. Discours des personnages feminins chez Seneque. *Collection Latomus*, 2019. URL `https://www.academia.edu/38169453/Discours_des_personnages_f%C3%A9minins_chez_S%C3%A9n%C3%A8que_Approches_logom%C3%A9triques_et_contrastives_dun_corpus_th%C3%A9%C3%A2tral`. ISBN: 9789042937970.

Vijaya Kumari Yeruva, Mayanka Chandrashekar, Yugyung Lee, Jeff Rydberg-Cox, Virginia Blanton, and Nathan A Oyler. Interpretation of sentiment analysis in aeschylus's greek tragedy. In *Proceedings of LaTeCH-CLfL 2020*, pages 138–146, 2020.

A Appendix: Figures

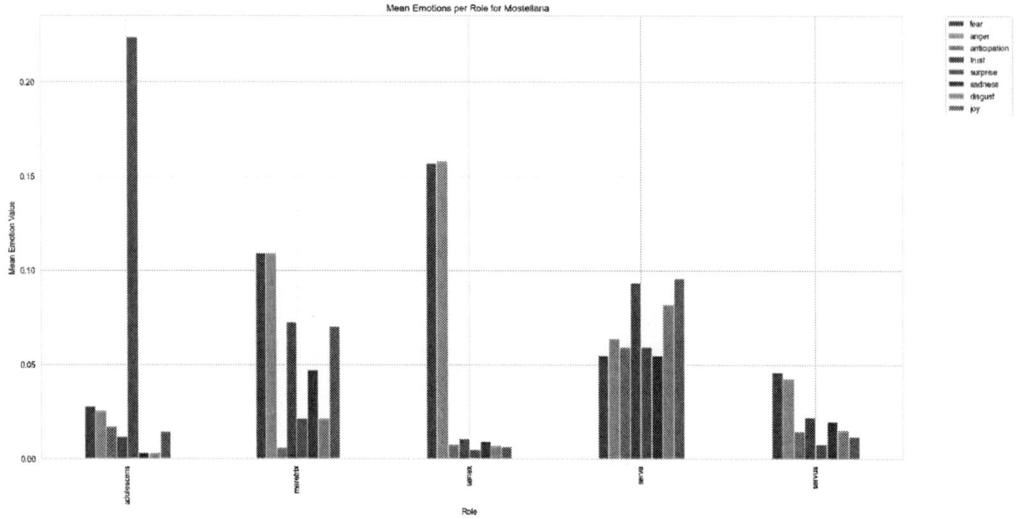

Figure 1: Emotional Distribution in Mostellaria

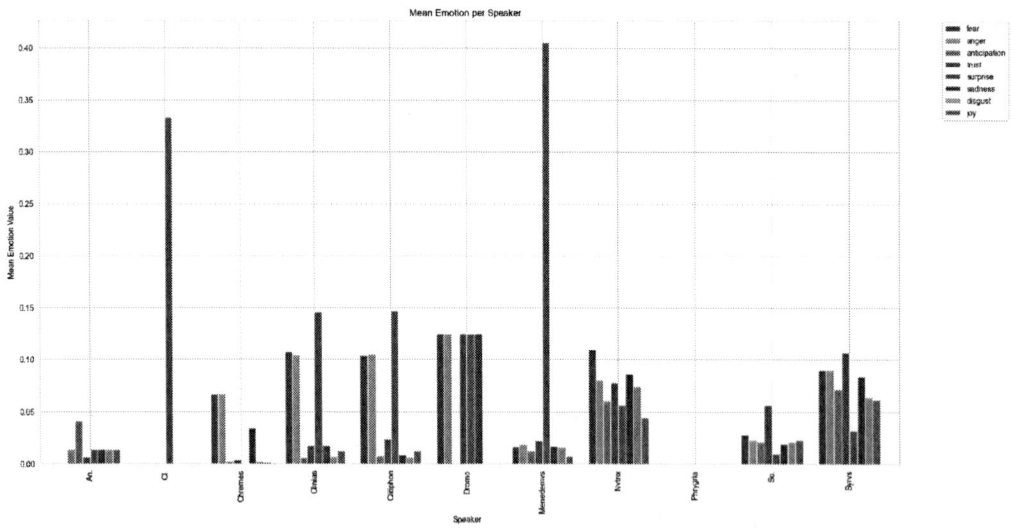

Figure 2: Emotional Landscape in the Heautontimoroumenos (Terentius)

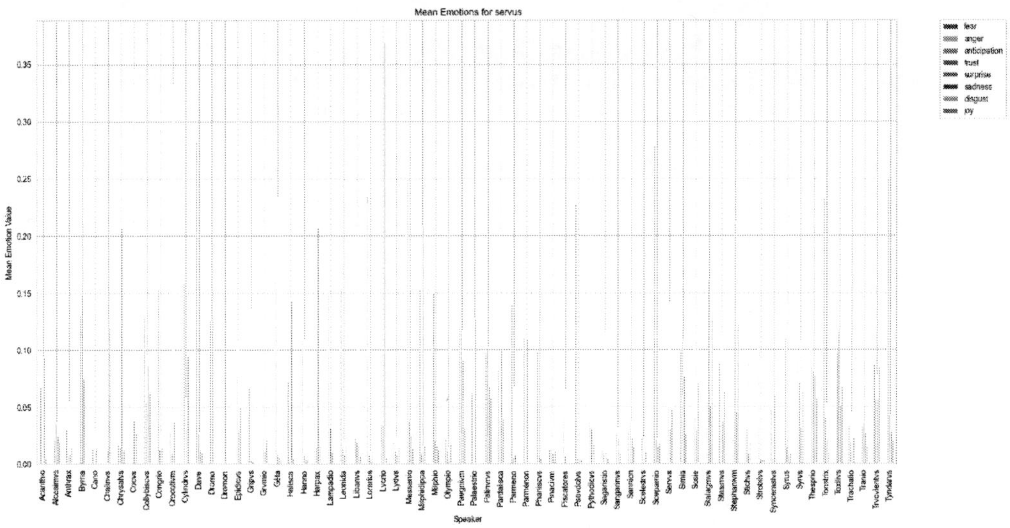

Figure 3: Representation of slaves' Emotional Spectrum

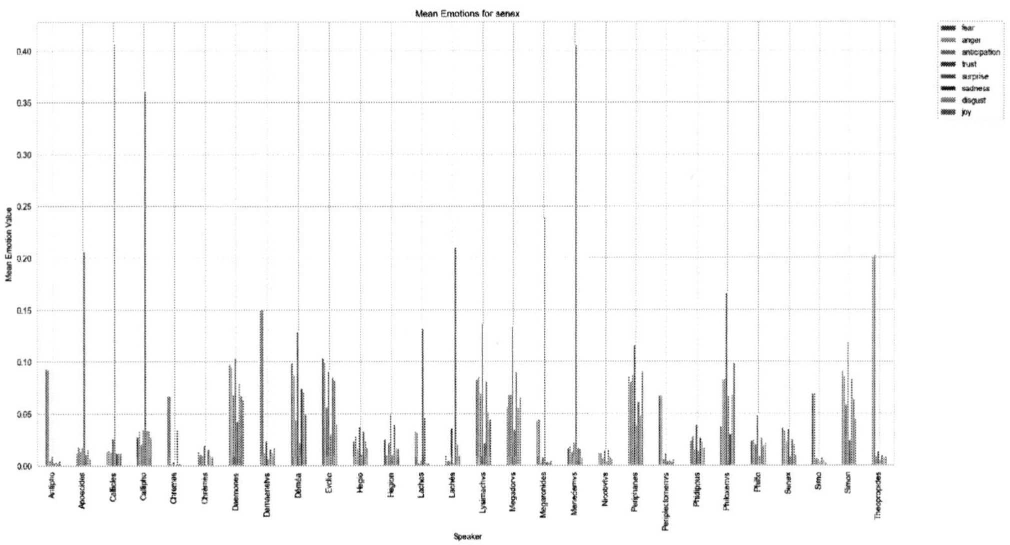

Figure 4: Emotions of *seneces* in Plautus and Terentius' drama

Morphological and Semantic Evaluation of Ancient Chinese Machine Translation

Kai Jin[1], **Dan Zhao**[1], **Wuying Liu**[2,3✉]

1. School of Foreign Languages, Qilu University of Technology, 250353, Jinan, Shandong, China
2. Shandong Key Laboratory of Language Resources Development and Application, Ludong University, 264025, Yantai, Shandong, China
3. Center for Linguistics and Applied Linguistics, Guangdong University of Foreign Studies, 510420, Guangzhou, Guangdong, China

{jk@qlu.edu.cn, dzhao639@gmail.com, wyliu@ldu.edu.cn}

Abstract

Machine translation (MT) of ancient Chinese texts presents unique challenges due to the complex grammatical structures, cultural nuances, and polysemy of the language. This paper focuses on evaluating the translation quality of different platforms for ancient Chinese texts using *The Analects* as a case study. The evaluation is conducted using the BLEU, LMS, and ESS metrics, and the platforms compared include three machine translation platforms (Baidu Translate, Bing Microsoft Translator, and DeepL), and one language generation model ChatGPT that can engage in translation endeavors. Results show that Baidu performs the best, surpassing the other platforms in all three metrics, while ChatGPT ranks second and demonstrates unique advantages. The translations generated by ChatGPT are deemed highly valuable as references. The study contributes to understanding the challenges of MT for ancient Chinese texts and provides insights for users and researchers in this field. It also highlights the importance of considering specific domain requirements when evaluating MT systems.

1 Introduction

Machine translation (MT) has been a prominent area of research and development in artificial intelligence since the 1950s. Over the years, it has undergone significant advancements, evolving from rule-based methods, statistical methods, and more recently, neural network-based learning methods. As the quality of MT continues to improve and the demand for translation work steadily increases, more and more translators are adopting the "machine translation + post-editing" mode for translation. At the same time, the quality of MT has been a subject of great interest and concern for both the MT and translation fields. Researchers, institutions, and conferences are continuously conducting studies in this area, and various evaluation metrics for MT have been proposed.

There have also been studies on MT of ancient texts. Some researchers have made algorithmic improvements specifically tailored for translating ancient texts (Gutherz et al. 2023; Park et al. 2020; Zhang et al. 2019; Zhou & Liu 2022). Researchers have also conducted evaluations of the quality of MT for ancient texts (Yao et al. 2013; Yang et al. 2021; Yousef et al. 2022). However, research on MT for ancient texts, including ancient Chinese texts, remains relatively scarce.

This paper primarily focuses on MT quality of ancient Chinese texts, and the subsequent discussions will concentrate on this specific domain. Compared to modern Chinese, ancient Chinese has its own unique characteristics. Firstly, ancient Chinese employs complex and distinctive grammatical structures, including syntax, word order, and rhetoric, among other aspects. These structures differ significantly from modern Chinese. MT struggles to accurately capture and parse the intricate grammatical relationships embedded in ancient Chinese texts. Secondly, ancient Chinese texts often employ rhetorical devices such as allusions, symbolism, and metaphors, which involve rich cultural connotations and backgrounds. These allusions and cultural nuances are often challenging for non-Chinese MT systems to comprehend, leading to translation errors or the loss of the original essence and aesthetic appeal. Thirdly, ancient Chinese texts often exhibit polysemy and ambiguity, where a single word or phrase may have multiple interpretations and

Proceedings of the Ancient Language Processing Workshop associated with RANLP-2023, pages 96–102,
held in Varna Bulgaria, Sept 8, 2023.
https://doi.org/10.26615/978-954-452-087-8_011

meanings. MT systems find it challenging to accurately select and judge among these complex semantic relationships, often leading to mistranslations or inaccuracies. The aforementioned characteristics pose significant challenges for MT of ancient Chinese texts.

This study aims to evaluate the translation quality of different platforms for ancient Chinese texts. Through this evaluation, we can gain insights and understanding in dealing with the complexities of ancient language and culture, contribute to the advancement in the field of natural language processing, and provide a supplement to MT quality assessment applications. Furthermore, these evaluation results will help users gain insights into the performance of different platforms, allowing them to identify potential issues and limitations.

2 Experiment design

This study takes the Chinese classic *The Analects*[1] as the research text and compares three classic human-translated versions and four versions generated by four platforms. Three MT quality evaluation metrics are used as evaluation criteria to assess the translation quality of the four platforms. For each human-translated text and each machine-translated text, quality scores are calculated individually. Then, the mean scores are calculated for each platform. The scheme is illustrated in Figure 1.

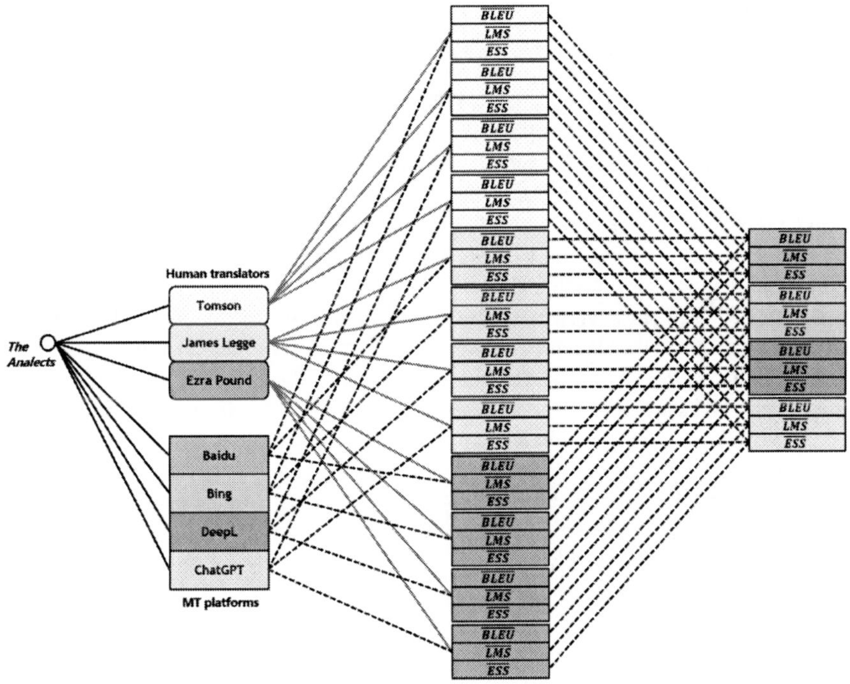

Figure 1: Research scheme.

2.1 Texts

In this study, we select *The Analects* as the sample ancient Chinese texts and its three translations as the reference human translations to compare with MT.

The Analects is one of the most influential texts in Chinese ancient philosophy and culture, regarded as a masterpiece in Chinese literature. Its impact extends not only within China but also across the globe, and it has been translated into multiple languages, generating significant influence worldwide (Li & Li 2013). As a

[1] The original Chinese title is "论语" (*lunyu*), and it has several different English versions. In this paper, apart from referring to specific translators, we use "The Analects" to refer to the book.

foundational work of Confucian thought, *The Analects* has garnered the largest number of English translations among classical Chinese texts.

We have compiled the original text of *The Analects* into a corpus, consisting of a total of 1,153 sentences.

We have also selected three highly influential versions of *The Analects* for our study, translated respectively by Tomson (辜鸿铭) (Tomson 2011), James Legge (Legge 2016) and Ezra Pound (Pound 1933). In 1861, James Legge, a missionary from the London Missionary Society, published the first English translation of *The Analects* in Hong Kong. Legge extensively studied the commentaries on *The Analects* from previous generations and used Victorian English in his translation, striving for faithfulness and comprehensiveness. Initially, Legge had a less favorable portrayal of Confucius in his translation. In contrast, Ezra Pound, who identified himself as a Confucian, aimed to transform the world through his translation of Confucian classics (Wang 2004). Pound's translation was published in 1951. Despite his limited proficiency in Chinese, Pound heavily relied on Legge's translation as a reference but also recognized its imperfections, leading him to make significant modifications in his own translation. Pound also emphasized linguistic conciseness (Wei 2005). Another noteworthy translation was by Tomson, published in 1898, which marked the earliest independent Chinese translation of *The Analects*. Tomson had a strong command of multiple languages, a solid linguistic foundation, and extensive knowledge. His English translation of *The Analects* gained wide recognition in the Western world. Tomson believed that Legge's translation often fell short of accurately or fully conveying the original meaning. Thus, Tomson's translation aimed to elucidate the cultural elements missing in the Western context, enabling readers to achieve a more comprehensive understanding (Meng et al. 2012).

In conclusion, while the translations by these three individuals are interconnected, they exhibit distinct characteristics in terms of vocabulary, style, and expression. As highly influential versions, they excel in terms of faithfulness, intelligibility, and elegance in their language. For the aforementioned reasons, we have selected these three translations as reference translations for the purpose of comparing and evaluating machine-translated texts.

2.2 Platforms

The platforms selected for this study include: Baidu Translate ("Baidu" for short), Bing Microsoft Translator ("Bing" for short), DeepL, and ChatGPT[2]. The former three are dedicated online MT systems, while the last one is a conversational generation system based on large-scale language models.

Given that the source text in our research is in ancient Chinese, it is essential for us to select at least one representative MT platforms from China. Baidu is one of the biggest and most influential MT platforms in China. According to industry reports and market data, Baidu consistently ranks first in terms of usage among Chinese MT platforms[3]. Therefore, Baidu has become our top choice as a MT platform developed in China.

For MT platforms outside of China, we have chosen Bing and DeepL. Both platforms are widely recognized and highly regarded for their usage and performance worldwide. Based on our extensive translation practice, we have observed that DeepL's translations occasionally exhibit noticeable differences in vocabulary and even sentence structure compared to other MT platforms.

ChatGPT is a language generation model that possesses the capability to comprehend and produce natural language text, encompassing translation tasks as well. While its primary utility lies in dialog and text generation, it can, to a certain extent, engage in translation endeavors. This attribute permits viable comparisons with conventional MT systems under specific circumstances. Recently, ChatGPT's performance in translation tasks has gained increasing attention and recognition. Although there is currently limited research on the translation quality of ChatGPT, some researchers have already drawn the conclusion that "ChatGPT has already become a good translator." (Jiao et al. 2023) Based on our observation, we have also found that the translations generated by ChatGPT exhibit differences from the three MT platforms. It is worth noting that each generation of translation by ChatGPT can vary, and the translation can also be adjusted based on the given prompts. Therefore, to

[2] ChatGPT-3.5 version is utilized in this study.

[3] Information source: http://bjx.iimedia.cn/app_rank, last accessed 2023/6/27.

ensure relatively reliable experimental results, we only select the first-generation translation produced by ChatGPT without adding any other prompts than "Translate… into English."

3 Evaluation metrics

The evaluation metrics adopted in this research include Bilingual Evaluation Understudy (BLEU) (Papineni et al. 2002), Levenshtein-distance-based Morphological Similarity (LMS) and Pretrained-model-based Embedding Semantic Similarity (ESS).

3.1 BLEU

In 2002, IBM proposed the BLEU metric, which has become the de facto standard for evaluating MT quality. This metric is based on the mechanical morphological evaluation method using n-gram grammar. In this paper, the BLEU referred to is BLEU4.

$$\overline{BLEU} = \frac{1}{nm}\sum_{j=1}^{n}\sum_{i=1}^{m} BLEU(r_{ij}, c_i) \qquad (1)$$

For a specific application scenario involving a machine-translated text collection (***C***) consisting of *m* sentences and the corresponding *n* sets of human reference translations (***R***), we evaluate using the arithmetic mean $\overline{BLEU}$, as shown in equation (1), of the BLEU metric.

3.2 LMS

To evaluate the morphological similarity between sentences, we introduce the LMS metric. This metric is based on the edit distance proposed by the Soviet mathematician Vladimir Levenshtein in 1965. The edit distance refers to the minimum number of editing operations required to transform one string into another, including substitution, insertion, and deletion. Let *LD*(*r*, *c*) represent the edit distance between a human reference translation (*r*) and a machine-translated candidate (*c*). The equation (2) represents the LMS. In the equation, length (*r*) represents the length of the reference translation and length (*c*) represents the length of the candidate translation. The LMS value ranges from 0 to 1, where a higher value indicates a greater morphological similarity between the sentences.

$$LMS(r, c) = 1 - \frac{LD(r, c)}{Max(Len(r), Len(c))} \qquad (2)$$

For a specific application scenario involving a machine-translated text collection (***C***) consisting of *m* sentences and the corresponding *n* sets of human reference translations (***R***), we evaluate using the arithmetic mean $\overline{LMS}$, as shown in equation (3), of the LMS metric. In this experiment, the getLevenshteinDistance library function from org.apache.commons.lang3.StringUtils is used.

$$\overline{LMS} = \frac{1}{nm}\sum_{j=1}^{n}\sum_{i=1}^{m} LMS(r_{ij}, c_i) \qquad (3)$$

3.3 ESS

To address the challenge of handling synonymous and morphologically variant expressions, we introduce the ESS metric as a semantic similarity evaluation index. This metric maps the human reference translation (*r*) and machine-translated candidate (*c*) to embedding vectors in a pre-trained model (Peters at al. 2018). Specifically, we obtain the embedding vectors ($\boldsymbol{v}_r$) for the reference translation and ($\boldsymbol{v}_c$) for the candidate translation. Then, we calculate the cosine similarity between vectors $\boldsymbol{v}_r$ and $\boldsymbol{v}_c$ in the embedding vector space (Reimers & Gurevych, 2019), representing the embedding semantic similarity between the reference and candidate translations as *ESS(r, c)*. According to the definition of this metric, the embedding semantic similarity values between two sentences is within [-1, 1]. To further normalize these values so that $ESS(r, c) \in [0, 1]$, we apply a proportional scaling transformation.

For a specific application scenario involving a machine-translated text collection (***C***) consisting of *m* sentences and the corresponding *n* sets of human reference translations (***R***), we evaluate using the arithmetic mean $\overline{ESS}$, as shown in equation (4), of the ESS metric. In this study, the all-roberta-large-v1 pre-trained model[4] was used.

[4] https://huggingface.co/sentence-transformers/all-roberta-large-v1

$$\overline{ESS} = \frac{1}{nm}\sum_{j=1}^{n}\sum_{i=1}^{m} ESS(r_{ij}, c_i) \quad (4)$$

4 Experiment results and analysis

First, we compare each human-translated text with each machine-translated text respectively under the three metrics BLEU, LMS and ESS, and the results are shown in Table 1. The highest value obtained when comparing the texts from different platforms to the same human translator is highlighted in bold. We can see that, except for one LMS value from DeepL, all the other highest values belong to Baidu.

Platforms	Human translators	Metrics		
		$\overline{BLEU}$	$\overline{LMS}$	$\overline{ESS}$
Baidu	Tomson	**0.1059**	0.2857	**0.8494**
	James Legge	**0.4901**	**0.3731**	**0.9162**
	Ezra Pound	**0.539**	**0.5382**	**0.9516**
Bing	Tomson	0.0469	0.2987	0.8109
	James Legge	0.0251	0.239	0.8468
	Ezra Pound	0.0905	0.3868	0.8597
DeepL	Tomson	0.0621	**0.3323**	0.8408
	James Legge	0.0356	0.2656	0.8611
	Ezra Pound	0.1049	0.3731	0.8321
ChatGPT	Tomson	0.0474	0.2996	0.8117
	James Legge	0.0253	0.2408	0.8478
	Ezra Pound	0.0907	0.3878	0.8606

Table 1. BLEU, LMS and ESS results of human-translated texts and machine-translated texts.

Then, we calculate the mean of the three values for each platform under each metric, resulting in the evaluation results for the translation quality of each platform. The results are shown in Table 2. It can be observed that Baidu has the best performance under all the metrics, with the BLEU value significantly surpassing the other three platforms.

Platforms	$\overline{BLEU}$	$\overline{LMS}$	$\overline{ESS}$
Baidu	**0.3783**	**0.3990**	**0.9057**
Bing	0.0542	0.3078	0.8391
DeepL	0.0545	0.3091	0.8400
ChatGPT	0.0675	0.3234	0.8446

Table 2. Evaluation results of the four platforms.

In this study, Baidu outperforms other platforms in translating ancient Chinese texts into English. Aside from technical architecture and optimized algorithms, the most possible reason is that Baidu, as a Chinese company, may have access to a larger and more diverse dataset of bilingual English-Chinese texts compared to other platforms, allowing their models to learn from a wide range of language patterns and translation examples. This extensive training data contributes to improving the accuracy and fluency of it Chinese-English translations.

5 Other findings: ChatGPT's advantages

From Table 2 we can observe that ChatGPT has the second-best performance in translation, right after Baidu. Also, we have found that ChatGPT has also demonstrated exceptional advantages in certain aspects.

(1) Semantic interpretation

In ancient Chinese, the phenomenon of polysemy, where a single word has multiple meanings, is very common. MT must make accurate judgments regarding the selection of the intended meaning for such words. These judgments often rely on the contextual information provided by the surrounding text. However, when the context does not provide sufficient information, MT systems often make errors in determining the correct meaning. On the other hand, ChatGPT demonstrates superior performance in the disambiguation of polysemous words, excelling in making accurate sense selection judgments even in cases where context is limited.

Example 1

Source Text ("ST" for short): 君子不器。

Baidu: A gentleman is not a weapon.

Bing: A gentleman is not a weapon.

DeepL: A gentleman is not a tool.

ChatGPT: A noble person is not defined by their possessions or material objects.

In this context, "器" refers to "utensil." This sentence conveys the idea that a noble person (君子) should have a broad and inclusive mindset, rather than being limited to a specific role or function like a utensil (器具). However, Baidu and Bing mistakenly interpret "器" as "weapon" (武器) and DeepL "tool" (工具).

Example 2

ST: 诲女知之乎！

Baidu: Teach women to know!

Bing: The girl knows!

DeepL: Teach your daughter to know!

ChatGPT: Have you learned to understand this?

In ancient Chinese, the character "女" (female) is often used as a phonetic loan character, representing the pronoun "汝" (thou). In Example 2, Baidu, Bing, and DeepL do not correctly identify the true intended meaning of "女," while ChatGPT do. We have found that, in our research, the translation of all instances of the character "女" as a phonetic loan character in *The Analects* exhibits the same pattern across different MT translations.

(2) Fault tolerance

During the process of data compilation, we have discovered that there were several errors in the original text (These errors were meticulously rectified, ensuring the source text's accuracy prior to commencing the MT task). When the text with errors is input into the platforms, Baidu, Bing and DeepL generate translations based on the faulty text. However, ChatGPT often demonstrate the ability to recognize and identify these errors and generate translations based on the correct characters. ChatGPT possesses this capability that is not present in traditional MT systems.

Example 3

ST: 邦君之妻，君称之曰夫人，夫人自称日小童……

Baidu: Bangjun's wife, whom you call Madame, and whose wife calls herself Rixiaotong…

Bing: The wife of the prince, the prince is called Mrs. Wang, and the lady calls herself Ri Xiaotong…

DeepL: The wife of the king of the state, the king called it the wife, the wife called herself the day child…

ChatGPT: The wife of the ruler of a state is called "Madam" by the ruler, and she refers to herself as "Little Child"…

In Example 3, the underlined character "日" (pronounced as "*ri*", meaning the sun or day) in the source text should be "曰" (say), and "小童" that follows means "little child". This sentence means that the madam calls herself "小童." Both Baidu and Bing transliterate this character mistakenly and DeepL interprets "日" as "day," while ChatGPT recognizes this fault.

Example 4

ST: 恭而无礼则劳，慎而无礼则葸……

Baidu: Respectful but impolite leads to labor, cautious but impolite leads to anthracene…

Bing: If you are respectful and rude, you will work, if you are cautious and rude, you will be rude…

DeepL: Respectful but no ritual is labor, prudent but no ritual is anthracite…

ChatGPT: If one is respectful without propriety, it leads to laboriousness. If one is cautious without propriety, it leads to timidity…

"蒽" (anthraquinone) in the original text is a faulty character which should be "葸" (afraid, bashful). Both Baidu and DeepL take "蒽" directly, and Bing simply omits it. ChatGPT recognizes the fault and translates it into "timidity," which aligns with the intended meaning of the original text.

6 Conclusion

Based on the evaluation of translation quality of the Chinese classic *The Analects* by Baidu, Bing, DeepL, and ChatGPT using the BLEU, LMS, and ESS metrics, we have found that among the four platforms, Baidu, as a MT platform developed in China, performs the best in handling ancient Chinese texts. Its scores in all three metrics are significantly higher than the other three platforms. ChatGPT, as a general-purpose language model, ranks second among the four, and has demonstrated unique advantages, and the translations it produces are highly valuable as references. It is worth mentioning that in this study, the translations generated by ChatGPT were done without any prompts (except for the one mentioned in 2.2) or adjustments. We plan to discuss in our future research the translation quality of ChatGPT by incorporating prompts for adjusting the translation of ancient Chinese into English.

Acknowledgments

The research is supported by the Scientific Research Project of China National Committee for Terminology in Science and Technology (No. YB2021027), the Art Science Key Project of Shandong Provincial Association for Science of Arts & Culture (L2022Z06170304), the New Liberal Arts Research and Reform Practice Project of Ministry of Education of China (No. 2021060049), the Postgraduate Education and Teaching Reform Research Project of Shandong (No. SDYJG21185), the Key Project of Undergraduate Teaching Reform Research of Shandong (No. Z2021323), the Science and Technology Program of Guangzhou (No. 202201010061), and the Humanity and Social Science Research Project of Ministry of Education of China (No. 20YJAZH069).

References

Kishore Papineni, Salim Roukos, Todd Ward, et al. 2002. Bleu: A Method for Automatic Evaluation of Machine Translation. In *Proceedings of the 40th Annual Meeting of the Association for Computational Linguistics*, 311-318.

Gai Gutherz, Shai Gordin, Luis Sáenz, et al. 2023. Translating Akkadian to English With Neural Machine Translation. *PNAS nexus*, 2(5): pgad096.

Chanjun Park, Chanhee Lee, Yeongwook Yang, et al. 2020. Ancient Korean Neural Machine Translation. *IEEE Acces,* 8: 116617-116625.

Zhiyuan Zhang, Wei Li, Qi Su. 2019. Automatic Translating Between Ancient Chinese and Contemporary Chinese with Limited Aligned Corpora. In *Natural Language Processing and Chinese Computing: 8th CCF International Conference, NLPCC 2019, Dunhuang, China, October 9–14, 2019, Proceedings, Part II 8.* Springer International Publishing, 157-167.

Chengbin Zhou, Zhongbao Liu. 2022. Machine Translation of Ancient Chinese Text Based on Transformer of Semantic Information Sharing. *Technology Intelligence Engineering*, 8(06): 114-127.

Zhenjun Yao, Xuhong Zheng, Pengtao Xu, et al. 2013. An Exploration of Phrase-Based SMT for English Translation of Tao Te Ching. *Shandong Foreign Language Teaching*, 34(03): 109-112.

Kexin Yang, Dayiheng Liu, Qian Qu, et al. 2021. An Automatic Evaluation Metric for Ancient-Modern Chinese Translation. *Neural Computing and Applications*, 33: 3855-3867.

Tariq Yousef, Chiara Palladino, David J. Wright, et al. 2022. Automatic translation alignment for ancient Greek and Latin. In *Proceedings of the Second Workshop on Language Technologies for Historical and Ancient Languages*, 101-107.

Gang Li, Jinshu Li. 2013. On the English Translation of *The Analects*: A Survey. *Journal of Social Science of Hunan Normal University*, 42(01).

Tomson. (Trans.). 2011. *The Discourse and Sayings of Confucius*. Yunnan People's Publishing House, Kunming, China.

James Legge. (Trans.). 2016. *Confucian Analects*. Liaoning People's Publishing House, Shenyang, China.

Ezra Pound. (Trans.). 1933. *Confucian Analects*. Peter Owen Limited, London, UK.

Hui Wang. 2004. A Comparison of Confucian Analects Translated by James Legge and Ezra Pound. *Foreign Language and Literature*, (05), 140-144.

Wangdong Wei. 2005. A Multi-Perspective Comparison of Three Translations of Lun Yu: From James Legge, Ezra Pound to Edward Slingerland. *Chinese Translators Journal*, (03), 52-57.

Jian Meng, Tao Qu, Yang Xia. 2012. English Translation of Chinese Classics under Adaptation Theory – Reflections on the English Translation of *Lunyu* by Gu Hong-ming. *Foreign Language Research*, (03), 104-108.

Wenxiang Jiao, Wenxuan Wang, Jen-tse Huang, et al. 2023. Is ChatGPT a Good Translator? A Preliminary Study. *arXiv preprint arXiv:2301.08745.*

Kishore Papineni, Salim Roukos, Todd Ward, et al. 2002. Bleu: A Method for Automatic Evaluation of Machine Translation. *Proceedings of the 40th Annual Meeting of the Association for Computational Linguistics*, 311-318.

Matthew E. Peters, Mark Neumann, Mohit Iyyer, et al. 2018. Deep Contextualized Word Repretations. *arXiv:1802.05365.*

Nils Reimers, Iryna Gurevych. 2019. Sentence-Bert: Sentence Embeddings Using Siamese Bert-Networks. *arXiv preprint arXiv:1908.10084.*

A tailored Handwritten-Text-Recognition System for Medieval Latin

Philipp Koch[1◇] **Gilary Vera Nuñez**[1◇] **Esteban Garces Arias**[1♠]
Christian Heumann[1♠] **Matthias Schöffel**[2♣] **Alexander Häberlin**[2,3♡]
Matthias Aßenmacher[1,4♠]

[1] Department of Statistics, LMU, Munich, Germany
[2] Bavarian Academy of Sciences, BAdW, Munich, Germany
[3] Universität Zürich, Zurich, Switzerland
[4] Munich Center for Machine Learning (MCML), LMU, Munich, Germany

◇{philipp.koch,gi.vera}@campus.lmu.de ♣matthias.schoeffel@badw.de ♡alexander.haeberlin@sglp.uzh.ch
♠{esteban.garcesarias,chris,matthias}@stat.uni-muenchen.de

Abstract

The Bavarian Academy of Sciences and Humanities aims to digitize its Medieval Latin Dictionary. This dictionary entails record cards referring to lemmas in medieval Latin, a low-resource language. A crucial step of the digitization process is the Handwritten Text Recognition (HTR) of the handwritten lemmas found on these record cards. In our work, we introduce an end-to-end pipeline, tailored to the medieval Latin dictionary, for locating, extracting, and transcribing the lemmas. We employ two state-of-the-art (SOTA) image segmentation models to prepare the initial data set for the HTR task. Furthermore, we experiment with different transformer-based models and conduct a set of experiments to explore the capabilities of different combinations of vision encoders with a GPT-2 decoder. Additionally, we also apply extensive data augmentation resulting in a highly competitive model. The best-performing setup achieved a Character Error Rate (CER) of 0.015, which is even superior to the commercial Google Cloud Vision model, and shows a more stable performance.

1 Introduction

The Medieval Latin Dictionary (MLW)[1] deals with Latin texts that were created between 500 and 1280 in the German-speaking region. The foundations for this project have been developed from 1948 onwards and since then, the dictionary has been continuously published in individual partial editions since 1959. The basis of the dictionary consists of 50 selected texts that have been fully transcribed onto DIN-A6 record cards (cf. Fig. 1) constituting about 40% of the note material. Later, another 2,500 texts were excerpted and transcribed manually onto DIN-A6 record cards, using a typewriter. In addition, there are so-called "index cards", a type of record card, that helps to uncover often

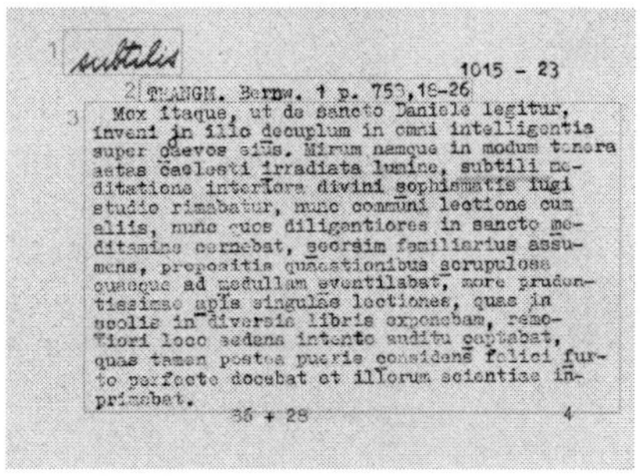

Figure 1: Record card from the MLW data set.

hundreds of additional references. In total, it is estimated that 1.3 million reference points have been recorded for the MLW. These record cards were sorted alphabetically by the first letter of the keyword (lemma), and serve as the foundation for creating a dictionary. Around 200,000 record cards have been scanned and annotated with their respective lemma. The accurate extraction and transcription of the lemma present a challenge, which is further compounded by the limited resources available for medieval Latin.

Our contributions are as follows: **(1)** We present a novel end-to-end HTR pipeline specifically designed for detecting and transcribing handwritten medieval Latin text. Notably, it surpasses commercial applications currently considered SOTA for related tasks. **(2)** We train a lemma-detection model without relying on human-annotated bounding boxes. **(3)** We conduct extensive experiments to compare various vision encoders and evaluate the effectiveness of data augmentation techniques.

2 Related Work

We provide an overview for HTR, which is the main challenge of this work. For object detection, which is an intermediate step of this work, we refer to Zaidi et al. (2021) for a detailed overview.

Connectionist Temporal Classification (CTC)

[1] In German: ***Mittellateinisches Wörterbuch (MLW)***

Proceedings of the Ancient Language Processing Workshop associated with RANLP-2023, pages 103–110,
held in Varna Bulgaria, Sept 8, 2023.
https://doi.org/10.26615/978-954-452-087-8_012

(Graves et al., 2006) is a technique in which a neural network – initially a Recurrent Neural Network (RNN) but other networks might also be used (Chaudhary and Bali, 2022) – is trained to predict a matrix of conditional transition probabilities. The input image, represented as a vector representation through a Convolutional Neural Network (CNN), is fed to the network, and for each input (i.e. the activation maps of the CNN) the network predicts the character. CTC, combined with CNNs and RNNs, often yielded competitive results, such as shown by Puigcerver (2017) and Bluche and Messina (2017). Furthermore, approaches applying only CNNs and CTC also exist (Chaudhary and Bali, 2021, 2022). Easter2.0 achieved competitive results on IAM (Marti and Bunke, 2002), a frequently used HTR data set consisting of English handwritten text.

A recent work that achieved SOTA results on IAM is TrOCR (Li et al., 2022), based on the transformer (Vaswani et al., 2017), consisting of a vision encoder and a text decoder. This deviated from previous approaches where primarily CNNs and RNNs were used. This development is closely linked to the emergence of the transformer in the vision domain (Dosovitskiy et al., 2021; Bao et al., 2022). Barrere et al. (2022) introduce another transformer model also using CTC, with the main difference to TrOCR being a different embedding technique for visual features based on a CNN. The results have also been shown to be competitive on the IAM data set. Diaz et al. (2021) compare encoder-decoder models' performance on HTR, using different models in the encoder and decoder parts, e.g. a transformer encoder plus a CTC-based decoder. Furthermore, they found that enriching this architecture with a language model yields SOTA results on IAM. The TrOCR framework has already been successfully applied to historical data akin to our task. Ströbel et al. (2022) fine-tune a TrOCR instance to handwritten Latin from the 16th century (Stotz and Ströbel, 2021, referred to as *Gwalther*), achieving competitive results.

3 Data

Our data set comprises 114,653 images, holding 3,507 distinct lemmas. All images are in RGB, but not uniform in size. The information on the corresponding lemma is available on the image level. Most lemmas start with the letter `"s"`, followed by a large number of lemmas starting with the letters `"m"`, `"v"`, `"t"`, `"u"`, `"l"`, and `"n"`. We observe lemmas from a length of one character up to 19 characters, with an average length between five and six characters. A total of 2,420 lemmas (69%) appear on ten record cards or less; 854 lemmas (24.4%), on 10 to 100 record cards, and just 233 lemmas (6.6%) on more than 100 record cards. 1,123 lemmas (36.7%) only occur on one card.

4 Lemma Extraction Pipeline

4.1 Visual Detection

Since the lemmas are always located in the upper left corner, but not annotated with their exact locations, training a custom object detection model for extraction is not feasible. In order to still retrieve the locations of the bounding boxes for some lemmas, we use the One For All (OFA) transformer (Wang et al., 2022), fine-tuned on RefCOCO (Kazemzadeh et al., 2014). To ensure the quality of the extracted lemma, we experiment with multiple prompts and examine their results (cf. Appendix A). After obtaining a training data set of 20,000 instances, we train a YOLOv8 model (Jocher et al., 2023) based on the You Only Look Once (YOLO) architecture (Redmon et al., 2016). The model predictions from our YOLO model, are then subject to two post-processing steps to ensure the quality of the images:

For 17,674 images (15.42% of the data), the model predicted **multiple bounding boxes**. We visually examined the cases and found that other handwritten text was often recognized as a lemma, sometimes scattered throughout the record cards (cf. Fig. 5, Appendix B). We further visually examined 202 cases where **no bounding box** was detected, stemming mostly from machine writing or scanning errors. For some images that follow the standard layout of the record cards, the model also failed. We disregard this set constituting less than 0.2% of the entire data set.

Taking all aspects into account, we introduce two rules to determine the appropriate bounding box: (1) choose the largest bounding box in (2) the upper left quarter of the entire image. The result after applying these rules is displayed in Figure 6 (Appendix B). The final data set consists of 114,451 samples, exhibiting a difference of the 202 samples to the initial 114,653 image-label pairs. We make our data available on HuggingFace.[2]

[2] `https://huggingface.co/misoda`

4.2 HTR Model

We use a transformer as the main model akin to TrOCR. For the encoder, we consider three different architectures, while we use GPT-2 (Radford et al., 2019) as a decoder model for all setups. All models are trained from scratch, although we use pre-trained image processors for the encoder models and train a tokenizer for our custom alphabet.

Tokenizer We use a customized byte-level BPE tokenizer (Sennrich et al., 2016) (trained on the labels from our data) for the dictionary's vocabulary.

Vision Encoders We consider three different encoder architectures, namely Vision Transformer (ViT) (Dosovitskiy et al., 2021), Bidirectional Encoder representation for Image Transformers (BEiT) (Bao et al., 2022), and Shifted Window Transformer (Swin) (Liu et al., 2021).

Text Decoder We use the GPT-2 (Radford et al., 2019) architecture, a decoder-only transformer, which we train from scratch, i.e., we do not use the pre-trained weights since we deal with a specific task in a low-resource language setting.

Implementation Details We use the HuggingFace transformers library (Wolf et al., 2020) and PyTorch (Paszke et al., 2019) to train the HTR pipeline. Our codebase, containing all scripts (experiments and training) is available via GitHub[3], and the final model is on pypi.[4] All the experiments were conducted using a Tesla V100 GPU (16 GB).

5 Experiments

5.1 Standard Training Settings

After shuffling the data, we randomly split it into a train (85% – 97,283 samples) and a test (15% – 17,168 samples) set. In the train split, 94.53% (3,315) of the lemmas are present. For all training procedures, we use the AdamW optimizer (Loshchilov and Hutter, 2019) and did not engage in hyperparameter tuning. Further details are reported in Appendix C. For standard training, the model is trained using a data set that includes the cut images from the record cards as input and their respective lemmas as the labels to be predicted. We train each of the models for a total of 5 epochs. We assess the model performance using the CER, which is computed by summing up edit operations and dividing by the label length. To account for the varying length, we further utilize the weighted CER.

[3]https://github.com/slds-lmu/mlw-htr

[4]https://pypi.org/project/mlw-lectiomat/

5.2 Data Augmentation

To increase the diversity of the training data, we apply random rotation, blurring, or modifications related to color perception. For the augmentation setting, we increase the number of epochs to 20 (compared to 5 for the standard training). We use three different augmentation pipelines, one of which is randomly chosen with $p = \frac{1}{3}$.

Pipeline A applies blurring and modifications to sharpness. The intensity of these modifications is determined randomly and can range from no modification to higher intensity. **Pipeline B** alters brightness, contrast, saturation, sharpness, and hue. The specific alterations for each instance are again determined randomly, also including the possibility of no modifications at all. **Pipeline C** combines the modifications from the previous two. In addition to the described techniques, all augmentation pipelines include random masking, where rectangles of the images are blackened, and random rotation within a range of -10 to 10 degrees.

Decoder Pre-Training We experiment with decoder pre-training (10 epochs) on a corpus of the concatenated lemmas to incorporate prior knowledge about medieval Latin. After pre-training, we combine it with the encoder and continue training for 20 epochs as described in Section 5.1, using the same augmentation techniques outlined before.

5.3 Experimental Results

The main results of our work are reported in Table 1. The BEiT+GPT-2 architecture achieved the best results in case of the standard training regime, exhibiting a CER of 0.258, followed by Swin+GPT-2 (0.349) and ViT+GPT-2 (0.418). Applying the augmentation pipelines notably improves model performance compared to the standard training for all three models. The best model with augmentation is Swin+GPT-2, achieving a CER of 0.017. As for the other two models, the CER is 0.073 for ViT+GPT-2 and 0.110 for BEiT+GPT-2.

	ViT	Swin	BEiT
Standard	0.418	0.349	0.258
+ Data Augmentation	0.073	**0.017**	0.110
+ Decoder Pre-Training	0.049	0.018	0.114

Table 1: CERs for different encoder configurations.

Pre-training of the decoder does, on average, not lead to further improvement. ViT+GPT-2 is the exception, for which the CER drops to 0.049. We observe no improvements for the other models. To summarize, the best results are achieved when using a Swin+GPT-2 model with data augmentations, reaching a CER value of 0.017.

5.4 Ablation Study

To investigate the impact of data augmentation, we perform three ablations, removing individual steps from the augmentation pipelines. To quantify the individual effects of each augmentation technique, we train the model without a specific augmentation method and report the resulting CER.

Swin+GPT-2 (Full augmentation pipelines)	0.017
w/o masking augmentation	**0.015**
w/o rotation augmentation	0.021
w/o color augmentation	0.017

Table 2: CER-Results of different model configurations.

Excluding the masking step from the pipeline leads to an actual improvement of model performance while excluding random rotations or color-related augmentations results do not (cf. Tab. 2).

5.5 Google Cloud Vision Comparison

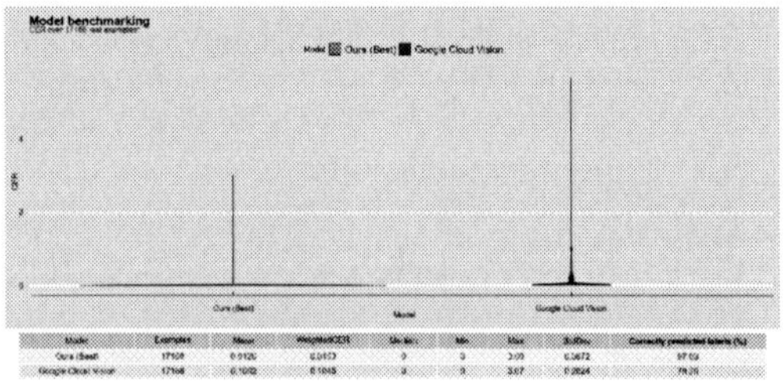

Figure 2: Comparison of Swin+GPT-2 to GCV.

To compare the results of our model, we decided to use Google Cloud Vision (GCV) a highly competitive HTR model, which has proven effective in practical applications (Thammarak et al., 2022). GCV often predicts extra characters and/or suffixes that are not part of the true lemma, which is why we post-process the predictions by GCV for a fair comparison by deleting extra characters and words after the first word or after a '-' or a '('. Figure 2 shows the comparison of our model with GCV. The violin plots of the (unweighted) CERs show a concentration of the CER values around 0 for both models. For our model, the most extreme values are at a CER of 3, for GCV the maximum is nearly twice as high and we observe an overall higher standard deviation compared to our model. To conclude, our best model exhibits a weighted CER of 0.0153, while GCV only reaches 0.1045. Overall, our model correctly predicts 97,09% of all lemmas, while GCV only does so for 78.26%.

5.6 Performance of other HTR systems

Table 3 illustrates the CERs of other systems on different HTR data sets. Ströbel et al. (2022) use Gwalther, while all other papers evaluate their systems on IAM. Our model achieves the lowest CER. However, it must be considered that we did not evaluate the same data set, which makes a direct comparison impossible. In contrast to the other transformer-based models, our best model uses Swin as an encoder.

Model	CER	Data set	Architecture
Ours (Best)	**0.0153**	MLW	Transformer
TrOCR Large (Ströbel et al., 2022)	0.0255	Gwalther	Transformer
TrOCR Large (Li et al., 2022)	0.0289	IAM	Transformer
EASTER2.0 (Chaudhary and Bali, 2022)	0.0621	IAM	CNN+CTC
Light Transformer (Barrere et al., 2022)	0.0570	IAM	CNN+Transformer
Self-Att.+CTC+LM (Diaz et al., 2021)	0.0275	IAM	Trf.+CTC+ LM

Table 3: Performance of contemporary HTR systems.

6 Conclusion and Outlook

Since the record cards include much more information than the one we extracted, we recommend further research into various extraction techniques. With the recent publication of Segment Anything Model, Kirillov et al. (2023) introduce a model that might be able to extract further features from the record cards with much higher accuracy.

We present a novel end-to-end pipeline for the Medieval Latin dictionary. Our library includes an image-detection-based model for lemma extraction and a tailored HTR model. We experiment with training different configurations of transformers using the ViT, BEiT, and Swin encoders while using a GPT-2 decoder. Employing data augmentation, our best model (Swin+GPT-2) achieves a CER of 0.015. The evaluation of the results exhibits a weaker performance on longer lemmas and on lemmas that appear less frequently in the training data. Further experiments with generative models to produce synthetic data (not reported in the paper) were not successful, however, we recommend further research into this direction. To conclude, our approach presents a promising HTR solution for Medieval Latin. Future research can build upon our work, and explore its generalizability to other languages and data sets by making use of our pip-installable Python package.

Limitations

Our approach has several limitations that can be addressed to improve its efficiency further. There are issues regarding the data set (cf. Sec. 3) that might be reflected in the model's performance. As discussed in Section 3, some lemmas are stroked out partially or entirely, introducing a notable noise to the data. Further, handwritten comments or other annotations have been added to some of the record cards, and some images are not correctly labeled, which might have distorted the recognition capabilities of our model.

Since our pipeline was mostly trained on data from the *S*-series of the dictionary, many words starting with other letters were not seen by the model during training. Therefore, the performance of the proposed approach, when applied to other series, remains somewhat uncertain. As elaborated in section 6, the model tends to perform weaker on unseen lemmas. Further, there are indications that the model might perform worse on longer lemmas.

The lemma-detection model (YOLOv8) is not guaranteed to predict the correct bounding box for the lemma consistently. Errors at this early stage of the pipeline may severely impact the result. Although the failure rate for the training dataset in which no bounding box was predicted is close to zero, the problem can still appear during inference.

We did neither experiment with the initial TrOCR architecture nor did we fine-tune a pretrained TrOCR instance for this task. However, the results of Ströbel et al. (2022) suggest a strong performance of TrOCR. Thus, we recommend training it on the MLW data set.

Ethics Statement

We affirm that our research adheres to the ACL Ethics Policy. This work involves the use of publicly available data sets and does not involve human subjects or any personally identifiable information. We declare that we have no conflicts of interest that could potentially influence the outcomes, interpretations, or conclusions of this research. All funding sources supporting this study are acknowledged. We have made our best effort to document our methodology, experiments, and results accurately and are committed to sharing our code, data, and other relevant resources to foster reproducibility and further advancements in research.

Acknowledgements

We would like to thank the three anonymous referees for their constructive comments and suggestions, which helped improve this paper considerably. We wish to thank the Bavarian Academy of Sciences for providing us with the guidance and required access to the handwritten material. This work has been partially funded by the Deutsche Forschungsgemeinschaft (DFG, German Research Foundation) as part of BERD@NFDI - grant number 460037581.

References

Hangbo Bao, Li Dong, Songhao Piao, and Furu Wei. 2022. Beit: Bert pre-training of image transformers.

Killian Barrere, Yann Soullard, Aurélie Lemaitre, and Bertrand Coüasnon. 2022. A light transformer-based architecture for handwritten text recognition. In *Document Analysis Systems*, pages 275–290, Cham. Springer International Publishing.

Théodore Bluche and Ronaldo Messina. 2017. Gated convolutional recurrent neural networks for multilingual handwriting recognition. In *2017 14th IAPR International Conference on Document Analysis and Recognition (ICDAR)*, volume 01, pages 646–651.

Kartik Chaudhary and Raghav Bali. 2021. Easter: Simplifying Text Recognition using only 1d Convolutions. *Proceedings of the Canadian Conference on Artificial Intelligence*. Https://caiac.pubpub.org/pub/fm5sy88o.

Kartik Chaudhary and Raghav Bali. 2022. Easter2.0: Improving convolutional models for handwritten text recognition.

Daniel Hernandez Diaz, Siyang Qin, Reeve Ingle, Yasuhisa Fujii, and Alessandro Bissacco. 2021. Rethinking text line recognition models.

Alexey Dosovitskiy, Lucas Beyer, Alexander Kolesnikov, Dirk Weissenborn, Xiaohua Zhai, Thomas Unterthiner, Mostafa Dehghani, Matthias Minderer, Georg Heigold, Sylvain Gelly, Jakob Uszkoreit, and Neil Houlsby. 2021. An image is worth 16x16 words: Transformers for image recognition at scale.

Alex Graves, Santiago Fernández, Faustino Gomez, and Jürgen Schmidhuber. 2006. Connectionist temporal classification: Labelling unsegmented sequence data with recurrent neural networks. In *Proceedings of the 23rd International Conference on Machine Learning*, ICML '06, page 369–376, New York, NY, USA. Association for Computing Machinery.

Glenn Jocher, Ayush Chaurasia, and Jing Qiu. 2023. YOLO by Ultralytics.

Sahar Kazemzadeh, Vicente Ordonez, Mark Matten, and Tamara Berg. 2014. ReferItGame: Referring to objects in photographs of natural scenes. In *Proceedings of the 2014 Conference on Empirical Methods in Natural Language Processing (EMNLP)*, pages 787–798, Doha, Qatar. Association for Computational Linguistics.

Alexander Kirillov, Eric Mintun, Nikhila Ravi, Hanzi Mao, Chloe Rolland, Laura Gustafson, Tete Xiao, Spencer Whitehead, Alexander C. Berg, Wan-Yen Lo, Piotr Dollár, and Ross Girshick. 2023. Segment anything.

Minghao Li, Tengchao Lv, Jingye Chen, Lei Cui, Yijuan Lu, Dinei Florencio, Cha Zhang, Zhoujun Li, and Furu Wei. 2022. Trocr: Transformer-based optical character recognition with pre-trained models.

Ze Liu, Yutong Lin, Yue Cao, Han Hu, Yixuan Wei, Zheng Zhang, Stephen Lin, and Baining Guo. 2021. Swin transformer: Hierarchical vision transformer using shifted windows.

Ilya Loshchilov and Frank Hutter. 2019. Decoupled weight decay regularization.

Urs-Viktor Marti and H. Bunke. 2002. The iam-database: An english sentence database for offline handwriting recognition. *International Journal on Document Analysis and Recognition*, 5:39–46.

Adam Paszke, Sam Gross, Francisco Massa, Adam Lerer, James Bradbury, Gregory Chanan, Trevor Killeen, Zeming Lin, Natalia Gimelshein, Luca Antiga, Alban Desmaison, Andreas Köpf, Edward Yang, Zach DeVito, Martin Raison, Alykhan Tejani, Sasank Chilamkurthy, Benoit Steiner, Lu Fang, Junjie Bai, and Soumith Chintala. 2019. Pytorch: An imperative style, high-performance deep learning library.

Joan Puigcerver. 2017. Are multidimensional recurrent layers really necessary for handwritten text recognition? In *2017 14th IAPR International Conference on Document Analysis and Recognition (ICDAR)*, volume 01, pages 67–72.

Alec Radford, Jeffrey Wu, Rewon Child, David Luan, Dario Amodei, Ilya Sutskever, et al. 2019. Language models are unsupervised multitask learners. *OpenAI blog*, 1(8):9.

Joseph Redmon, Santosh Divvala, Ross Girshick, and Ali Farhadi. 2016. You only look once: Unified, real-time object detection.

Rico Sennrich, Barry Haddow, and Alexandra Birch. 2016. Neural machine translation of rare words with subword units.

Peter Stotz and Phillip Ströbel. 2021. bullinger-digital/gwalther-handwriting-ground- truth: Initial release.

Phillip Benjamin Ströbel, Simon Clematide, Martin Volk, and Tobias Hodel. 2022. Transformer-based htr for historical documents.

Karanrat Thammarak, Prateep Kongkla, Yaowarat Sirisathitkul, and Sarun Intakosum. 2022. Comparative analysis of tesseract and google cloud vision for thai vehicle registration certificate. *International Journal of Electrical and Computer Engineering*, 22:1849–1858.

Ashish Vaswani, Noam Shazeer, Niki Parmar, Jakob Uszkoreit, Llion Jones, Aidan N. Gomez, Lukasz Kaiser, and Illia Polosukhin. 2017. Attention is all you need.

Peng Wang, An Yang, Rui Men, Junyang Lin, Shuai Bai, Zhikang Li, Jianxin Ma, Chang Zhou, Jingren Zhou, and Hongxia Yang. 2022. Ofa: Unifying architectures, tasks, and modalities through a simple sequence-to-sequence learning framework.

Thomas Wolf, Lysandre Debut, Victor Sanh, Julien Chaumond, Clement Delangue, Anthony Moi, Pierric Cistac, Tim Rault, Rémi Louf, Morgan Funtowicz, Joe Davison, Sam Shleifer, Patrick von Platen, Clara Ma, Yacine Jernite, Julien Plu, Canwen Xu, Teven Le Scao, Sylvain Gugger, Mariama Drame, Quentin Lhoest, and Alexander M. Rush. 2020. Huggingface's transformers: State-of-the-art natural language processing.

Syed Sahil Abbas Zaidi, Mohammad Samar Ansari, Asra Aslam, Nadia Kanwal, Mamoona Asghar, and Brian Lee. 2021. A survey of modern deep learning based object detection models.

Appendix

A Annotatong the Bounding Boxes

This Appendix holds the details of the Visual Detection part of the pipeline, described in Section 4.1, and the challenges we were confronted with.

A.1 The Task

To annotate the bounding boxes, the model is provided with a prompt describing the lemma and the image. The model then returns a bounding box for the requested object, which is the lemma in our case. Different prompts are described in Table 4.

Prompt 1		`Cursive text upper left`
Prompt 2		`Handwritten cursive word upper left`
Prompt 3	Length: 1-5:	`Blue drawing in the upper left`
	Other:	`Handwritten cursive word upper left`
Prompt 4	Length: 1-6:	`Blue drawing in the upper left`
	Other:	`Handwritten cursive word upper left`

Table 4: Different prompts used for OFA.

A.2 Assumption about Bounding Boxes

Since we do not have any ground truth about the bounding boxes, we rely on heuristics to verify the correctness of the boxes. One such heuristic is the assumed linear relationship between the lemma length and the bounding box's width. While the height of the boxes is assumed to be similar across instances, the lemma length must significantly impact the bounding box's width. To verify the results of the annotation process, we use box plots to visualize the relationship between lemma length and width (cf. Fig. 3a – 3d).

A.3 Initial Implementation and Results

We use the RefCOCO-OFA model[5] and modify it four our purposes. Prompt one (cf. Tab. 4) is used to obtain the lemmas for all images.

After running the model on the first instances with *Prompt 1*, we find that the relationship between the box's width and the lemma length does not look as expected. Figure 3 illustrates this problem. Investigating the short lemmas, we observe that the model often fails to annotate the record cards appropriately. Often other textual objects are annotated, or the bounding box stretches throughout the entire record card.

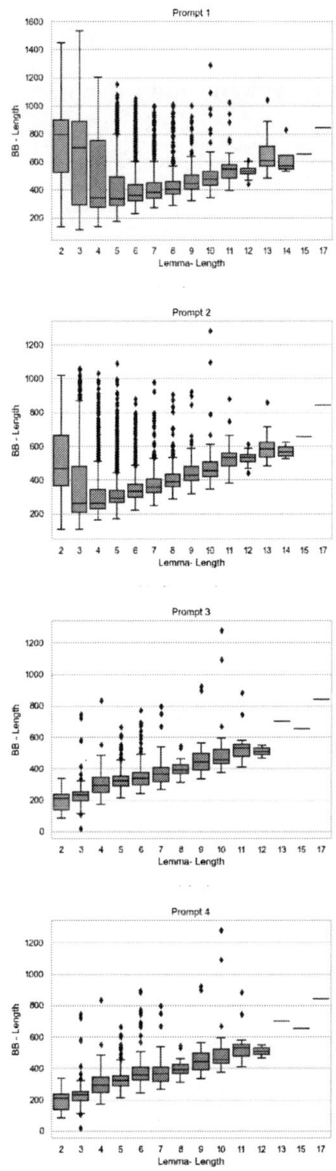

(d) Fourth and final Prompt

Figure 3: Box-Plots for the width of the bounding boxes based on the lemma's length.

A.4 Two Different Prompts for Shorter and Longer Lemmata

After different experiments, *Prompt 2* turned out to work appropriately for shorter lemmas, but was, however, not suitable for longer ones. To combine the strength of both prompts, we apply a conditional prompt based on the length of the lemma using different cut-offs (5 or 6 characters). We find that using *Prompt 4* is the best-suited approach. The analysis of the relationship between the bound-

[5]Huggingface: `OFA-Base-RefCOCO`

ing box widths and the length of the lemma for different prompts can be seen in Figure 3.

B YOLO: Training and Inference

B.1 Training Results

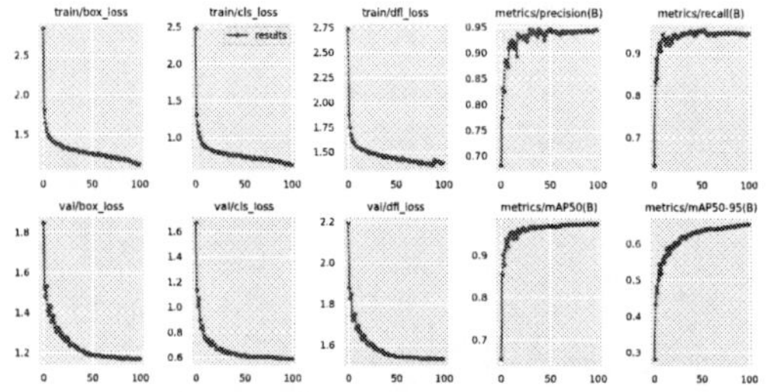

Figure 4: YOLO Training Results.

B.2 Multiple Lemmas Detected by YOLO

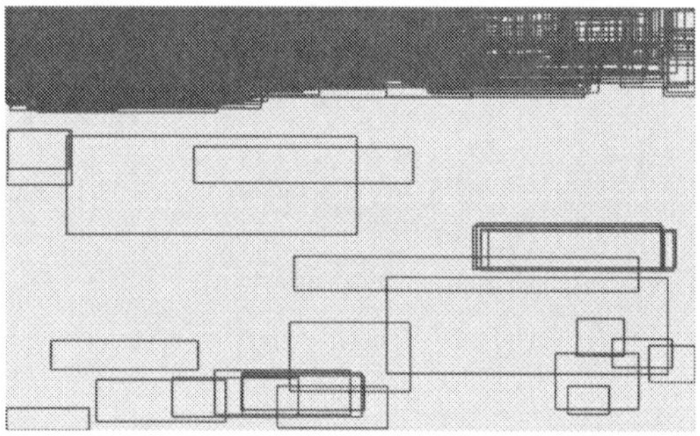

Figure 5: All bounding boxes from instances where YOLO has detected more than one bounding box.

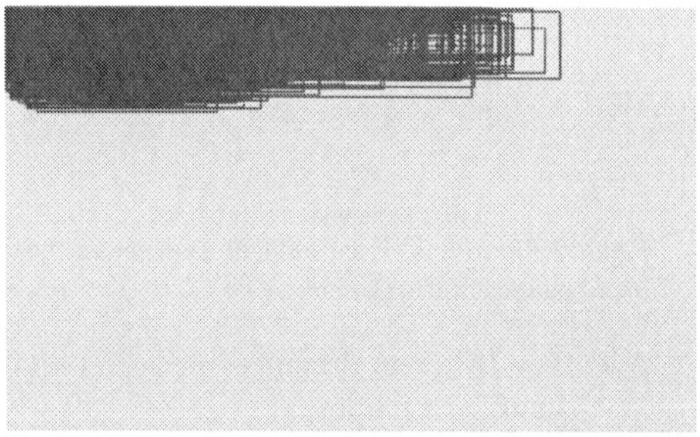

Figure 6: Bounding boxes of all instances to which the rule *largest bounding box in the upper left corner* was applied to.

C Training details

We used the defaults from `transformers` (4.26.1), if not reported otherwise.

C.1 Standard Training

Parameter	Value
Seed	42
Optimizer	AdamW
Epochs	5
Decoder	GPT-2
Encoder	{BEIT, Swin, ViT}
Batch Size (Train & Test)	64

Table 5: Parameters for the standard training.

C.2 Training with Augmentation

Parameter	Value
Seed	42
Optimizer	AdamW
Epochs	{5, 20}
Decoder	GPT-2
Encoder	{BEIT, Swin, ViT}
Batch Size (Train & Test)	64

Table 6: Parameters for training with augmentation.

C.3 Natural Language Generation

Parameter	Value
Max Length	32
Early Stopping	True
No Repeat Ngram Size	3
Length Penalty	2.0
Number of Beams	4

Table 7: Parameters for natural language generation.

C.4 Decoder Pre-Training

Parameter	Value
Seed	42
Epochs	10
Batch Size (Train & Test)	192

Table 8: Parameters for pre-training of the decoder.

Evaluating Existing Lemmatisers on Unedited Byzantine Greek Poetry

Colin Swaelens[1], **Ilse De Vos**[2] and **Els Lefever**[1]
[1] LT3, Language and Translation Technology Team
Department of Translation, Interpreting and Communication, Ghent University
[2] Department of Linguistics, Ghent University
9000 Ghent, Belgium
{colin.swaelens, i.devos, els.lefever}@ugent.be

Abstract

This paper reports on the results of a comparative evaluation of four existing lemmatizers, all pre-trained on Ancient Greek texts, on a novel corpus of unedited, Byzantine Greek texts. The aim of this study is to get insights into the pitfalls of existing lemmatisation approaches as well as the specific challenges of our Byzantine Greek corpus, in order to develop a new lemmatizer that can cope with its peculiarities. The results of the experiment show an accuracy drop of 20% on our corpus, which is further investigated in a qualitative error analysis.

1 Introduction

If Ancient Greek is considered a low-resourced language, Byzantine Greek is even lower-resourced. What Ancient and Byzantine Greek have in common, is that their texts have been continuously copied by hand until the end of the 15th century. So when we read, for instance, Plato's *Apology*, we read a collation of a philologist who aspires to reconstruct Plato's original 4th-century text *based on* the existing Medieval manuscripts; *based on* but not copied from these manuscripts, as linguistic inconsistencies or orthographic mistakes are adapted to fit the dialect in which the text was conceived. Existing NLP tools for historical Greek are developed for this variant of Greek, that was edited to perfection.

However, because of a growing research interest and progress in optical character recognition (OCR) and, even more relevant, handwritten text recognition (HTR) (e.g. Tsochatzidis et al. 2021; Platanou et al. 2022; Ströbel et al. 2022), more and more unedited Greek texts will become available. These unedited texts contain, among other things, lacunae due to a damaged piece of parchment, omissions of words due to sloppiness or fatigue of the scribe or funky orthography due to phonetic changes. Although no substantial HTR-based corpus is available for Greek, two online available corpora do offer the unedited texts from manuscripts: the Trismegistos (Depauw and Gheldof, 2014) project and the Database of Byzantine Book Epigrams (DBBE) (Ricceri et al., 2023). Both Trismegistos and DBBE do store the edited as well as the unedited version of texts found in papyri and manuscripts, respectively. The DBBE provides Byzantine[1] book epigrams, which are metrical paratexts as they are written in the margin, next to (παρά, para) the main text of a manuscript. The literal transcription of these poems are stored as so-called *Occurrences*, which are linked to a normalised version called *Type*.

Our aim is to develop a linguistic annotation pipeline for the latter, unedited Greek texts. The differences between Ancient and Medieval Greek are thoroughly described by Swaelens et al. (Forthcoming 2023), the features relevant for this work are elaborated upon in Section 3. A new approach for part-of-speech tagging and morphological analysis was developed (Swaelens et al., 2023), as the existing techniques are not capable of handling the idiosyncrasies these unedited texts display. Before diving into the development of the last step of the pipeline, i.e. the lemmatizer, we wanted to evaluate existing systems for lemmatisation on our gold standard of unedited, Byzantine Greek texts.

2 Related Research

The first lemmatizer for Greek was developed by Packard (1973), as part of the first lin-

[1] Byzantine and Medieval will be used as synonyms to refer to the period from the 5th until 15th century.

Proceedings of the Ancient Language Processing Workshop associated with RANLP-2023, pages 111–116,
held in Varna Bulgaria, Sept 8, 2023.
https://doi.org/10.26615/978-954-452-087-8_013

guistic annotation pipeline. In order to perform morphological analysis, first suffixes are removed to retrieve the stem of every token. Then, a dictionary made by Packard, is searched with a binary search algorithm to find the matching stem. Based on this dictionary search, the algorithm returns the lemma that is linked to the matching stem. If multiple lemmas are possible, a philologist is needed to discern which lemma was the correct one.

In 2003, the biggest online resource of Greek texts, the Thesaurus Linguae Graecae (TLG) (Pantelia, 2022) started their lemmatization project. Few details on the methodology are provided in the paper, except that the TLG *digitised and extracted a large number of headwords from dictionaries*[2]. The authors, however, claim that the lemmatizer is capable of recognising automatically 98.3% of all tokens in the TLG.

RNN Tagger (Schmid, 2019) was developed as the combination of a morphological tagger and lemmatizer for historical texts. Schmid has made use of a character-based bi-LSTM network to cope with – systematic – spelling variations and improve tagging accuracy. The lemmatizer is also based on a recurrent neural network, making use of the dl4mt machine translation system (He et al., 2016). In his experiments, Schmid did also train and test his tagger on the Ancient Greek Dependency Treebank, which resulted in a tagging accuracy of 91.29%.

The Classical Language Toolkit (CLTK), is an NLP framework developed for pre-modern languages (Johnson et al., 2021). This framework stores several lemmatizers, among which a back-off lemmatizer (Burns, 2020) that makes use of several, sequenced lemmatizers. CLTK's default lemmatizer for Ancient Greek makes use of the Stanza (Qi et al., 2020) lemmatization algorithm, that has been pretrained on the PROIEL treebanks (Haug and Jøhndal, 2008). This algorithm consists of a dictionary-based lemmatizer combined with a neural sequence-to-sequence lemmatizer. On the encoder's output of this combination, an additional classifier is added to cope with, among other things, lowercasing. The authors, however, did not provide an accuracy score of how well the algorithm performs on Ancient Greek.

Burns' back-off lemmatizer, which is included in the CLTK, is a sequence of five lemmatizers. The token first passes a dictionary-based lemmatizer to tag frequently occurring, indeclinable words; then it passes through a unigram-model lemmatizer that is based on training data of the Ancient Greek and Latin Dependency Treebanks (Celano, 2019); third in the sequence is a rule-based lemmatizer that makes use of regular expressions; the fourth lemmatizer is a variation of the previous, regular expression-based lemmatizer that factors in principal-part information; finally, the token is passed through another dictionary-based lemmatizer making use of Morpheus' (Crane, 1991) lemma dictionary. Should none of these lemmatizers output a proper lemma, the token itself is returned as lemma. Vatri and McGillivray (2020) report an accuracy of 91% on poetry and 93% on prose.

Where CLTK's default lemmatizer disambiguates ambiguous tokens based on frequency, the GLEM lemmatizer (Bary et al., 2017) makes use of part-of-speech information to disambiguate. Even more interesting, is that GLEM provides a lemma for out-of-vocabulary words. This is achieved by combining a dictionary-based approach with a memory-based machine learning algorithm, called FROG (Bosch et al., 2007). If the to-be-tagged word occurs only once in the lexicon, consisting of the PROIEL and Perseus (Celano, 2019) corpora, GLEM returns the lexicon's lemma; if not, the word is considered ambiguous and FROG is applied. If several lemmas are possible, GLEM evaluates whether there is exactly one match with the part-of-speech tag predicted by the FROG algorithm and the lexicon. If so, the lemma is assigned; if there are several possible or no matching part-of-speech tags, frequency information is used to assign a lemma from the lexicon.

The interest in lemmatizing Greek has increased, proved by Keersmaekers and Van Hal (2022) and de Graaf et al. (2022). That is, both articles discover how corpora which cannot be lumped together with classical, literary Greek prose, could be lemmatized. Keersmaekers and Van Hal, on the one hand, aim to

[2]`https://stephanus.tlg.uci.edu/history.php`

lemmatize the papyri texts stored in Trismegistos, de Graaf et al., on the other hand, look into lemmatizing Greek inscriptions. Just like the unedited texts we want to tag, these corpora had some peculiarities that deviate from the polished, classical Greek on which the existing lemmatizers are based.

Although several other lemmatizers do exist, they are not part of this assessment because they are either not freely available or do not disambiguate ambiguous word forms. We did not test TreeTagger (Schmid, 1994) since the parameter files[3] do not contain any information on lemmas. Neither Morpheus (Crane, 1991) nor Eleuxis[4] have been part of our comparison as neither of those disambiguate ambiguous tokens.

3 Comparative Experiment

To evaluate the lemmatizers described in Section 2, we annotated about 10,000 tokens from the DBBE *occurrences* (Swaelens et al., 2023). The DBBE *occurrences* are the literal transcription, viz. without any editing, of the text that is found in a manuscript. As already mentioned in Section 1, these *occurrences* are linked to edited, normalised versions called *Types*, as shown in Example 1. Example 1a shows the *occurrence*, the text as it is found in the manuscript Vat.gr.1908[5], Example 1b the *Type* to which the *Occurrence* is linked and its translation (translated by the authors) is given in Example 1c.

(1) a. ὧς περ' ξένη χἔρονιτες ἡδῆν π(ατ)ρίδα
DBBE Occurrence 17870

b. Ὥσπερ ξένοι χαίρουσιν ἰδεῖν πατρίδα
DBBE Type 2820

c. Just like travellers rejoice upon seeing their homeland

[3]Available at https://www.cis.uni-muenchen.de/~schmid/tools/TreeTagger/

[4]https://outils.biblissima.fr/en/eulexis-web/index.php

[5]This book epigram is situated on f.118v and online consultable via https://digi.vatlib.it/view/MSS_Vat.gr.1908/0121

This example displays one of the main characteristics of the Greek found in manuscripts before they are edited: orthographic inconsistencies. Since the itacism – a phonetic shift that turned η, ι, υ, ει and οι into the phoneme /i/ – has made its introduction in the 3rd century, quite some orthographic inconsistencies are to be found in the manuscripts. In Example 1a both the first syllable, ἡδ- (the stem of the word), and the second, -ῆν (the suffix indicating the Greek infinitive), are affected by the itacism. This makes the word ἰδεῖν almost unrecognisable, which is why we hypothesise that a dictionary-based approach might be put at a disadvantage.

For our comparative study, all lemmatizers discussed in Section 2, CLTK, GLEM, RNN Tagger, and the Stanza tagger, are used to lemmatize our gold standard containing 10,000 tokens of unedited, Byzantine Greek text. Before feeding the data to the lemmatizers, we removed all redundant white spaces and deleted all punctuation.

4 Results

The results of the comparitive experiments are shown in Table 1. First of all, We observe a general accuracy drop of 20% or more compared to the results of the lemmatizers on Ancient, edited Greek. This was expected, because our data is very challenging. Second, the sequential back-off lemmatizer comes out best, performing almost 7% better than the Stanza lemmatizer, which performed worst. To gain more insight in the results of the tested lemmatizers,we performed a qualitative analysis of the system output, which revealed some tendencies of the problems related to our corpus.

Lemmatizer	Accuracy
Stanza	64.99%
RNN Tagger	66.67%
GLEM	70.82%
CLTK	71.69%

Table 1: Performance of existing lemmatizers on Byzantine Greek poetry.

This comparative study uncovered an encoding problem in our test set: the transcriptions of the manuscripts stored in DBBE make use of multiple unicode characters for identical characters. The acute accent, for example, is present in the DBBE as two different unicode characters. That is, the ί in πατρίδα (Example 1) has two different unicode representations within the DBBE corpus. Consequently, every deviation from the unicode character that is stored in DBBE or its annotations has been evaluated as incorrect. What is more, the Stanza lemmatizer outputs unicode characters that are different from those CLTK and RNN Tagger output.

The diachronic and/or diatopic alterations that are inherent to the Greek language, hinders the evaluation of the taggers as well. Verbs whose stem ends in a velar occlusive, have a lemma that ends either in -ττω (the classic, Athenian variant), or -σσω (other dialects' variant). The token φύλαττε (*keep guard*) has been annotated as coming from the lemma φυλάττω, while all lemmatizers returned φυλάσσω as lemma. Although this is a correct prediction, it was considered as incorrect by the automatic evaluation. In this same category belongs the alteration between ι and υ, observable in the – identical – words βίβλος and βύβλος (*papyrus roll*).[6] The alteration of a word's final consonant, is the last example that fits within this category. The preposition ἐκ (*out*) is written as ἐξ when followed by a vowel. Again, these double forms caused unjust penalties in the lemmatizers' output. In order to cope with these inconsistencies, we harmonised the different outputs, mainly caused by the unicode difference between the *tonos* and *oxia* accent (Tauber, 2019). The new lemmatisation results, however, show a minor impact of the encoding problems and inconsistencies, resulting in improvements of only 0.04 to 0.6 %, which makes no difference for the final ranking of the tested lemmatizers.

The lemmatizers also have a hard time assigning the correct lemma to a verb in the perfect tense. This might be due to the very low presence of this tense in general in Greek. It is, however, surprising that the back-off lemmatizer cannot extract and match the stem of, e.g., πεφευγώς (*having fled*) to its lemma φεύγω (*to flee*). What is even more surprising, is that GLEM did not even return a lemma of this quite frequent word, while it was stated that GLEM could output lemmas it had never seen before.

A GLEM-specific remark is how much this lemmatizer is affected by the absence of the iota subscriptum[7] in, e.g., the dative case. In DBBE this iota is sometimes written, now underneath the vowel, then next to it, and sometimes not written. Not once did it correctly lemmatize τω as a form of the article ὁ, while τῷ has been lemmatized correctly. The iota adscriptum is not yet part of the test set.

5 Conclusion & Future Research

As a last step in the development of our new annotation pipeline that cannot only handle classical Greek texts but also unedited, Byzantine texts, we are exploring the field of lemmatizing Greek. We compared four freely available lemmatizers that are capable of coping with ambiguity: CLTK back-off lemmatizer, GLEM, RNN Tagger and the Stanza lemmatizer. The back-off lemmatizer performed best, which might be attributed to the fact that it combines five different lemmatizers. The error analysis provided us with useful insights, which we will take into account while developing our own lemmatizer for Byzantine Greek.

At the moment of writing, we are looking into a cascaded system that combines a rule-based module with a dictionary look-up as a first step. In addition, a machine-learning component will be developed to handle all tokens that cannot be lemmatized by the first part. We are investigating several possible algorithms, going from a decision tree model to a neural approach. Furthermore, we will need to cope with the abundance of unicode characters and provide a mapping to evaluate our output correctly. We also need to develop a strategy to deal with the alterations that are inherent to the language to make evaluation easier and more correct, namely a mapping of (1) the five ways to write the /i/ sound, (2) the iota subscriptum or adscriptum and (3) forms like -σσω/-ττω. Finally, we will experiment with the presence or absence of diacritics and their possible impact on the machine learning.

[6]This alteration is not to be confused with the itacism; this alteration is already attested before the itacism appeared.

[7]When a long vowel is followed by a iota, ι /j/, the iota is written either underneath (*subscriptum*) or next to that vowel (*adscriptum*).

References

Corien Bary, Peter Berck, and Iris Hendrickx. 2017. A memory-based lemmatizer for ancient greek. In *Proceedings of the 2nd International Conference on Digital Access to Textual Cultural Heritage*, DATeCH2017, page 91–95, New York, NY, USA. Association for Computing Machinery.

Antal van den Bosch, Bertjan Busser, Sander Canisius, and Walter Daelemans. 2007. An efficient memory-based morphosyntactic tagger and parser for dutch. *LOT Occasional Series*, 7:191–206.

Patrick J Burns. 2020. Ensemble lemmatization with the classical language toolkit. *Studi e Saggi Linguistici*, 58(1):157–176.

Giuseppe G.A. Celano. 2019. *The Dependency Treebanks for Ancient Greek and Latin*, pages 279–298. De Gruyter Saur, Berlin, Boston.

Gregory R. Crane. 1991. Generating and Parsing Classical Greek. *Literary and Linguistic Computing*, 6(4):243–245.

Evelien de Graaf, Silvia Stopponi, Jasper K. Bos, Saskia Peels-Matthey, and Malvina Nissim. 2022. AGILe: The first lemmatizer for Ancient Greek inscriptions. In *Proceedings of the Thirteenth Language Resources and Evaluation Conference*, pages 5334–5344, Marseille, France. European Language Resources Association.

Mark Depauw and Tom Gheldof. 2014. Trismegistos: An interdisciplinary platform for ancient world texts and related information. In *Theory and Practice of Digital Libraries – TPDL 2013 Selected Workshops*, pages 40–52, Cham. Springer International Publishing.

Dag TT Haug and Marius Jøhndal. 2008. Creating a parallel treebank of the old indo-european bible translations. In *Proceedings of the second workshop on language technology for cultural heritage data (LaTeCH 2008)*, pages 27–34.

Di He, Yingce Xia, Tao Qin, Liwei Wang, Nenghai Yu, Tie-Yan Liu, and Wei-Ying Ma. 2016. Dual learning for machine translation. *Advances in neural information processing systems*, 29.

Kyle P. Johnson, Patrick J. Burns, John Stewart, Todd Cook, Clément Besnier, and William J. B. Mattingly. 2021. The Classical Language Toolkit: An NLP framework for pre-modern languages. In *Proceedings of the 59th Annual Meeting of the Association for Computational Linguistics and the 11th International Joint Conference on Natural Language Processing: System Demonstrations*, pages 20–29, Online. Association for Computational Linguistics.

Alek Keersmaekers and Toon Van Hal. 2022. In search of the flocks: How to perform onomasiological queries in an Ancient Greek corpus? In *Proceedings of the Second Workshop on Language Technologies for Historical and Ancient Languages*, pages 73–83, Marseille, France. European Language Resources Association.

David W. Packard. 1973. Computer-assisted morphological analysis of Ancient Greek. In *COLING 1973 Volume 2: Computational And Mathematical Linguistics: Proceedings of the International Conference on Computational Linguistics*.

Maria C. Pantelia. 2022. *Thesaurus Linguae Graecae, A Bibliographic Guide to the Canon of Greek Authors and Works*. University of California Press, Berkeley.

Paraskevi Platanou, John Pavlopoulos, and Georgios Papaioannou. 2022. Handwritten paleographic Greek text recognition: A century-based approach. In *Proceedings of the Thirteenth Language Resources and Evaluation Conference*, pages 6585–6589, Marseille, France. European Language Resources Association.

Peng Qi, Yuhao Zhang, Yuhui Zhang, Jason Bolton, and Christopher D. Manning. 2020. Stanza: A Python natural language processing toolkit for many human languages. In *Proceedings of the 58th Annual Meeting of the Association for Computational Linguistics: System Demonstrations*.

Rachele Ricceri, Klaas Bentein, Floris Bernard, Antoon Bronselaer, Els De Paermentier, Pieterjan De Potter, Guy De Tré, Ilse De Vos, Maxime Deforche, Kristoffel Demoen, Els Lefever, Anne-Sophie Rouckhout, and Colin Swaelens. 2023. The database of byzantine book epigrams project: Principles, challenges, opportunities. *Journal of Data Mining & Digital Humanities*.

Helmut Schmid. 1994. Probabilistic part-of-speech tagging using decision trees. In *Proceedings of the International Conference on New Methods in Language Processing*, Manchester, UK.

Helmut Schmid. 2019. Deep learning-based morphological taggers and lemmatizers for annotating historical texts. In *Proceedings of the 3rd International Conference on Digital Access to Textual Cultural Heritage*, DATeCH2019, page 133–137, New York, NY, USA. Association for Computing Machinery.

Phillip Benjamin Ströbel, Martin Volk, Simon Clematide, Raphael Schwitter, Tobias Hodel, and David Schoch. 2022. Evaluation of HTR models without ground truth material. In *Proceedings of the Thirteenth Language Resources and Evaluation Conference*, pages 4395–4404, Marseille, France. European Language Resources Association.

Colin Swaelens, Ilse De Vos, and Els Lefever. 2023. Medieval social media: Manual and automatic annotation of byzantine Greek marginal writing. In *Proceedings of the 17th Linguistic Annotation Workshop (LAW-XVII)*, pages 1–9, Toronto, Canada. Association for Computational Linguistics.

Colin Swaelens, Ilse De Vos, and Els Lefever. Forthcoming 2023. Linguistic annotation of byzantine book epigrams. *Language Resources and Evaluation*.

James K. Tauber. 2019. *Character Encoding of Classical Languages*, pages 137–158. De Gruyter Saur, Berlin, Boston.

Lazaros Tsochatzidis, Symeon Symeonidis, Alexandros Papazoglou, and Ioannis Pratikakis. 2021. Htr for greek historical handwritten documents. *Journal of Imaging*, 7(12).

Alessandro Vatri and Barbara McGillivray. 2020. Lemmatization for ancient greek: An experimental assessment of the state of the art. *Journal of Greek Linguistics*, 20(2):179 – 196.

Vector-Based Stylistic Analysis on Ancient Chinese Books: Take the *Three Commentaries on the Spring and Autumn Annals* as an Example

Yue Qi [1],Liu Liu [1]*, Bin Li [2], Dongbo Wang [1]
[1]College of Information Management, Nanjing Agricultural University,Nanjing,China
[2]School of Chinese Language and Literature, Nanjing Normal University,Nanjing,China
liuliu@njau.edu.cn

Abstract

Commentary of Gongyang, *Commentary of Guliang*, and *Commentary of Zuo* are collectively called the *Three Commentaries on the Spring and Autumn Annals*, which are the supplement and interpretation of the content of *Spring and Autumn Annals* with value in historical and literary research. In traditional research paradigms, scholars often explored the differences between the *Three Commentaries* within the details in contexts. Starting from the view of Stylistic Analysis, this paper examines the differences in the language style of the *Three Commentaries* through the representation of language, which takes the methods of deep learning. Specifically, this study vectorizes the context at word and sentence levels. It maps them into the same plane to find the differences between the use of words and sentences in the *Three Commentaries*. The results show that the *Commentary of Gongyang* and the *Commentary of Guliang* are relatively similar, while the *Commentary of Zuo* is significantly different. This paper verifies the feasibility of deep learning methods in stylistics study under computational humanities. It provides a valuable perspective for studying the *Three Commentaries on the Spring and Autumn Annals*.

1 Introduction

Style is an additional component in the process of language expression and expression. It changes due to the social era and environment in which language is used and in various forms due to the user's expression habits and intentions. This characteristic has received longstanding attention from stylistics. Among the study of ancient Chinese classics, *the Spring and Autumn Annals* was known as "having profound meaning in simple words." and the *Historical Records* were called "*Li Sao* without rhyme." These are classic summaries of ancient Chinese books. The language style can also be used to compare and analyze authors, such as Li Bai and Du Fu honored as "Poetic Immortal" and "Poetic Sage". For the study of stylistics, the traditional paradigm generally starts from vocabulary, rhetoric, sentence patterns, etc., with the help of examples, and forms an interpretive logic that is now called "close reading". Corresponding to this is the "distance reading" after the rise of digital humanities. With the help of many computational methods such as lexical statistics, quantitative linguistics, and natural language processing, the study of textual style has increasingly inclined towards results with precision value. This research paradigm, or computational humanities, provides new exploration perspectives for studying stylistics.

This study focuses on the style of ancient books in computational humanities. Compared with traditional methods, the advantage of the computational humanities lies in quantification, which is based on data and computation to obtain objective and verifiable conclusions. The study of stylistics under this paradigm also presents a variety of technical and theoretical frameworks due to the intersection of fields, forming a developing trend of mutual integration. This study of the style of ancient books depends on multi-level observations from Chinese characters to vocabulary and sentences. Representation learning can also provide more comprehensive quantification for the style analysis of ancient books.

This research focuses on the *Three Commentaries on the Spring and Autumn Annals* and related ancient books. The *Three Commentaries* are the most important classics among ancient Chinese books and have also received much attention in computational humanities. On the other hand, stylistic studies on the difference between the *Three Commentaries* have also gained much attention. Specifically, this study will take Hong Ye's *Index on Spring and Autumn Annals and the Three Commentaries* as the data source and use text representation learning in deep learning to examine the style differences between the *Three Commentaries*. As

Proceedings of the Ancient Language Processing Workshop associated with RANLP-2023, pages 117–121,
held in Varna Bulgaria, Sept 8, 2023.
https://doi.org/10.26615/978-954-452-087-8_014

an essential content of computational humanities, this study will provide a compelling computational research idea and reference for studying style in ancient books.

2 Related Research

The *Three Commentaries on the Spring and Autumn Annals* revolve around the history of the Lu State recorded in the Spring and Autumn Period in terms of content and ideological system. Still, there are apparent differences in the writing and language style focus. Scholars often draw relevant conclusions based on a careful reading of the *Three Commentaries*(Chen, 2021), which have significantly contributed to the development of historiography but need more accurate, verifiable, and reproducible digital indicators to prove it. Moreover, the entry point for investigation is single, often only starting from a specific problem, needing a macroscopic inspection from a global perspective.

As one of the research directions of ancient Chinese text mining, the metrological research of old books has the characteristics of mature technology and diverse perspectives. According to the different properties of the research objects, it can be divided into different research levels, such as vocabulary, sentences, and text. The measurement research of ancient books based on vocabulary includes word segmentation(Huang et al., 2015), part-of-speech tagging(Zhang et al., 2021), named entity recognition(Liu and Wang, 2018), keyword extraction(Qin and Wang, 2020), etc. In the quantitative research conducted around the sentence level, taking sentence segmentation (Zhao et al., 2022), sentence classification(Liu et al., 2013), and sentence extraction(Zhou et al., 2021) as examples, it is possible to explore the implicit features and inter-sentence relationships of sentences in ancient books. Research at the chapter level includes research on automatic summarization(Xu et al., 2022), bibliographic information measurement(Tong et al., 2021), etc. In summary, studying computational humanities in ancient books has extended research in various directions at different levels and has gradually formed a mature research paradigm. However, there is still a gap in the study of the style and style of ancient books, and there needs to be more research that takes ancient books as the main body and uses quantitative analysis to observe the differences in digital indicators of ancient books. This study takes the *Three Commentaries on the Spring and Autumn Annals* as the research object. It aims at texts of different levels to explore the language style differences formed in writing the three biographies. This is significant for exploring ancient books in the Spring and Autumn Periods.

3 Style Comparison With Text Representation

Words and sentences are important objects in stylistics research; different from the measurement of word frequency in traditional diagrams, this study uses representation learning models in deep learning to automatically obtain the vectorized representation of words and sentences to acquire knowledge about vocabulary and sentence style. Specifically, Word2vec and Sentence-BERT were chosen respectively for vectorizing words and sentences in the *Three Commentaries*, and mapping scatter points with dimensionality reduction was used for the style comparison.

3.1 Model Introduction

Word2vec is a neural network language model that can capture semantic information between contexts, map each word into a word vector, and mine connections between words(Mikolov et al., 2013). The Word2vec model contains two models for training word vectors: the CBOW (Continuous Bag-of-Words Model) model and the Skip-gram model. The former uses N words before and after the feature word to predict the word, and the latter uses the word's context to predict N words before and after. The Word2vec model adds contextual analysis to the context, which makes the semantic analysis more abundant.

Sentence BERT (SBERT for short) is a sentence vector computing model proposed (Reimers and Gurevych, 2019), which maps text into Vector space in sentence units. One vector can represent the semantics expressed by a sentence in the text. Compared with the BERT model, SBERT can better generate sentences. The Embedding vector enables the vectorized expression to carry more semantic information.

3.2 Word Vectorization Mapping

As was written in the name, the *Three Commentaries* were all commentaries on *Spring and Autumn Annals*, which provided detailed descriptions of historical events of the State of Lu in the Spring and Autumn period. Their themes and contents

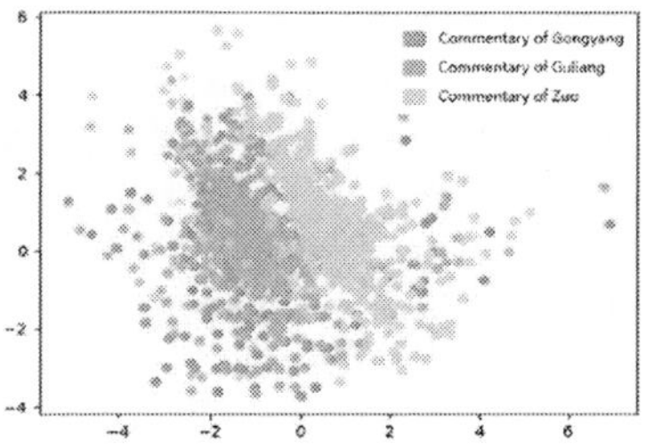

Figure 1: The mapping of words in the *Three Commentaries*

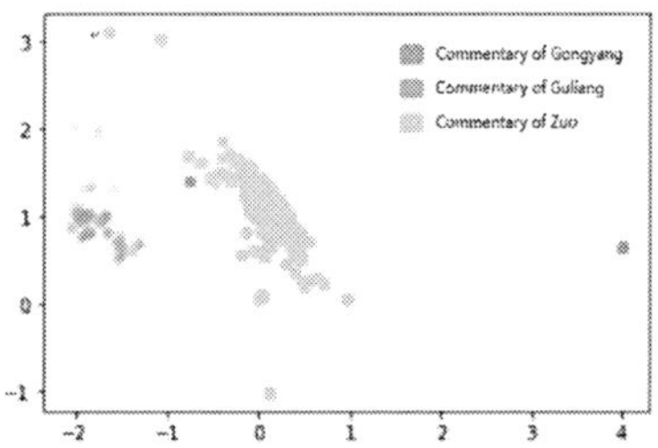

Figure 2: The mapping of single-occurrence words in the *Three Commentaries*

are similar to a certain extent, but their language styles are different. Based on this, it can be considered that the differences shown in the mapping on the scatterplot are more due to the differences in the language styles of the *Three Commentaries*, rather than the "fixed collocation" between words, that is, the differences caused by different recorded content. We use the word-segmented text to train the Word2vec model and generate words into multi-dimensional word vectors. To map in two-dimensional space, PCA is used to reduce the dimensionality of word vectors and map them on the graph through different colors.The distribution of words and single-occurrence words of the three biographies is shown in Figure 1 and Figure 2.

Each dot represents a word in the scatter plot, and the three colors correspond to the *Three Commentaries*. For example, a blue dot represents a word in the Commentary of Zuo. The number of points determines the depth of the color at the coordinate position. Since a point represents a word, the distance between points represents the degree of similarity between the two words. It can be observed that the three biographies have a slight overlap near the point (0, 0) in Figure 1. In addition, the blue word points representing the *Commentary of Zuo* are mainly concentrated in the upper right corner of Figure 1, with a relatively clear and intuitive boundary between the *Commentary of Gongyang* and the *Commentary of Guliang*. Based on this, from the perspective of words, even though the content is similar, the three biographies still have differences in language style. The *Commentary of Gongyang* and the *Commentary of Guliang* are identical in language style and preferred word definition. At the same time, the *Commentary of Zuo* has a unique narrative style that prefers supplementary historical events.

Single-occurrence words refer to the words that occurred only in one of the *Three Commentaries*.Compared with some more general words, these words that only appear in certain commentaries can better reflect the language habits in the process of writing the book. On the map of single-occurring words, there is almost no overlapping part, which conforms to the definition concept of single-occurring words, which can explain that based on similar content, the language styles of the *Three Commentaries* are different in terms of words. And the distribution of each commentaries point is consistent with that shown in Figure 2. The above image also reflects the orange dots near points (4,1). The distribution of single-occurrence words deepens the accuracy and credibility of the above picture from the side.The distribution of single-occurrence words deepens the accuracy and credibility of the above picture from the side, which confirms that the *Three Commentaries* not only show differences in the overall language style but also have different habits in the use of single-occurrence words.

3.3 Sentence Vectorization Mapping

The process of generating sentence vectors is to use the text after the sentence to train the SBERT model, and each generated vector represents a sentence. Similar to the word vector dimensionality reduction method, PCA is used to reduce the dimensionality of the sentence vector so that it can be presented on a two-dimensional graph. The distribution of sentence vectors is shown in Figure 3.

Each point in Figure 3 represents a sentence, and the distance between points represents the sentence's similarity. In the sentence vector, it is observed that the dispersion of the sentence vector is slightly smaller than that of the word vector, and the overlapping area is larger around the point (0,0). Most of Figure 3's color blocks are composed of

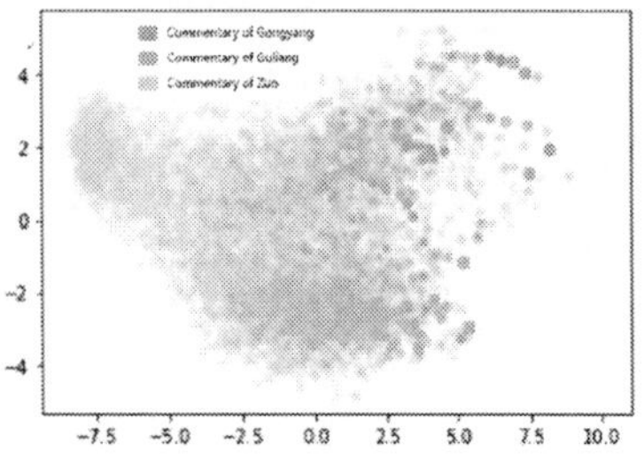

Figure 3: The distribution of sentence vectors in the *Three Commentaries*

mixed and interlaced colors. But the *Commentary of Zuo* still shows differences, converging into a single color block around the point (-7.5, 2). This phenomenon is consistent with what the word vectors offer, and it reflects that the *Commentary of Zuo* is significantly different from the other two biographies in style.

Based on the mapping results of word vectors and sentence vectors, the style of the *Commentary of Gongyang* and the *Commentary of Guliang* are relatively similar, and the *Commentary of Zuo* shows distinct style differences. This result aligns with the views of ancient and modern scholars who have carefully read *Three Commentaries on the Spring and Autumn Annals* and can deepen the conclusion that the *Commentary of Zuo* is different in language style.

4 Conclusion

From the perspective of Natural language processing, uses a deep learning model with good versatility to calculate the language style differences between different levels of the *Three Commentaries on the Spring and Autumn Annals*. It concludes that the *Commentary of Zuo* differs from the *Commentary of Gongyang*, and the *Commentary of Guliang*, realizing the mining research on the language characteristics of ancient books.

In the follow-up research, we will use other methods to examine the differences between the *Three Commentaries*. From the perspective of natural language processing, this study has verified the feasibility of the general language model in discovering the differences in the *Three Commentaries*, and subsequent language models suitable for ancient Chinese, such as GuwenBERT, SikuBERT, and other pre-training based on ancient Chinese domain data enhancement model to further observe differences in language styles. In addition, the difference between the *Three Commentaries* can be observed from multiple perspectives, such as automatically mining different types of entities, or observing the usage habits of words from the part of speech.

From the perspective of quantitative linguistics, the language style differences between the *Three Commentaries* will be observed through different levels of language measurement indicators. At the word level, the index selects the average word length to measure the difference in word length, selects the word density, standard type ratio, and single word ratio to measure the difference in the richness of the *Three Commentaries* vocabulary, and observes the information carrying capacity of the richness of the *Three Commentaries* by calculating the entropy of text information. At the sentence level, the writing characteristics of the *Three Commentaries* were examined through average sentence length, sentence dispersion, sentence fragmentation, and other indicators. From the above two perspectives, the linguistic characteristics and stylistic differences of the *Three Commentaries on the Spring and Autumn Annals* can be examined from a new perspective, which provides new verification ideas for the research related to *Three Commentaries on the Spring and Autumn Annals*.

5 Acknowledgments

This work was supported by the National Natural Science Foundation of China [grant number 72004095], and the National Social Science Fund of China [grant number 21&ZD331].

References

Wangheng Chen. 2021. Political Aesthetic Thoughts of the Three Commentaries on the Spring and Autumn Annals. *Wuhan University Journal (Philosophy & Social Science)*, 74(6):80–94.

Shuiqing Huang, Dongbo Wang, and Lin He. 2015. Discussion on Automatic Word Segmentation of Pre-Qin Classics Using Sinological Index Series as the domain vocabulary. *Library and Information Service*, 59(11):127–133.

Liu Liu, Bin Li, Weiguang Qu, and Xiaohe Chen. 2013. Automatic Acquisition of Age Characteristics of Pre-Qin Vocabulary and Automatic Judgment of Document Age. *Journal of Chinese Information Processing*, 27(5):107–113.

Liu Liu and Dongbo Wang. 2018. A Review of Named Entity Recognition. *Journal of the China Society for Scientific and Technical Information*, 37(3):329–340.

Tomas Mikolov, Kai Chen, Greg Corrado, and Jeffrey Dean. 2013. Efficient estimation of word representations in vector space. *arXiv preprint arXiv:1301.3781*.

Heran Qin and Dongbo Wang. 2020. Application of Keyword Extraction in Pre-Qin Ancient Chinese under the Digital Humanities——Taking Chun Qiu Jing Zhuan as an Example. *Library Journal*, 39(11):97–105.

Nils Reimers and Iryna Gurevych. 2019. Sentence-BERT: Sentence Embeddings using Siamese BERT-Networks. ArXiv:1908.10084 [cs].

Lin Tong, Bing Liu, Jingpeng Deng, Dajun Liu, Yongsheng Yang, Xueyuan Hu, Zefeng Kang, and Ruili Huo. 2021. Quantitative analysis and thinking on bibliographic information of existing ancient Chinese ophthalmology books. *Journal of Traditional Chinese Ophthalmology*, 31(6):449–452.

Runhua Xu, Dongbo Wang, Huan Liu, Yuan Liang, and Kang Chen. 2022. Research on Automatic Summarization of History as a Mirror for the Digital Humanities of Ancient Books——Taking the SikuBERT Pre-training Model as an Example. *Library Tribune*, 42(12):129–137.

Qi Zhang, Chuan Jiang, Youshu Ji, Minxuan Feng, Bin Li, Chao Xu, and Liu Liu. 2021. Construction of an automatic tagging model for part-of-speech integration of word segmentation for multi-domain pre-Qin classics. *Data Analysis and Knowledge Discovery*, 5(3):2–11.

Lianzhen Zhao, Yiqin Zhang, Jiangfeng Liu, Dongbo Wang, Minxuan Feng, and Bin Li. 2022. Research on Automatic Punctuation of Pre-Qin and Han Classics for Digital Humanities—Taking SikuBERT Pre-training Model as an Example. *Library Tribune*, 42(12):120–128+137.

Hao Zhou, Dongbo Wang, and Shuiqing Huang. 2021. Research on Automatic Recognition of Context of Citations in Ancient Books——Taking Commentary Documents as an Example. *Information studies: theory & application*, 44(9):169–175.

A Joint Model of Automatic Word Segmentation and Part-Of-Speech Tagging for Ancient Classical Texts Based on Radicals

Bolin Chang[1,2], **Yiguo Yuan**[2], **Bin Li**[1,2✉], **Zhixing Xu**[1,2], **Minxuan Feng**[1,2], **Dongbo Wang**[3,2]
[1]School of Chinese Language and Literature, Nanjing Normal University, Nanjing, China
[2]Center of Language Big Data and Computational Humanities, Nanjing Normal University, Nanjing, China
[3]College of Information Management, Nanjing Agricultural University, Nanjing, China
✉libin.njnu@gmail.com

Abstract

The technique of word segmentation and part-of-speech tagging in ancient Chinese plays a crucial role in the field of information processing in ancient Chinese. The current state of ancient Chinese word segmentation and part-of-speech tagging technology presents pressing issues that require immediate attention, such as low accuracy and efficiency. This study employs a methodology that combines word segmentation and part-of-speech tagging. It establishes a correlation between fonts and radicals, trains the Radical2Vector radical vector representation model, and integrates it with the SikuRoBERTa word vector representation model. Finally, it connects the BiLSTM-CRF neural network.The study investigates the combination of word segmentation and part-of-speech tagging through an experimental approach using a specific data set. In the evaluation dataset, the F1 score for word segmentation is 95.75%, indicating a high level of accuracy. Similarly, the F1 score for part-of-speech tagging is 91.65%, suggesting a satisfactory performance in this task. This model enhances the efficiency and precision of the processing of ancient books, thereby facilitating the advancement of digitization efforts for ancient books and ensuring the preservation and advancement of ancient book heritage.

1 Introduction

The challenge of automatically segmenting words and assigning part-of-speech tags to ancient Chinese text is a crucial area of study within the discipline of natural language processing. The primary objective of this project is to employ computer technology for the precise identification of word boundaries in ancient Chinese writings, as well as the exact assignment of appropriate part-of-speech labels to these words, including nouns, verbs, conjunctions, and others. By implementing this procedure, the conventional task of manual labelling can be efficiently alleviated, leading to notable enhancements in both labelling efficiency and accuracy. The progress of this technology not only facilitates the processing of ancient Chinese texts, but also exerts a significant influence on interconnected disciplines, including literature, history, philology, and digital humanities.

The maturation of ancient Chinese automatic word segmentation and part-of-speech tagging technologies is occurring with the ongoing advancement of computer technology. Nevertheless, the current utilisation of these methodologies is confronted with two distinct obstacles as a result of the numerous distinctive characteristics of ancient Chinese. Firstly, it is worth noting that there remains potential for enhancing the precision of word segmentation and part-of-speech labelling in the context of ancient Chinese. While several technologies currently available have the capacity to partially substitute manual labelling, their level of accuracy falls short of totally replacing manual labelling. Consequently, a significant amount of proofreading labour is necessary during the later stages. Secondly, there is a need for additional enhancement in the effectiveness of word segmentation and part-of-speech tagging in the context of ancient Chinese. The prevailing approach involves conducting word segmentation as the initial step, followed by part-of-speech tagging. Nevertheless, this sequencing will result in diminished processing efficiency and has the potential to propagate errors in word segmentation to the subsequent part-of-speech tagging phase, so exacerbating the influence of these errors and subsequently diminishing overall accuracy.

This paper utilizes the Word2Vec model to incorporate the radical information of Chinese characters. It proceeds to train the Radical2Vector model and combines it with SikuRoBERTa to form the Embedding layer. Subsequently, the BiLSTM-CRF neural network is connected to conduct an experiment on the integration of word segmentation and part-of-speech tagging in ancient Chinese. The

Proceedings of the Ancient Language Processing Workshop associated with RANLP-2023, pages 122–132,
held in Varna Bulgaria, Sept 8, 2023.
https://doi.org/10.26615/978-954-452-087-8_015

utilization of ancient Chinese word segmentation and part-of-speech tagging facilitates the exploration of profound insights within ancient texts, thereby advancing the digital advancement and utilization of these texts. Furthermore, it contributes to the preservation and progression of ancient literary works.

2 Related Work

The co-examination of automatic word segmentation and part-of-speech tagging in the context of ancient Chinese is a common area of research. Huang (2002) conducted a study on part-of-speech tagging in ancient Chinese using the hidden Markov model. They applied this model to analyze "The Analects of Confucius" and "Tao Te Ching". Although the study employed a set of 22 part-of-speech tags, it made significant contributions to the field. In their study, Fang (2009) developed a text segmentation program called Yu Segmentation Program. The researchers focused on ancient books such as "The Classic of Tea" and employed a model algorithm that utilized tree pruning to achieve efficient text segmentation of these classical texts. The F1 score for word segmentation has been reported to be approximately 86% by Min Shi (2010). A comparative experiment was conducted to evaluate the performance of the Conditional Random Fields (CRF) model in the tasks of automatic word segmentation, part-of-speech tagging, and integration of ancient Chinese. Both features and integrated processing contribute to the enhancement of the F1 value. Runhua Xu (2012) proposed a method that utilizes structured annotations to enhance the word segmentation process. In their study, Shuiqing Huang (2015) employed the CRF model to analyze word categories, phonetics, and probability features. Notably, their analysis yielded a remarkable F1 value of 97.47%. According to the study conducted by Xiaoyu Wang (2017), This paper examines the issue of automatic word segmentation in Middle Ancient Chinese by employing a combination of the CRF model and a dictionary. It also investigates the impact of inconsistent word segmentation on the results of artificial word segmentation in Middle Ancient Chinese through experimental analysis. Additionally, the paper introduces character classification as part of the research methodology. The dictionary information exhibits two notable features. Firstly, the word segmentation F1 value achieved a remarkable accuracy rate of over 99% in the closed test. Secondly, in the open test, the word segmentation F1 value ranged between 89% and 95%, further highlighting the effectiveness of the dictionary information. Ning Cheng (2020) employed the Word2Vec-BiLSTM-CRF model to investigate the amalgamation of part-of-speech tagging for sentence segmentation and part-of-speech analysis in ancient Chinese texts.

Numerous studies have been conducted on the utilization of vector representations of strokes, parts, components, and radicals to facilitate Chinese information processing, both in contemporary and ancient contexts. In their study, Tao (2019) introduces a new model called Dual-channel Word Embedding (DWE) that aims to effectively capture both sequential and spatial information of characters. The author argues that this model demonstrates a logical and advantageous approach in representing the morphology of Chinese language. In their study, Zhang (2021) presents a novel model called the Feature Subsequence based Probability Representation Model (FSPRM) for the purpose of acquiring Chinese word embeddings. The model incorporates both morphological and phonetic features, specifically stroke, structure, and pinyin, of Chinese characters. By designing a feature subsequence, the model captures a wide range of semantic information pertaining to Chinese words. The efficacy of the proposed method is substantiated through a series of comprehensive experiments conducted on various tasks including word analogy, word similarity, text classification, and named entity recognition. The results of these experiments consistently indicate that the proposed method surpasses the performance of the majority of existing state-of-the-art approaches. In the study conducted by Shi (2015), a novel deep learning technique referred to as "radical embedding" is introduced. The author provides a rationale for this approach by drawing upon principles derived from Chinese linguistics. Furthermore, the feasibility and usefulness of this technique are assessed through a series of three experiments. In their study, Yu (2017) presents a method for simultaneously embedding Chinese words, characters, and subcharacter components at a detailed level. The performance of our model is shown to be superior through evaluation on both word similarity and word analogy tasks. In their study, Han (2018) utilized a shared radical level embedding approach to address the task of Simplified and Traditional Chinese Word Segmentation. Notably, their method does not require any additional conversion from Traditional to Simplified Chinese. The integration of radical and character embeddings results in a reduction in parameter count, while facilitating the sharing and transfer of semantic knowledge between the two levels. This integration significantly enhances performance. In their recent publication, Tang (2021) introduces a pioneering model named Moto, which aims to enhance embedding through the incorporation of multiple joint factors. The empirical findings indicate that our Moto model attains state-of-the-art performance with an F1-score of 0.8316, representing a 2.11% improvement, when applied to Chinese news titles. Furthermore, it achieves an accuracy of 96.38 (a 1.24% improvement) on the Fudan Corpus dataset and 0.9633 (a 3.26% improvement) on the THUCNews dataset. Among the various research endeavors, the investigation into the utilization of radical vectors stands out as the most prominent. On one hand, this phenomenon can be attributed to the relatively straightforward acquisition of the corresponding relationship data between Chinese characters and their radicals. On the other hand, the inclusion of radical vectors has been found to enhance the efficacy of Chinese information processing tasks.

It is evident that among the aforementioned studies, only one specifically addresses the topic of ancient Chinese classical Chinese, with a specific focus on automating sentence segmentation tasks. The absence of vector representations for strokes, parts, components, and radicals in ancient Chinese information processing has the potential to enhance the morphology of ancient books. This article endeavors to analyze the impacts of research. This study exclusively focuses on the radical vector representation and application of ancient Chinese characters, primarily due to limited resources.

3 Model Architecture

3.1 Embedding

The embedding layer, also known as the input layer, is a fundamental component in neural network architectures. It is responsible for transforming input data into enhancing the caliber of vectorized representation of historical Chinese text within the coding layer of the model constitutes a pivotal aspect in advancing the automated processes of sentence segmentation and word segmentation in ancient Chinese. In order to utilize natural language as input for the neural network model, it is necessary to convert it into a vector representation. The BERT model, constructed by Transformer's bidirectional encoder, is currently one of the most advanced technologies for language vector representation. Therefore, this research has opted to utilize the BERT model. The SikuRoBERTa model serves as the foundational approach for generating vector representations of Chinese characters. SikuRoBERTa is a vector representation model developed by Wang Dongbo et al. that is specifically designed for ancient Chinese. This model is built upon the BERT architecture. The training corpus utilized in this study is the renowned Wenyuange "Siku Quanshu" collection, which consists of approximately 500 million word instances. The word list encompasses a total of 21,128 characters.

The exclusive reliance on Chinese character vectors is insufficient in fully capturing the interrelationships among Chinese characters. It is imperative to delve into a comprehensive characterization of the intrinsic information embedded within Chinese characters. Chinese characters are a form of semantic and phonetic characters, wherein the radicals, components, and even strokes of these characters possess a certain capacity to convey meaning. Hence, in the domain of character-based sequence labeling, the inclusion of semantic information from these entities is frequently employed to enhance the precision of lexical analysis. precision. Firstly, it is imperative to differentiate between the four concepts of strokes, parts, component, and radicals of Chinese characters. This article aligns with the principles outlined in "A General Theory of Modern Chinese" edited by Jingmin Shao (2017).

(1) The stroke represents the fundamental building block of regular script glyphs.

(2) The part refers to a unit of character construction in the Chinese writing system. It is comprised of strokes, can be utilized autonomously, and serves the purpose of constructing Chinese characters. Components can also be considered as units of word formation that are derived through one or more segmentations of the complete word.

(3) The component refers to the structural component obtained through a single segmentation of the combined character using the dichotomy method.

(4) The radical is component or subcomponent that can combine to create characters in groups. The characters that share a common component

are grouped together in the "character set", with this component being positioned at the forefront as the leading unit. This arrangement serves as the foundation for character retrieval.

Using the character "時" as a case study, Table 1 reveals the presence of a shared denotative symbol "日" in the parts, components, and radicals of "時". This symbol serves as a pictograph, also known as a meaning, for "時" characters. However, it is important to note that there is no direct and exclusive correspondence between the pictographs and radicals found in Chinese characters. In certain instances, the complete representation of a Chinese character necessitates the inclusion of all its constituent components or radicals. For instance, the pictograph for the character "闖" is denoted by the combination of "門" and "馬", which collectively convey the meaning of door. This character "膾", in turn, signifies "肉".

Word building unit	Composition of "時"
strokes	丨乛一一一丨一一亅丶
parts	日土寸
components	日寺
radicals	日

Table 1: The strokes, parts, components and radicals of "時"

This paper establishes a mapping between fonts and radicals based on a dataset comprising over 70,000 Chinese characters and their corresponding radicals. Subsequently, the ancient Chinese traditional corpus known as "Siku Quanshu" is converted into radicals using the established mapping relationship between fonts and radicals. Please refer to Figure 1. This study utilizes the radical corpus and employs the Word2Vec training methodology to train the Radical2Vector model, which represents radical vectors. The Word2Vec algorithm is widely recognized as a prominent method for training word vectors. It effectively maps words or radicals onto a continuous vector space, enabling the identification and representation of semantic and morphological similarities among them. By utilizing the Radical2Vector model that has undergone rigorous training, it is possible to acquire the vectorized representation of individual radicals.

While the radical vector does contain internal information pertaining to Chinese characters, its informational capacity is restricted. Consequently, it cannot serve as a standalone vector representation for Chinese characters, necessitating its utilization in conjunction with word vectors. There exist two methods for integrating character vectors and radical vectors. The first approach involves concatenating the radical vectors and character vectors to form extended vectors, which are subsequently fed into a Bidirectional Long Short-Term Memory (BiLSTM) feature extractor. The second method entails combining the radical vectors and character vectors without further elaboration. The vectors are inputted into two distinct BiLSTM feature extractors, with the exception of the hidden size, the hyperparameters of these two feature extractors remain consistent. In conclusion, it is imperative to meticulously adjust the hyperparameters in order to achieve the most optimal radical vector representation model and input methodology.

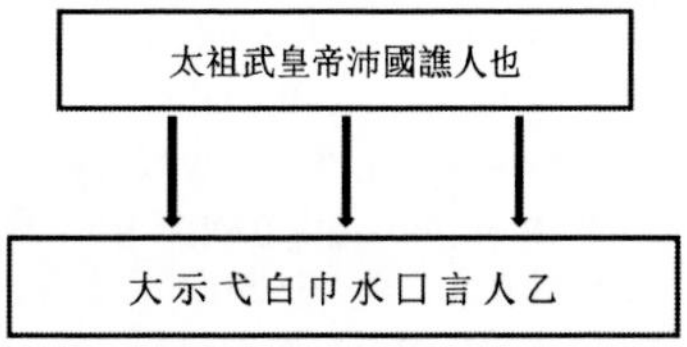

Figure 1: Transformation from traditional Chinese corpus to radical corpus

3.2 Neural Networks

The neural network layer is connected subsequent to the Embedding layer. The neural network architecture comprises two distinct layers, BiLSTM layer and CRF layer.

The BiLSTM is a type of neural network that incorporates bidirectional long short-term memory units. The recurrent neural network under consideration possesses the capability to effectively model sequential data. The BiLSTM model encompasses both forward and backward directions, enabling the simultaneous consideration of contextual information. This characteristic renders it highly effective for tasks involving sequence labeling. By utilizing BiLSTM, the model is able to acquire a greater amount of global semantic information.

The CRF model, also known as the conditional random field, is a statistical model used in machine learning and pattern recognition. The proposed approach is a statistical model designed for sequence labeling tasks, with the capability to optimize the labeling results on a global scale. Given that the output of the BiLSTM model is a probability matrix, it can be observed that the outcomes at each time step are mutually independent. Consequently, the impact of the preceding label on the current label cannot be taken into account. To address this issue, the current innovation opts for CRF model and integrates it following BiLSTM model. The CRF is a graph model that can be used to represent the joint probability distribution of a label sequence given an observation sequence. It is commonly employed to enforce constraints on the labeling results produced by BiLSTM model, ensuring that the output labels adhere to the rules of a valid sequence. Furthermore, the CRF can also be utilized to compute the optimal solution of the BiLSTM output sequence, thereby enhancing the effectiveness of sequence labeling.

The Embedding layer incorporates both word vectors and radical vectors, resulting in the formation of two distinct model structures when the neural network is spliced. These structures are illustrated in Figure 2 and Figure 3. Based on the analysis of Figure 2 and Figure 3, it is evident that the two input methods for radical vectors exhibit distinct characteristics. The former approach involves the concatenation of word vectors and radical vectors within the embedding layer, requiring the construction of a set of hidden layers using BiLSTM. Conversely, the latter method necessitates the integration of radical vectors with other components. The word vector and radical vector are separately fed into two distinct BiLSTM hidden layers in order to generate two sets of BiLSTM feature vectors. These LSTM feature vectors are subsequently concatenated.

4 Integrated Labeling Strategy

The tasks of Chinese automatic word segmentation and part-of-speech tagging are typically performed independently, with the outcome of automatic word segmentation serving as the foundation for part-of-speech tagging. Hence, the general approach in Chinese lexical analysis involves the sequential implementation of automatic word segmentation followed by part-of-speech tagging. The concept of integrated tagging can be attributed to Shuanhu Bai (1996), who proposed a combined approach for word segmentation and part-of-speech tagging to address the issue of ambiguous domains in contemporary Chinese automatic word segmentation. However, Shuanhu Bai did not conduct a comprehensive assessment of the practicality of integrated tagging. Ng (2004) provide a comprehensive analysis of the viability of integrated tagging in their scholarly work. The authors conducted a comparative analysis of two strategies for Chinese word segmentation, namely part-of-speech tagging and integrated tagging, using the maximum entropy model. The findings indicate that the integrated method, which relies on word annotation, demonstrates superior performance. The initial utilization of the integrated tagging method in the domain of ancient Chinese can be attributed to the research conducted by Min Shi (2010). The CRF model was employed to carry out experiments on word segmentation and part-of-speech tagging for Pre-Qin Chinese. The findings of the study indicated that the integrated strategy was effective. In comparison to the two-step strategy, it demonstrates a notable enhancement in the efficacy of word segmentation and part-of-speech tagging. Hence, this study also employs an integrated labeling approach. To achieve integrated labeling, the output label of each word is determined by combining the word's position and its corresponding part of speech. The lexical tagging system for word position information consists of a set of four lexemes: B for begin, I for middle, E for end, and S for a single word. The "Basic Collection of Pre-Qin Chinese Parts of Speech Tags" prescribes the use of part-of-speech tags. For instance, the tag "v" is employed to indicate verbs, while the tag "n" is used to indicate nouns, among others. The hyphen (-) serves as a connector between the lexeme marker and the part-of-speech marker. An illustration of this can be seen in the token B-v, which represents a word that initiates a verb.

5 Experiment

5.1 Dataset

The selection of "Zuo Zhuan" as the experimental corpus is based on the following rationales: The "Zuo Zhuan" holds the distinction of being the inaugural chronicle history book in our nation's history, encompassing a comprehensive narrative. Furthermore, it boasts the highest word count among all pre-Qin literature publications. The extensive body of literature, consisting of over 200,000 characters, is well-suited for conducting automated word segmentation and part-of-speech tagging experiments on ancient Chinese through the application of deep learning techniques. Furthermore, the reliability of the electronic corpus of "Zuo Zhuan" utilized in this study is reasonably assured. In ad-

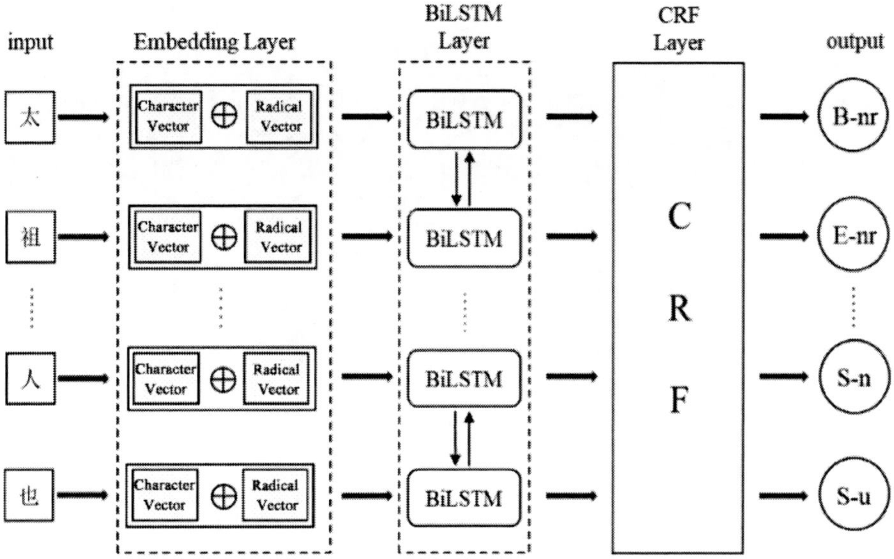

Figure 2: The first input method of radical vector

dition to addressing punctuation and collation, the research group also examined the matter of variant texts in relation to Yang Bojun's (1990) work titled "Spring and Autumn Zuozhuan Zhuan". Furthermore, our research team has conducted artificial segmentation and tagging of the electronic corpus of "Zuo Zhuan". The aforementioned tagged corpus exhibits a commendable level of quality and is deemed appropriate for utilization as an experimental corpus. In their respective studies, Min Shi (2010), Chengming Li (2018), and Ning Cheng (2020) employed the "Zuo Zhuan" as the corpus for conducting automated lexical analysis of ancient Chinese. In order to facilitate a meaningful comparison with their experimental findings, it is imperative for this study to employ the identical "Zuo Zhuan" annotated corpus during the experimentation process.

Hence, the partitioning of the "Zuo Zhuan" dataset in this study aligns with the experimental design of the baseline model. Specifically, the initial ten volumes of "Zuo Zhuan" serve as the training corpus, while the final two volumes are utilized as the test corpus. Table 2 displays the precise scale of the experimental set.

Dataset	Tokens	Types
Training set	194,995	166,141
Test set	33,298	28,131

Table 2: "Zuo Zhuan" training set and test set size

Among the datasets, the ratio of word case occurrences in the training set to the test set is approximately 5.86, while the ratio of overall word case occurrences is approximately 5.91. In general, the training set is approximately six times larger than the test set in terms of size ratio.

This study employs the conventional word tagging technique to accomplish the task of automated lexical analysis. To do so, we must develop a tag set that is suitable for both word segmentation and part-of-speech tagging tasks.

5.2 Equipment and Environment

The model employed in this study was constructed using the PyTorch 1.7.1 framework, with the programming language of choice being Python 3.8. Regarding the system configuration, the central processing unit (CPU) employed is the Intel i7-13700F operating at a clock speed of 2.90GHz. The memory capacity of the system amounts to 64GB, while the graphics processing unit (GPU) utilized is the NVIDIA GeForce RTX 4090. Furthermore, the memory size associated with the GPU is 24GB. This particular system configuration has the capability to guarantee both the efficiency and speed of model training.

5.3 Hyper-parameters

Radical2Vector can be described as a vector representation model that captures the essence of ancient

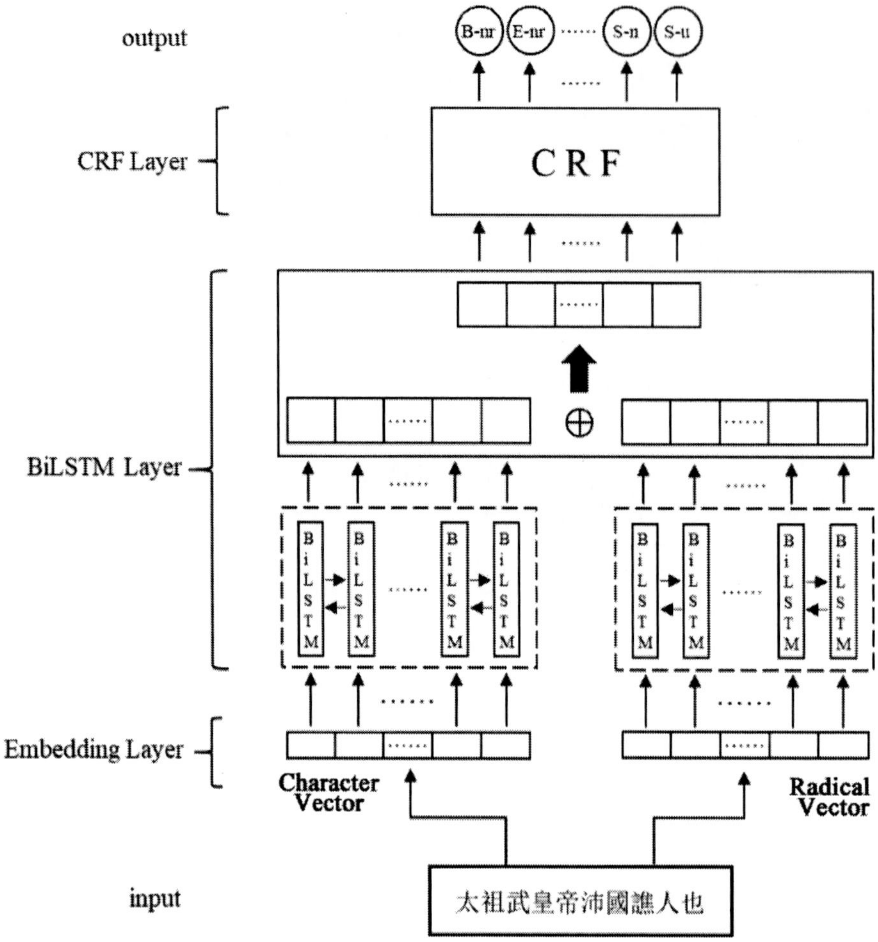

Figure 3: The second input method of radical vector

Chinese radicals. This model is constructed by applying the Word2Vec training method to a radical corpus sourced from "Siku Quanshu," which contains over 700 million word examples. During the training process of Word2Vec models, it is common to encounter the need for adjusting four key hyperparameters. These hyperparameters include the choice of training algorithm, which encompasses both Continuous Bag of Words (CBOW) and Skip-Gram methods, as well as the feature vector dimension, the number of iterations, and the window size. The CBOW model is a technique that utilizes contextual information to predict the current word or words as part of a training task. On the other hand, the Skip-Gram model is a method that employs the current word or words to predict the surrounding context as part of a training task. The training tasks. The dimension of the feature vector is a crucial parameter in the Word2Vec model as it dictates the size of the vector representation for words or radicals in the continuous space. The term "number of iterations" pertains to the frequency at which the corpus is traversed during the training process. In each iteration, the parameters of the model will be updated in order to optimize the vector representation of words or radicals. The term "window size" pertains to the maximum distance separating the context and the present word (or words), thereby determining the extent of the context. This paper combines various hyperparameter selections as outlined in Table 3 and conducts an initial experiment for parameter tuning.

This study initially selects the initial splicing technique of word vector and radical vector, and proceeds to conduct a comparative experiment on the training algorithm. Initially, the CBOW and Skip-Gram models underwent training with vector dimensions of 128, 256, and 512, respectively. This

Hyperparameters	Value
training algorithm	CBOW/Skip-Gram
vector dimension	128/256/512/768
iterations	5/10/15/20/25
window size	3/4/5/6/7/8

Table 3: Hyperparameters for Radical2Vector Model

Model name	Word segmentation	POS tagging
CBOW-128d	95.73	91.54
CBOW-256d	95.56	91.45
CBOW-512d	**95.75**	**91.65**
Skip-128d	95.58	91.38
Skip-256d	95.73	91.35
Skip-512d	95.63	91.35

Table 4: F1 value (%) of CBOW and Skip-Gram models with different radical vector dimensions

training was conducted with iteration number 10 and window size 5. The resulting models were labeled as CBOW-128d, CBOW-256d, CBOW-512d, Skip-128d, Skip-256d, and Skip-512d. Next, employ the initial radical vector input approach to carry out a comprehensive experiment involving word segmentation and part-of-speech tagging on the "Zuo Zhuan" dataset. The empirical findings are presented in Table 4.

Figures 4 and 5 display the performance of CBOW-512d across various iterations with a window size of 5, as well as the performance of CBOW-512d across different window sizes with a fixed number of iterations at 10. These figures aim to investigate the impact of the number of iterations and window size on the model's influence.

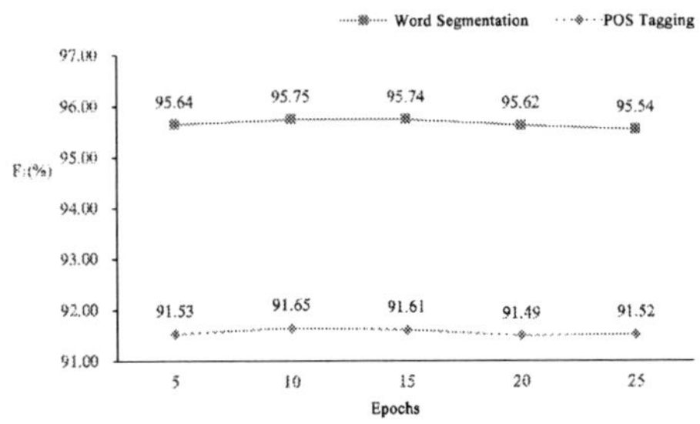

Figure 4: The performance of CBOW-512d at different iterations when the window size is 5

The chart illustrates that the CBOW-512d model demonstrates the most favorable outcome. Additionally, the Word2Vec method's radical vector

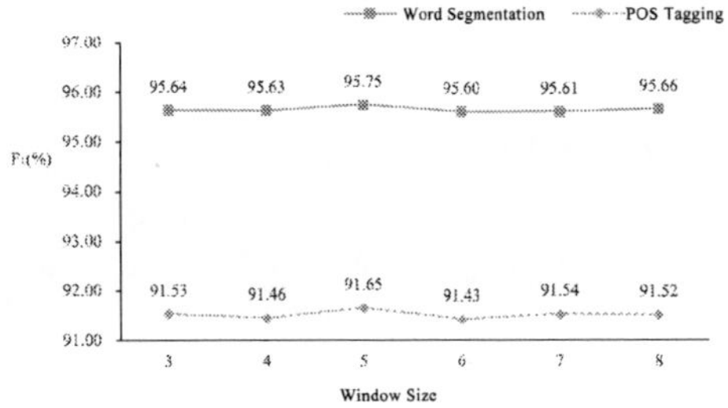

Figure 5: The performance of CBOW-512d at different iterations when the window size is 5

training does not significantly contribute to word segmentation; however, it does enhance the efficacy of part-of-speech tagging. The Skip-Gram approach is not deemed appropriate for the training of radical vectors. To ascertain the potential enhancement of the model's performance with a larger radical vector dimension, this study employs the Continuous Bag-of-Words (CBOW) approach to train a model with a vector dimension of 768, referred to as CBOW-768d. In comparison to the CBOW-512d model, the integrated tagging of this model exhibits a decrease of 0.1 in the F1 value for word segmentation and a decrease of 0.17 in the F1 value for part-of-speech tagging.

In general, the selection of the CBOW training method and the configuration of a vector dimension of 512 are deemed more suitable. This study made adjustments to the number of iterations and window size of CBOW-512d, based on the given rationale. Based on the findings presented in Figure 4 and Figure 5, this study ultimately determines that the optimal number of iterations for CBOW-512d is 10, while the most effective window size is 5. The model is referred to as Radical2Vector.

5.4 Vector Composition

The preceding data represents the performance of Radical2Vector in the initial approach of radical vector input, wherein the word vector and radical vector are combined and fed into a series of BiLSTM hidden layers to produce LSTM feature vectors. In this particular instance, there is a slight enhancement observed in the impact of part-of-speech tagging. This study employs the Radical2Vector methodology to carry out experiments pertaining to the second input modality. The experimental results of the two input methods are presented in Table ??. The second input method of the radical vector, Radical2Vector, exhibits minimal improvement efficacy.

6 Evaluation

In this study, the Radical2Vector model was selected as the representation model for ancient Chinese radicals. The radical vector was combined with the word vector and fed into the same set of BiLSTM hidden layers. This approach, referred to as the first radical vector input method, was employed. The incorporation of radical vectors enhances the efficacy of part-of-speech tagging; however, its impact remains somewhat constrained.

To assess the impact of the model proposed in this research paper, the evaluation metrics employed include accuracy rate (P), recall rate (R), and harmonic mean (F1). The model presented in this study is then compared to the outcomes achieved by participating teams in the open test TestA of the first international ancient chinese word segmentation and pos tagging bakeoff(Li et al., 2022). The findings are juxtaposed, as illustrated in Table 6. The training and test sets utilised in this study align with the evaluation dataset. Furthermore, the training approach and outcome statistics presented in this article adhere to the criteria outlined for open evaluation. Consequently, the model's computational findings can be compared to the evaluation results to assess its impact on word segmentation and part-of-speech tagging.

7 Discussion

Innovation can improve ancient Chinese word segmentation and part-of-speech labeling. Reasons include these. Ancient Chinese radicals are related with form and meaning. The word segmentation and part-of-speech tagging model captures ancient Chinese character structural similarities better by integrating radical information. The resemblance helps the model reliably identify and categorize ancient Chinese characters, improving word segmentation precision. Radicals also relate to ancient Chinese character semantics. Radical information helps the model learn radical semantics and apply them to part-of-speech labeling. Some radicals associate with nouns, whereas others with verbs or adjectives. Semantic information can improve part-of-speech labeling. Ancient Chinese word segmentation and part-of-speech tagging require knowledge of ancient literature and culture. Radicals are a vital part of ancient Chinese characters. Innovative information improves the word segmentation and part-of-speech tagging model's understanding of historical manuscripts' lexicon and expressions, improving ancient Chinese language processing computational capabilities.

Lexical analysis is better with integrated tagging. The integrated labeling technique reduces category labels during multi-classification tasks like lexical analysis. This improves lexical analysis. This work uses the four-lexeme tag set for automatic word segmentation and 21 part-of-speech tags for tagging. Integrated tagging reduced the training set of "Zuo Zhuan" to 59 integrated tags. Strategy has 84 category labels. This is because ancient Chinese auxiliary words (u), quantifiers (q), and concurrent words (j) were single-character terms. These linguistic elements are only combined with the single-word marker (S), not with beginning (B), medial (I), or final (E) markers. The "Zuo Zhuan" dataset contains terms without three-character words. This applies to prepositions, adverbs, modal particles, and onomatopoeia. This method reduces class labels further by adding in-word (I) tagging. Certain characters vary and limit the part-of-speech scope of their words on different lexemes. This limits character consequences. Thus, the integrated tagging technique integrates external knowledge and automated processing by leveraging the interrelated and complimentary nature of word segmentation and part-of-speech information. Thus, this study labels everything.

8 Conclusion

This study employs deep learning techniques to extract the radical information of Chinese characters, thereby achieving the integration of automatic word segmentation and part-of-speech tagging in ancient texts. This study utilizes a dataset comprising over 70,000 Chinese characters and their corresponding radicals to establish a correlation between fonts and radicals. Additionally, it employs the Radical2Vector model to train a radical vector representation. An experiment was conducted on the "Zuo Zhuan" dataset to examine the integration of word segmentation and part-of-speech tagging, utilizing the SikuRoBERTa-Radical2Vector-BiLSTM-CRF model in conjunction with the original SikuRoBERTa. The model's automatic word segmentation achieved an F1 value of 95.75% on the test set, while the automatic part-of-speech tagging achieved an F1 value of 91.65%. The present

Input Method	Task	P	R	F1
First	Word Segmentation	95.52	95.97	**95.75**
	POS Tagging	91.44	91.86	**91.65**
Second	Word Segmentation	95.38	95.85	95.61
	POS Tagging	91.08	91.53	91.31

Table 5: The integrated labeling effect of Radical2Vector on the two input methods (%)

Evaluation	Word Segmentation			POS Tagging		
	P	R	F1	P	R	F1
FDU	95.81	96.88	**96.34**	92.05	93.07	**92.56**
	95.73	96.84	96.28	91.88	92.94	92.41
ZNNU	92.78	90.18	91.46	88.97	86.48	87.71
HIT	91.2	93.49	92.33	85.41	87.56	86.47
	91.09	93.41	92.24	85.27	87.45	86.35
BLCU	90.91	92.4	91.65	83.55	84.92	84.23
	90.56	92.29	91.41	83.13	84.72	83.92
NJUPT	78.14	86.31	82.02	57.35	63.35	60.2
This article	95.52	95.97	95.75	91.44	91.86	91.65

Table 6: Comparison between the model in this paper and the results of the evaluation teams (%)

study introduces an integrated model that utilizes radicals for word segmentation and part-of-speech tagging in ancient Chinese. This model demonstrates a high level of performance, significantly enhancing the efficiency and accuracy of tagging ancient book corpora. Consequently, it facilitates the digitization process of ancient books and actively contributes to the advancement of research in this field. The topic of discussion pertains to the concepts of inheritance and development.

9 Acknowledgments

This research was supported by National Language Commission Project (YB145-41), Key Project of Ancient Books Work (22GJK006) and National Social Science Foundation of China major project (21&ZD331, 22&ZD262). We are grateful to the reviewers for comments which helped us to improve the paper.

References

Shuanhu Bai. 1996. An integrated method of chinese word segmentation and part-of-speech automatic tagging. *Chinese Information*, 2:46–48.

Ning Cheng, Bin Li, Sijia Ge, Xingyue Hao, and Minxuan Feng. 2020. A joint model of automatic sentence segmentation and lexical analysis for ancient chinese based on bilstm-crf model. *Journal of Chinese Information Processing*, 34(4):1–9.

Miao Fang, Yi Jiang, Qi Zhao, and Xin Jiang. 2009. Automatic word segmentation for chinese classics of tea based on tree-pruning. In *2009 Second International Symposium on Knowledge Acquisition and Modeling*, volume 1, pages 438–441. IEEE.

Han He, Lei Wu, Xiaokun Yang, Hua Yan, Zhimin Gao, Yi Feng, and George Townsend. 2018. Dual long short-term memory networks for sub-character representation learning. In *Information Technology-New Generations: 15th International Conference on Information Technology*, pages 421–426. Springer.

Liang Huang, Yinan Peng, Huan Wang, and Zhenyu Wu. 2002. Pcfg parsing for restricted classical chinese texts. In *COLING-02: The First SIGHAN Workshop on Chinese Language Processing*.

Shuiqing Huang, Dongbo Wang, and Lin He. 2015. Exploring of word segmentation for fore-qin literature based on the domain glossary of sinological index series. *Library and Information Service*, 59(11):127.

Bin Li, Yiguo Yuan, Jingya Lu, Minxuan Feng, Chao Xu, Weiguang Qu, and Dongbo Wang. 2022. The first international ancient chinese word segmentation and pos tagging bakeoff: Overview of the evahan 2022 evaluation campaign. In *Proceedings of the Second Workshop on Language Technologies for Historical and Ancient Languages*, pages 135–140.

Chengming Li. 2018. *Research on Lexical Analysis of Ancient Books Based on Deep Learning*. Ph.D. thesis, Nanjing, China: Nanjing Normal University.

Hwee Tou Ng and Jin Kiat Low. 2004. Chinese part-of-speech tagging: One-at-a-time or all-at-once? word-based or character-based? In *Proceedings of the*

2004 Conference on Empirical Methods in Natural Language Processing, pages 277–284.

Jingmin Shao. 2017. *General Theory of Modern Chinese.* Shanghai Educational Publishing House.

Min Shi, Bin Li, and Xiaohe Chen. 2010. Crf based research on a unified approach to word segmentation and pos tagging for pre-qin chinese. *Journal of Chinese Information Processing*, 24(2):39–45.

Xinlei Shi, Junjie Zhai, Xudong Yang, Zehua Xie, and Chao Liu. 2015. Radical embedding: Delving deeper to chinese radicals. In *Proceedings of the 53rd Annual Meeting of the Association for Computational Linguistics and the 7th International Joint Conference on Natural Language Processing (Volume 2: Short Papers)*, pages 594–598.

Xunzhu Tang, Rujie Zhu, Tiezhu Sun, and Shi Wang. 2021. Moto: Enhancing embedding with multiple joint factors for chinese text classification. In *2020 25th International Conference on Pattern Recognition (ICPR)*, pages 2882–2888. IEEE.

Hanqing Tao, Shiwei Tong, Tong Xu, Qi Liu, and Enhong Chen. 2019. Chinese embedding via stroke and glyph information: A dual-channel view. *arXiv preprint arXiv:1906.04287*.

Xiaoyu Wang and Bin Li. 2017. Automatically segmenting middle ancient chinese words with crfs. *Data Analysis and Knowledge Discovery*, 1(5):62–70.

Runhua Xu and Xiaohe Chen. 2012. A method of segmentation on zuo zhuan by using commentaries. *Journal of Chinese Information Processing*, 26(2):13r17.

Bojun Yang. 1990. *Annotations to the Spring and Autumn Annals.* Zhonghua Book Company.

Jinxing Yu, Xun Jian, Hao Xin, and Yangqiu Song. 2017. Joint embeddings of chinese words, characters, and fine-grained subcharacter components. In *Proceedings of the 2017 conference on empirical methods in natural language processing*, pages 286–291.

Yun Zhang, Yongguo Liu, Jiajing Zhu, and Xindong Wu. 2021. Fsprm: A feature subsequence based probability representation model for chinese word embedding. *IEEE/ACM Transactions on Audio, Speech, and Language Processing*, 29:1702–1716.

Introducing an Open Source Library for Sumerian Text Analysis

Hansel Guzman-Soto and **Yudong Liu**
Computer Science Department
Western Washington University
Bellingham, Washington 98225
{guzmanh, liuy2}@wwu.edu

Abstract

The study of Sumerian texts often requires domain experts to examine a vast number of tables. However, the absence of user-friendly tools for this process poses challenges and consumes significant time. In addressing this issue, we introduce an open-source library that empowers domain experts with minimal technical expertise to automate manual and repetitive tasks using a no-code dashboard. Our library includes an information extraction module that enables the automatic extraction of names and relations based on the user-defined lists of name tags and relation types. By utilizing the tool to facilitate the creation of knowledge graphs, which is a data representation method offering insights into the relationships among entities in the data, we demonstrate its practical application in the analysis of Sumerian texts.

1 Introduction

The study of Sumerian texts offers a valuable opportunity to gain insights into the earliest written languages and its associated historical context. Assyriologists have conducted studies such as prosopography (Jacobs, 2007; Dahl, 2007; Liu, 2021) and social network analyses (Kulikov et al., 2021; Pottorf, 2022) on these texts, enabling a deeper understanding of administrative and economic history as well as the involved families and individuals during the Ur III period (ca. 2112-2004 BC). However, this type of studies often necessitates the identification of named entities and their relationships within a specific timeframe, demanding domain experts to meticulously examine a vast number of ancient Sumerian tablets. This process can be time-consuming and challenging.

Currently, non-technical users primarily depend on SQL and Excel to perform repetitive tasks such as manually locating and recording instances of individuals and their relationships across tablets. Not only does this result in a less intuitive interface, but it also is not scalable. Additionally, given that Sumerian is a low-resource language, the availability of dedicated software tools is scarce, limiting scholars' access to user-friendly NLP (natural language processing) toolkits.

To address these issues, we introduce an open-source library that facilitates the seamless integration of processing and NLP models, thereby enabling more comprehensive and expedited analysis of Sumerian texts. The library consists of two key components: a pipeline and a dashboard. Currently the pipeline provides functionalities for data processing and information extraction, equipping users with the necessary tools to build robust and efficient software solutions. The dashboard offers a user-friendly interface which requires minimal technical preparing for domain experts to automate their workflow in analyzing Sumerian tablets, ultimately accelerating their research progress.

2 Related Work

There are existing tools that process or perform NLP tasks tailored for specific tasks such as Machine Translation (Pagé-Perron et al., 2017; Punia et al., 2020) and Sumerian text annotation (Tablan et al., 2006; Smith, 2010; Liu et al., 2015; Luo et al., 2015; Chiarcos et al., 2018). Most notably, the Cuneiform Digital Library Initiative (CDLI) hosts several repositoriesthat process Sumerian in various data formats such as CoNLL-U and RDF (Resource Description Framework), and perform various NLP tasks. Although these tools may provide versatility for different tasks, they require adequate technical knowledge for modifying their utilization. Without such expertise, modifying these resources to accommodate the diverse requirements of Assyriology can be daunting. Therefore, the need for a more accessible platform becomes apparent, underscoring the importance of our work in this space. To the best of our knowledge, no existing dashboard currently allows scholars to easily uti-

Proceedings of the Ancient Language Processing Workshop associated with RANLP-2023, pages 133–137,
held in Varna Bulgaria, Sept 8, 2023.
https://doi.org/10.26615/978-954-452-087-8_016

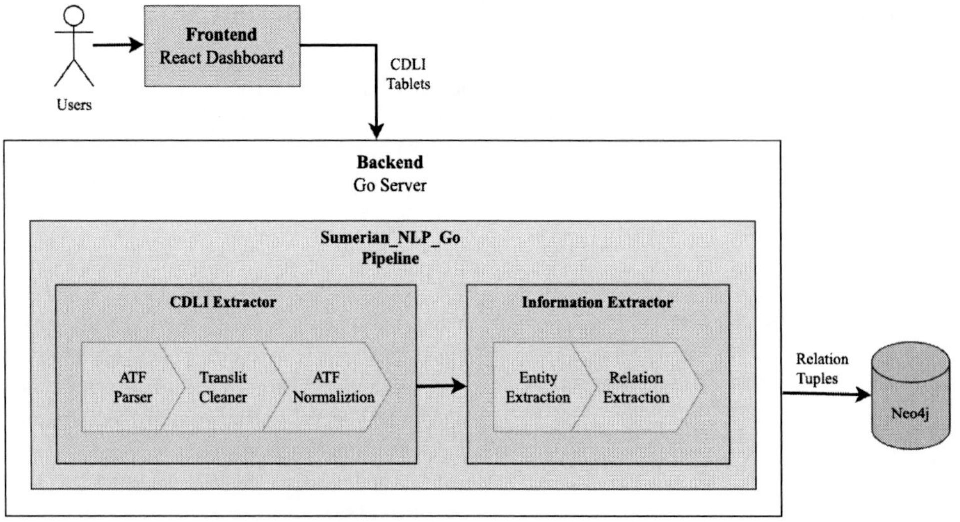

Figure 1: Architecture of the system.

lize tools or scripts specifically designed for the analysis of Sumerian tablets.

3 System Description

3.1 System Architecture

Fig. 1 illustrates our system's structure. It features a dashboard interface for users to upload their own data such as tablets or a customized list of named entity tags used by the backend pipeline. The backend pipeline handles user requests, such as data annotation, entity extraction or relation extraction, using specific library components which can be configured by the users on the fly. Additionally, users can create knowledge graphs, stored in a Neo4j database, leveraging the system's entity and relation extraction capabilities.

The library, accessible via this link[1] is designed to enable researchers to seamlessly integrate their workflow into our pipeline for their specific use cases. While the implementations are still relatively preliminary, the modular nature of the components involved ensures their adaptability for a wide range of applications. In the following sections, we will provide detailed descriptions of each component we have developed.

3.2 CDLI Extractor

The entry point to the pipeline is the CDLI Extractor, comprising three components: ATF (a text markup format used by CDLI to describe inscriptions on Cuneiform tablets and other artifacts) (Robson, 2014) Parser, Transliteration Cleaner, and ATF Normalizer. This component is built to load and process tablets from the CDLI repository, which are written in ATF.

ATF Parser reads tablets in ATF format and stores it into an internal data structure that preserves all metadata, tablet content and positional information. For now, we support data from CDLI which has tablets in ATF format. Other formats exist such as Open Richly Annotated Cuneiform Corpus (ORACC) (Robson, 2014) and the Database of Neo-Sumerian Texts (BDTNS) (Molina, 2002) for which we plan to offer support.

Transliteration Cleaner then handles broken tablets and normalizes transliterations to follow a specific format. For example, for the transliteration of "1(disz)", we may want this to map simply to "1" because the meaning is intact but it is easier for us to process.

ATF Normalizer aims to establish a standardized format enabling the uniform processing of data from diverse sources, including CDLI, ORAAC, and BTDNS. Currently, this component normalizes CDLI data to a unified format, with plans to extend its functionality to standardize data formats from other sources.

Fig. 2 shows a working example of this module.

[1] https://github.com/WWU-Sumerian-NLP

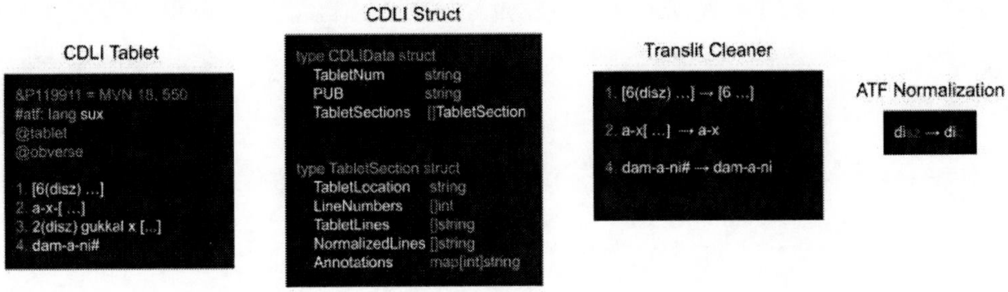

Figure 2: A working illustration of the CDLI Extractor. The ATF parser takes a CDLI tablet and parses and stores it into an internal data structure. The Translit Cleaner then performs cleaning on numeric symbols, damaged annotations, and annotator's correction or guesses markers. Finally, the Normalizer standardizes transliterations from various tablet sources.

3.3 Information Extractor

As named entities and entity relationships are often the key information for Sumerian text analysis, our Information Extractor module currently contains two modules: Entity Extractor and Relation Extractor.

Entity Extraction We use a simple approach based on string matching. In this process, each word is examined, and target words are labelled with entity types drawn from a list of known entities (Bansal et al., 2021). As aforementioned, the pipeline is designed to be flexible, allowing users to input a customized list of named entity labels to be processed. While simple, this approach effectively automates the manual annotation work and establishes a centralized platform to leverage the annotated data for downstream tasks. Future iterations will port existing Named Entity Recognition models to our library and provide them as option to users.

Relation Extraction It involves finding connections between entities. The process involves the application of user pre-defined rules for relations using regular expressions. The pipeline allows users to define and pass a list of regular expressions for the system to search through.

3.4 Dashboard for Non-technical Users

A No-Code Dashboard To facilitate the use of our library, we have developed a user-friendly dashboard that enables users to view, modify, and upload their data (see Fig. 3). It currently supports the following features: 1) Upload, add or delete entity names with their corresponding entity tag. 2) Define relation types with specific pattern rules. Our application takes these patterns, iterate through all data, and display the results to the user. 3) Configure different components within the pipeline. For example, users could configure ATF parser to filter by tablet metadata such providence or by broken tablets. 4) Search or filter for the results of each components output. 5) Download data or use the relationship tab to feed relations to a knowledge graph stored in Neo4j.

Server Architecture We have a server in place that acts as an intermediary between our dashboard and NLP libraries. Our server's backend imports our NLP libraries to use for each task and stores data in a relational database to maintain the state of data across multiple services. For server implementation, we use the Mux library in Go. The dashboard is designed for easy extension. To support a new tab for a service, users only need to create a new form in the frontend, add an entry in our server's database, and create a corresponding endpoint in our backend that uses the service. We are also developing features that will allow users to access their own Sumerian tablets for a variety of downstream tasks.

4 Evaluation and Implementation Considerations

We aim to create reproducible, replicable tools that can be easily customized and interchanged within the Assyriologist community. This is reflected in our pipeline architecture which will allow for the seamless integration of various components, enabling users to modify and adapt the tools according to their specific needs. This modularity not only promotes the reuse and repurposing of individual

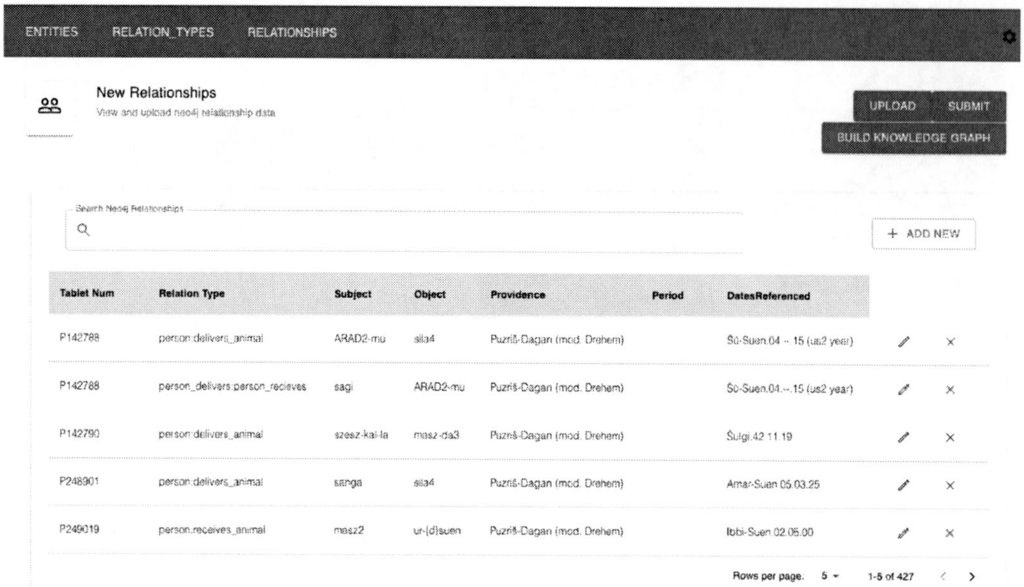

Figure 3: Dashboard interface designed for the streamlined data upload and knowledge graph generation through interactive widgets: "Entities", "Relation_Types", and "Relationships". With the "Entities" widget, users can input entity lists with tags, triggering entity extraction across their dataset. Extracted entities are then cataloged in a database and displayed in a corresponding table.

components but also encourages collaboration and knowledge sharing within the Assyriologist community.

Our decision to utilize the Go programming language, is primarily motivated by its speed. It offers up to a 30-fold speed increase, resulting a highly responsive user dashboard. For example, tasks such as entity extraction, which could require 5-20 minutes in Python, now demand only 1-5 seconds in Go. As we continue to introduce more customization options, algorithms and features, maintaining this speed becomes essentials for a good user experience. Furthermore, this efficiency extends to server interactions, ensuring swift communication between the frontend and backend.

5 Use Case: Creating Knowledge Graphs with Our Tools

Knowledge graphs serve as a powerful tool for representing data as a network of interrelated entities, enabling us to answer queries such as "who did what to whom". For illustrative purposes, we draw upon the work (Liu, 2021) to demonstrate the use of knowledge graphs in studying prosopography of a family engaging in an animal delivery business during the Ur III period. In this knowledge graph, nodes represent entities such as people, animals, and locations. Connections between nodes depict relationships or actions, and each connection is enriched with tablet metadata, including tablet number, year, and region. For instance, the node 'ARAD2-mu' (a person) is connected to the node 'sila4' (lambs) with an edge labeled 'delivers'. The graph not only illustrates the volume of deliveries, recipients, and geographic routes but also provides a comprehensive view of individual interactions over time and space. It gives insights into the networks of individuals and the broader prosopological landscape, shedding light on societal structures, relationships, and economic dynamics.

6 Conclusion and Future Work

This paper introduces an open-source library designed to empower domain experts in processing and analyzing Sumerian cuneiform tablets through an no-code dashboard. The application of knowledge graphs enhances the analysis via large-scale entities and relation visualization. The current implementation shows an initial but promising step in accommodating configurable components that are agnostic to various NLP tasks. As the pipeline's capabilities expand, we invite collaborations to broaden its applications, potentially encompassing a wider range of ancient Mesopotamian languages.

References

Rachit Bansal, Himanshu Choudhary, Ravneet Punia, Niko Schenk, Jacob L Dahl, and Émilie Pagé-Perron. 2021. How low is too low? a computational perspective on extremely low-resource languages. arXiv:2105.14515.

Christian Chiarcos, Ilya Khait, Émilie Pagé-Perron, Niko Schenk, Jayanth, Christian Fäth, Julius Steuer, William Mcgrath, and Jinyan Wang. 2018. Annotating a low-resource language with llod technology: Sumerian morphology and syntax. *Information*, 9(11):290.

J.L. Dahl. 2007. *The Ruling Family of Ur III Umma: A Prosopographical Analysis of an Elite Family in Southern Iraq 4000 Years Ago.* Peeters Publishers Booksellers.

Dennis Jacobs. 2007. The secret life of judges. *75 Fordham L. Rev. 2855.*

Anya Kulikov, Adam Anderson, and Niek Veldhuis. 2021. Sumerian Networks: Classifying Text Groups in the Drehem Archives. *IDEAH*. Https://ideah.pubpub.org/pub/q22859lx.

Changyu Liu. 2021. Prosopography of individuals delivering animals to Puzriš-Dagan in Ur III Mesopotamia," Akkadica 142/2, 2021, pp. 113-142. *Akkadica*, 2021(24.0):112–142.

Yudong Liu, Clinton Burkhart, James Hearne, and Liang Luo. 2015. Enhancing sumerian lemmatization by unsupervised named-entity recognition. In *Proceedings of the 2015 Conference of the North American Chapter of the Association for Computational Linguistics: Human Language Technologies*, pages 1446–1451.

Liang Luo, Yudong Liu, James Hearne, and Clinton Burkhart. 2015. Unsupervised sumerian personal name recognition. In *The Twenty-Eighth International Flairs Conference*.

Manuel Molina. 2002. Bdtns: Database of neo-sumerian texts.

Émilie Pagé-Perron, Maria Sukhareva, Ilya Khait, and Christian Chiarcos. 2017. Machine translation and automated analysis of the Sumerian language. In *Proceedings of the Joint SIGHUM Workshop on Computational Linguistics for Cultural Heritage, Social Sciences, Humanities and Literature*, pages 10–16, Vancouver, Canada. Association for Computational Linguistics.

Andrew Pottorf. 2022. *Social Stratification in Southern Mesopotamia during the Third Dynasty of Ur (ca. 2100–2000 BCE)*. Ph.D. thesis, Harvard University Graduate School of Arts and Sciences.

Ravneet Punia, Niko Schenk, Christian Chiarcos, and Émilie Pagé-Perron. 2020. Towards the first machine translation system for sumerian transliterations. In *Proceedings of the 28th International Conference on Computational Linguistics*, pages 3454–3460.

Steve Tinney Eleanor Robson. 2014. Oracc: The open richly annotated cuneiform corpus.

Eric JM Smith. 2010. *Query-Based Annotation and the Sumerian Verbal Prefixes*. University of Toronto.

Valentin Tablan, Wim Peters, Diana Maynard, Hamish Cunningham, and K Bontcheva. 2006. Creating tools for morphological analysis of sumerian. In *LREC*, pages 1762–1765.

Coding Design of Oracle Bone Inscriptions Input Method Based on "ZhongHuaZiKu" Database

Dongxin Hu

College of Liberal Arts , Capital Normal University , 10089 Beijing , China
602201042@qq.com

Abstract

Based on the oracle bone glyph data in the "**ZhongHuaZiKu**"database, this paper designs a new input method coding scheme which is easy to search in the database, and provides a feasible scheme for the design of oracle bone glyph input method software in the future. The coding scheme in this paper is based on the experience of the past oracle bone inscriptions input method design. In view of the particularity of oracle bone inscriptions, the difference factors such as component combination, phonetic code and shape code (letter) are added, and the coding format is designed as follows : The single component characters in the identified characters are arranged according to the format of " **structural code + pronunciation full spelling code + tone code** " ; the multi-component characters in the identified characters are arranged according to the format of " **structure code + split component pronunciation full spelling code + overall glyph pronunciation full spelling code**"; unidentified characters are arranged according to the format of " **y + identified component pronunciation full spelling + unidentified component shape code (letter)** ".Among them, the identified component code and the unidentified component shape code are input in turn according to the specific glyph from left to right, from top to bottom, and from outside to inside. Encoding through these coding formats, the heavy code rate is low, and the input habits of most people are also taken into account.

1 Previous design and inspiration of oracle bone inscriptions input method

In the past, some scholars designed the input method of oracle bone inscriptions from the perspective of shape code in coding. For example, Mr.Xu Song of Central China Normal University developed a method in 1995, which applied 26 English letters and 9 Arabic numerals to correspond to more than 500 characters in oracle bone inscriptions, and realized the input of oracle bone inscriptions by keyboard input characters. By 2012, researchers such as Li Qingsheng of Anyang Normal University jointly developed an input method of oracle bone inscriptions based on the dynamic description library of oracle bone inscriptions. On the basis of the coding and writing specifications of modern Chinese characters, the input side uses the dynamic description method to describe the oracle bone inscriptions with directed strokes and strokes, and combines the extended coding area with the external description character library. It is more effective to solve the input problem of variant characters and unliteracy in oracle bones.

Some scholars have developed image method, visual input method and handwritten input method from the perspective of non-coding to solve the input problem of oracle bone inscriptions. In 1990, Zhou Demin et al.of Henan University first developed the Calculator Oracle Information Processing System (CJPS), which laid an important foundation for the subsequent research and development of related input methods. In 2004, Mr. Liu Yongge and Li Qingsheng of Anyang Normal University developed a visual oracle bone inscriptions input method. The principle of the input method is to provide the input person with a table of oracle bone inscriptions. The input person selects the corresponding radicals contained according to the oracle bone inscriptions that he wants to input. The program presents the results containing these radicals to the input person in the form of candidates. The input person clicks on the glyph he wants to input to complete the input. After that, in 2020, Mr.Liu Yongge, Mr.Li Qiang and others from the Key Laboratory of Oracle Bone Inscription Information Processing of Anyang Normal University jointly developed a new oracle bone script handwriting input method. Based on the latest research results of artificial intelligence

Proceedings of the Ancient Language Processing Workshop associated with RANLP-2023, pages 138–147,
held in Varna Bulgaria, Sept 8, 2023.
https://doi.org/10.26615/978-954-452-087-8_017

deep learning and convolutional neural network, the oracle bone script recognition network and recognition module were developed. The method of using this input method is to operate the mouse to write the oracle bone script that you want to input to the virtual handwriting board to complete the recognition of oracle bone script, and then generate the glyph candidate, and then click the candidate glyph to complete the input of oracle bone script.

From the above content, there are two main problems in the design of oracle bone inscriptions input method in the past. On the one hand, computer professionals only design the input method of oracle bone inscriptions from the two directions of shape code and non-coding, and do not use phonetic code to participate in coding. The reason is that phonetic code can not encode the unidentified characters in oracle bone inscriptions.[1] Whether it is from the perspective of speech or keyboard input, most of us are used to associating phonetic symbols with text . Considering that people whose mother tongue is Chinese or people whose mother tongue is not Chinese, the first thing they learn when learning Chinese is the Chinese pinyin scheme, we think that setting phonetic codes in the input method coding is very convenient. .From the perspective of ancient Chinese characters , since oracle bone inscriptions are already identified , they must have a clear pronunciation. The commonly used characters in oracle bone inscriptions are basically identified glyphs, it is precisely these identified glyphs that we often use when inputting characters . According to these , we should not abandon the phonetic code when designing input method encoding .

On the other hand, the shortcomings of using only shape code to encode are generally not convenient for input learners to learn and use. Some are used to input the roots to retrieve alternative characters. This method is similar to the five-stroke input method to split today's regular script characters, but its drawbacks are reflected in the fact that the keyboard is as inconvenient for users to master as the five-stroke input method. It is not in line with the character theory for some oracle bone inscriptions, and it is not convenient to distinguish the large number of variant characters in oracle bone inscriptions. Some search for alternative glyphs according to the method of stroke input（*Nie Yanzhao and Liu Yongge . 2010.*）, but most of the modern so-called strokes are applicable to the glyph decomposition of Li and Kai characters, while many of the more pictorial characters in oracle bone inscriptions cannot be described by the concept of strokes.For example, the relatively representative glyphs of oracle bone inscriptions [2], 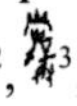[3], etc., strokes cannot truthfully describe the shape at the top of the glyph ; the 车 characters of oracle bone inscriptions are [4] and [5]. This special glyph of the record segment and the nuances between the glyphs cannot be combined and split simply by strokes. Some combine the similar four-corner number retrieval method with the configuration codes such as closed curve stroke and its extension line structure , cross stroke structure , discrete stroke structure, etc（*Liu Yongge and Li Qiang . 2020.*）. The **"Oracle Bone Inscription Six-digit Code Search Font Library"** is based on these three aspects as the basis for coding, but this search font library does not contain as many glyphs as ours.The most difficult thing for users is to learn this coding rule, which does not meet our requirements in simplicity and efficiency. Some use the method of dynamic description, based on the coding and writing norms of modern Chinese characters, using concepts and techniques such as directed strokes and pen elements to describe oracle bone inscriptions.（*Li Qingsheng, Wu Qinxia, Wang Lei . 2012.*）. The premise of this method is that the input must have a deep understanding of oracle bone glyphs, and the writing norms of modern Chinese characters are a kind of rules with strong regularity and serious symbolization, which is not very suitable for oracle bone glyphs with strong realism.

Since oracle bone inscriptions have a high degree of pictography, from the professional point of ancient Chinese characters' view, we hope to provide the academia with a coding scheme that

[1] Although "Yin Qi Wen Yuan" Data Platform (http://jgw.aynu.edu.cn) has provided this input method, it does not provide input method software that can be used away from the website, so its coding principle is not clear.

[2] *Jia Gu Wen He Ji* 6816

[3] *Jia Gu Wen He Ji* 27888

[4] *Jia Gu Wen He Ji* 584 front side

[5] *Jia Gu Wen He Ji* 10405 front side

conforms to the professional cognition of ancient Chinese characters. We urgently need a set of input method coding scheme that can be easily accepted by professionals to the greatest extent, faithful to the correct description of oracle bone inscriptions as much as possible, and convenient for users to learn and use.

2 A new design scheme of oracle bone inscriptions input method

2.1 Technical route of oracle bone inscriptions input method design

The Oracle Bone Inscriptions Input method is designed using Microsoft 's Text Service Framework (TSF : Text Service Framework). It is a COM-based input method framework that does not depend on specific input devices and can support multiple languages. It provides a simple and scalable technology for implementing text input and natural language processing technology. The text service framework includes three main components : application, TSF manager and text service. The architecture is shown in the following figure.

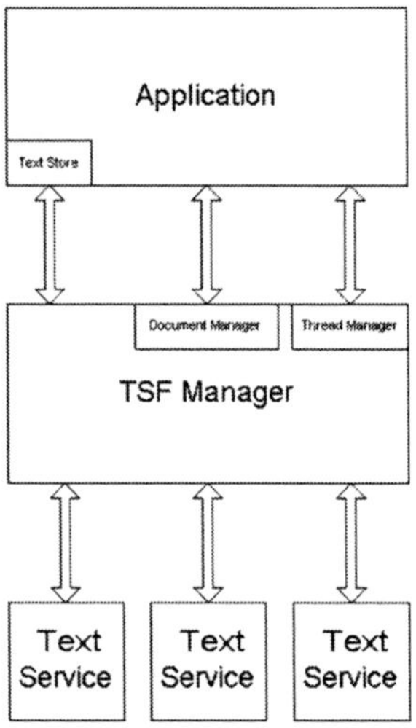

Picture 1 : TSF architecture

"Application" refers to the application software that supports and has adopted TSF, such as Microsoft 's MS Office, Notepad and other word processing programs. The application accesses text by implementing a COM server that supports a specific interface, and communicates with TSF by using an interface exposed by the TSF manager. Applications that support TSF do not need to consider the specific details of the input method, and can receive text input from the "text service" to achieve a series of operations such as displaying, editing, and storing text.

"Text service" refers to the text input processor, which can be keyboard input, handwritten recognition input or speech recognition input and other input programs. After registering with TSF, users can use language bar or keyboard shortcuts to interact with the text service. The text service can obtain text from the application or write text to the application. Text services can also associate data and attributes with text blocks. The oracle bone inscriptions input method implemented in this paper is a text service that inputs oracle bone inscriptions characters through the keyboard.

"TSF Manager" is an intermediary between an application and one or more text services, implemented by the operating system to enable applications and text services to share text. The text service does not interact directly with the application, and all communications are performed through the TSF manager.

Oracle Bone Inscriptions Input method implements the basic elements of TSF, such as Thread Manager, Client Identifiers, Document Manager, Edit Context, Ranges, Compartment, Properties and Composition.

The **"Thread Manager"** is responsible for completing the task of connecting the application and the text service. These tasks include activating or suspending the TSF text service, creating the document manager, and maintaining the correct association between the document and the input focus.

The **"client identifier "** is an identifier assigned by the thread manager that is received and must be maintained by clients such as applications and text services. The client needs to provide its own identifier when calling various TSF methods.

The continuous text stream created by the **"edit context"** through the interface can be created by the application and provided to the text service. In some cases, the text service can also create an edit context as needed.

The **"document manager"** is responsible for maintaining the last-in-first-out buffer, and the content stack stores the list of edited content managed by the document manager.

An **"input combination"** is a temporary input state that enables the text service to keep the application and user input text in a state of constant change. The application can obtain the display attribute information of the input combination and use this information to display the input combination state to the user. The application determines how to display the text and what kind of operation to the text according to whether there is an input combination.

2.2 Coding scheme designed by oracle bone inscriptions input method

Professor Huang Tianshu of Tsinghua University presided over the press and publication of major scientific and technological projects of the Chinese characters project **"中华字库- Oracle bone inscriptions collection and collation"** (0610-1041BJNF2328-03), its network platform has been sorted out 12685 Oracle bone inscriptions, the number of this glyph is the past Oracle Bone Inscriptions Input method can not be compared. We divide the 12685 oracle glyphs into two categories : literate and unliterate, and encode them separately. Among them, literate is divided into two categories : single component and multi-component. Unliteracy is divided into three categories : components that are identified but not identified as a whole, some components can be identified but the rest are not identified, and components are not identified at all.

2.2.1 Coding scheme of identified glyphs

2.2.1.1 Coding scheme of single component character

On the basis of **" natural classification "** , Mr.Huang Tianshu summarized and sorted out the radicals of oracle bone inscriptions into four categories :**"象物" "象人" "象工"** and **"other"** (*Huang Tianshu. 2020.*) . The **"象物"** refers to all non-living and living things in nature, **"象人"** refers to the shape of people and their five senses and limbs, **"象工"** refers to the products of human wisdom, **"other"** refers to parts that cannot be classified .For the input method itself, a constraint condition is added to the limited coding position, which can greatly reduce the repetition rate. Therefore, we roughly divide the structure of single-component characters into four categories : 象物, 象人, 象工, and others. According to the full spelling of the first letter of the character **"物"**, and at the same time, in order to distinguish it from **"合文"** in the following text, **"v"** is used to refer to **"象物"** . According to this setting method, the other three types of codes can be set as follows: **"象人"**corresponds to**"r"**,**"象工"**corresponds to**"g"**, and **"other"** corresponds to**"t"** (**"other"** in Chinese is **"其他"**, based on the full spelling of the first letter of the character **"他"** is **"t"**) . It may be the first time in the history of input method development to classify and encode single component characters by natural classification.

We set this type of coding in the first place of the input order. Because the identified characters in oracle bone inscriptions generally have corresponding interpretation opinions, there will be corresponding pronunciations of regular script characters in later generations. This pronunciation also belongs to the important coding attribute of single component characters in oracle bone inscriptions, so we set the corresponding Chinese pinyin spelling in the second place of the input order. From the perspective of reducing the repetition rate, under the constraints of the first two codes, sometimes there may be situations where the accuracy of the alternative characters is not enough. For example, under the premise that the expected input phonetic code **"you"** is added, the input situation is divided into vyou , ryou , gyou , tyou. The corresponding vyou codes are **"柚" "囚"** etc., and the corresponding ryou codes are **"又" "尤"** etc. Corresponding to gyou codes, there are **"酉" "卣"** etc., corresponding to tyou codes, there are **"㞢" "由" "䀁"** etc., and it can be seen that the repetition rate is already very low, but there are many variant characters of the same character in oracle bone inscriptions. After entering the coding, the number of options becomes the number of variant characters of one character plus the number of all variant characters of another or two characters. The number is still a lot. In the input method software or patents that have appeared, there is no design for encoding tones. The tone symbols and corresponding codes we designed are listed below :

Intonation	Coding
High-level tone (first tone)	y
rising tone (second tone)	p
falling-rising tone (third tone)	s
falling tone (fourth tone)	q

Table 1 : Tones table

If we add the attribute difference of tone on this basis. Coding becomes vyouy, vyoup, cvyous, cvyouq, ryouy, cryoup, ryous, ryouq, gyouy, gyoup, gyous, gyouq, tyouy, tyoup, tyous, tyouq and so on. In this way, in the previous coding, except that the characters **"酉"** and **"卣"** under the **"gyou"** code are not distinguished, the characters under the other three codes can be distinguished. Therefore, the coding format of **" structure code + pronunciation full spelling code + tone code"** is completely feasible.

In the following, we show some practical examples of single component character coding.

Intermediate code of "中华字库"	Oracle glyphs	Input coding
0E9C7B		gzheny
0E9C86		trenp
0E9C88		vyueq
0E9C79		tdingy
0E9C75		gzus
0E79E0		vyangp
0E79D1		rhuangp
0E86DA		vzhiq
0E86E9		vlaip
0E86D6		rruoq

Table 2： Single component characters coding table

2.2.1.2 Coding scheme of multi-component characters

The classification of multi-component characters is the most detailed. We divide the structure of multi-component characters in oracle bone glyphs into 14 categories， and according to the general shape of the structure, it is coded with English letters with similar shapes : the left and right structure correspond to the position of "⿰" , and the corresponding code is **"h"** ; the corresponding position of the upper and lower structure is "⿱", and the corresponding code is **" z "** ; the corresponding position of the full inclusion structure is "⿴" , and the corresponding code is **" o "** ; the corresponding position of the upper three-inclusion structure is "⿵" , and the corresponding code is **" n "**; the corresponding position of the lower three-inclusion structure is "⿶", and the corresponding code is **" u "** ; the corresponding position of the left three-inclusion structure is "⿷" , and the corresponding code is **"c "** ; the right three-inclusion structure corresponds to the position of "⿼" , and the corresponding code is **" b "** ; the corresponding position of the upper left contains structure is "⿸", and the corresponding code is **" p "** ; the corresponding position of the upper right contains structure is "⿹", and the corresponding code is **" q "** ; the corresponding position of the lower left inclusion structure is "⿺", and the corresponding code is **" l "** ; the corresponding position of the lower right inclusion structure is "⿽" , and the corresponding code is **" j "** ; the corresponding position of the covering structure is "⿻", and the corresponding code is **" f "** ; The corresponding position of the upper, middle and lower structure is "⿳", and the corresponding code is **" e "** ; the corresponding position of the left, middle and right structure is "⿲", and the corresponding code is **" m "**. The above-mentioned glyph structure and the corresponding coded letters are set up on the basis of the principle that the structural form of the first-level component is as close as possible to the letters .

We believe that the full-spelling syllable coding, which conforms to the typing and recognition habits of modern Chinese people, is very suitable for encoding multi-component characters, but it is also a problem to match the full-spelling coding with what coding. Tone coding is very suitable for distinguishing single-component characters. If multi-component character coding is designed to use tone coding on the basis of full pinyin syllables, the distinguishing ability of this coding will be greatly reduced. For example, in oracle bone inscriptions, the multi-component characters with pronunciation of fú are supported, 扶，俘 and 蘠 etc., the three-character components are completely different but cannot be distinguished. In addition, some of the components in the multi-component characters have been deformed and voiced during the evolution of the glyph. The changes in this component can not be distinguished by the pronunciation of the characters. For example, 兴 characters are generally from the same  deformed into  ;  left component is deformed into 因（簟）, and the overall evolution is . The above two aspects of coding problems, **"full spelling + tone"** method is not able to solve.

Therefore, we add two coding items, the whole glyph pronunciation and the disassembly component pronunciation, to the structural coding, that is, the coding format of **"structural code + disassembly component pronunciation full spelling + whole glyph pronunciation full spelling"** . This three-stage coding design scheme for multi-component characters of Chinese characters may be original.

In the following, we show some practical examples of multi-component character coding.

Intermediate code of “中华字库”	Oracle glyphs	Input coding
0E9C83		zrourouduo
0E79D3		zzhiwangwang
0E79DC		zshengmuxing
0E79D9		nmianwanbin
0E86E4		hyiliyi
0E9C42		nmianshizong
0E860E		mchiwujieyu
0E7342		ezhiweizhiwei
0E95E6		ozhubeigu
0E9965		uzhikanchu
0E8765		pyanziyou
0E94C5		fmeigemie
0E86AF		fjiannvyan
0E7BD2		broushitun
0E75F0		oweichuangzang

Table 3： Multi-component characters coding table

However, there are some of the multi-component characters that can be analyzed for structure and components, but they cannot identify the overall pronunciation of the characters. For the convenience of coding, we classify all these characters into the category of “ **unidentified characters** ” during coding, such as can be analyzed as 犬 and 大, can be analyzed as 殳 and 米, can be analyzed as 目 and 口 , but these are not the exact overall pronunciation, we for the convenience of coding, this kind of multi-component characters into the category of literacy.

There are a large number of **“合文”** in oracle bone inscriptions. This kind of glyph refers to the phenomenon of combining several original independent glyphs into one glyph. For **“合文”** , although the identity of each part of the new glyph is a character rather than a component, the combination of **“ 合 文 ”** is actually similar to **“ multi-component character ”** in terms of structure. In order to take into account the independent and common characteristics of **“合文”** , we regard **“合文”** as an input method structure category that can be independently classified, and the subsequent coding writes the pronunciation of each part according to the reading order of **“ 合 文 ”** , and the coding format is roughly **“ w + split component full spelling ”** , The coding order of each character in **“合文”** is arranged according to the order of reading.

When encoding the **“合文”**, we need to pay attention to the following aspects : some combinations of **“合文”** are connected or even have overlapping parts, such as 大 and 丁 is , 柚 and 京 is , 上 and 甲 is , 三 and 牛 is , and so on . Some combination methods are similar to the “借笔” in the combination characters, such as 大 and 甲 is , 五 and 璧 is , 五 and 牢 is , 妣 and 丙 is and so on. Although some two characters are separated, the “character spacing” is slightly closer than the normal character spacing, such as 大 and 庚 is , 母 and 癸 is , 祖 and 己 is and so on , this is also the most common **“合文”** . In some combination forms, one of the components is separated, and even the separated components are quite close to the other character. This kind of combination is not easy to identify, such as 武 and 乙 is , 三 and 牡 is , 龐 and 母 is , 武 and 丁 is and so on. Although some of the combined texts are separated from each other, one of the characters is simple, such as 多 and 子 is . In addition, in order to facilitate the explanation of the rules of the input method, we also incorporate the situation of **“ 重 文 ”** into the category of compound characters. At present, only one phenomenon of **“重文”** is found in oracle bone inscriptions, that is, 有 and 佑 duplicate characters is .

In the following, we show some practical examples of “合文” coding.

Intermediate code of“中华字库”	Oracle glyphs	Input coding
0E8848		wzuding
0E8B2E		wshangjia
0E7D0E		wshiyiyue
0E9A2E		wbaoyi
0E9A20		wwubi
0E7D90		wxiaogao
0E8F1F		wyoujing
0E9A82		wfuding
0E977E		wxiaolao
0E94E3		wyouyou
0E8128		wsanniu
0E91FB		wliuyue
0E79C1		wwushi
0E7DCD		wduozi

Table 4： “合文”characters coding table

2.2.2 Unidentified glyph coding scheme

2.2.2.1 All components are identified but the whole character does not identified

This part is relatively simple, although we do not identify the pronunciation of the glyphs, do not identify which glyphs they correspond to later generations, but each component in the glyphs is identified, so this part of the code can be coded according to the **"y + component"** format, and the pinyin of the component can be written in the order from left to right, from top to bottom, and from outside to inside.

In the following, we show some practical examples of coding.

Intermediate code of "中华字库"	Oracle glyphs	Input coding
0E8618	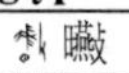	yyanripu
0E7786	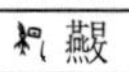	yyanripu
0E7966		yriyan
0E7D7E	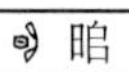	yrishi
0E79A2		yriyuan
0E8F54	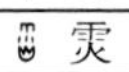	yyuhuo
0E906C	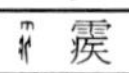	yyuji
0E7F03	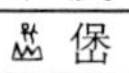	ybaohuo
0E93D9		yzhuilihuo
0E9157	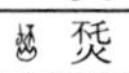	yzhebuhuo

Table 5 : All components are identified characters coding table

2.2.2.2 Some components can be identified but the rest do not.

In addition to the glyphs that are clearly fit structures, we forcibly separate the uncharacterized glyphs that may be part of the single body into several parts for the convenience of the input method design. The coding order of this part is written in accordance with **" y + identified components + unidentified components"** . The order of identified components and unidentified components is also arranged in the order from left to right, from top to bottom, and from outside to inside. The unidentified components are represented by the selection of 26 letters similar to their shapes according to the specific glyphs.

In the following, we show some practical examples of coding.

Intermediate code of "中华字库"	Oracle glyphs	Input coding
0E7D86		ytianoo
0E734D		ymunn
0E75E6		ycaijie
0E9D74		yhzhui
0E8858		yyux
0E79CB		yyangmumin
0E9FF4/0E9118		yiikou
0E7353/0E73A7	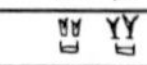	yyykou
0E8109		yrioda
0E735D		yzuoyyou
0E7E94		yodao
0E8FB0		yochu
0E967A		ypanren
0E9683		yshuio
0E82FA		yxjie
0E73BF		ymjiewang
0E7D2D		yygan
0E8675		ywixing
0E7F13		yfuy
0E933C		ymuyx
0E95B2		ykoukoux
0E74F1		ywda

Table 6 : Some components can be identified characters coding table

The middle part of the font of 0E7D86 is like "田", and the closed semicircle on both sides is replaced by two **"o"**.

The lower part of the glyph of 0E734D is "目", and the upper part looks like two upward raised curved pens, so it is replaced by two **"n"**.

The left side of the font of 0E75E6 is "才", and the right side is both an undetermined and inseparable component. The component on the right side is composed of the head of "鳫" and "卩". In this case, if the coding is designed according to this splitting, the coding will become very long, so we choose the "卩" which is easier to identify to replace the component on the right side.

The lower part of the glyph of 0E9D74 is "隹", and the upper part looks like **"H"**.

The upper part of the glyph of 0E8858 is "雨", and the lower part does not know what animal it refers to. Because there are cross strokes in the lower part of this component, and the repetition rate of coding **"yyux"** is very low, we use **"x"** to replace the following components.

The glyph periphery of 0E79CB may be "皿".Although the inner component does not know what it is, it can be forcibly disassembled into two parts : "羊" and "木".

The left side of the glyph of 0E967A is "爿", and the right side of the component is not "人" but still like the shape of human.

The glyph of 0E73BF has half part of the "王", and the left half is like the kneeling figure. The upper side of the left component that cannot be split is like **"m"**, so it can be forced to split into **"m+卩"**.

Part of the glyph of 0E8675 is an obvious "行". the upper side of the non-separable part that almost encloses the "行" is like **"w"**, the lower side is like **"I"**.

0E933C may be a single font. The top is "目" and "屮", and the lower part can no longer be split. But the part like "屮" is not "屮", so we use the approximate trident **"Y"** instead. Because the repetition rate of encoding **"ymuyx"** is also very low, the lower part is replaced by **"x"**.

2.2.2.3 Components completely unidentified

In this case, we can only split these glyphs into several parts, and arrange the letters similar to each part according to their order in the glyph. In order to make the input of this part of the glyph easier, we try to arrange the parts with roughly similar shapes in the same letter as much as possible.

In the following, we show some practical examples of coding.

Intermediate code of "中华字库"	Oracle glyphs	Input coding
0E774A		yooox
0E94F7		youx
0E8AB9/0E97C5/0E72FC		youuy
0E7E8E		ym
0E8482		yy
0E999E		yi
0E7BB3		yii
0E7180		yam
0E87B9		yyooa
0E8B29		yooy
0E8B2D		yuooy
0E7EDC		yox
0E9A2D/0E8275/0E96CF		yox
0E778B		ymmy
0E832D		yco
0E97B3		yhh
0E717C		yh
0E8283		yi
0E813C		yo
0E899D		yww
0E9740		yuo
0E9822		yyooo
0E7E23		yoooy
0E850A		yiiixx
0E7687		yuu
0E8326		ys
0E8327		ys
0E97F8		yk
0E8E6F		yk
0E9172		yx
0E9096		yy
0E78F8		yl
0E78FD		yoo
0E8C8A		yl
0E9F9B		yy
0E9FC3		yh
0E98B2		yui
0E7814		yeo
0E8680		yto
0E7E64		yox
0E7EAA		yi
0E7E3D		ym
0E8100		yuu
0E761F		yl
0E80F6		yj
0E7F29		yi
0E818E		yf
0E89F5		ycj
0E8A23		ym
0E8E21		yomx
0E8415		yoy

Table 7： Components completely unidentified characters coding table

In order to facilitate the reader to understand our ideas, we split the description of complex characters . Due to space constraints, we list some of the more special examples to illustrate.

According to the strokes, we can see that the upper two curved pens of 0E774A[6] form three rings, and only **"o"** is a ring in the 26 letters. Therefore, we have compiled three **"o"**, and there are two crossed strokes. The image of **"x"** is more consistent, so this character is coded as **"yooox"**.

From top to bottom, 0E94F7 is an image of a ring, a "凵" shape, two eyes, and a combination of a person's upper limb and a frog's lower limb. This glyph has many and obvious distinguishing features. For the convenience of input, the part of the eye shape that can not be encoded. In other aspects, the "凵" shape can be encoded by **"u"** , and the rest of the glyph is similar to "☆", but the 26 letters are not similar to it, so the **"x"** with cross

[6] For the convenience of writing, we use the intermediate code to replace the original character, and the corresponding character can refer to the above table.

stroke features is used to encode. So this character is coded as **"youx"**.

From top to bottom, 0E8AB9 is a ring, two **"凵"** shapes, and the rest can be seen as an inverted **"Y"** shape, so the character is encoded as **"youuy"**. The glyphs 0E97C5 and 0E72FC look similar to 0E8AB9, so we think these three characters can use the same code.

The shape of 0E8482 is similar to that of oracle bone inscriptions **"步"** , but it should not be the same character. The whole shape of this character is three-line intersection, so it is encoded by the letter **"y"** .

The shape of 0E7180 is originally a single body, but in order to facilitate input and avoid coding repetition, we divide this font into two parts. The top tip shape is like **"A"**, so we use **"a"** to encode it. The lower part is like a bird spreading its wings, which is similar to **"M"**, so we use **"m"** to encode it.

The shape of 0E8B2D from top to bottom is approximately **"凵"** , two circles, inverted triangle, and other strokes. A vertical stroke is connected under the triangle below, and they are combined together to be similar to the **"Y"** shape, so the word is encoded as **"yuooy"** . Similarly, the coding of 0E8B29 is **"yooy"** .

The glyph of 0E7EDC can be divided into two parts. The periphery is a circle, and the inside is three lines that intersect at the same point. The intersecting lines can still be encoded by **"x"** . 0E9A2D, 0E8275 and 0E96CF all have similar characteristics, like the larger version of **"田"** . The periphery of the three is basically closed and can be coded with **"o"**.There are many dry cross lines at the center of the font, which can be coded with only one **"x"**. We use the same coding on the two types of glyphs, which may lead to high repetition rate, but there are few cases similar to 0E7EDC glyphs, and there are not many uncharacterized glyphs similar to 0E9A2D,0E8275 and 0E96CF.Therefore, these two types of glyphs are easy to distinguish in the input process and will not affect the efficiency of input.

Both 0E8326 and 0E8327 are on the 合集 22507, and it remains to be further investigated whether they are glyphs or characterization symbols. However, the shape and composition of the two are very strange. Like today's one-stroke, it is not common in oracle bone inscriptions. Because we use **"s"** to encode the curved linear components of the rope shapes in other glyphs, we also use **"s"** to encode here.

3 Conclusion

According to our internal test program, the above coding design is indeed feasible, and the coding repetition rate is very low, which is conducive to accurate search. The number of glyphs involved in the input method coding scheme we designed is unprecedented, so our coding design will be closer to the real situation of oracle bone inscriptions than previous coding designs. We try to provide a coding scheme for the input method in line with the professional cognition of ancient Chinese characters. Therefore, we are different from the previous design : the coding design is carried out for different types of Oracle glyphs, and the concept of **"natural classification"** is added to the coding of single component characters. For the unidentified glyphs, we also imitate the multi-component characters as much as possible to carry out the separation in line with the cognition of ancient Chinese characters to encode, and use the English letters to refer to the unidentified parts with similar shapes. Not only that, we have also implemented the coding form of **"shape code + phontic code"** that has not been tried in the past.

The remaining number of variants that are not often used is not a lot of unidentified glyphs. Although some of these are not encoded according to the knowledge of ancient Chinese philology, there are still general rules to follow. For example, we use **"o"** to refer to the closed form component, **"x"** to refer to the cross part of the two lines, **"y"** to refer to the trident part, **"x"** to refer to the unidentified component that cannot be split without increasing the repetition rate, and so on. The design of o, x and y is similar to Oracle Bone Inscriptions Six-digit Code Retrieval Font, but we refer to it from the perspective of "component" of ancient Chinese characters, not using the concept of "stroke" of subsequent of Chinese characters. Nevertheless, it still takes a lot of effort to form a regular coding design for the unidentified glyphs.

At present, the learning manual matching the input method formed on the basis of this coding design is still in preparation, and the preparation of the learning manual is the subject we will study next. In the following research, we will improve the part of the above coding design that is not convenient for fast input, and try to fit the coding rules with strong regularity as much as possible for the unidentified glyph part.

Acknowledgments

Thanks to Mo Bofeng, Liu Ying, and Li Aihui for their guidance on this research. Thanks to Mr. Deng Jian for his guidance in computer technology. Thanks to the anonymous reviewers for their valuable comments on this paper.

References

Huang Tianshu. 2020.*A Preliminary Study on the Side and Head of the Oracle Bone . Collection of Huang Tianshu 's Oracle Bone Science.* .Zhonghua Book Company. page172-181.(in Chinese)

Li Qingsheng, Wu Qinxia, Wang Lei . 2012 *Oracle Bone Inscription Input Method Based on Oracle Bone Inscription Character Dynamic Description Library* .Chinese Journal of Information Issue 4. (in Chinese)

Liu Yongge and Li Qingsheng . 2004. *Design and Implementation of Visual Oracle Bone Inscription Input Method* , Computer Engineering and Application Issue 17. (in Chinese)

Liu Yongge and Li Qiang . 2020.*Summary of Oracle Bone Inscription Input Method*. Yindu Journal . Issue 3.（in Chinese）

Liu Zhixiang and Liu Xiaorong . 2019. *Oracle Bone Inscriptions Six-digit Code Retrieval Font.* Sichuan Dictionary Publishing House.（in Chinese）

Nie Yanzhao and Liu Yongge . 2010. *Free Stroke Input Method of Oracle Bone Inscriptions* , Chinese Journal of Information. Issue 6.(in Chinese)

Xu Song and Hu Jinzhu . 1995. *Realization of Oracle Image Code Input Method* , Journal of Central China Normal University (Natural Science Edition). Issue 3. (in Chinese)

Zhou Demin, Wang Guoan, Zheng Tongbin, Su Yue, Li Feng . 1990. *Design and Implementation of Computer Oracle Bone Inscriptions Information Processing System (CJPS).*Henan Science and Technology. Issue 1. (in Chinese)

Word Sense Disambiguation for Ancient Greek: Sourcing a training corpus through translation alignment

Alek Keersmaekers, Wouter Mercelis, Toon Van Hal
University of Leuven, Belgium
{alek.keersmaekers,wouter.mercelis,toon.vanhal}@kuleuven.be

Abstract

This paper seeks to leverage translations of Ancient Greek texts to enhance the performance of automatic word sense disambiguation (WSD). Satisfactory WSD in Ancient Greek is achievable, provided that the system can rely on annotated data. This study, acknowledging the challenges of manually assigning meanings to every Greek lemma, explores strategies to derive WSD data from parallel texts using sentence and word alignment. Our results suggest that, assuming the condition of high word frequency is met, this technique permits us to automatically produce a significant volume of annotated data, although there are still significant obstacles when trying to automate this process.

1 Aims

This contribution aims at making active use of translations of Ancient Greek texts in order to improve results in automatic word sense disambiguation (WSD). Section 2 outlines the general research context, showing that decent WSD in Ancient Greek is, in the current stage, feasible if the system can be trained on annotated data. Given the impracticality of manually annotating word meanings to all Greek lemmas, this paper explores the possibility of generating a significant volume of annotations automatically. Section 3 surveys related work both at the level of our general aim – word-sense disambiguation of Ancient Greek – and at the level of the methodology we adopt for attaining automatically annotated data for word-sense disambiguation, viz. sourcing from parallel texts via sentence and word alignment. After detailing the methodology adopted (Section 4), we subsequently discuss the results obtained, possible avenues for improvement and perspectives for applications (Sections 5-7).

2 Research context: towards onomasiological searches

It is generally known that in natural languages there is not a one-to-one mapping between form and meaning: one form or term can express various meanings or concepts (e.g. 'bright' can refer to light or intelligence) and vice versa (e.g. there are various ways to express that a person is intelligent, including 'bright', 'clever', 'smart' etc.). In semantic theory, studying the various meanings that a specific form expresses is called the 'semasiological' perspective, while studying the various forms that can be used to express a certain meaning is called the 'onomasiological' perspective (see Geeraerts, 2010).

This has important practical consequences: while it is straightforward to query most annotated corpora for specific terms, querying it for specific concepts is usually far less straightforward (see, for instance, Goossens, 2013). Most corpora have not been annotated semantically, given that the annotation is labor-intensive and often subjective, and semantics is multifaceted. However, to avoid manual annotation, one could make use of so-called 'vector-based models of meaning' or 'word embeddings', which retrieve computational representations of meaning in a bottom-up manner from a large, unannotated dataset (Lenci, 2018).

In the context of Ancient Greek, exploratory studies of vector-based models for detecting onomasiology have begun to emerge, starting from the premise that these models can be harnessed to identify words bearing a similar or related meaning to a given target word (Keersmaekers and Van Hal, 2021 & 2022). In this case, if the researcher already knows some terms that can express a particular concept (say γλῶσσα and φωνή for the concept 'language'), they can use these models to look for terms that are similar to these target words and by

Proceedings of the Ancient Language Processing Workshop associated with RANLP-2023, pages 148–159,
held in Varna Bulgaria, Sept 8, 2023.
https://doi.org/10.26615/978-954-452-087-8_018

doing so fully map the onomasiology of this concept.

However, one complication is polysemy. When using a vector-based model[1] to find the ten nearest neighbors of the term γλῶσσα, for example, the results are all body parts, such as οὖς 'ear', ὀδούς 'tooth', ὀφθαλμός 'eye', χεῖλος 'lip' and φάρυγξ 'throat'. The explanation for this is predominantly linked to the polysemy of γλῶσσα, which can denote both 'language' and 'tongue'. The latter meaning is particularly prominent due to the corpus's extensive inclusion of medical data, which constitutes 14% of all training data, in which 'tongue' is more frequently referred to.

One possible solution is WSD: if we could separate all tokens of γλῶσσα that mean 'tongue' from those meaning 'language', we could look for the nearest neighbors of γλῶσσα when only the tokens meaning 'language' are taken into account. Again, vector-base models can be employed for this: indeed, several transformer-based embedding models such as BERT (Devlin et al., 2019) do no longer model the 'general' meaning of a word but the meaning of a word in context. Such an approach for Ancient Greek is discussed in Mercelis et al. (Forthc.), using ELECTRA (Clark et al., 2020) as a language model. When this model was used in an unsupervised way, the results were disappointing, possibly due to data sparsity. However, when used in a supervised way, by finetuning the transformer network, decent results could be achieved with only about 150 training examples (for binary meaning distinctions) or 300 (for ternary meaning distinctions).

To overcome the problems related to the acquisition bottleneck in obtaining annotated data (Lefever et al., 2011: 320; Pasini, 2020), this paper will discuss an automated way of creating datasets for WSD, by exploiting parallel texts (Greek original texts and English translations). This approach initially involves aligning sentences. Subsequently, within the aligned sentences, individual words are aligned. This two-step process will enable us to annotate polysemous words in Greek with English labels, thus trying to get a hold of their polysemy.

3 Related work

3.1 WSD for Ancient Greek

While the problem of automatic WSD has been tackled for decades already for English, interest in computational semantics has only raised recently for Ancient Greek, and the literature on this topic is therefore very limited. The only studies that we are aware of are Mercelis et al. (Forthc.), as discussed in Section 2, and McGillivray et al. (2019). While Mercelis et al. (Forthc.) directly explored supervised and unsupervised WSD using large language models, the angle of McGillivray et al. (2019) is somewhat different in that they explore how computational methods can be used for lexical semantic change detection. Focusing on three polysemous words (viz. μῦς, ἁρμονία and κόσμος), they explore their polysemy over time and genre using a Bayesian topic model, and match the results to manually annotated datasets of these words.

3.2 Word and sentence alignment

Word alignment used to be one of the key steps in the process of statistical machine translation. Statistical word alignment, represented by GIZA++ (Och and Ney, 2003) formed a strong baseline, which was only surpassed recently by large language models such as BERT (Devlin et al., 2019) and RoBERTa (Liu et al., 2019), based on transformer techniques. Nowadays, attention mechanisms in these large language models have made the word alignment task obsolete in machine translation pipelines. Nonetheless, in recent years word alignment made a comeback, albeit not solely in function of machine translation (Li, 2022). Our paper can be situated in this newfound interest in word alignment, as we focus on aligning words to create datasets for WSD.

Li (2022) provides a comprehensive summary of the history of word alignment, along with an overview of potential strategies for executing this task. Given that the word alignment task is inherently multilingual, most approaches employ a multilingual language model such as mBERT (Devlin et al., 2019) or XLM-RoBERTa (Conneau et al., 2020), which is then fine-tuned for the alignment task. In our case, this is more complex, given that Ancient Greek is in general not incorporated in such multilingual models. Hence,

[1] This example is retrieved from the vector models described in Keersmaekers & Van Hal 2021, which are based on word vectors created using singular value decomposition incorporating syntactic dependency features.

we used the recently released PhilBERTa model (Riemenschneider and Frank, 2023), a trilingual model trained on English, Ancient Greek, and Latin texts.

Yousef et al. (2022a) recently investigated translation alignment at the word level, with a particular focus on Ancient Greek. They utilized multilingual embeddings from which they selected the most similar pairs, signifying aligned words. They employed two alignment techniques: the approach of Jalili Sabet et al. (2016) and that of Dou and Neubig (2021). While according to Li (2022) both techniques handle the word alignment task proficiently, the highest-performing technique in Li's (2022) dataset was a span-extraction model by Nagata et al. (2020). This approach is widely recognized for its application in Question Answering, as the Stanford Question Answering Dataset (SQuAD) (Rajpurkar et al., 2016) was designed with this technique in mind.

Chousa et al. (2020) released a similar model – also based on span-extraction – for sentence alignment. This model achieved state-of-the-art results on various modern language combinations (German – English, French – English, Japanese – English), beating previous approaches such as VecAlign (Thompson and Koehn, 2019).

3.3 Translation alignment for WSD

Parallel texts have a long-standing tradition in WSD, with its roots traced back to the work of Ng et al. (2003) (cf. Pasini, 2020: 4939 for more details). Our approach in this contribution is bilingual, viz. Ancient Greek – English. Over the past decade or so, there has been an emphasis on a multilingual rather than bilingual approach to parallel corpora for WSD (see e.g. Lefever et al., 2011). Most of these approaches rely on the massive European parliament corpus (see, e.g. Delli Bovi et al., 2017). Rather than concentrating solely on direct annotation transfer on the token level, certain researchers propose a more holistic approach. This involves taking into account the wider context provided by the entire parallel corpus, rather than merely focusing on parallel sentences (van der Plas and Apidianaki, 2014). More recently, scholars have proposed multilingual approaches in which translation parallels are replaced with propagation methods. Starting from contextualized word embeddings in English and relying on multilingual data from knowledge bases (such as WordNet and Wikipedia), such approaches can automatically generate training data for languages without labeled data for WSD (Barba et al., 2020). Recent research has also pointed out that the generation of translations can improve the quality of WSD (see e.g. Luan, 2020).

4 Methodology

4.1 Data

In our undertaking Ancient Greek is the source language and English the target language, given the abundance of English translations and manually aligned data. For our source language, we started from the GLAUx corpus (Keersmaekers, 2021), which encompasses approximately 32M Greek tokens, spanning roughly from the 8th century BC to the 4th century AD. As for the target language, the majority of our English data was drawn from the Perseus project (Smith et al., 2000).[2] However, we also incorporated openly accessible online editions for certain lengthy texts not available in Perseus, such as Dionysius of Halicarnassus's *Roman Antiquities*. Both the GLAUx data and the English translation data incorporate information about the texts' structure (e.g., division into books, chapters, sections, verses, etc.). This facilitated the alignment of 'paragraphs' in both languages. We use the term 'paragraph' loosely here, referring to the shortest shared structural unit between the Greek text and its translation, which can be, for instance, a section, chapter (if no sections are provided), or, in the case of poetic texts, a group of verses. In total, we were able to link around 7.2 million Greek tokens (approximately a quarter of the GLAUx corpus) to an English translation.

We trained word alignment models using data from the Alpheios project[3] and from the UGARIT project (Yousef et al., 2022b) as training data (66929 tokens). For the sentence alignment task, we used the same data sources, supplemented with Pedalion data (Keersmaekers et al., 2019), as well as a parallel New Testament corpus and data from the Greek Learner Texts Project.[4] In addition to this, we also annotated data ourselves. In total, this amounted to 15178 training sentences.

[2] Data taken from https://github.com/PerseusDL/canonical-greekLit.

[3] https://alpheios.net/pages/tools/

[4] See https://greek-learner-texts.org and https://github.com/jtauber/plato-texts.

During the development stage, we assessed the word alignment task using the same gold standard data (5076 tokens) employed by Yousef et al. (2022a). This facilitated a direct comparison of our results with their work. We evaluated the sentence alignment model using our own held-out data (879 sentences). This dataset was the most appropriate for evaluating performance as it consisted of parallel paragraphs, whereas for other datasets, we were forced to artificially combine sentences into existing or sometimes even entirely new paragraphs (fixed at a length of 10 sentences), since they did not provide paragraph data. Given the length of some of these paragraphs in our evaluation dataset, this dataset posed a significant challenge for the model in accurately predicting sentence alignments.

4.2 Sentence alignment

Our target corpus, GLAUx, is paragraph-aligned, requiring us to first conduct sentence alignment to enable word alignment within these sentences.

Segmenting Ancient Greek paragraphs into sentences is a straightforward process, given the existence of meticulous editions of the available texts and the general lack of abbreviations that might complicate splitting at full stops. Thus, our aim is to extract the English sentences that correspond to a particular Ancient Greek sentence from an entire English paragraph.

To achieve this, we employ a span-extraction approach, based on the work of Chousa et al. (2020), as discussed in Section 3.2. This method represents the state-of-the-art approach and is methodologically quite similar to the word alignment model. The key distinction lies in the focus of extraction: tokens from sentences in the case of word alignment, and sentences from paragraphs for sentence alignment.

4.3 Word alignment

As noted earlier, there are several strategies for word alignment. For this task, we selected the span-extraction approach as well. This method was the top performer in the study by Li (2022),[5] and it utilizes annotated data, to which we had access. Additionally, choosing a different approach to word alignment than Yousef et al. (2022a) allowed us to compare the outcomes.

For each pair of parallel sentences, we used the English sentence as the context. Then, for every token in the Ancient Greek sentence, we treated this sentence as a 'question', similar to the terminology used in SQuAD. In this sentence, the current token was demarcated with a special separation token. Both the context and the 'question' were processed by a PhilBerta model (Section 3.2), fine-tuned for the span-extraction task. The model then predicted the start and end indices of the corresponding English token in the context, or the English sentence, thereby aligning the Ancient Greek and English tokens.

Upon completing this process, we secured a corpus that was aligned at the word level.

Lemma's	Frequency band
γλῶσσα; λόγος; φωνή	1
ῥῆμα	2

Table 1: Linguistic terms.

Lemma	Frequency band
αἴσθησις; καταλύω; ἀλλότριος	1
βίοτος; ἀπαντάω; μιαρός	2
ἱστός; ἀνύω; ξηρός	3

Table 2: Randomly selected terms.

4.4 From translation alignment to WSD

To investigate how useful the word-aligned results are for WSD, we created two test sets of (a) words referring to metalinguistic concepts and (b) randomly selected polysemous words, as shown in Tables 1 and 2 respectively. The first set of words was handpicked by our team, as this work was initiated within the framework of a project focused on the onomasiology of linguistic concepts. The second set was chosen to extend the validation of our approach beyond the confines of this specific project. To be precise, we utilized the word list by Van Hal (2013), which provides information on the frequency (in four frequency bands) and polysemy of various Greek words, excluding those that are extremely common. From the first three frequency bands of Van Hal (2013), we randomly selected one noun, one adjective, and one verb.

[5] Note, however, that the target languages of these studies are all modern languages that are less inflectional than Greek and can utilize larger language models.

Next, for each of the target words listed in Table 1-2, we extracted the word alignments retrieved with our automatic models. The results were quite messy, containing many one-to-many alignments (likely due to our training data): an example (γλῶσσα) is shown in Table 3. Additionally, they contain inflected forms ('tongues') as well as function words such as articles and prepositions, due to linguistic differences between the two languages (i.e. Greek uses case marking, does not have an indefinite article and uses definite articles differently from English etc.). We therefore further cleaned the data by (a) tokenizing the results, (b) removing punctuation, (c) removing stop words and (d) lemmatizing each word in the results, using the NLTK packages *stopwords* and *WordNetLemmatizer* (Bird et al. 2009). After doing so, we further removed noise by calculating the frequency of each remaining lemma and removing all the lemmas that occur less than 1% in the total results. An example of the final output for γλῶσσα is given in Table 4. Although the table still contains some noise (e.g. the adjectives 'rare', 'good' and 'ordinary'), most of the results are clear translations of the word γλῶσσα.

Nevertheless, the results contained several synonyms or very closely related words (e.g. 'lip' and 'mouth' in Table 4). To use these results for WSD, they therefore need to be clustered in some way. In order to obtain a first idea which criteria the clustering should use, we performed the clustering manually, although automatic clustering is obviously necessary if one wants to scale up this approach to the full Greek corpus. Concretely, we used both frequency and meaning relatedness as criteria: in all cases, we clustered very closely related meanings (i.e. near-synonyms) together, but also clustered meanings when they were only somewhat closely related but were infrequent. In other words, we used a pragmatic criterion: if there were too little examples of a specific meaning, it would be problematic to learn this meaning through WSD, so it would be worth it to combine them with examples of another related meaning, even if some meaning granularity was lost by doing so. We did not assign irrelevant words to a cluster (e.g. 'rare', 'good', 'ordinary' in Table 4), but simply discarded them from the dataset. The results of the manual meaning clustering can be seen in Tables 5-8 in Appendix. To create a final dataset for WSD, for each cleaned up word alignment we checked if it contained any of the words assigned to one of the clusters, and if not, the example was discarded. Next, one could use these results to train models for WSD, take the tokens from the Greek corpus that were assigned to one of the meanings that they are interested in (e.g. the linguistic meaning of γλῶσσα in our case) and calculate the nearest neighbors based on these tokens, as detailed in Section 2. However, we did not perform this step in the scope of this paper.

Alignment	#	Alignment	#
tongue	57	my tongue	5
the tongue	18	in a tongue	5
tongues	11	of	5
with tongues	9	the tongues	5
a	7	speech	4
of the tongue	6	a tongue	4
.	5	lips	3
his tongue	5	...	...

Table 3: Example of word alignment results: γλῶσσα.

Alignment	#	Alignment	#
tongue	168	language	4
word	15	good	4
speech	12	voice	3
rare	8	mouth	3
lip	6	ordinary	3

Table 4: Cleaned results of γλῶσσα

5 Results

5.1 Sentence alignment

Firstly, we evaluated the model on the held-out data described in Section 4.1. This resulted in an accuracy (exact matches) of 73% (644/879). The F1-score, which also takes into account partial matches, was 86%.

Since such a quantitative evaluation can be misleading (since the test data might not entirely match our target corpus), we also manually conducted an evaluation of sentence alignment performance using 133 sentences from the target corpus chosen at random. The accuracy was 65% (86/133), somewhat lower than the 73% of the automatic evaluation, indicating that these results might be too rosy.[6] Out of the remaining 35% of sentence alignments that were not correct, half of them (25/47) were partially correct, i.e. the Greek sentence contained the English translation but included more text, or vice versa.

The size of the training corpus at the sentence alignment task appears to be of great importance. It was our hypothesis that non-problematic corresponding sentences (in a 1-to-1 ratio, i.e. without Greek sentences that are mapped to multiple English sentences, or vice-versa) that were combined into artificial paragraphs (cf. Section 4.1) would contribute little. This turned out not to be the case. A model trained on data without these artificial paragraphs performed significantly worse, with an accuracy of 43% and an F1-score of 41% on the held-out data.

5.2 Word alignment

In contrast with the results shown in Li (2022), the span-extraction approach implemented in our model performed worse than the approach of Jalili Sabet et al. (2016) and Dou and Neubig (2021), as used by Yousef et al. (2022a). The comparison is difficult however, as they not only used another alignment approach, but also utilized another training dataset. Their best-performing model achieved an F1-score of 81.5, and an Alignment Error Rate (AER) of 18.7. It is, however, not exactly clear how the metrics are computed, viz. how punctuation and source words that do not have an alignment (e.g. untranslatable particles) are exactly handled. In the gold dataset, tokens without alignment are not annotated. Thus, it is not clear whether they are included in the evaluation or not.

The scores including these source tokens and punctuation, are an F1 of 47.7 and an AER of 43.5 (5076 tokens in total). If we leave these out, the F1 score rises to 59.6, and the AER is 35.9. For the scope of this project, the former evaluation is the most important, as the WSD task is mainly interested in content words such as verbs, nouns and adjectives. In contrast with these part-of-speech classes, the left-out tokens are mainly punctuation marks and untranslatable particles, which are of less importance for the WSD task.

5.3 Manual clustering of the results

The results derived from applying word alignment and subsequently manually clustering them, as outlined in Section 4.4, are presented in Tables 5-8 (found in the Appendix). A notable observation is that a considerable proportion of the data, accounting for 49% of all aligned tokens on average across all target words, included many translations that could not be neatly clustered (labelled as 'other' in these tables). This percentage varied from 24% (for μιαρός) to as high as 84% (for ιστός). These typically fall into two categories: (a) words that were excluded by the frequency filter (see Section 4.4) or (b) incorrect word alignments. Concerning category (a), there are instances where the frequency filter eliminates relevant terms. A case in point is 'Latin' for γλῶσσα, which was filtered out despite clearly referring to the linguistic sense of γλῶσσα (contextually appearing in 'λέγειν ἱκανῶς ἑκατέραν γλῶτταν' which was roughly translated to 'to speak both Latin and Greek fluently'). Conversely, when the frequency filter is not used, the data evidently becomes cluttered with irrelevant results. For instance, some of the single-occurrence results for γλῶσσα include 'she-bear', 'of frigidity', and 'power of lubricating', which are unquestionably incorrect translations for γλῶσσα. Given that translation alignment at both the sentence and word levels only reaches a respective F1-score of 86 and 60 percent, it is inevitable that the data will contain numerous errors, resulting from either inaccurate sentence or word alignment.

Since the frequency threshold was relatively low, for less frequent words (viz. βίοτος, μιαρός, ιστός, and ἀνύω) no words were filtered out, allowing us to assess how many alignment pairs were relevant for the task described in this paper. As can be deduced from Tables 5-8, for βίοτος 40% of all alignments were irrelevant, for μιαρός 24%, for ιστός 84% and for ἀνύω 67%. This averages out to 54%, meaning that only half of the alignments were relevant for compiling a WSD dataset.

This has serious consequences for the possibilities of automating this approach. On the one hand, the frequency filter was absolutely necessary, given the amount of noise present in the data, which would make automatic clustering problematic. On the other hand, if an absolute frequency filter would have been used (e.g.

[6] Although the differences are barely statistically significant, with p=0.05 with Fisher's exact test.

filtering out translations that occur less than 3 times), this would lead to data sparsity for less frequent words. Therefore an obvious solution would be expanding the data, either by improving the alignment results or by adding more parallel English translations to the data.

On a brighter note, this method is clearly capable of retrieving a sufficient number of relevant examples for more frequent terms, thus creating a useful dataset for WSD. Nevertheless, there are several important considerations. Firstly, it is worth noting that the manual clustering was highly subjective: another researcher may well have grouped the words differently than we did. In such instances, an automatic clustering method might offer greater objectivity, even though automatic methods carry their own inherent biases. Generally speaking, the use of parallel translations is more effective when meanings can be more clearly differentiated (e.g., in the case of ἱστός, where there is a stark difference between 'mast' and 'loom'), rather than when the differences are somewhat vague (for instance, for λόγος, the distinctions between 'word', 'statement', and 'report' are not always easily discernible).

Secondly, the level of granularity that is possible to distinguish is dependent on the number of examples for a specific sense, especially when taking into account that some senses are more present in the data that we are using than other senses. While for λόγος many fine-grained distinctions can be made, for γλῶσσα only a general 'linguistic' sense can be distinguished, conflating the translations 'voice', 'speech', 'language' and 'word'. Meanwhile, for some WSD is not possible at all: for ξηρός all translations pointed to 'dry' (while the word also has other meanings in Greek, such as 'slim' and 'harsh').

Finally, one obvious issue is that this method assumes that the English translation equivalents do not have the exact same sense ambiguity as the Greek words. This does not always hold true. In the γλῶσσα-case, for instance, the English term 'tongue' can occasionally signify 'language', as exemplified in phrases like 'mother tongue'. This interpretation is also found in some of the more antiquated translations within our corpus. Another example is αἴσθησις, where 'sense' in English is similarly ambiguous between the meaning 'sensation, perception' and 'faculty for experiencing the outside world'. This issue could be solved in multiple ways, e.g. by using parallel translations from other languages that do not have this sense ambiguity. Alternatively, WSD could be conducted on the English data. However, this adds another automated step, which may potentially compromise the quality of the final results.

6 Avenues for better results

6.1 Improving alignment

Clearly, as the previous section demonstrates, inaccurate alignment results significantly curtail the volume of data that can be employed for WSD. Therefore, enhancing automatic alignments is a vital step towards further improvements.

On a foundational level, our work relied on an existing multilingual RoBERTa model, namely PhilBerta. However, given potential mismatches between the data format of PhilBerta and GLAUx data (for instance, in terms of Unicode encoding of accents or tokenization), it might prove beneficial to adopt an English-Greek model that is more closely attuned to the GLAUx data.

Regarding sentence alignment, potential improvements could be realized by augmenting the training data. Considering our current training set is rather limited (comprising 15,178 sentences), expanding it is one possible avenue for enhancing results (a step we are presently exploring; cf. Section 6.4). However, this inevitably entails a significant amount of manual work. An alternative strategy is to refine the alignment method itself. Our current method relies solely on word embedding information. While this might function effectively for language models with extensive data, Greek embedding models could be too sparse to be effectively deployed in isolation. Supplemental information might thus bolster the results, such as sentence position within a paragraph (naturally, Greek and English sentences tend to occupy similar positions within identical paragraphs) and the frequency of matches between the English translation of a Greek word, using a bilingual dictionary, and the English sentence. Moreover, the word alignment task could inform sentence alignment: very low probabilities in word alignment might signal that sentence alignment has misidentified a sentence. Lastly, an entirely different approach than the one employed in this study could also be considered. Adopting an unsupervised approach like VecAlign (Thompson and Koehn, 2019) could address the problem of having to depend excessively on annotated examples.

Given that our method for word alignment is based on the same technique as sentence alignment, all the above considerations hold true for the former task as well. However, manually annotating word alignment proves to be even more labor-intensive than sentence alignment. Hence, unsupervised models may prove particularly advantageous for this task.

6.2 Improving the clustering

While the alignment results could be improved further, the task is inherently challenging and it is therefore likely that a significant amount of noise will always persist in the data. Thus, it is vital to implement effective techniques for filtering this noise. The simple frequency filter used in this study could potentially be too restrictive in some instances, such as with the Greek word μιαρός, which has several one-time translations for the concept 'miserable'. To address this, we might consider semantic similarity (operationalized through language models) as an additional criterion, specifically by including low-frequency translations if they show substantial semantic similarity to a higher-frequency translation.

For this study, we manually performed the clustering, but naturally, automatic clustering is necessary if we aim to extend this approach to the entire Greek corpus. A feasible method might involve clustering words with similar static embeddings in English.

6.3 Alternative methods

The applicability of new techniques for WSD and translation alignment, as discussed in Section 3.3, to Ancient Greek remains uncertain. When it comes to multilingual approaches, there is a scarcity of multilingual parallel corpora featuring Ancient Greek, with the exception of Biblical texts. However, repositories like <remacle.org> and *hodoi elektronikai* <hodoi.fltr.ucl.ac.be> could facilitate the creation of a trilingual Greek, English, and French corpus. The potential of propagation methods (which necessitate knowledge bases) and automatic translations in enhancing WSD in Ancient Greek is unclear.

One reviewer commented that instead of the method proposed in this paper, one could collect training data from dictionaries, as was done by Bamman and Burns (2020). Indeed, this was the strategy we initially pursued, using a digital version of the Liddell-Scott-Jones (LSJ) dictionary that we automatically linked with the GLAUx corpus. However, it soon became clear that relying exclusively on this dataset was only possible for a few highly frequent words with many examples in the dictionary: even when excluding the irrelevant word alignments (classified as 'other' in Table 5-8), the amount of data we could retrieve from word alignment was ten times larger than from the LSJ dictionary, and there was only one word (λόγος) for which we could retrieve more than 100 examples from LSJ (243 in total, which is still much smaller than the 3128 examples from word alignment). However, these dictionaries might still provide supplementary data, or provide a solid base for clustering the word alignments (i.e. by showing which English translations 'group together' for one specific meaning).

6.4 Progress made after peer review

While the results discussed in this paper might not seem too promising initially, we found that we were able to substantially improve the results by expanding and cleaning up the training data for both sentence and word alignment, and expanding our parallel Greek-English corpus with some other openly available translations.[7] For example, for the word γλῶσσα we now obtained 829 relevant results, after removing 187 results by applying the frequency filter, while previously we only had 210 relevant results after removing 152 results (see Table 8).

7 Conclusions and perspectives

In view of the extensive research conducted on WSD for modern languages, the comparative neglect of classical languages is striking. However, significant progress can be made in the near future to rectify this disparity, thanks in part to the comprehensive philological studies conducted in the past. With a robust lexicographical tradition replete with translated example sentences, and a prolific translation history, classical language resources, once available in a digital shape, have

[7] For sentence alignment, the accuracy rose from 73% to 85%, while the F1 score increased from 86% to 92%. For word alignment, the F1 score improved from 59.6 to 70.6, while the AER dropped from 35.9 to 24.0.

the potential to unlock promising possibilities for WSD applications.

The methodology presented in this paper appears to be a promising means to achieve our goals – coming to an onomasiological disclosure of the Ancient Greek corpus. A critical prerequisite, however, is the availability of a substantial volume of data, suggesting that the approach is effective predominantly for frequently used words.

Apart from this, we believe that this approach holds intrinsic value. For texts that have digital English translations available, we can make educated predictions regarding the meanings of the individual tokens. Additionally, this approach provides insights into the distribution of word senses as distinguished by lexicographers in Ancient Greek.

Acknowledgments

We would like to thank the reviewers for their valuable comments and suggestions. The research in this article was made possible by grant numbers HBC.2021.0210/KRIS:0508000001361 (VLAIO) and G052021N (FWO, Research Council – Flanders).

References

Bamman, David, and Patrick J. Burns. 2020. "Latin BERT: A Contextual Language Model for Classical Philology." ArXiv:2009.10053 [Cs], September. http://arxiv.org/abs/2009.10053.

Barba, Edoardo, Luigi Procopio, Niccolò Cam polungo, Tommaso Pasini, and Roberto Navigli. 2020. "MuLaN: Multilingual Label Propagation for Word Sense Disambiguation." In Proceedings of IJCAI, 3837–44.

Bird, Steven, Edward Loper, and Ewan Klein. 2009. Natural Language Processing with Python. O'Reilly Media Inc.

Chousa, Katsuki, Masaaki Nagata, and Masaaki Nishino. 2020. "SpanAlign: Sentence Alignment Method Based on Cross-Language Span Prediction and ILP." In Proceedings of the 28th International Conference on Computational Linguistics, 4750–61. Barcelona (Online): International Committee on Computational Linguistics. https://doi.org/10.18653/v1/2020.coling-main.418.

Clark, Kevin, Minh-Thang Luong, Quoc V. Le, and Christopher D. Manning. 2020. "ELECTRA: Pre-Training Text Encoders as Discriminators Rather Than Generators." CoRR abs/2003.10555. https://arxiv.org/abs/2003.10555.

Conneau, Alexis, Kartikay Khandelwal, Naman Goyal, Vishrav Chaudhary, Guillaume Wenzek, Francisco Guzmán, Edouard Grave, Myle Ott, Luke Zettlemoyer, and Veselin Stoyanov. 2020. "Unsupervised Cross-Lingual Representation Learning at Scale." arXiv. https://doi.org/10.48550/arXiv.1911.02116.

Delli Bovi, Claudio, Jose Camacho-Collados, Alessandro Raganato, and Roberto Navigli. 2017. "EuroSense: Automatic Harvesting of Multilingual Sense Annotations from Parallel Text." In Proceedings of the 55th Annual Meeting of the Association for Computational Linguistics (Volume 2: Short Papers), 594–600. Vancouver: Association for Computational Linguistics. https://doi.org/10.18653/v1/P17-2094.

Devlin, Jacob, Ming-Wei Chang, Kenton Lee, and Kristina Toutanova. 2019. "BERT: Pre-Training of Deep Bidirectional Transformers for Language Understanding." In Proceedings of the 2019 Conference of the North American Chapter of the Association for Computational Linguistics: Human Language Technologies, Volume 1 (Long and Short Papers), 4171–86. Minneapolis).

Dou, Zi-Yi, and Graham Neubig. 2021. "Word Alignment by Fine-Tuning Embeddings on Parallel Corpora." arXiv. http://arxiv.org/abs/2101.08231.

Geeraerts, Dirk. 2010. Theories of Lexical Semantics. Oxford & New York: Oxford University Press.

Goossens, Diane. 2013. "Assessing Corpus Search Methods in Onomasiological Investigations." Corpus Perspectives on Patterns of Lexis 57: 271.

Jalili Sabet, Masoud, Philipp Dufter, François Yvon, and Hinrich Schütze. 2021. "SimAlign: High Quality Word Alignments without Parallel Training Data Using Static and Contextualized Embeddings." arXiv. http://arxiv.org/abs/2004.08728.

Keersmaekers, Alek. 2021. "The GLAUx Corpus: Methodological Issues in Designing a Long-Term, Diverse, Multi-Layered Corpus of Ancient Greek." In Proceedings of the 2nd International Workshop on Computational Approaches to Historical Language Change 2021, 39–50. Online: Association for Computational Linguistics. https://doi.org/10.18653/v1/2021.lchange-1.6.

Keersmaekers, Alek, Wouter Mercelis, Colin Swaelens, and Toon Van Hal. 2019. "Creating, Enriching and Valorizing Treebanks of Ancient Greek." In Proceedings of the 18th International Workshop on Treebanks and Linguistic Theories (TLT, SyntaxFest 2019), 109–17. Paris: Association for Computational Linguistics. https://doi.org/10.18653/v1/W19-7812.

Keersmaekers, Alek, and Toon Van Hal. 2021. "A Corpus-Based Approach to Conceptual History of Ancient Greek." In Cognitive Sociolinguistics Revisited, edited by Gitte Kristiansen, Karlien Franco, Stefano De Pascale, Laura Rosseel, and Weiwei Zhang, 213–25. Berlin & Boston: Walter de Gruyter.

———. 2022. "In Search of the Flocks: How to Perform Onomasiological Queries in an Ancient Greek Corpus?" In Proceedings of the LREC 2022 Second Workshop on Language Technologies for Historical and Ancient Languages (LT4HALA 2022), 73–83. Marseille.

Lefever, Els, Véronique Hoste, and Martine De Cock. 2011. "ParaSense or How to Use Parallel Corpora for Word Sense Disambiguation." In Proceedings of the 49th Annual Meeting of the Association for Computational Linguistics: Human Language Technologies, 317–22. Portland: Association for Computational Linguistics. https://aclanthology.org/P11-2055.

Lenci, Alessandro. 2018. "Distributional Models of Word Meaning." Annual Review of Linguistics 4 (1): 151–71. https://doi.org/10.1146/annurev-linguistics-030514-125254.

Li, Bryan. 2022. "Word Alignment in the Era of Deep Learning: A Tutorial." arXiv. https://doi.org/10.48550/arXiv.2212.00138.

Liu, Yinhan, Myle Ott, Naman Goyal, Jingfei Du, Mandar Joshi, Danqi Chen, Omer Levy, Mike Lewis, Luke Zettlemoyer, and Veselin Stoyanov. 2019. "RoBERTa: A Robustly Optimized BERT Pretraining Approach." arXiv. https://doi.org/10.48550/arXiv.1907.11692.

Luan, Yixing, Bradley Hauer, Lili Mou, and Grzegorz Kondrak. 2020. "Improving Word Sense Disambiguation with Translations." In Proceedings of the 2020 Conference on Empirical Methods in Natural Language Processing (EMNLP), 4055–65. Online: Association for Computational Linguistics. https://doi.org/10.18653/v1/2020.emnlp-main.332.

McGillivray, Barbara, Simon Hengchen, Viivi Lähteenoja, Marco Palma, and Alessandro Vatri. 2019. "A Computational Approach to Lexical Polysemy in Ancient Greek." Digital Scholarship in the Humanities 34 (4): 893–907. https://doi.org/10.1093/llc/fqz036.

Mercelis, Wouter, Toon Van Hal, and Alek Keersmaekers. Forthcoming. "Tongue, language or noise? Word Sense Disambiguation in Ancient Greek with corpus-based methods." In International Colloquium of Ancient Greek Linguistics.

Nagata, Masaaki, Katsuki Chousa, and Masaaki Nishino. 2020. "A Supervised Word Alignment Method Based on Cross-Language Span Prediction Using Multilingual BERT." In Proceedings of the 2020 Conference on Empirical Methods in Natural Language Processing (EMNLP), 555–65. Online: Association for Computational Linguistics. https://doi.org/10.18653/v1/2020.emnlp-main.41.

Ng, Hwee Tou, Bin Wang, and Yee Seng Chan. 2003. "Exploiting Parallel Texts for Word Sense Disambiguation: An Empirical Study." In Proceedings of the 41st Annual Meeting of the Association for Computational Linguistics, 455–62. Sapporo: Association for Computational Linguistics. https://doi.org/10.3115/1075096.1075154.

Och, Franz Josef, and Hermann Ney. 2003. "A Systematic Comparison of Various Statistical Alignment Models." Computational Linguistics 29 (1): 19–51.

Pasini, Tommaso. 2020. "The Knowledge Acquisition Bottleneck Problem in Multilingual Word Sense Disambiguation." In Proceedings of the Twenty-Ninth International Joint Conference on Artificial Intelligence, 4936–42. Yokohama: International Joint Conferences on Artificial Intelligence Organization. https://doi.org/10.24963/ijcai.2020/687.

van der Plas, Lonneke, and Marianna Apidianaki. 2014. "Cross-Lingual Word Sense Disambiguation for Predicate Labelling of French." In Proceedings of TALN 2014 (Volume 1: Long Papers), 46–55. Marseille: Association pour le Traitement Automatique des Langues. https://aclanthology.org/F14-1005.

Rajpurkar, Pranav, Jian Zhang, Konstantin Lopyrev, and Percy Liang. 2016. "SQuAD: 100,000+ Questions for Machine Comprehension of Text." arXiv. https://doi.org/10.48550/arXiv.1606.05250.

Riemenschneider, Frederick, and Anette Frank. 2023. "Exploring Large Language Models for Classical Philology." arXiv. https://doi.org/10.48550/arXiv.2305.13698.

Smith, David A., Jeffrey A. Rydberg-Cox, and Gregory R. Crane. 2000. "The Perseus Project: A Digital Library for the Humanities." Literary and Linguistic Computing 15 (1): 15–25.

Thompson, Brian, and Philipp Koehn. 2019. "Vecalign: Improved Sentence Alignment in Linear Time and Space." In Proceedings of the 2019 Conference on Empirical Methods in Natural Language Processing and the 9th International Joint Conference on Natural Language Processing (EMNLP-IJCNLP), 1342–48. Hong Kong: Association for Computational Linguistics. https://doi.org/10.18653/v1/D19-1136.

Van Hal, Toon. 2013. Ankura. Basiswoordenlijst Oudgrieks. Antwerpen & Apeldoorn: Garant.

Yousef, Tariq, Chiara Palladino, Farnoosh Shamsian, Anise d'Orange Ferreira, and Michel Ferreira dos Reis. 2022. "An Automatic Model and Gold Standard for Translation Alignment of Ancient Greek." In Proceedings of the Thirteenth Language Resources and Evaluation Conference, 5894–5905. Marseille: European Language Resources Association. https://aclanthology.org/2022.lrec-1.634.

Yousef, Tariq, Chiara Palladino, Farnoosh Shamsian, and Maryam Foradi. 2022. "Translation Alignment with Ugarit." Information 13 (2): 65. https://doi.org/10.3390/info13020065.

A Appendices

Lemma	Translations	N
αἴσθησις	perception, sensation	118
	sense, faculty	43
	memory, knowledge, consciousness, opinion	20
	other (unclassified)	173
καταλύω	subvert, overthrow, undermine, suppress, destroy, abolish, depose, dissolution	109
	end, break, cease, stop	33
	lodge	7
	other (unclassified)	234
ἀλλότριος	another, property, others, belongs, belonging, else, possessions	148
	alien, foreign, strange, strangers	77
	other (unclassified)	210

Table 5: Results for randomly chosen terms (frequency band 1).

Lemma	Translations	N
βίοτος	life, age	40
	mean, victual, property, substance, gold, wealth, livelihood	16
	estate, house	6
	food	4
	other (unclassified)	44
ἀπαντάω	meet, encounter	96
	come, go	42
	confront	5
	other (unclassified)	238
μιαρός	infamous, wretch, bad, cruel, abominably, wretched, abominable, rogue, foul, trouble, ...	54
	polluted, pestilential, stain, blood, defiled, unclean, pestilent, filthy	14
	other (unclassified)	21

Table 6: Results for randomly chosen terms (frequency band 2).

Lemma	Translations	N
ἱστός	raft, keel, ship, mast	7
	weaving, loom, tambour	6
	other (unclassified)	68
ἀνύω	attain, prove, accomplish, gain, achieve, finish, obtain, complete, reach, stop, fulfil	22
	haste, proceed, renew	4
	other (unclassified)	53
ξηρός	dry, withered, arid, wet, dried, barren, liquid, moist, dessicant, watery	126
	other (unclassified)	78

Table 7: Results for randomly chosen terms (frequency band 3).

Lemma	Translations	N
γλῶσσα	tongue, mouth, lip	177
	voice, speech, language, word	33
	other (unclassified)	152
φωνή	voice, cry, vocal	355
	speech, language, utterance, word, tongue	112
	sound	60
	other (unclassified)	294
λόγος	say, talk, speech, statement, said, saying, speak	1032
	word	850
	argument, reason	520
	story, report, discourse	433
	formula	92
	discussion	82
	account	66
	eloquence	53
	other (unclassified)	3616
ῥῆμα	name, saying, word, expression, term	108
	verb	17
	sentence, phrase	16
	speech	4
	other (unclassified)	92

Table 8: Results for linguistic terms.

Enhancing State-of-the-Art NLP Models for Classical Arabic

Tariq Yousef **Lisa Mischer** **Hamid Reza Hakimi** **Maxim Romanov**

"The Evolution of Islamic Societies (c. 600-1600): From Algorithmic Analysis into Social History"
Emmy Noether Junior Research Group, Hamburg University
{firstname.lastname}@uni-hamburg.de

Abstract

Like many other historical languages, Classical Arabic is hindered by the absence of adequate training datasets and accurate "off-the-shelf" models that can be readily used in processing pipelines. In this paper, we discuss our ongoing work to develop and train deep learning models specially designed to manage various tasks related to classical Arabic texts. We specifically concentrate on Named Entity Recognition, classification of person relationships, toponym classification, detection of onomastic section boundaries, onomastic element classification, as well as date recognition and classification. Our efforts aim to confront the difficulties tied to these tasks and to deliver effective solutions for analyzing classical Arabic texts. Though this work is still under development, the preliminary results presented in the paper suggest excellent to satisfactory performance of the fine-tuned models, successfully achieving the intended objectives for which they were trained.

1 Introduction

Arabic chronicles and biographical collections preserve a plethora of information on long-term environmental and societal processes that shaped and molded Islamic societies. Numerous and extensive, these written texts are the richest "mine" of information and are particularly valuable for the period before the 15th century, for which exceptionally few archival documents are available.

Our work focuses on constructing the social history of the Islamic world from historical and biographical texts that constitute a significant part of the Arabic written tradition. The project studies a vast corpus of digitized texts and relies on a series of computational methods for identifying and linking relevant information from the corpus. Currently, the project is at the stage of fine-tuning relevant NLP-based approaches. The work described in this paper is the methodological foundation for the creation of the network of knowledge. This network will serve as the main research framework of the project for the study of the social history of the Islamic world.

Classical Arabic, like all other historical and ancient languages, lacks adequate training datasets and accurate "off-the-shelf" models that can be directly employed in the processing pipelines. In light of this, our objective is to make a valuable contribution to the field by creating comprehensive training datasets for various tasks related to classical Arabic text processing and analysis. Furthermore, we aim to develop, train, and fine-tune models that can be easily integrated and shared with fellow researchers in the community, facilitating their work and promoting further advancements in the field of classical Arabic language processing.

In the following sections, we present our in-progress work in developing and training deep learning models tailored for handling diverse tasks relevant to classical Arabic texts. Specifically, we focus on NER, person relationships classification, toponyms classification, onomastic section boundaries detection, onomastic entities classification, as well as date recognition and classification.

2 Related Work

Recent advancements in deep learning and language modeling have significantly propelled the development of Natural Language Processing (NLP) models for the Arabic language. Several transformer-based language models are currently available and provide state-of-the-art performance in various downstream tasks.

ARABERT (Antoun et al., 2020) is the first transformer-based language model for the Arabic language. The CAMEL LAB (Obeid et al., 2020) introduced a collection of pre-trained models for several Arabic NLP tasks such as Part-of-speech (POS) tagging, named entity recognition (NER), sentiment analysis, and text classification.

Proceedings of the Ancient Language Processing Workshop associated with RANLP-2023, pages 160–169,
held in Varna Bulgaria, Sept 8, 2023.
https://doi.org/10.26615/978-954-452-087-8_019

Figure 1: An example illustrating a typical biography.

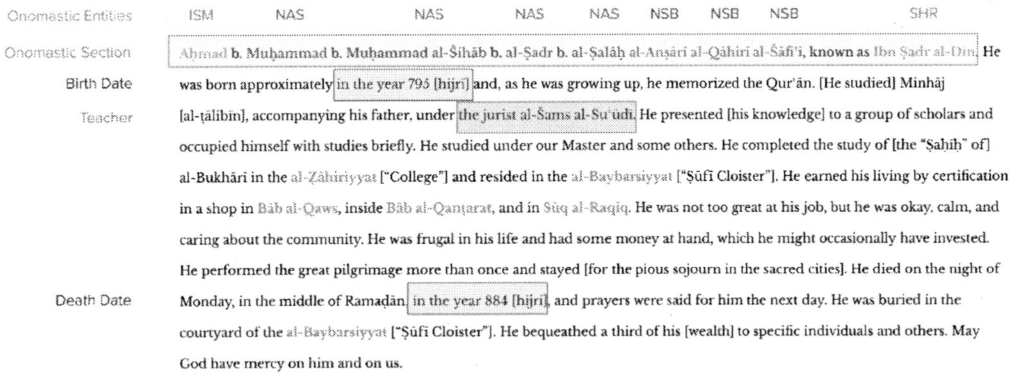

Figure 2: Translation of the example in Figure 1.

These models have been trained using different corpora, namely, classical Arabic CA, dialectal Arabic DA, modern standard Arabic MSA, and the MIXED corpus which comprises all available corpora. FARASA[1] (Abdelali et al., 2016) offers diverse solutions and models for Arabic text processing. It also provides a RESTful API, allowing users to access its functionalities and leverage language-independent solutions.

Further, several pre-trained models have been trained for different downstream tasks such as ARAT5 (Nagoudi et al., 2021) and ARAGPT2 (Antoun et al., 2021b) for Arabic language generation and understanding; ARAELECTRA (Antoun et al., 2021a), ARBERT, and MARBERT (Abdul-Mageed et al., 2021) for language representation. The majority of the models mentioned in this context have been trained primarily on modern Arabic texts. However, their applicability to classical Arabic texts varies in terms of performance. Notably, the CAMELBERT-CA model[2] is the only model that is specifically trained on classical Arabic texts. It offers the highest initial performance, if compared to all the other models. Serving as a cornerstone for our research, this model formed the basis for our initial annotations and subsequent fine-tuning, allowing us to adapt it to our specific tasks and requirements.

3 Corpus

Texts utilized in our project are a sub-corpus of the OpenITI corpus (Nigst et al., 2023).[3] At the moment, our sub-corpus includes 101 multi-volume texts (c. 71 million tokens), which include approximately 495 thousand biographical records. Most of these texts—about 70 of them—come from the period of 1000–1600 CE and from all the major regions of the Islamic world, spanning from Spain (al-Andalus) and North Africa (al-Maġrib), to Egypt

[1] `https://farasa.qcri.org/`.

[2] `CAMeL-Lab/bert-base-arabic-camelbert-ca`

[3] `https://github.com/openiti/`, Open Islamicate Texts Initiative.

(Miṣr) and Syria (al-Šām), to Iraq (al-'Irāq), Iranian provinces (Fārs, Khurasān, etc.) and Central Asia (Mā-warā'-l-nahr).

Figure 1 illustrates a typical structure of biographies in our corpus (Figure 2 offers a translation for additional clarity). The onomastic section, which provides details about the biographee's name, genealogy, origins, as well as some social and religious background, is typically located at the beginning of the biography. The onomastic section may also mention members of the immediate and extended family. This section is usually followed by information about the biographee's education: with whom they studied, in which cities, and, sometimes, what specifically they studied. The section on teachers is often followed by a section on biographee's students, who are listed in a structurally similar manner. In some biographies, descriptions of the biographee's characteristics are given as well, either as the opinion of the main text's author or as opinions of other earlier biographers. In the middle, biographies often include other important facts from the life of biographees. Usually, concluding sections of biographies provide information on the date and place of biographee's death, and, occasionally, the location of biographee's burial.

4 Methodology

Manually created data plays a crucial role in the training process of machine learning models. Large and accurate training datasets are particularly important to the development of more precise models with improved performance. Historical and classical languages pose a unique challenge as there is often a lack of readily available training datasets. Creating such datasets requires domain experts with specialized knowledge to perform accurate data annotation. Given the limited resources available, we have decided to employ the active learning process (Wang and Hua, 2011) as a solution to generate training data for the various tasks we aim to tackle. Figure 3 illustrates the active learning paradigm we adapted as an efficient strategy to produce accurate training data to be used for model training. Figure 4 illustrates a lightweight annotation scheme that we developed to increase the easiness, speed, and accuracy of manual annotation.[4]

[4]Inspired by markdown, our scheme relies on short opening tags, where the end of the tagged entity is determined by a number indicating the number of tokens. For example, a tag `P3T` can be placed at the beginning of a 3-token entity indicating a person, who was a teacher of the biographee.

After preparing our sub-corpus, we began working with a random subset of biographies. Initially, we utilized CAMeL Lab models for lemmatization, Named Entity Recognition (NER), and Part-of-Speech (POS) tagging to perform the initial annotation steps. Also, in the initial stage, we employed our own rule-based models for date recognition and classification. Following this, we proceeded with the first round of manual refinement and correction conducted by domain experts, resulting in the successful correction of 1,100 biographies. To ensure consistency and accuracy, annotators performed cross-validation to ensure the correctness and consistency of the annotations. Using this refined dataset, we fine-tuned the NER model and trained a model specifically designed to detect boundaries of the onomastic section. Subsequently, we employed these models to annotate a subset of biographies and repeated the cycle of manual correction and fine-tuning. This iterative process will continue until we achieve a stable performance that meets our expectations, enabling the models to accurately perform the intended tasks.

5 NER for Classical Arabic

Named Entities Recognition aims to identify entities within the biographies and classify them into three main categories, namely, Toponym, Person, and Misc. This task can be viewed as a token classification task, where each token in the text is assigned a specific label. There is a notable distinction between modern Arabic names and traditional Arabic (Islamic) names. Modern names often follow a similar structure to Western names, including a given name and a surname or family name. Traditional Arabic names typically consist of up to six different elements, though not all of these elements have to be present in each case and they may appear in any order. Traditional Arabic names and their elements are explained in more detail in the section 6.2.

In the initial phase, we employed `CAMeLBERT-CA-NER` model to create the first round of annotations. Then, annotators refined the automatic annotations and added the missing annotations according to our annotation scheme. The first manual correction round resulted in a training dataset comprising 1,100 sentences, including 3,244 persons, 692 toponyms, and 198 miscellaneous entities. Next, we used this dataset to fine-tune `CAMeLBERT-CA-NER` model and used the

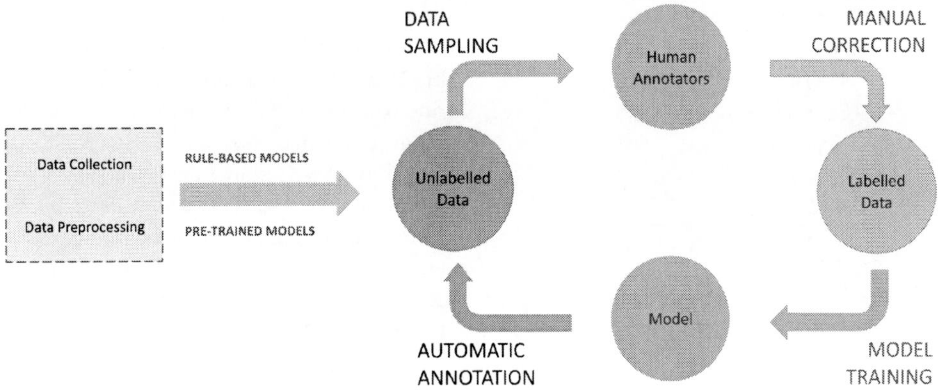

Figure 3: Development Process.

	TOPONYM		PERSON		MISC	
	zero-shot	fine-tuned	zero-shot	fine-tuned	zero-shot	fine-tuned
Precision	83.45%	92.95%	56.56%	94.29%	3.28%	71.21%
Recall	91.10%	95.94%	64.25%	95.35%	2.50%	74.21%
F1	87.11%	94.42%	60.16%	94.82%	2.84%	72.68%

Table 1: NER Model Performance.

trained model to automatically annotate a set of biographies. Subsequently, the next step resulted in a bigger training dataset 3,826 sentences containing 10,333 persons, 1,906 toponyms, and 612 miscellaneous entities. Table 1 provides a comparative analysis of the performance between the `CAMeLBERT-CA-NER` model (zero-shot) and the most recent fine-tuned model. Notably, there is a significant improvement in the identification of persons' names, with an increase of approximately 34.6% in the F1 score. This improvement can be attributed to the fact that the initial model is trained on modern Arabic person names which are structurally different if compared to traditional Arabic names.

Furthermore, our MISC entities did not overlap much with the MISC entities of the original `CAMeLBERT-CA-NER` model. Our fine-tuned model started to learn from our annotations, resulting in a promising performance with an F1 score of 72.68%.

5.1 Person Relationships Classification

The NER model achieved great performance in detecting persons in the biographies. Further, we wanted to determine the relationships between these detected persons and the biographee, a person in whose biography they appear. For this purpose, we defined six main classes (as shown in table 2). Detailed classification of the roles of individuals mentioned in biographies will allow us to model and generate complex networks, which will help the project to study the social organization of communities of Muslims across different periods and regions of the growing Islamic world. Table 2 illustrates the dataset utilized for training. The role classification information was manually added to person tags, which were generated automatically using the fine-tuned NER model.

Based on our reading of annotated biographies, we have singled out several consistently present classes of persons. Some of these classes can be described as unimportant, especially those that do not indicate any kind of direct contact to biographees.[5] We ended grouping them into the UNDEFINED class. Aiming for better performance and reliable classification, we trained two models with a reduced number of classes. The first model classifies the detected persons in the biography into three main classes TEACHER, STUDENT, and UNDEFINED. The second model classifies persons into four classes FAMILY, OPINION, CONTACT, and UNDEFINED. Then we merge the classes from both

[5]Lots of persons appear in so-called "chains of transmission" (Ar. *isnād*); most of these individuals never met the biographee and therefore are not part of that biographee's immediate social network.

Classes	# Entities
TEACHER (T)	2,891
STUDENT (S)	2,117
OPINION (O)	905
FAMILY (F)	603
CONTACT (C)	562
UNDEFINED (X)	3,372
Total	10,325

Table 2: Training Dataset for the *Persons Classification* Task.

models allowing persons to be associated with two classes simultaneously. For instance, a person may be classified as both STUDENT and FAMILY, in cases, for example, when a biographee is a student of his father.

Table 3 shows the classification results revealing that the TEACHER and STUDENT classes achieved good performance compared to other classes because the dataset contains a substantial number of entities belonging to these specific types. Currently, we are working to expand the training dataset by correcting and refining the automatic annotations created by the models. We believe that having a bigger training dataset would enhance the performance, especially for the labels of the second model.

5.2 Toponym Classification

In addition to the recognition of toponyms in the biographies, we are also interested in the relation between the biographee and the place mentioned. We defined six main classes, namely, places of: BIRTH, DEATH, BURIAL, KNOWLEDGE transfer, RESIDENCE, and UNDEFINED places. For the training of the preliminary model, we used a dataset of 1,047 biographies; for the subsequent fine-tuning of the preliminary model, we used 824 biographies. Table 4 illustrates the datasets utilized for the training.

This model was trained with two datasets. The first dataset was initially annotated with a rule-based model which classified toponyms based on certain keywords preceding them. This data, without any manual revisions, was then used to train our preliminary model. We then used this preliminary model to annotate the second dataset. We then manually corrected this second dataset, creating a revised set of training data.

The evaluation of the model is based on this second dataset that has been pre-annotated with the preliminary fine-tuned CAMELBERT-CA-based model and then manually corrected. We used the rule-based model as our baseline to compare the results of the fine-tuned CAMELBERT-CA-based model to. Table 5 shows the evaluation of the classification task results. For now, the achieved performance of both models—the rule-based one as well as the fine-tuned CAMELBERT-CA-based one—is not satisfying. The low results for the fine-tuned CAMELBERT-CA model are due to a lack of sufficient training data as our manually labeled dataset only contains 437 classified toponyms. Since we achieved high-accuracy results for all other token classification tasks with our fine-tuned CAMELBERT-CA models with bigger training datasets, we are currently expanding our training datasets.

6 Onomastic Entity Recognition for Classical Arabic

Each biography starts with a robust onomastic section on the biographee. The onomastic section is particularly valuable as it gives information on various backgrounds of the biographee. To identify the respective descriptors in the text, two different models are required. The first model identifies the boundaries of the onomastic section in the text of a biography. Applied to the identified onomastic section, the second model recognizes and classifies different onomastic elements.

6.1 Onomastic Section Boundaries Detection

We formulated this problem as a token classification task. In this approach, the model assigns labels to individual tokens within the given text. Specifically, we utilized three labels. 1) `B-ONOM` represents the beginning of the onomastic section, indicating that the token marks the start of the relevant section; 2) `I-ONOM` indicates that the token is inside the onomastic section, and 3) `O`, which is assigned to tokens that are outside the onomastic section.

The model was trained with 3,848 biographies labeled using with the active learning cycle over two rounds. The recent fine-tuned model achieved a precision 87.39%, a recall of 88.24%, and an F1 score of 87.81%. However, it is important to mention certain challenges and factors that influenced the numerical evaluation results. Largely, this is due to minor inconsistencies in the manu-

	TEACHER	STUDENT	OPINION	CONTACT	FAMILY	UNDEFINED
Precision	92.60%	94.16%	95.28%	60.26%	80.88%	90.19%
Recall	94.44%	94.65%	84.87%	56.88%	75.86%	93.54%
F1	93.51%	94.40%	89.78%	58.52%	78.29%	91.83%

Table 3: Person Relationships Classification Results.

Classes	# Entities
BIRTH (B)	23
DEATH (D)	60
BURIAL (G)	16
KNOWLEDGE (K)	77
RESIDENCE (R)	183
UNDEFINED (X)	78
Total	437

Table 4: Training Datasets for the *Toponym Classification* Task.

ally labeled training data, e.g. whether or not to include punctuation marks at the end of the onomastic section. Despite these challenges, however, it is important to stress that for the purposes of our project, the achieved level of accuracy is perfectly sufficient. The minor discrepancies, which are mainly due to closing tags being placed after an extra punctuation mark or an extra token, have no effect on the accuracy of the final outcome of the main research task.

6.2 Onomastic Entity Classification

Traditional Arabic (Islamic) names, as they appear in biographical collections, are quite different from their modern counterparts and are more akin to the short social profiles of individuals. With up to six different onomastic elements that may occur in any order and not all of them are always available, they give us the biographee's:[6] 1) "personal name" (`ISM`, Ar. *ism*); 2) the list of mainly male ancestors, which has the structure of "the son of ... the son of ... etc." (`NAS`, Ar. *nasab*); 3) "descriptive names", which describe tribal, religious, professional, geographical, and other affiliations (`NSB`, Ar. *nisba*); 4) a "patronymic" name that has the form of "The Father of ... / Abū Fulān" or "The Mother of ... / Umm Fulān" (`KUN`, Ar. *kunya*); 5) "honorific titles" (`LQB`, Ar. *laqab*); and 6) the "name of renown" (`SHR`, Ar. *šuhra*). The "descriptive names" (`NSB`, Ar. *nisba*) are the most valuable onomastic element for the goals of our project as they allow us to model different social and historical processes in the context of the development of the Islamic world.

Once the onomastic section within the biographical text has been identified, our next objective is to recognize and classify discrete onomastic elements present within it. For this purpose, we trained a token classification model that distinguished among the six main classes, described above (`ISM`, `NSB`, `NAS`, `SHR`, `KUN`, and `LQB`).

First, we pre-annotated the initial data set with our rule-based model (Table 6), which was built on data from the ONOMASTICON ARABICUM (Institute de Recherche et d'Histoire des Texts).[7] More specifically, we developed an onomastic gazetteer from data elements which were classified as *ism*, *kunya*, *laqab*, *nisba* and *šuhra* in the descriptions of persons collected in the ONOMASTICON ARABICUM. Further, the gazetteer included technical terms, used in texts to explain the spelling of rare names. We used our rule-based model to assign classes to all tokens inside onomastic sections; these assignments were then manually corrected. The model was trained with 2,011 biographies. Table 7 shows the training results. Notably, `ISM` achieved the best performance since it is unique in each onomastic section and it comes almost always as the first entity in the section. The training process adhered to the project's active learning cycle. The initial training data was generated by manually correcting labels derived from the rule-based model. Subsequently, the onomastic entity recognition model was trained using this corrected sample. The subsequent samples were then annotated using the onomastic entity recognition model.

7 Date Recognition, Classification, and Parsing

The aim of this model is threefold: 1) recognition of dates; 2) classification of dates; 3) parsing dates

[6] The main source of methodological guidance for this work is Malti-Douglas and Fourcade 1976, which summarizes the main research method of the ONOMASTICON ARABICUM Project.

[7] See, `https://onomasticon.irht.cnrs.fr`.

	rule-based			fine-tuned		
	Precision	Recall	F1	Precision	Recall	F1
BIRTH	78.57%	100%	88%	45.45%	100%	62.5%
DEATH	85.45%	78.33%	81.74%	50%	58.33%	53.85%
BURIAL	77.78%	77.78%	77.78%	0%	0%	0%
KNOWLEDGE	68.25%	59.72%	63.70%	96.55%	73.68%	83.58%
RESIDENCE	88.59%	52.38%	65.84%	57.14%	77.61%	65.82%
UNDEFINED	36.99%	75%	49.54%	41.67%	22.73%	29.41%

Table 5: Toponym Classification Results.

Classes	# Entities
ISM	1,888
NSB	3,260
NAS	3,856
KUN	910
LQB	285
SHR	179
Total	10,378

Table 6: Training Dataset for the *Onomastic Entities Classification* Task.

to numerical values. The research focus of the project is on the period of *c.* 600-1600 C.E. and information from the texts is assigned to a certain point in time somewhere within this period. We are particularly interested in what kind of information—historical events—can be associated with specific points in time.

First, the model searches the Arabic text with a regular expression (`regex`) which will match phrases reporting on dates. The regex matches days, days of the week, months, and years. Additionally, it captures ten preceding tokens, which are considered the context of a date. At the moment, we are primarily interested in years and their thematic contexts.[8] When the regex finds an occurrence of a date phrase, it usually returns two main groups of elements. One of the groups is the context; another one is a series of spelled-out numerals of the date statement, including ones, tens (decades), hundreds (centuries), and, in late texts, a thousand (for the first millennium). The model then uses a dictionary that returns numerical values of date statement element. Summing up these numerical values gives us the actual value of the date. Additional regex is then applied to the date context to check if it has any of the most common contextual vocabulary. For example, tokens like *wulida* (he was born) or *wulidat* (she was born) are used to classify dates as dates of birth. If the context contains more than one term from the date classification dictionary, we use the one closest to the date statement. We defined six main classes of dates, which are BIRTH, DEATH, KNOWLEDGE transfer, appointment or termination of an OFFICE, PILGRIMAGE, and UNDEFINED dates.

Table 9 shows the classes and their number of occurrences in the test dataset. The model was evaluated with 1,047 biographies. The numerical value extraction by this model achieved a mean average percentage error (MAPE) of 1.55% and a mean average error (MAE) of 4.76 years if the date phrase was correctly recognized as such.

Table 8 shows the results for this rule-based model. One of the reasons for a low precision for the class UNDEFINED is that this class is assigned whenever no other indicator was in the ten preceding tokens. Those ten tokens are not enough for every case, so sometimes the indicator was the 11th preceding token, and therefore the date was mistakenly classified as UNDEFINED. Overall, the results by this rule-based model show promising performance, especially since the parsing is already working very well for recognized dates. Still, date recognition presents a lot of obstacles.

So far, the model only returns information about a date if it's explicitly stated in the recognized phrase. However, not all information is always presented explicitly. A common instance is the omission of the century, as authors often expect readers to infer the exact century from the context. Consequently, we need to enhance our model to derive any missing data from other dates provided in the biography, headers of chapters containing the biography (especially when biographies are grouped into periods—a common practice in our

[8] Year statements are the most frequent type of date statements; more precise indications of time are significantly less frequent and, structurally, are more diverse and less consistent.

	ISM	KUN	NSB	NAS	LQB	SHR
Precision	99.07%	99.42%	97.15%	96.55%	75.32%	79.07%
Recall	97.72%	97.73%	97.99%	98.07%	80.56%	70.83%
F1	98.39%	98.57%	97.57%	97.30%	77.85%	74.73%

Table 7: Onomastic Elements Classification Results.

	BIRTH	DEATH	KNOWLEDGE	OFFICE	PILGRIMAGE	UNDEFINED
Precision	96.03%	94.64%	89.66%	66.67%	80.00%	52.41%
Recall	90.98%	84.57%	59.09%	16.67%	50.00%	81.46%
F1	93.44%	89.33%	71.23%	26.67%	61.54%	62.20%

Table 8: Date Recognition and Classification Results.

Classes	# Entities
BIRTH (B)	133
DEATH (D)	376
KNOWLEDGE (K)	44
OFFICE (O)	12
PILGRIMAGE (P)	8
UNDEFINED (X)	85
Total	658

Table 9: Evaluation Dataset for the *Date Classification* Task.

sources), or the scope of the historical source where the biography was found. We are still assessing the most efficient approach to implement this disambiguation.

Another challenge involves handling date statements that refer to periods or approximate years. For example, instead of exact numbers, we may find words like *ba'ḍ* and *nayyif*, which refer to an unspecified year within a specified decade. While these date statements cannot be translated into precise numerical values, this limitation does not severely impact our project. Given the extensive period we are studying, we typically operate on the granularity of decades, rounding exact years to the nearest decade when necessary.

Additionally, authors sometimes report alternative dates for the same event, either by detailing both dates fully or by abbreviating the second date. In such cases, we make an effort to collect and process both dates.

8 Conclusions and Future Work

In the preceding sections, we have outlined our efforts in adapting existing state-of-the-art Arabic NLP models to specific research tasks. We fine-tuned an NER model, specifically tailored for historical and biographical texts in classical Arabic, which exhibits excellent performance in detecting persons and toponyms. Moreover, we trained models to further classify detected persons, based on how they are related to the biographee. This model achieved good performance, particularly in the classification of teachers and students within the biographical context. The model for toponym classification is still under development as we are lacking sufficient training data. We are currently working on increasing our training dataset for this task.

Further, we trained a boundaries detection model to locate the onomastic section inside biographies, and yet another model that identifies onomastic elements within that section. The model for date recognition, classification, and parsing achieved promising results for the main goals of the project. Still, date recognition is not a trivial task and we are researching ways to overcome limitations such as the missing centuries.

Although this work is still in progress, the preliminary results reported in the paper indicate the excellent-to-satisfactory performance of the fine-tuned models, effectively meeting the intended goal for which they were trained. However, our ongoing efforts involve expanding the training datasets and further fine-tuning the models with the aim of achieving even better results.

Finally, our contribution extends beyond the trained models themselves. We have also developed and curated valuable training datasets that can serve as a resource for other researchers and contribute to the advancement of work in the field of classical Arabic. These datasets provide a foundation for further exploration and improvements in the current models.

Figure 4: Example of automatically annotated biography from al-Saḫāwī's *al-Ḍaw' al-lāmi'*.

Our future work can be summarized as follows. In the short term, our primary focus lies in generating additional training data to facilitate further fine-tuning of the models. This iterative process is aimed at continuously improving the performance of the models until reaching a stage where they can effectively annotate the entire corpus. Figure 4 illustrates an exemplar output of our annotation pipeline, wherein the annotated text has undergone processing by all the discussed models. After annotating all biographies in our corpus and extracting all relevant metadata (onomastic elements, persons, toponyms, dates, etc.), our subsequent objective is to organize this information into networks comprised of overlapping thematic clusters. These thematic clusters will serve as an analytical framework, enabling us to explore and derive insights from the interconnections and relationships among various social, professional, and religious groups, within extensive historical and geographical contexts as they are recorded in our vast corpus. Additionally, the project explores the development of these networks through spatial and temporal analysis, which is grounded in the recognition of dates and toponyms. Overall, this network will serve as the main research framework of the project for the study of the social history of the Islamic world. Further, this project will help to identify weakly researched topics in the field of Arabic studies and at the same time provide a new research tool for fellow researchers to start working on these topics.

Limitations

Ancient and classical languages, including classical Arabic, face significant challenges in terms of the availability of adequate training datasets and pre-trained models. Creating such datasets is a non-trivial task, demanding considerable time and resources. It necessitates the involvement of domain experts possessing the requisite knowledge to perform annotations in accordance with prescribed guidelines or annotation schemes. The scale of the dataset and the complexity of classification tasks present additional challenges. To tackle these obstacles, we have adopted an active learning development cycle, which allows us to efficiently and rapidly generate training data. Furthermore, in certain cases, we decided to reduce the number of labels or split the labels into two sets and train two separate models instead of one model in order to get better performance.

Acknowledgement

This research is a part of the work within the Emmy Noether Research Group (№445975300), "The Evolution of Islamic Societies (c.600-1600 CE): Algorithmic Analysis into Social History" (EIS1600), funded by the German Research Foundation (DFG) and hosted at Universität Hamburg.

References

Ahmed Abdelali, Kareem Darwish, Nadir Durrani, and Hamdy Mubarak. 2016. Farasa: A fast and furious segmenter for Arabic. In *15th Annual Conference of the North American Chapter of the Association for Computational Linguistics: Human Language Technologies*, pages 11–16. Association for Computational Linguistics.

Muhammad Abdul-Mageed, AbdelRahim Elmadany, et al. 2021. ARBERT & MARBERT: Deep bidirectional transformers for Arabic. In *Proceedings of the 59th Annual Meeting of the Association for Computational Linguistics and the 11th International Joint Conference on Natural Language Processing (Volume 1: Long Papers)*, pages 7088–7105.

Wissam Antoun, Fady Baly, and Hazem Hajj. 2020. Arabert: Transformer-based model for arabic language understanding. In *LREC 2020 Workshop Language Resources and Evaluation Conference 11–16 May 2020*, page 9.

Wissam Antoun, Fady Baly, and Hazem Hajj. 2021a. AraELECTRA: Pre-training text discriminators for Arabic language understanding. In *Proceedings of the Sixth Arabic Natural Language Processing Workshop*, pages 191–195, Kyiv, Ukraine (Virtual). Association for Computational Linguistics.

Wissam Antoun, Fady Baly, and Hazem Hajj. 2021b. AraGPT2: Pre-trained transformer for Arabic language generation. In *Proceedings of the Sixth Arabic Natural Language Processing Workshop*, pages 196–207, Kyiv, Ukraine (Virtual). Association for Computational Linguistics.

Institute de Recherche et d'Histoire des Texts. Onomasticon Arabicum.

Fedwa Malti-Douglas and Geneviève Fourcade. 1976. *The Treatment by Computer of Medieval Arabic Biographical Data: An Introduction and Guide to the Onomasticum [i.e., Onomasticon] Arabicum*. Number 6 in Série Onomasticon Arabicum. Editions du Centre national de la recherche scientifique.

E Moatez Billah Nagoudi, A Elmadany, and M Abdul-Mageed. 2021. Arat5: Text-to-text transformers for Arabic language understanding and generation. *arXiv preprint arXiv:2109.12068*.

Lorenz Nigst, Maxim Romanov, Sarah Bowen Savant, Masoumeh Seydi, and Peter Verkinderen. 2023. OpenITI: a Machine-Readable Corpus of Islamicate Texts.

Ossama Obeid, Nasser Zalmout, Salam Khalifa, Dima Taji, Mai Oudah, Bashar Alhafni, Go Inoue, Fadhl Eryani, Alexander Erdmann, and Nizar Habash. 2020. CAMeL tools: An open source python toolkit for Arabic natural language processing. In *Proceedings of the Twelfth Language Resources and Evaluation Conference*, pages 7022–7032, Marseille, France. European Language Resources Association.

Meng Wang and Xian-Sheng Hua. 2011. Active learning in multimedia annotation and retrieval: A survey. *ACM Transactions on Intelligent Systems and Technology (TIST)*, 2(2):1–21.

Logion: Machine-Learning Based Detection and Correction of Textual Errors in Greek Philology

Charlie Cowen-Breen[1], **Creston Brooks**[2], **Johannes Haubold**[3], **Barbara Graziosi**[3]
[1]Department of Applied Mathematics and Theoretical Physics, University of Cambridge
ccbreen@mit.edu
[2]Department of Computer Science, Princeton University
[3]Department of Classics, Princeton University
{cabrooks, jhaubold, barbara.graziosi}@princeton.edu

Abstract

We present statistical and machine-learning based techniques for detecting and correcting errors in text and apply them to the challenge of textual corruption in Greek philology. Most ancient Greek texts reach us through a long process of copying, in relay, from earlier manuscripts (now lost). In this process of textual transmission, copying errors tend to accrue. After training a BERT model on the largest premodern Greek dataset used for this purpose to date, we identify and correct previously undetected errors made by scribes in the process of textual transmission, in what is, to our knowledge, the first successful identification of such errors via machine learning. The premodern Greek BERT model we train is available for use at `https://huggingface.co/cabrooks/LOGION-base`.

1 Introduction

Ancient texts have been passed down by scribes over hundreds of years, in a process known as textual transmission. Scribes occasionally make mistakes, some of which lie undiscovered to this day. As unchecked errors have the potential to change the meaning of a text, finding and correcting scribal errors is a central aim in Greek philology.

In a proof-of-concept paper, we presented the first scribal mistakes detected by contextual language models (Graziosi et al., 2023). In this paper, we describe and study the approaches used to arrive at those results and evaluate the algorithm's effectiveness on artificially generated errors.

Prior to Graziosi et al. (2023), to the best of our knowledge, scribal errors were found only by hand—that is, with domain experts carefully reading the text until they find potential errors, and then using database searches to assess textual problems and propose solutions. These errors include simplifying difficult expressions, omissions, replacing one word for another with a similar sound, shape, or function, etc. Discovery of such errors typically requires a sophisticated understanding of an author's writing tendencies and the context of a particular text.

This motivates the use of contextual language models for the detection of scribal errors. In this paper, we propose *Logion*, a framework for detecting scribal errors based on contextual language models.[1] Logion consists of three stages: in the first stage, a contextual language model learns conditional word distributions for a selected corpus; in the second stage, potential errors are identified according to statistics derived from the learned distribution; lastly, in the third stage, corrections are proposed for the words identified as potentially erroneous. While not all words flagged by the algorithm will be genuine scribal errors, a "shortlist" of potential scribal errors can point philologists to previously undetected errors which, after being corrected, restore the original meaning.

To summarize, our main contributions are as follows:

- We present a premodern Greek BERT trained with what we believe to be the largest dataset used for this purpose to date.
- We propose Logion, a framework for scribal error detection and emendation based on contextual language models.[2]
- We study the effectiveness of Logion at detecting artificially generated scribal errors, and showcase real errors which it has already discovered.

In this paper, we concentrate on the discovery of scribal errors in the works of the Byzantine author Michael Psellus, who is a convenient choice at

[1]The name "Logion" derives from an ancient Greek word meaning "oracle" to emphasize that model-generated results benefit from human interpretation.

[2]Our code and shareable data is available at `https://github.com/charliecb/Logion/tree/main/error_detection_and_correction`.

Proceedings of the Ancient Language Processing Workshop associated with RANLP-2023, pages 170–178,
held in Varna Bulgaria, Sept 8, 2023.
https://doi.org/10.26615/978-954-452-087-8_020

a proof-of-concept stage for philological reasons. However, we remark that these methods may be applied to any premodern text passed down by scribes, provided sufficient data is available.

2 Related Work

In a study also related to the restoration of premodern Greek, Assael et al. (2022) train a multi-task transformer-based model to date, place, and fill gaps in ancient Greek inscriptions. Inscriptions display the original text on stone, pottery, or other media, whereas most of what survives from antiquity reaches us via a long tradition of hand-copying from earlier exemplars. For this reason, Assael et al. (2022) focus on gaps in inscriptions caused by physical damage but not on copying errors in texts.

In English and other modern languages, previous work on textual error detection has typically focused on spelling and grammar checking (Etoori et al., 2018) (Ganiz et al., 2020) (Naber, 2003), while textual errors introduced by scribes are often more complex (e.g. Figure 4). For this reason, identifying scribal errors more closely aligns with *out-of-distribution* detection, in which the task is to discern whether samples—in our case, words—are likely to have been generated by a given distribution—in our case, the author's body of work—or instead are out of distribution—i.e., the result of an error in transmission. Ren et al. (2019) propose the use of likelihood ratios to determine out-of-distribution samples for images and genomic sequences, a metric which we slightly modify. Sometimes error detection is validated by philological experts; at other times it is confirmed directly by manuscripts that were either sidelined or misread by previous scholars in the course of preparing the first or subsequent printed editions. To our knowledge, this paper is the first to identify and correct scribal errors via machine learning.

3 Methodology

Logion is a three-stage framework for the discovery and emendation of textual errors in a given corpus.[3] The initial stage involves training a BERT model, which undergoes broad pre-training on premodern Greek text followed by subsequent fine-tuning on specific works of interest, as outlined in subsection 3.1.

The second and third stages harness the learned distributions of the fine-tuned BERT to detect and emend errors, respectively. Before describing the later stages in full, we briefly recount the conditional distributions which BERT learns. Given a sequence of tokens $w_1, \ldots, w_n$, consider a single token w_i and denote the surrounding (bidirectional) context by $w_{-i} = (w_1, \ldots, w_{i-1}, w_{i+1}, \ldots, w_n)$. From the masked-language model (MLM) training task, the model learns the distribution

$$p(w|w_{-i}) \tag{1}$$

over tokens w which occur in the ith position of a sentence when surrounded by context w_{-i} (Devlin et al., 2019). For inference on words comprised of multiple tokens, we extend p to a distribution over sequences of tokens via beam search. Therefore, in what follows, when $(w_1, \ldots, w_k)$ is a sequence of words, rather than tokens, we will let $p(w|w_{-i})$ denote the corresponding distribution over words w which is derived from Expression 1 via beam search.

In the second and third stages, described in subsection 3.2 and subsection 3.3, respectively, existing statistical theory is applied to the learned distribution p to determine the tokens which are most likely to contain errors, and subsequently to propose emendations. The stages are illustrated together in Figure 1.

3.1 BERT Training

We initially trained a BERT model on a dataset of 6.4 million words of premodern Greek, which we gratefully received from Pranaydeep Singh. This is the base model used in Graziosi et al. (2023). Singh et al. (2021) assembled this data from open-source databases, such as the Perseus Digital Library and the First1KGreek corpus, in the course of training a BERT model for ancient and medieval Greek. We subsequently assembled a much larger dataset of roughly 70 million words.[4] We divided this data into a 90-10 train-test split and trained the BERT model using two NVIDIA A100 GPUs for 200 epochs until validation loss stabilized. To prepare the tokenized input, we maximized the amount of punctuation-separated text in each input, up to a limit of 512 input tokens. We used a batch size of

[3]It also has other philological functionalities we do not describe here, but which we explore in Cowen-Breen et al. (2023) and Graziosi et al. (2023).

[4]See Appendix A.

16 and a mask ratio of 0.15.[5]

To evaluate the impact of Singh et al.'s pre-training on modern Greek, we trained two models, one with random initialization and one initialized from Singh et al. (2021)'s Ancient Greek BERT. Both times, we used Singh et al. (2021)'s tokenizer which had been created for Modern Greek sub-words, since they themselves fine-tuned a Modern Greek BERT. We find that both trainings converge to the same validation loss after a small number of epochs, indicating no discernible benefit from pre-training on Modern Greek. A future model may be more effective with a tokenization optimized for Ancient Greek: see section 6. The resulting premodern Greek BERT model is available for use at `https://huggingface.co/cabrooks/LOGION-base`.

To learn more accurately the distribution of particular works in which we would like to identify errors, we then perform a fine-tuning of the broadly trained premodern Greek BERT. We partition selected works into a 90-10 train-test split and continue training using the MLM objective until validation loss stabilizes.

3.2 Error Detection

In this section, we show how certain metrics derived from the distribution p learned by BERT function as indicators of the likelihood that a given word contains an error.

Given a corpus, the goal is to flag words which are most likely to be erroneous, in order to provide domain experts with a shortlist of potential errors and emendations. A word is flagged if it satisfies certain conditions based on the metrics we define below.

3.2.1 Metrics

We propose three metrics for flagging potential errors. Additional metrics may achieve higher accuracy at error detection in the future.[6] That said, the metrics presented here have the benefit of certain theoretical guarantees, as shown by Proposition 1 in subsubsection 3.2.3.

1. Given a word w_i with (bidirectional) context w_{-i}, the **chance** of word i is defined as

$$p(w_i|w_{-i})$$

that is, the probability that the word exists in its given context, as determined by the model.

2. The model's **confidence** at word i is defined as

$$\max_{\text{word } w} p(w|w_{-i})$$

that is, the probability of the top suggested replacement in the given context around position i, as determined by the model.

3. The **scribal distance** at word i is defined as

$$d\left(w_i, \quad \operatorname*{argmax}_{\text{word } w} p(w|w_{-i})\right)$$

where $d(x, y)$ denotes the Levenshtein distance between strings x and y.

3.2.2 Rare Words

While low chance may seem to be the most intuitive indicator of errors, we find that the other two metrics are helpful for avoiding false positives. If chance were the only metric considered, genuine but rare words would be incorrectly flagged as errors.[7] Moreover, scribal errors are sometimes graphically or phonetically similar to the correct text. Thus, we choose to flag low-chance portions of text which are close in sound or shape to high-confidence model suggestions. As experimentally demonstrated in subsection 4.3, accuracy at detecting artificially generated errors is greatly improved by considering both chance and confidence, in comparison to using either metric alone.

3.2.3 Combining Metrics

Depending on the application of interest, one can combine metrics in various ways to generate error flags. In what follows, we present two ranking schemes that appear to be effective at finding either real scribal errors or artificial errors introduced in order to test the effectiveness of our approach.

[5] At the task of 1-token prediction on our test set, the model achieves 84.4% top-1 accuracy and 95.2% top-5 accuracy, and obtains a low pseudo-perplexity of 2.162 (Wang and Cho, 2019). We note that these metrics are dependent on specific tokenizations and should not be compared to models with different tokenizations.

[6] These metrics are certainly not the only ones that would lead a human philologist to consider a word suspicious, but they serve for now as a useful tool, as evidenced by Graziosi et al. (2023). In the future, we expect that more end-to-end methods—such as training for detecting errors directly—and regressions accounting for more metrics will outperform what is shown here.

[7] This is because chance considers only the absolute probability of a word w_i in context w_{-i}, instead of the relative probability when compared to plausible alternatives. Such relative probabilities are achieved by the chance-confidence ratio, which we present in the next section.

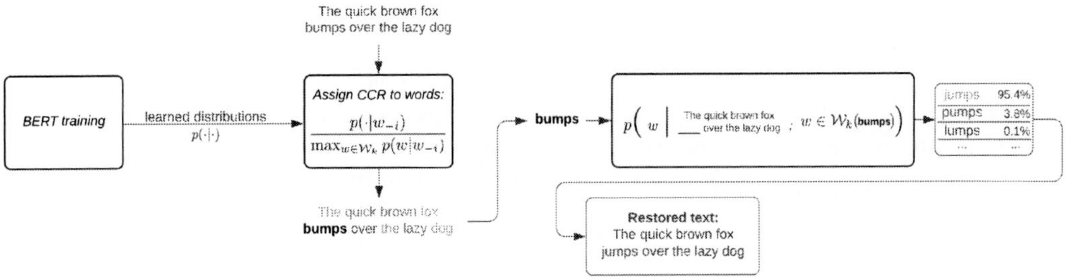

Figure 1: Logion pipeline. Here, the given text has been corrupted with a change from "jumps" to "bumps." In the first stage (left), a BERT model is fine-tuned to learn $p(\cdot|w_{-i})$ for a given corpus. In the second stage (middle), to identify the error, Logion computes the CCR of each word in the sentence (this is depicted as the brightness of each word) and identifies "bumps" as having the lowest CCR. In the third stage (right), to correct the error, a change from "bumps" to "jumps" is proposed based on the learned distribution, when restricted to words which are one-character modifications of "bumps" (here, $k = 1$). Error and emendation proposals are then vetted by domain experts.

Chance-confidence ratio rankings

Suppose that we are given a sequence of words $s = (w_1, \dots, w_n)$. As a measure of likelihood for the ith word to be an error, we propose the quantity

$$\rho_i(s) := \frac{p(w_i|w_{-i})}{\max_{w\in\mathcal{W}_k(w_i)} p(w|w_{-i})} \tag{2}$$

where

$$\mathcal{W}_k(x) = \{y : d(x, y) \leq k\}$$

and k is a fixed positive integer. To motivate $\rho_i(s)$ as a measure of the likelihood that the ith word is erroneous, we note that, intuitively, $\rho_i(s)$ is small when its numerator is small and its denominator is large, i.e. when word i has low chance and is close in Levenshtein to a high-confidence model suggestion. By the discussion in subsubsection 3.2.2, then, we expect erroneous words to correlate with words for which $\rho_i(s)$ is small.

We will refer to $\rho_i(s)$ as the **chance-confidence ratio** (CCR) of the ith word of s. This name derives from the fact that if the distributions $p(\cdot|w_{-i})$ used to compute chance and confidence are further conditioned on the event that $d(\cdot, w_i) \leq k$, then the ratio of the (conditioned) chance and confidence is equal to $\rho_i(s)$.

One natural motivation for the CCR is the following: suppose we are allowed to change only one character of a sentence and want to do so in such a way that it most resembles what a given author has written. Then, the character which we should change is exactly the one which would result in the smallest CCR of the affected word. This is formalized in the following proposition, which we prove in Appendix B.[8]

Proposition 1. (Correspondence between CCR and relative probabilities of sentences) *Let $p(s)$ be a joint distribution on sentences s. Given a sentence s, suppose that*

$$s^* = \operatorname*{argmax}_{s'\in\mathcal{W}_1(s)} p(s')$$

Then $s^* = s$ if and only if $\rho_i(s) > 1$ for all i. Moreover, if $s^* \neq s$ and i^* is the word index at which s^* differs from s, then

$$i^* = \operatorname*{argmin}_i \rho_i(s)$$

Furthermore, s^* is obtained by replacing w_{i^*} with the model top suggestion at i^* restricted to $\mathcal{W}_1(w_{i^*})$.

In other words, the proposition states that, assuming a joint probability distribution exists,[9] the CCR indicates the one-character alteration of s which the model determines most likely to have been written by the author.[10] This motivates ranking words by their CCR (i.e., by the values $\rho_i(s)$) in order to detect plausible errors. In section 4, we artificially generate errors and find that the word with index

$$\operatorname*{argmin}_i \rho_i(s)$$

[8] For alterations of $k > 1$ characters, the proposition generalizes to the corresponding statement with the assumption instead that s' lies in the set of all sentences which differ from s in a single word by at most k characters.

[9] For methods of constructing joint distributions from masked language model conditionals, see Torroba Hennigen and Kim (2023).

[10] That said, care must be taken in concluding that s^* was the original formulation of the author. Scribal errors may skew toward easier readings of the text and may thus increase p. This is an effect we consider further in section 6.

indeed contains an error 90% of the time, showing that such rankings are effective at detecting artificially generated errors (see Table 1 and Figure 3). Moreover, in 98% of such instances, the top model suggestion at the erroneous word w_i, $\text{argmax}_{w \in \mathcal{W}_1(w_i)} p(w|w_{-i})$, recovers the correct ground-truth word.

Another interpretation of ρ_i is that it is the likelihood-ratio statistic, assuming the prior on w which is uniform on $\mathcal{W}_k$ and vanishes elsewhere. In this sense, the CCR builds on Ren et al. (2019) and Gangal et al. (2020), which achieved success at detecting out-of-distribution samples with the likelihood-ratio statistic. This interpretation amounts to treating the ground truth word at position i as an unknown parameter w, the value of which determines the conditional distribution $p(w_{-i}|w)$ of the surrounding words. In this case—again assuming that scribes only make errors which do not exceed a Levenshtein distance of k from the original text—we can formulate error detection as the hypothesis testing problem

$$\begin{aligned} H_0 &: \text{ The word } w_i \text{ is correct as written.} \\ H_1 &: \text{ The original word has been altered} \\ &\quad \text{ and lies in } \mathcal{W}_k \setminus \{w_i\}. \end{aligned}$$

The corresponding likelihood-ratio statistic for this hypothesis test is given by

$$\frac{p(w_{-i}|w_i)}{\max_{w \in \mathcal{W}_k} p(w_{-i}|w)}$$

In a Bayesian framework with uniform prior on $\mathcal{W}_k$, one can see that this is equivalent to the CCR. In Figure 2 (i), we plot the distribution of the likelihood-ratio statistic under the hypotheses H_0 and H_1. The distributions under each hypothesis are distinct, allowing for formal hypothesis testing via the likelihood-ratio test.

Thresholding

In some applications, thresholding for each metric individually can provide more flexibility for generating a shortlist of errors. In Graziosi et al. (2023), the results were generated by thresholding for confidence of at least 50%, scribal distance at most 3, and ranking the remaining words in order of increasing chance. A selection of flags resulting from this scheme is shown in section 5. The choice of a 50% threshold for confidence is convenient because it respects the property that, among words which pass the threshold, the model's top suggestion is the same before and after thresholding for scribal distance.

Thresholds determine the precision and recall of the model when it is used to identify erroneous words. For applications where one wishes to find a list of strong candidates for erroneous words (i.e. high precision is desirable), one can set the confidence threshold to be high (e.g. 90%) and the chance and scribal distance thresholds to be low (e.g. 10^{-6} and 2, respectively). For applications in which one wishes to find more corrupted words and can tolerate sifting through weaker candidates (i.e. high recall is desirable), one can set the confidence threshold to be low (e.g. 50%) and the chance and scribal distance thresholds to be high (e.g. 10^{-4} and 4, respectively).

3.3 Emendation

Once a subset of the corpus has been flagged as potentially erroneous, we can easily propose emendations via Proposition 1. In the case $k = 1$, for example, Proposition 1 suggests that the highest probability one-character alteration of the input text is found by replacing the flagged word (say, w_i) with the model top suggestion at position i when restricted to only one-character alterations:

$$\underset{w \in \mathcal{W}_1(w_i)}{\text{argmax}}\ p(w|w_{-i})$$

This is the scheme which is employed for the experiments in the following section. Since producing more than one suggested emendation can be helpful for domain experts, in practice, we report any number of the most likely words $w \in \mathcal{W}_k(w_i)$ according to the distribution

$$p(w|w_{-i})$$

for any $k \geq 1$.

4 Experiments

In this section, we study the effectiveness of the proposed approach at finding artificially generated errors, while noting that the proposed approach has already resulted in the discovery of real errors, as outlined in Graziosi et al. (2023). A sample of that work is shown in section 5.

4.1 Artificially Generated Errors

Artificially generating scribal errors is made difficult by the fact that the data-generating mecha-

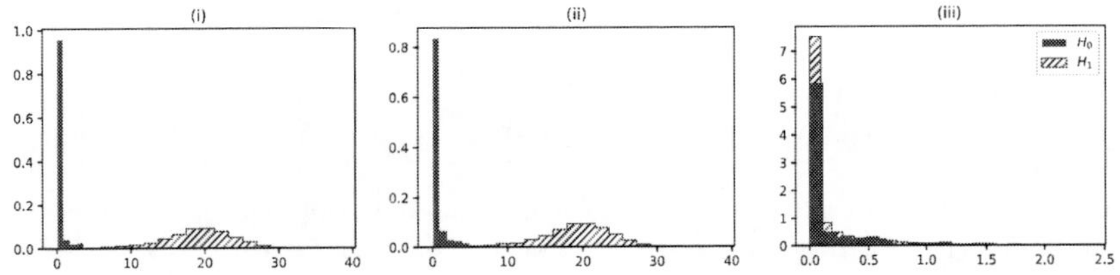

Figure 2: Distribution of metrics under hypotheses H_0 and H_1. The metrics shown are (i) CCR as in Expression 2, (ii) chance, (iii) confidence. Each horizontal scale is $-\log T$, where T is the metric associated with the plot. Here, H_1 is modeled by the scheme to generate artificial errors described in section 4, where we restrict to only single token replacements in order to produce samples efficiently. Each plot contains roughly 500,000 samples from H_0 and 1,000 samples from H_1.

nism is inherently complex and difficult to reproduce. Such errors are often dependent on individual scribes, the context in which they were working, and their interest in what they were copying: scribal errors can be quite varied and complex.

That said, some errors are fairly banal, such as changes in pronunciation that can result in spelling errors due to phenomena such as itacism.[11] For the purpose of this simulation, we generate scribal errors in the following manner: within every paragraph, we replace a randomly chosen character with another random character such that the modified word is in the dictionary of words used by the author at least ten times. If the modified word does not meet this criterion, we continue substituting characters until it does. This process ensures that a simple dictionary check could not catch the errors we generate.

4.2 Results

Within every paragraph, we rank words by CCR (Equation 2), as described in subsubsection 3.2.3 with $k = 1$. Out of 615 randomly generated instances, the erroneous word ranked first 556 times, yielding a 90.5% top-1 accuracy. Among instances in which the erroneous word ranked first, the ground-truth word was the top suggested replacement for the erroneous word 98.1% of the time. The results are summarized in Table 1.

4.3 Ablation Study

To demonstrate that consideration of all three metrics introduced in Section 2.3 improves accuracy at detecting artificial errors, here we compare ranking by CCR to two alternative ranking schemes which do not involve all three metrics: (i) ranking by confidence when restricted to scribal distance 1, and (ii) ranking by chance alone.

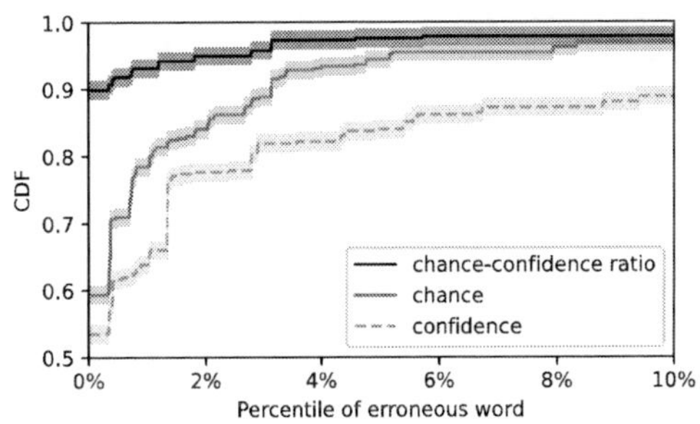

Figure 3: Artificial errors are inserted into one word per paragraph (average 230 words). The metrics of every word in the paragraph are computed (CCR, chance alone, confidence restricted to scribal distance 1), and the percentile of the erroneous word is measured when ranked by metric within the paragraph. This plot shows the cumulative distribution function of these percentiles. 90.5% of words rank first (i.e. 0th percentile) in their paragraph by CCR, and 59.7% of words rank first by chance, in agreement with Table 1. Error bands are computed via the DKW inequality with 99% coverage probability.

Figure 3 shows the distribution of artificially corrupted words when ranked by the ranking schemes proposed. The distribution of each ranking scheme is heavily left-skewed: more than 85% of erroneous words lie in the bottom 10% of words when ranked by any metric. This suggests that each of the rankings proposed correlates with artificial errors.

However, when ranking by either scheme (i) or scheme (ii), the corrupted word is ranked first in less than 60% of cases; in comparison, the CCR metric ranks the corrupted word first in 90.5% of cases (see Table 1). Therefore, we conclude that

[11]The term itacism describes a confusion between different vowels and diphthongs, all of which came to be pronounced /i/.

Accuracy	CCR	Chance alone	Confidence alone
Top-1	90.5%	59.7%	54.2%
Top-5	95.9%	88.2%	81.1%
Top-10	97.6%	93.1%	83.5%

Table 1: Accuracy at detecting a single artificial error out of 230 words according to different schemes of combining metrics. Best performance is achieved by using CCR, although chance is also a viable metric. Since the task is to generate shortlists of potential errors for review (and domain experts can often verify quickly whether a flagged word is a true error) top-10 accuracy is a significant metric here.

ranking words by either scheme (i) or scheme (ii) is less effective in identifying artificial errors than ranking by the CCR.

5 Philologically Significant Results

The metrics presented here have successfully identified errors that were previously undetected, ranging from scribal errors in the manuscripts, typographical errors in printed editions, and errors caused by digitization. These findings underwent philological peer review and have been published in *TAPA*, the research journal of the Society for Classical Studies.

In Graziosi et al. (2023), we show at proof-of-concept stage how the approaches introduced here improve on previous knowledge of premodern Greek texts by identifying and sometimes solving several different philological problems. For detailed examples and further discussion, please see Graziosi et al. (2023). Below, we offer a single example to illustrate one type of error which may be detected (in this case a misreading of the manuscript on the part of modern scholars rather than an actual error in the manuscript itself).

In Psellus's *Hist. brev.* at lines 81.89–90, Aerts' edition reads:

> οὗτος δὶς βασιλεύσας ηὔχετο καὶ τρὶς καὶ τετράκις· ἧ δὲ γάρ, φησι, μετὰ νέφος ὁ ἥλιος.
> Houtos dis basileusas ēucheto kai tris kai tetrakis: ē de gar, fēsi, meta nephos, ho hēlios.
> 'This man, having been king twice, prayed for a third and fourth term. For indeed, he said, there is sun after clouds.'

When thresholding for confidence and scribal distance, the token δε was one of the lowest chance tokens in the test set. The algorithm output depicted in Figure 4 and the subsequent examination of the manuscript on which this edition is based led to the realization that the manuscript actually reports "ἡδὺ", not "ἧ δὲ". The sentence can now be translated as follows: "This man, having been king twice, prayed for a third and fourth term. For, he said, 'sun after clouds is sweet'." In this case, then, the error turned out to be not in the early manuscript but in subsequent readings of it.

6 Future Work

One major line of future work concerns developing an application which is adopted by domain experts and used to assist their work. Given any text, such an application would be capable of generating shortlists of suspected errors and proposed emendations for review. Future research directions in this area include developing efficient and linguistically motivated sub-word tokenization schemes and the capability to include or exclude sections of the dataset from consideration at inference time: this is relevant when one is interested in performing error detection on a section of text which was included in the training set without retraining the model entirely. In working towards the latter goal, one promising architecture is DEMix, which enables dynamic expert mixtures at inference time (Gururangan et al., 2021). Another idea for future work, and one which sets scribal error detection apart from traditional error detection, concerns treating scribal modifications as diffusion processes. As scribal errors are often contextually driven, text altered by scribes may paradoxically evaluate to having higher probability than the original text.[12] On this view, then, the text evolves over time as a diffusion process with a transition kernel derived from p (for example, one option is to model the trajectory of the text by Gibbs sampling according

[12] In philology, this is the principle known as *lectio difficilior potior*. Because "the normal tendency is to simplify, to trivialize, to eliminate the unfamiliar word or construction," the more difficult reading (i.e., *lectio difficilior*) should in some circumstances be taken to be the authentic one (West, 1973).

ουτος δις βασιλευσας ηυχετο και τρις και τετρακις η δε γαρ, φησι, μετα νεφος ο ηλιος.

ηκε	1.3%
ηδει	0.06%
ηδυ	0.05%

Figure 4: Algorithm output that led to the discovery of a scribal error in the words η δε. *Top line:* words are given a grayscale color according to their CCR, as in Equation 2; the word δε was flagged because it obtained the smallest CCR of all words in its given context (the surrounding 512 tokens, not all of which are pictured here). *Below top line:* algorithm-generated suggestions, given a grayscale color according to their likelihood. In each case, the algorithm suggests merging two words by deleting the space before δε. The third suggestion, ηδυ, is, in fact, transmitted in the relevant manuscript and must be what was originally written by the author (Graziosi et al., 2023). The small probability awarded here reflects the complexity of scribal errors. Some are trivial, including the ones we generate artificially; others, including this one, are harder to emend.

to the conditionals $p(w_i|w_{-i})$. Diffusion models are designed to recover original data from diffused data, so it may be fruitful to apply such models for recovery of original text from scribally-modified text (Sohl-Dickstein et al., 2015). While not itself a diffusion model, ELECTRA is a promising architecture for such future work (Clark et al., 2020).

7 Conclusion

In this study, we have trained a BERT model to support philological work on premodern Greek texts: in particular, we use statistical and machine-learning-based approaches to identify scribal errors that accrue in the process of textual transmission and to propose emendations. In a broader sense, this research aims to contribute to the future of philology, understood as a discipline concerned with preserving, elucidating, and making publicly accessible the global archive of premodern texts. Some of what we have presented here is of relevance also for authors and languages we have not considered, as well as for modern text editing in general.

Acknowledgements

We are grateful to the three anonymous peer reviewers, Kasia Kobalczyk, Simon Babb, Suma Bhat, David Cox, Justin Curl, Bernhard Haubold, Max Haubold, Peter Heslin, Mika Hyman, Mirjam Kotwick, Karthik Narasimhan, Maria Pantelia, Stratis Papaioannou, Pranaydeep Singh, and David Smith for helpful feedback and advice for future steps.

References

Y. Assael, T. Sommerschield, B. Shillingford, et al. 2022. Restoring and attributing ancient texts using deep neural networks. *Nature*, 603:280–283.

K. Clark et al. 2020. ELECTRA: Pre-training text encoders as discriminators rather than generators. In *Proceedings of the 8th International Conference on Learning Representations*, Addis Ababa, Ethiopia. International Conference on Learning Representations.

C. Cowen-Breen, C. Brooks, J. Haubold, and B. Graziosi. 2023. Logion: Machine learning for greek philology.

J. Devlin, M.-W. Chang, K. Lee, and K. Toutanova. 2019. Pre-training of deep bidirectional transformers for language understanding. In *Proceedings of the 2019 Conference of the North American Chapter of the Association for Computational Linguistics: Human Language Technologies*, volume 1 (Long and Short Papers), pages 4171–4186. Association for Computational Linguistics.

P. Etoori, C. Manoj, and M. Radhika. 2018. Automatic spelling correction for resource-scarce languages using deep learning. In *Proceedings of the 56th Annual Meeting of the Association for Computational Linguistics. Student Research Workshop*, pages 146–152. Association for Computational Linguistics.

V. Gangal, A. Arora, A. Einolghozati, and S. Gupta. 2020. Likelihood ratios and generative classifiers for unsupervised out-of-domain detection in task oriented dialog. In *Proceedings of the Thirty-Fourth AAAI Conference on Artificial Intelligence (AAAI-20)*, pages 7764–7771. Association for the Advancement of Artificial Intelligence.

M. Can Ganiz et al. 2020. Grammar and spell checking for turkish language. Cse4197 – analysis and design document, T.C. Marmara University, Faculty of Engineering, Computer Engineering Department.

B. Graziosi, J. Haubold, C. Cowen-Breen, and C. Brooks. 2023. Machine learning and the future of philology: A case study. *TAPA*, 153(1):253–284.

S. Gururangan et al. 2021. Demix layers: Disentangling domains for modular language modeling.

D. Naber. 2003. A rule-based style and grammar checker. Diplomarbeit Technische Fakultät, Universität Bielefeld.

J. Ren, P. J. Liu, E. Fertig, J. Snoek, R. Poplin, M. A. DePristo, J. V. Dillon, and B. Lakshminarayanan. 2019. Likelihood ratios for out-of-distribution detection. In *Advances in Neural Information Processing Systems 32 (NeurIPS 2019)*, volume 19, pages 14640–14651, Red Hook, NY. Curran Associates Inc.

P. Singh, G. Rutten, and E. Lefever. 2021. A pilot study for bert language modelling and morphological analysis for ancient and medieval greek. In *Proceedings of the 5th Joint SIGHUM Workshop on Computational Linguistics for Cultural Heritage, Social Sciences, Humanities and Literature*, pages 128–137. Association for Computational Linguistics.

J. Sohl-Dickstein et al. 2015. Deep unsupervised learning using nonequilibrium thermodynamics. In *Proceedings of the 32nd International Conference on Machine Learning*, volume 37 of *Proceedings of Machine Learning Research*, pages 2256–2265. PMLR.

L. Torroba Hennigen and Y. Kim. 2023. Deriving language models from masked language models. In *Proceedings of the 61st Annual Meeting of the Association for Computational Linguistics (Volume 2: Short Papers)*, pages 1149–1159, Toronto, Canada. Association for Computational Linguistics.

A. Wang and K. Cho. 2019. BERT has a mouth, and it must speak: BERT as a Markov Random Field Language Model. In *Proceedings of the Workshop on Methods for Optimizing and Evaluating Neural Language Generation*, pages 30–36, Minneapolis. Association for Computational Linguistics.

M. L. West. 1973. *Textual Criticism and Editorial Technique Applicable to Greek and Latin Texts*. Teubner, Stuttgart.

Appendix A

Data for premodern Greek faces a specific problem which needs to be addressed. The best online database is the Thesaurus Linguae Graecae (TLG). It is not open access (unlike the best databases for other ancient languages, e.g. Latin). We are grateful to the TLG Director for providing us with some of the data we used for our models; we were instructed, however, that it cannot be disseminated further, because of the license currently restricting access to the TLG. The global archive of premodern texts is an important reservoir of linguistic and cultural diversity which should be accurately digitized and made freely available. For now, we make available the models we trained along with all training data that can be disseminated; we further include instructions and code for reproducing the error detection methods we present here at `https://github.com/charliecb/Logion`.

Appendix B

Proof of Proposition 1.

$$\begin{aligned}
\max_{s' \in \mathcal{W}_1(s)} p(s') &= \max_{1 \leq i \leq n} \max_{w \in \mathcal{W}_1(w_i)} p(w_1, \ldots, w, \ldots w_n) \\
&= \max_{1 \leq i \leq n} \max_{w \in \mathcal{W}_1(w_i)} p(w|w_{-i}) p(w_{-i}) \\
&= \max_{1 \leq i \leq n} \max_{w \in \mathcal{W}_1(w_i)} \frac{p(w|w_{-i}) p(w_{-i})}{p(w_i|w_{-i}) p(w_{-i})} p(s) \\
&= p(s) \max_{1 \leq i \leq n} \max_{w \in \mathcal{W}_1(w_i)} \frac{p(w|w_{-i})}{p(w_i|w_{-i})} \\
&= p(s) \max_{1 \leq i \leq n} \frac{1}{\rho_i(s)}
\end{aligned}$$

which establishes that, for $s^* \in \mathcal{W}_1(s)$,

$$p(s^*) = \max_{s' \in \mathcal{W}_1(s)} p(s')$$

if and only if s^* differs from s in word i^* and

$$\rho_{i^*}(s) = \min_i \rho_i(s).$$

On the other hand, we have

$$\begin{aligned}
\rho_i(s) &= \frac{p(w_i|w_{-i})}{\max_{w \in \mathcal{W}_1(w_i)} p(w|w_{-i})} \\
&= \min_{s' \in \mathcal{W}_1(s): s' \text{ differs from } s \text{ at word } i} \frac{p(s)}{p(s')} > 1
\end{aligned}$$

if and only if $\forall s'$ such that s' differs from s only in word i, and only by one character, we have $p(s) > p(s')$. If this holds for all i, then $s = s^*$ by definition. If not, then for some i, it holds that $p(s) \leq p(s')$. In this case, by uniqueness of the maximum, for some i for which this holds, we must have $p(s) < p(s')$. Thus $s \neq s^*$. $\square$

Classical Philology in the Time of AI: Exploring the Potential of Parallel Corpora in Ancient Languages

Tariq Yousef
University of Southern Denmark
yousef@imada.sdu.dk

Chiara Palladino
Furman University
chiara.palladino@furman.edu

Farnoosh Shamasian
Leipzig University
farnoosh.shamsian@uni-leipzig.de

Abstract

This contribution presents an overview of Parallel Text Processing, particularly Translation Alignment, and illustrates the current status of this task in ancient languages. In the first part, we provide the fundamental principles of Parallel Texts and give an overview of their applications for the study of ancient texts. In the second part, we indicate how Parallel Texts can be leveraged to perform other NLP tasks, including automatic alignment, dynamic lexica induction, and Named Entity Recognition. In the conclusion, we emphasize current limitations and future work.

1 Introduction

Parallel Text Processing refers to various computational tasks based on parallel corpora (Véronis, 2000). Parallel corpora are collections of texts that show some level of equivalence between them: for example, a text and its translations, or different versions of the same text.

The most important task in Parallel Text Processing is Text Alignment, that is, the automatic establishment of equivalences across various types of units: document, chunk, sentence, and word (Kay and Röscheisen, 1993). The task of aligning a text against its translation(s) is called Text-Translation Alignment (from now on, TA). The output of TA is defined as Translation Pairs (TPs), which correspond to pairs of the various units aligned (chunks, sentences, words, etc.).

TA can be considered a subfield of Text Alignment: however, it has very unique challenges attributed to the complex dynamics underlying the relationship between texts and their translations. In particular, word-level TA poses considerable complexity due to the inherent uncertainty in establishing individual equivalences: translations are not perfect transpositions of the originals, and tend to alter, normalize, expand or simplify parts of the text. Moreover, structural differences across languages, such as morphology and word order, contribute to additional difficulties.

The goal of this paper is to offer a programmatic survey of the current status of TA research in the specific domain of ancient languages, particularly Ancient Greek. As such, we will cover many different applications, both in Philology and Computer Science, with the intent of demonstrating the potential of this method in the study of ancient languages. Our aim is to illustrate how TA and parallel corpora can be used for a wide range of research, to contribute to existing debates and to inspire new questions.

2 Design and Concept of Translation Alignment Tools

Since TA was established, several tools have been designed to collect TPs, with or without integrated reading environments for visualizing the alignments (overviews are provided in our previous works Yousef and Janicke 2020; Yousef 2023). In the context of ancient languages, a limited number of tools have been developed. These include Alpheios (Almas and Beaulieu, 2013), DUCAT Citation Alignment Tool (Blackwell et al., 2020), Benner's tool for aligning the Bible (Benner, 2014), and UGARIT[1], designed to enable word-level alignments in low-resourced languages (Yousef et al., 2022c). Currently, UGARIT counts about 50 aligned languages, 700 users, and more than a million TPs[2], establishing itself as the most popular tool in this area.

UGARIT was designed as a crowd-sourcing project to collect training data for automatic alignment methods for ancient languages, but it expanded into a range of diverse applications, mostly thanks to its global community of scholars and

[1]https://ugarit.ialigner.com/

[2]Of this number, about 240,000 TPs are automatically generated through traditional statistical automatic alignment tool (Giza++).

Proceedings of the Ancient Language Processing Workshop associated with RANLP-2023, pages 179–192,
held in Varna Bulgaria, Sept 8, 2023.
https://doi.org/10.26615/978-954-452-087-8_021

students. The alignment workflow, which allows bilingual and trilingual alignments, is simple and intuitive.UGARIT allows different types of TPs: word-to-word (1-1), word-to-phrase (1-N), phrase-to-word (N-1) and phrase-to-phrase (N-N).

Alignments are immediately published online. The visualization of published alignments allows the user to compare aligned texts token by token, providing a transliteration service for non-Latin alphabets, statistical information about the percentage of aligned and not-aligned tokens, types of links, a downloadable list of TPs, and an embedding option (Figure A.1).

The tool integrates a dynamic lexicon, which can be triggered through the search function or simply by clicking on a word in an aligned text. The results are visualized as a radial cluster dendrogram, a tree view, and as a list of words with frequency (Figure A.2). The lexicon extracts all the translation equivalents of a given word across the whole database, providing a list of all languages in which that word has been translated.

3 Applications of Translation Alignment

In many modern languages, TA is successfully employed in a wide range of NLP tasks. For example, it is essential in word- and phrase-based Statistical Machine Translation (SMT) pipelines (Brown et al., 1993; Koehn et al., 2003); it can be used to analyze the output of Neural Machine Translation models (NMT) and assess their performance quality (Neubig et al., 2019); to filter and clean noisy parallel corpora (Kurfalı and Östling, 2019; Zariņa et al., 2015); to transfer linguistic annotation from one text to its translation, such as Semantic Role labels, POS tags, Named Entity tags (Yousef, 2015; Ni et al., 2017; Huck et al., 2019). Parallel Corpora aligned at word-level can support the work of professional translators (Liu, 2020), bilingual lexicon induction (Marchisio et al., 2021), and word sense disambiguation (Procopio et al., 2021). Moreover, they provide extremely useful information for vocabulary assimilation and language teaching (Vyatkina and Boulton, 2017), and for the study of the history of transmission of a corpus (Laviosa, 2021).

In the following sections, we will survey the current state of TA research for ancient languages, illustrating how the parallel corpora created on UGARIT are used for qualitative and quantitative research.

3.1 Qualitative Studies: Pedagogy and Translation Studies

Manual or supervised TA is essential for the creation of high-quality Gold Standards and training datasets. However, it can also be configured as a close reading task for translation study and language learning. In recent years, efforts have been undertaken in the realm of Digital Philology, in the context of a major emphasis on the development of open resources for innovative approaches to learning Classical languages (Crane et al., 2023).

3.1.1 Pedagogy and User Behavior

Parallel corpora on UGARIT are currently being used to teach Ancient Greek, Latin, and Persian in several universities, including Leipzig, Furman, São Paulo, Tufts, University of Zagreb, Göttingen, Cattolica University, but also in schools across Europe, such as the Liceo G. Peano Tortona in Italy.

The active engagement with the text through the effort of establishing fine-grained equivalences stimulates a reflective approach to the text and creates an opportunity to design exercises that invite language learners to reflect upon the cultural and linguistic specificities of ancient texts through the contrastive comparison with modern translations: through specific exercises tailored to the level, students are stimulated to reflect on the depths of semantic and linguistic differences, and their impact on the very operation of translating (Palladino, 2020). Moreover, this process encourages a critical approach to translations as interpretations, rethinking their role in understanding ancient texts, and enabling the students to be part of a broader conversation about the reception and significance of a text over time. Palladino et al. 2021 provide a series of use cases showing how TA can be used for learning Ancient Greek or Latin at various levels, through a series of reflective and project-based exercises. Most importantly, the comparison of different translations of the same texts provides a tangible sense of the different strategies employed by professional translators, and gives a strong pragmatic understanding of the fluidity of translations and their (in)ability to transmit the original in its full meaning. Shamsian and Crane 2022 showed how TA can be integrated with grammar explanations and other types of annotations to create born-digital pipelines for learning ancient languages, even at beginner level. Through TA, students are able to critique existing scholarly translations and reflect on how to create more accurate representations of the original. This process is particularly useful in linguistic contexts where available translations are mostly derivative from translations in other languages, like in the case of Persian.

3.1.2 Empirical study of translations and intertextual phenomena

While translations constitute a crucial aspect in the history of the transmission of ancient texts, very few studies have used computational approaches to investigate them. In this area, manual and automatic TA provides an extremely promising resource. Bizzoni et al. 2017 used an automatic alignment workflow based on the Needleman-Wunsch algorithm, using proper names as anchors to align selected passages of the *Odyssey* against a large corpus of French translations, to identify large-scale trends in translation practices across the 16th and 17th century. Shukhoshvili 2017 used UGARIT to support the creation of a complete translation of Plato's *Theaetetus* into Georgian and used the resulting corpus to investigate cross-linguistic dynamics between the two languages. Somewhat in the opposite direction, Xie 2023 used UGARIT to examine the Ancient Greek translation of the Latin text of the *Res Gestae*: the method applied combined close reading to inspect specific semantic phenomena, and distant reading through the consultation of the alignment statistics provided by the tool. Interestingly, while Xie 2023 found a remarkable degree of accuracy in the corpus, the trilingual alignment of the Rosetta Stone performed by Amin et al. 2023 on UGARIT demonstrated that the three versions of the text bear considerable differences and they cannot be considered one and the same text. Finally, Palladino et al. 2022a propose a workflow that combines close reading and quantitative indicators to support alignment-based evaluation of translations of Ancient Greek texts: the set of criteria includes frequency of link types, percentage of aligned and not-aligned words, intersection across translators, POS intersection, in combination with close reading of selected passages.

The ever-increasing amount of corpora in UGARIT also allows for big-data exploration scenarios. Palladino and Yousef 2023 used the UGARIT database to investigate cross-linguistic dynamics, studying how language and culture affect the establishment of word equivalents between text and translation. Their data show how different language systems influence the process of translation, creating very distinctive results for specific language pairs, but also that cultural context, text genre and modalities of transmission have an impact in determining structural differences in translations.

3.2 Quantitative Studies: AI and Parallel Corpora

The various applications described above show the importance of parallel corpora for the study of texts from different perspectives. For this reason, it is important to develop workflows for automated alignment tasks, which support the scalability of both qualitative and quantitative research. While this area is very well developed for modern languages, it is still in its infancy for ancient ones. In the following section, we will show current efforts in the improvement of automatic alignment models, and indicate how automatic TA can be used to enhance the performance of important NLP tasks.

Until the advent of transformer-based models, the state of the art of automatic TA was statistical methods, such as Giza++ (Och and Ney, 2003), fast_align (Dyer et al., 2013) and EfLomAl (Östling and Tiedemann, 2016). However, the performance of statistical alignment models relies on the presence and size of training datasets in the form of parallel sentences.

Recently, however, Neural Machine Translation (NMT) and multilingual transformer models have introduced the possibility of creating accurate alignments even with no training datasets (Jalili Sabet et al., 2020). Most notably, transformer models facilitate the creation of contextualized word embeddings, which encode information about a meaning of a word based on its context. Pre-trained multilingual transformer models, such as Multilingual Bert (mBERT) and XLM-RoBERTa, achieved significant performance improvements for numerous cross-lingual tasks (Conneau et al., 2019b; Devlin et al., 2018a).

Language models are now increasingly used for various NLP tasks in ancient languages (Sommerschield et al. 2023 provide a comprehensive survey in the field). Most current applications are developed with a strong interest in POS tagging and morphological analysis. To the best of our knowledge, we are pioneers in employing transformer models to automate TA tasks in ancient corpora, and to leverage on the resulting parallel texts to explore new possibilities in other NLP tasks. We

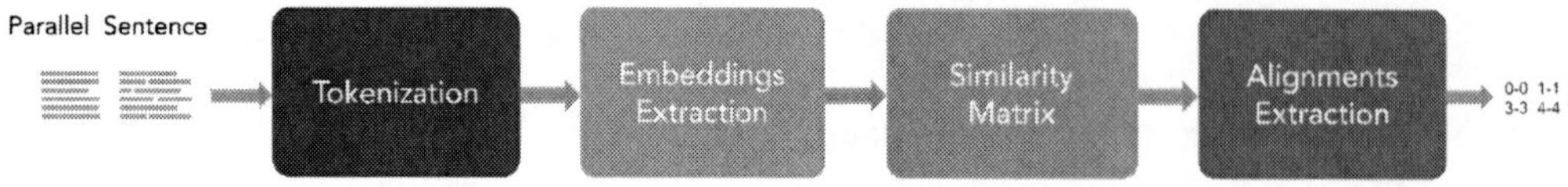

Figure 1: The alignment workflow.

use Ancient Greek as a case study, but the model we developed is multilingual and can be fine-tuned for other ancient languages.

3.2.1 Alignment Guidelines and Gold Standards

In order to evaluate the performance of automatic alignment models, it is essential to have high-quality gold standard datasets. Gold Standards are typically created by two or more annotators, whose Inter-Annotator Agreement (IAA) is measured to ensure consistency in the dataset. Guidelines are created and used to ensure that annotators are following a similar strategy.

While there is no lack of guidelines and standards for modern languages,[3] we developed the first ones specifically aimed at ancient languages: using Ancient Greek as case study, we considered translations into English, Portuguese, Persian,[4] and scholarly Latin. These guidelines can be used for the evaluation of automatic alignment tasks, but also as a general reference for students and scholars who wish to create their own parallel corpus for other purposes (Ferreira et al., 2022; Palladino et al., 2022b; Palladino and Shamsian, 2022).

The resulting Gold Standards are based on a corpus of 5,500 words from Ancient Greek epic poetry and prose (Homer, Xenophon, and Plato) and on 100 fragments of Ancient Greek translated into Latin from the Digital Fragmenta Historicorum Graecorum (DFHG)[5]. Two annotators aligned each corpus separately, after having drafted the Guidelines. The resulting IAA was measured at 86.17% for GRC-ENG and 83.31% for GRC-POR, and GRC-LAT 90.50%.

Our guidelines considered the same general principles established for modern languages (Lambert et al., 2005), but working within the specificities of an ancient language: for example, we had to carefully address the impact of high inflection and the inconsistency shown in the translation of linguistic and rhetorical structures. As a result, while most guidelines cover 7-10 classes of phenomena, ours covered 14 main classes with several subclasses. Therefore, it is easy to understand how the alignment of an ancient text may result in higher ambiguities than modern corpora traditionally used in TA: moreover, modern corpora are usually technical texts, which leave little space for variation, but that is not the case for ancient texts, which are necessarily literary or even poetical. Although our guidelines reach and exceed the 80% threshold of optimal consistency, it is important to reflect on the origins of disagreements across annotators in order to individuate areas of improvement for both the Gold Standards and automatic TA models: factors such as the native language of the annotators, their proficiency with the language/s, their familiarity with the text and specific dialect, and the time at their disposal may all have an impact on their performance. This qualitative study is part of our future work.

3.2.2 The UGARIT Ancient Greek Alignment Model

In our previous works (Yousef et al., 2022b,d), we have trained an automatic TA model that employs the recent advances in language modelling and is able to generate accurate word-level alignments even with small amounts of training data. In this context, we adapted the pipeline illustrated in Figure 1 proposed by (Jalili Sabet et al., 2020; Dou and Neubig, 2021).

The core concept is to leverage pre-trained multilingual contextualized language models such as MBERT (Devlin et al., 2018b) and XLM-ROBERTA (Conneau et al., 2019a) or fine-tuned versions of them. A similarity matrix can be derived based on distance/similarity metrics that calculate the similarity for every two tokens based on their embeddings. Then, the word-level alignments can be predicted by employing an extraction algorithm over the similarity matrix.

The initial experiments we conducted on the pre-

[3] An overview of available resources can be found on the UGARIT website: `https://ugarit.ialigner.com/guidelines.php`.

[4] This set of guidelines has not yet been used for the creation of Gold Standards, therefore we did not employ it for evaluation purposes.

[5] `https://www.dfhg-project.org/`

Experiment	Languages	Data Size	Source
Phase 1	GRC Monolingual	12 Millions Tokens	Perseus DL, TreeBanking, First1kGreek
Phase 2	GRC-ENG, GRC-LAT GRC-KAT	45.000 sentences	Perseus DL, DFHG, UGARIT
Phase 3	Mixed dataset	5000 sentences 190k TPs	UGARIT

Table 1: The proposed fine-tuning strategy.

		mBERT				XLM-RoBERTa			
		Precision	Recall	F1	AER	Precision	Recall	F1	AER
ENG	Softmax	80.80%	56.91%	66.78%	32.72%	92.62%	66.85%	77.65%	21.88%
	Match	65.42%	72.76%	68.90%	31.31%	79.22%	**87.26%**	**83.05%**	**17.17%**
	Argmax	84.95%	52.47%	64.87%	34.57%	**94.44%**	63.32%	75.81%	23.70%
	Itermax	78.43%	64.08%	70.53%	29.14%	91.05%	71.65%	80.19%	19.42%
LAT	Softmax	85.67%	84.64%	85.15%	14.83%	94.64%	92.39%	**93.50%**	**6.47%**
	Match	62.18%	87.97%	72.86%	27.55%	80.61%	**96.30%**	87.76%	12.50%
	Argmax	88.46%	80.80%	84.46%	15.09%	**95.52%**	91.38%	93.40%	6.55%
	Itermax	81.27%	84.78%	82.99%	17.06%	92.21%	93.33%	92.77%	7.25%
POR	Softmax	63.84%	61.27%	62.53%	37.40%	76.11%	75.61%	75.86%	24.13%
	Match	50.00%	72.61%	59.22%	41.50%	58.79%	**86.17%**	69.89%	31.01%
	Argmax	66.01%	54.92%	59.96%	39.76%	**77.25%**	71.10%	74.05%	25.81%
	Itermax	59.67%	64.06%	61.79%	38.35%	72.22%	81.02%	**76.37%**	**23.91%**

Table 2: Evaluation results of the automatic alignment model on three gold standard datasets.

trained MBERT and XLM-ROBERTA (Zero-Shot) showed significantly poor performance on Ancient Greek-English, Ancient Greek- Latin, and Ancient Greek-Portuguese datasets. Therefore, fine-tuning those models was necessary to achieve better performance. Due to the availability of parallel sentences and in order to obtain the best outcome from the training process, we conducted several experiments employing multiple training objectives (Dou and Neubig, 2021) aiming to find the best training strategy. Each experiment tested various combinations of unsupervised and supervised training. Table 1 illustrates our proposed training strategy which consists of three phases. The initial stage involved training pre-existing models using monolingual Ancient Greek corpora, which encompassed a total of 12 million tokens. Subsequently, the model underwent an unsupervised fine-tuning process utilizing a collection of 45,000 parallel sentences. This fine-tuning phase encompassed sentences in Greek-English, Greek-Latin, and Greek-Georgian. Ultimately, the model underwent supervised fine-tuning, where it was refined using precise manual alignments extracted from the UGARIT database.

The performance of the model was evaluated against the gold standard datasets using *Precision*, *Recall*, *F*1 and Alignment Error Rate *AER*.

Table 2 presents the performance evaluation of our model during phase 3, utilizing three gold standard datasets: Greek-English, Greek-Latin, and Greek-Portuguese. We evaluated the model's performance using four alignment extraction heuristics and two fine-tuned models: mBert-based model and XLM-RoBERTa-based model. Notably, the fine-tuned XLM-RoBERTa models consistently outperformed the mBERT-fine-tuned models across all cases, demonstrating their superior performance in alignment extraction. The *Match* heuristic significantly outperformed other models regarding Recall. However, it achieved always the lowest Precision. On the other hand, the Argmax heuristic consistently achieved the highest precision but the lowest recall. Both the Softmax and Itermax heuristics demonstrated balanced performance, with a relatively equal consideration given to recall and precision. Itermax showcased superior recall compared to Softmax, while Softmax displayed better precision than Itermax. Overall, the performance of these heuristics varies in terms of recall and precision, with each exhibiting strengths and weaknesses. The choice of the appropriate heuristic will depend on the specific requirements and priorities of the task at hand, balancing the trade-off between recall and precision based on the desired outcomes.

Our alignment model is available on HUGGING FACE [6] and can be downloaded and used locally. In order to make it more accessible, however, we implemented an online tool[7] that integrates the pre-trained model and allows users to simply paste their texts and align them automatically, with an option to visualize and download the results (Figure A.1).

The pre-trained alignment model can be used to scale all the qualitative operations described above, but also for a variety of downstream tasks. In the following sections, we will describe our preliminary results in the areas of Bilingual Lexica Induction and Named Entity Recognition.

3.2.3 Bilingual Lexica Induction

The significance of aligned word-level parallel corpora as a data source for terminology banks and bilingual dictionaries is emphasized by Véronis 2000. These resources are highly valuable to improve the performance of professional translators, to enrich and train translation memory software, to retrieve terminology lists for technical texts, or in lexicographic studies. However, it is worth noting that not all language pairs can be easily aligned, especially when dealing with ancient and low-resourced languages. In this proof of concept, we applied automatic dictionary induction to produce high-quality translation pairs for languages that do not share parallel texts. Additionally, we represented the acquired translation pairs within a graph-based data structure. This approach allows us to integrate manual alignments and dictionary entries and facilitate performing clustering or pivoting to generate translation pairs of languages with no direct connections.

Corpora: we used 400,000 parallel sentences in 6 languages (Ancient Greek, Arabic, English, Hebrew, Latin, and Persian). Our corpus derives from the Bible[8], the Perseus Digital Library[9], and the DFHG corpus.

Alignment: we used our fine-tuned alignment model for Ancient Greek to perform the word/phrase alignments. We employed *Itermax* heuristic to extract the most accurate translation pairs from the similarity matrix since it achieved the highest Phrase Alignment Accuracy (Yousef et al., 2023; Yousef, 2023).

Graph Generation: Figure 2 illustrates the proposed graph structure. We model every translation pair as two nodes connected with an edge. Additional relations can be added to indicate different linguistic features if they are available. For example, connecting a phrase with its constituent words or linking a word with its lemma. These relations can be beneficial for running sophisticated queries. Shi et al. (2021) proposed a matching ratio that considers the alignment frequency and how frequently the two words co-occurred in the corpus. However, this ratio works only with one-to-one alignments. Therefore we proposed an alignment score that considers phrases as well:

$$score(s,t) = \frac{2 * A(s,t)}{A(s|L_t) + A(t|L_s)} \quad (1)$$

Where $A(s,t)$ indicates how many times the two words/phrases are aligned together, $A(s|L_t)$ indicates how many times s is aligned in total to words/phrases in the same language as t, and $A(t|L_s)$ indicates how many times t is aligned in total to words/phrases in the same language as s.

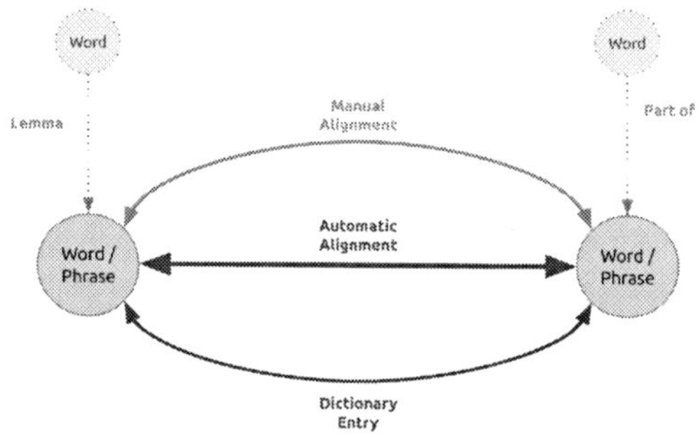

Figure 2: The graph structure of the induced TPs.

The resulting graph contains over 614k nodes and 1,620k edges from Automatic Alignment, and an additional 193k TPs collected from UGARIT as Manual Alignment. Moreover, graph clustering algorithms such as CHINESE WHISPER (Biemann, 2006), a hard partitioning and flat clustering algorithm, can be applied to cluster graph entries into sets containing words/phrases that are semantically related or share the same meaning. Figure 3 shows a cluster of aligned words/phrases in various languages. This cluster is one of 7300 clusters

[6] https://huggingface.co/UGARIT/grc-alignment
[7] http://ugarit-aligner.com
[8] https://github.com/christos-c/bible-corpus.
[9] http://www.perseus.tufts.edu/hopper/.

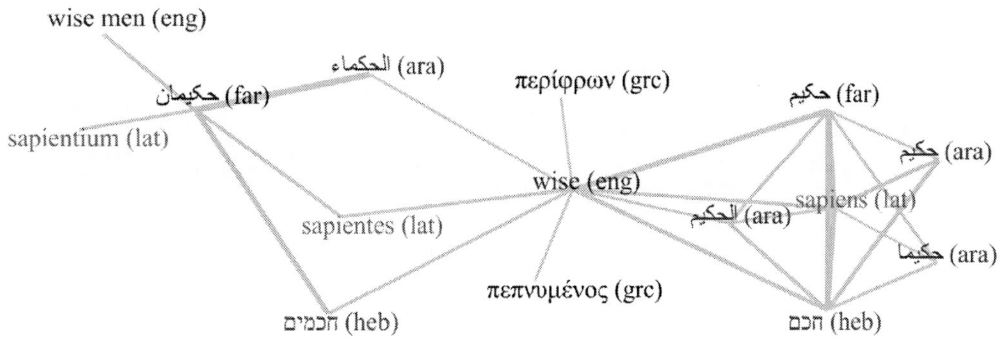

Figure 3: An example from graph clustering results.

obtained after filtering out the relations with frequency less than 5, alignment score less than 0.25, and running CHINESE WHISPER clustering algorithm for 20 iterations. Figure A.4 shows another cluster with an extended visualization, in which manual alignments and PART_OF relations are displayed.

The results of this work are available on our GitHub[10]: The resulting dictionaries can provide an invaluable resource to establish equivalences across languages that are not normally translated into each other: for example, a Persian speaker studying Ancient Greek can use this resource to extract Persian equivalents of Greek words, instead of relying on English or French translations. Moreover, the dictionaries provide insights into real-world use of the words, as they derive directly from contextual usages in texts. Therefore, the development of this application will considerably improve the use of parallel corpora for teaching, translating, and language learning.

Our future work in this regard includes expanding the corpus of accurate manual alignments for other low-resourced languages, and expanding the monolingual and bilingual datasets to improve the accuracy of the model in other languages. We will also develop a user interface with various search and visualization functions.

3.2.4 NER for Ancient Greek

An additional application of our alignment model pertains to enhancing the efficacy of Named Entity Recognition (NER) in the context of ancient languages through the employment of annotation projection. This workflow leverages on cross-lingual transfer: the basic principle is that, if NER models reach accurate results in one language, we can use an automatic alignment workflow to align an annotated text with another one, for which NER models do not achieve such a high performance. This principle, called annotation projection, consists in projecting NER annotations performed on English translations on an aligned text in an ancient language, so that Named Entities can be extracted and classified through the alignment process.

NER is in great demand among scholars of ancient languages. However, it comes with significant challenges including OCR-generated errors and noisy data, complexity of the sources, lack of gold standards and guidelines. The only survey on the topic for historical languages is provided by Ehrmann et al. 2021, with some recent updates in Sommerschield et al. 2023. New pipelines based on transformers have shown considerable improvement in this area, although NER remains a particularly challenging task (Palladino et al., 2020; Yousef et al., 2022a; Burns, 2023; Yoo et al., 2022).

While most of these experiments use a direct training approach with annotated datasets of Named Entities in the target language, we propose a novel workflow that integrates annotation projection and leverages on our automatic alignment model. Figure 4 illustrates our pipeline: we collect a parallel corpus of Ancient Greek and English translations; automatically annotate the text of the English translations using *AllenNLP*, an accurate off-the-shelf NER system[11]; then, we employ automatic word alignment to retrieve translation pairs,

[10] `https://github.com/UgaritAlignment/`

[11] We benchmarked three high-quality English NER models, namely, *spaCy*, *AllenNLP* and *flairNLP* to select the model with the highest accuracy on our corpus. The comparison revealed that *AllenNLP* and *flairNLP* significantly outperformed *spaCy*, and their performance was very close.

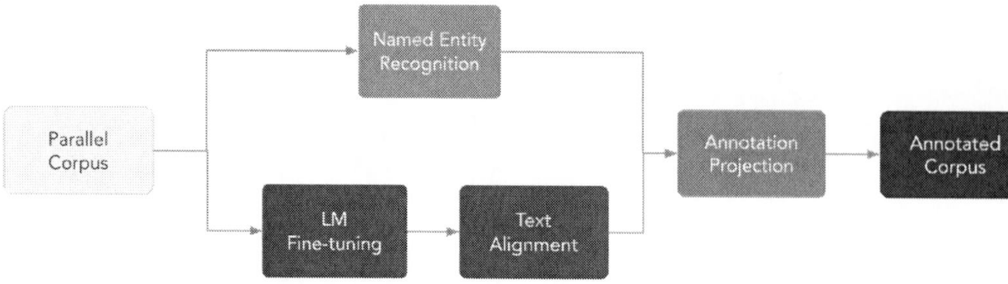

Figure 4: Named-Entity annotation projection pipeline.

and project the annotations from the English translations onto the corresponding tokens in the Ancient Greek text using a direct mapping heuristic.

While *AllenNLP* provides four entity classes (PERS, LOC, ORG, MISC), we only used PERS, LOC, and MISC, as the ORG entity label does not apply intuitively to ancient naming systems (see further on this issue Ehrmann et al. 2021; an alternative strategy for labeling is proposed for Latin by Burns 2023.).

We tested the workflow on the Bible corpus, using English for annotation and selecting versions in Ancient Greek, Latin, and Arabic[12]. We decided to expand the range of languages beyond Ancient Greek, which is still the most present in training datasets, to show the potential of the multilingual model.

Two domain experts performed qualitative evaluation on 100 random verses (about 550 entities per dataset) and assigned a score as shown in table 3. The evaluation results show an accuracy of 86.63% in Ancient Greek, 82.34% in Latin, and 75.54% in Arabic: understandably, Arabic showed the worst performance because we had much less corpora available for training. The most common errors were found in the misclassification of entities, sometimes as a consequence of the fact that English translations adopted a different entity type. Most notably, many ethnonyms (MISC in our dataset) were translated with place-names in English, and therefore classified as LOC in the ancient language. Moreover, incomplete or partial alignments were frequent in multi-token entities, such as "Jesus Christ", "Simon Zelotes", and "Pontius Pilate".

[12]All versions were taken from the Bible Corpus on GitHub, while the Ancient Greek version was retrieved from the Perseus Digital Library.

4 Conclusions and Future Work

Parallel Corpora are today's Rosetta Stones (Véronis, 2000). They can be used for a variety of philological and computational tasks, as they provide a medium between languages and cultures. This study shows the importance of parallel text processing, specifically in the context of Translation Alignment, for various activities in the study of low-resource languages. The value of TA emerges in its various applications, which include language learning, NLP development, dictionary extraction, and research on translations and cross-linguistic interactions.

Most importantly, the development of accurate TA models can significantly contribute to improve the performance of important NLP tasks in ancient languages through the mdeium of annotation projection. For this reason, we plan a significant expansion of monolingual and bilingual corpora for supervised and unsupervised training, in order to improve performance on other ancient languages. Moreover, we will test analogous workflows based on annotation projection for other NLP tasks, such as POS tagging and lemmatization. In this sense, the development of accurate sentence alignment workflows is fundamental, as it can significantly enhance the performance of word-alignment models.

Despite the great success of transformers and language models, we want to emphasize that manually annotated corpora and guidelines are still essential to ensure accurate performance and to detect patterns of error. Gold Standards and output evaluation require strong disciplinary expertise, especially in scenarios where the research questions are complex. For this reason, as already emphasized by Sommerschield et al. 2023, the best efforts in the domain of automatic text processing are achieved

Score	Ancient Greek	Latin	Arabic
Correct alignment / Correct NER	86.63%	82.34%	75.54%
Incorrect alignment / Correct NER	7.26%	12.87%	21.16%
Correct alignment / Incorrect NER	5.28%	3.96%	2.98%
Incorrect alignment / Incorrect NER	0.83%	0.83%	0.33%

Table 3: Manual evaluation of 100 randomly selected verses.

by multidisciplinary teams, where the contribution of scholars of the language and philologists can provide better information about the idiosyncrasies of the material, and crucially contribute to the evaluation of the results. High-quality philological work is essential for progress in this field, and the only way we can produce reliable tools that will be used by Digital Humanists and Humanists as well.

Acknowledgements

We are most grateful to all the people who contributed to the development of UGARIT, the Alignment Models, and who provided Gold Standards and annotated datasets: Gregory Crane, Monica Berti, Anise d'Orange Ferreira, Michel Ferreira dos Reis, Josh Kemp, David Wright, Maia Shukhoshvili, Sisi Xie, Brian Clark, and all the scholars and students who worked on Translation Alignment on Ugarit.

References

Bridget Almas and Marie-Claire Beaulieu. 2013. Developing a New Integrated Editing Platform for Source Documents in Classics. *Literary and Linguistic Computing*, 28(4):493–503.

Miriam Amin, Angelos Barmpoutis, Monica Berti, Eleni Bozia, Josephine Hensel, and Franziska Naether. 2023. The Digital Rosetta Stone Project. In Rita Lucarelli, Joshua A. Robertson, and Steve Vinson, editors, *Ancient Egypt, New Technology.*, volume 17 of *Harvard Egyptological Studies*, pages 58–84. Brill, Leiden - Boston.

Drayton Benner. 2014. A Tool for a High-Carat Gold-Standard Word Alignment. In *Proceedings of the 8th Workshop on Language Technology for Cultural Heritage, Social Sciences, and Humanities (LaTeCH)*, pages 80–85.

Chris Biemann. 2006. Chinese whispers - an efficient graph clustering algorithm and its application to natural language processing problems. In *Proceedings of TextGraphs: the First Workshop on Graph Based Methods for Natural Language Processing*, pages 73–80, New York City. Association for Computational Linguistics.

Yuri Bizzoni, Marianne Reboul, and Angelo Del Grosso. 2017. Diachronic Trends in Homeric Translations. *Digital Humanities Quarterly*, (2).

Christopher W. Blackwell, Chiara Palladino, Mackense Greico, and Allie Bolton. 2020. DUCAT: Passage/Translation Alignment with the CITE Architecture. In *Proceedings of the DH2020 Digital Humanities Conference 2020, Ottawa.*

Peter F. Brown, Stephen A. Della Pietra, Vincent J. Della Pietra, and Robert L. Mercer. 1993. The Mathematics of Statistical Machine Translation: Parameter Estimation. *Computational Linguistics*, 19(2):263–311. Place: Cambridge, MA Publisher: MIT Press.

Patrick J. Burns. 2023. LatinCy: Synthetic Trained Pipelines for Latin NLP. ArXiv:2305.04365 [cs].

Alexis Conneau, Kartikay Khandelwal, Naman Goyal, Vishrav Chaudhary, Guillaume Wenzek, Francisco Guzmán, Edouard Grave, Myle Ott, Luke Zettlemoyer, and Veselin Stoyanov. 2019a. Unsupervised cross-lingual representation learning at scale. *CoRR*, abs/1911.02116.

Alexis Conneau, Kartikay Khandelwal, Naman Goyal, Vishrav Chaudhary, Guillaume Wenzek, Francisco Guzmán, Edouard Grave, Myle Ott, Luke Zettlemoyer, and Veselin Stoyanov. 2019b. Unsupervised Cross-lingual Representation Learning at Scale. *CoRR*, abs/1911.02116. ArXiv: 1911.02116.

Gregory Crane, Alison Babeu, Lisa M. Cerrato, Amelia Parrish, Carolina Penagos, Farnoosh Shamsian, James Tauber, and Jake Wagner. 2023. Beyond translation: engaging with foreign languages in a digital library. *International Journal on Digital Libraries*.

Jacob Devlin, Ming-Wei Chang, Kenton Lee, and Kristina Toutanova. 2018a. BERT: Pre-training of Deep Bidirectional Transformers for Language Understanding. *CoRR*, abs/1810.04805. : 1810.04805.

Jacob Devlin, Ming-Wei Chang, Kenton Lee, and Kristina Toutanova. 2018b. BERT: pre-training of deep bidirectional transformers for language understanding. *CoRR*, abs/1810.04805.

Zi-Yi Dou and Graham Neubig. 2021. Word Alignment by Fine-tuning Embeddings on Parallel Corpora. In *Proceedings of the 16th Conference of the European Chapter of the Association for Computational Linguistics: Main Volume*, pages 2112–2128, Online. Association for Computational Linguistics.

Chris Dyer, Victor Chahuneau, and Noah A. Smith. 2013. A Simple, Fast, and Effective Reparameterization of IBM Model 2. In *Proceedings of the 2013 Conference of the North American Chapter of the Association for Computational Linguistics: Human Language Technologies*, pages 644–648, Atlanta, Georgia. Association for Computational Linguistics.

Maud Ehrmann, Ahmed Hamdi, Elvys Linhares Pontes, Matteo Romanello, and Antoine Doucet. 2021. Named Entity Recognition and Classification on Historical Documents: A Survey. ArXiv:2109.11406 [cs].

Anise d'Orange Ferreira, Michel Ferreira dos Reis, and Tariq Yousef. 2022. Critérios ou Convenções de Alinhamento do Grego às Traduções em Português. Publisher: Zenodo. Version Number: 1.0.

Matthias Huck, Diana Dutka, and Alexander Fraser. 2019. Cross-lingual Annotation Projection Is Effective for Neural Part-of-Speech Tagging. In *Proceedings of the Sixth Workshop on NLP for Similar Languages, Varieties and Dialects*, pages 223–233, Ann Arbor, Michigan. Association for Computational Linguistics.

Masoud Jalili Sabet, Philipp Dufter, François Yvon, and Hinrich Schütze. 2020. SimAlign: High Quality Word Alignments Without Parallel Training Data Using Static and Contextualized Embeddings. In *Findings of the Association for Computational Linguistics: EMNLP 2020*, pages 1627–1643, Online. Association for Computational Linguistics.

Martin Kay and Martin Röscheisen. 1993. Text-translation Alignment. *Computational Linguistics*, 19(1):121–142.

Philipp Koehn, Franz J Och, and Daniel Marcu. 2003. Statistical phrase-based translation. Technical report, University of Southern California Marina Del Rey Information Sciences Inst.

Murathan Kurfalı and Robert Östling. 2019. Noisy parallel corpus filtering through projected word embeddings. In *Proceedings of the Fourth Conference on Machine Translation (Volume 3: Shared Task Papers, Day 2)*, pages 277–281.

Patrik Lambert, Adrià De Gispert, Rafael Banchs, and José B. Mariño. 2005. Guidelines for Word Alignment Evaluation and Manual Alignment. *Language Resources and Evaluation*, 39(4):267–285. Publisher: Springer.

Sara Laviosa. 2021. *Corpus-based Translation Studies: Theory, Findings, Applications*, volume 17 of *Approaches to Translation Studies*. Brill, Leiden - Boston.

Kanglong Liu. 2020. *Corpus-Assisted Translation Teaching: Issues and Challenges*, volume 7 of *Corpora and Intercultural Studies*. Springer.

Kelly Marchisio, Philipp Koehn, and Conghao Xiong. 2021. An Alignment-Based Approach to Semi-Supervised Bilingual Lexicon Induction with Small Parallel Corpora. In *Proceedings of Machine Translation Summit XVIII: Research Track*, pages 293–304, Virtual. Association for Machine Translation in the Americas.

Graham Neubig, Zi-Yi Dou, Junjie Hu, Paul Michel, Danish Pruthi, and Xinyi Wang. 2019. compare-mt: A Tool for Holistic Comparison of Language Generation Systems. In *Proceedings of the 2019 Conference of the North American Chapter of the Association for Computational Linguistics (Demonstrations)*, pages 35–41, Minneapolis, Minnesota. Association for Computational Linguistics.

Jian Ni, Georgiana Dinu, and Radu Florian. 2017. Weakly Supervised Cross-Lingual Named Entity Recognition via Effective Annotation and Representation Projection. In *Proceedings of the 55th Annual Meeting of the Association for Computational Linguistics (Volume 1: Long Papers)*, pages 1470–1480, Vancouver, Canada. Association for Computational Linguistics.

Franz Josef Och and Hermann Ney. 2003. A systematic comparison of various statistical alignment models. *Computational Linguistics*, 29(1):19–51.

Chiara Palladino. 2020. Reading Texts in Digital Environments: Applications of Translation Alignment for Classical Language Learning. *The Journal of Interactive Technology and Pedagogy*, (18).

Chiara Palladino, Maryam Foradi, and Tariq Yousef. 2021. Translation Alignment for Historical Language Learning: a Case Study. *Digital Humanities Quarterly*, 015(3).

Chiara Palladino, Farimah Karimi, and Brigitte Mathiak. 2020. NER on Ancient Greek with minimal annotation. *DH2020 Ottawa. Book of Abstracts*.

Chiara Palladino and Farnoosh Shamsian. 2022. Translation Alignment: Ancient Greek to English. Annotation Style Guide and Gold Standard. Publisher: Zenodo Version Number: 1.0.

Chiara Palladino, Farnoosh Shamsian, and Tariq Yousef. 2022a. Using Parallel Corpora to Evaluate Translations of Ancient Greek Literary Texts. An Application of Text Alignment for Digital Philology Research. *Journal of Computational Literary Studies*, (1).

Chiara Palladino, David J. Wright, and Tariq Yousef. 2022b. Translation Alignment: Ancient Greek to Latin. Annotation Style Guide and Gold Standard. Publisher: Zenodo Version Number: 1.0.

Chiara Palladino and Tariq Yousef. 2023. To say almost the same thing? A study on cross-linguistic variation in ancient texts and their translations. *Digital Scholarship in the Humanities*.

Luigi Procopio, Edoardo Barba, Federico Martelli, and Roberto Navigli. 2021. MultiMirror: Neural Cross-lingual Word Alignment for Multilingual Word Sense Disambiguation. volume 4, pages 3915–3921. ISSN: 1045-0823.

Farnoosh Shamsian and Gregory R. Crane. 2022. Open Resources for Corpus-Based Learning of Ancient Greek in Persian. *Journal of Interactive Technology and Pedagogy*, (21).

Haoyue Shi, Luke Zettlemoyer, and Sida I Wang. 2021. Bilingual lexicon induction via unsupervised bitext construction and word alignment. *arXiv preprint arXiv:2101.00148*.

Maia Shukhoshvili. 2017. Methodology of Translation Alignment of Georgian Text of Plato's "Theaetetus". *International Journal of Language and Linguistics*, 4(4).

Thea Sommerschield, Yannis Assael, John Pavlopoulos, Vanessa Stefanak, Andrew Senior, Chris Dyer, John Bodel, Jonathan Prag, Ion Androutsopoulos, and Nando de Freitas. 2023. Machine Learning for Ancient Languages: A Survey. *Computational Linguistics*.

Nina Vyatkina and Alex Boulton. 2017. Corpora in Language Teaching and Learning. *Language Learning and Technology*, (3).

Jean Véronis, editor. 2000. *Parallel Text Processing: Alignment and Use of Translation Corpora*. Text, Speech and Language Technology. Springer Netherlands, Dordrecht-Boston-London.

Sisi Xie. 2023. Textual Alignment of Res Gestae: Translation in Historical Languages. *The Stoa: a Review for Digital Classics*.

Haneul Yoo, Jiho Jin, Juhee Son, JinYeong Bak, Kyunghyun Cho, and Alice Oh. 2022. HUE: Pretrained Model and Dataset for Understanding Hanja Documents of Ancient Korea. In *Findings of the Association for Computational Linguistics: NAACL 2022*, pages 1832–1844, Seattle, United States. Association for Computational Linguistics.

Tariq Yousef. 2015. Word alignment and named-entity recognition applied to greek text reuse. *MSc's Thesis. Alexander von Humboldt Lehrstuhl für Digital Humanities, Universität Leipzig*.

Tariq Yousef. 2023. *Translation Alignment Applied to Historical Languages*. Ph.D. thesis.

Tariq Yousef, Gerhard Heyer, and Stefan Jänicke. 2023. Evalign: Visual evaluation of translation alignment models. In *Proceedings of the 17th Conference of the European Chapter of the Association for Computational Linguistics: System Demonstrations*, pages 277–297.

Tariq Yousef and Stefan Janicke. 2020. A Survey of Text Alignment Visualization. *IEEE Transactions on Visualization and Computer Graphics*, PP:1–1.

Tariq Yousef, Chiara Palladino, and Stefan Jänicke. 2022a. Transformer-based named entity recognition for ancient greek.

Tariq Yousef, Chiara Palladino, Farnoosh Shamsian, Anise d'Orange Ferreira, and Michel Ferreira dos Reis. 2022b. An automatic model and Gold Standard for translation alignment of Ancient Greek. In *Proceedings of the Thirteenth Language Resources and Evaluation Conference*, pages 5894–5905, Marseille, France. European Language Resources Association.

Tariq Yousef, Chiara Palladino, Farnoosh Shamsian, and Maryam Foradi. 2022c. Translation Alignment with Ugarit. *Information*, 13(2):65. Number: 2 Publisher: Multidisciplinary Digital Publishing Institute.

Tariq Yousef, Chiara Palladino, David J. Wright, and Monica Berti. 2022d. Automatic Translation Alignment for Ancient Greek and Latin. In *Proceedings of the Second Workshop on Language Technologies for Historical and Ancient Languages*, pages 101–107, Marseille, France. European Language Resources Association.

Ieva Zariņa, Pēteris ikiforovs, and Raivis Skadiņš. 2015. Word alignment based parallel corpora evaluation and cleaning using machine learning techniques. In *Proceedings of the 18th Annual Conference of the European Association for Machine Translation*, pages 185–192.

Robert Östling and Jörg Tiedemann. 2016. Efficient Word Alignment with Markov Chain Monte Carlo. *The Prague Bulletin of Mathematical Linguistics*, 106.

A Appendix

Figure A.1: Ugarit manual alignment tool, Side-by-side visualization of bilingual aligned texts.

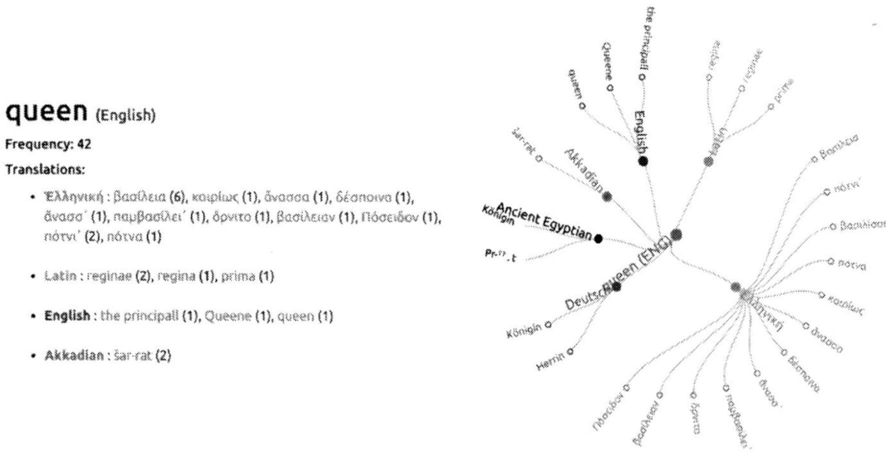

Figure A.2: Visualization of translation pairs search results.

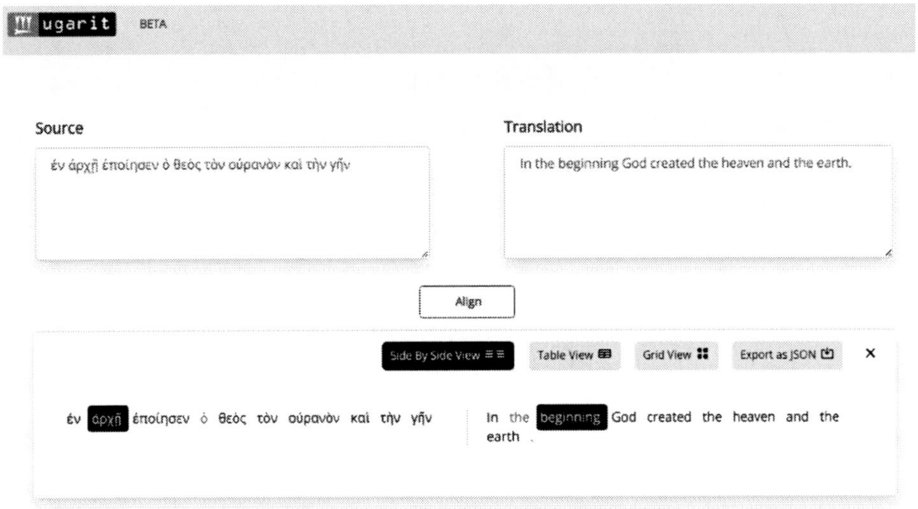

Figure A.3: Ugarit automatic alignment tool.

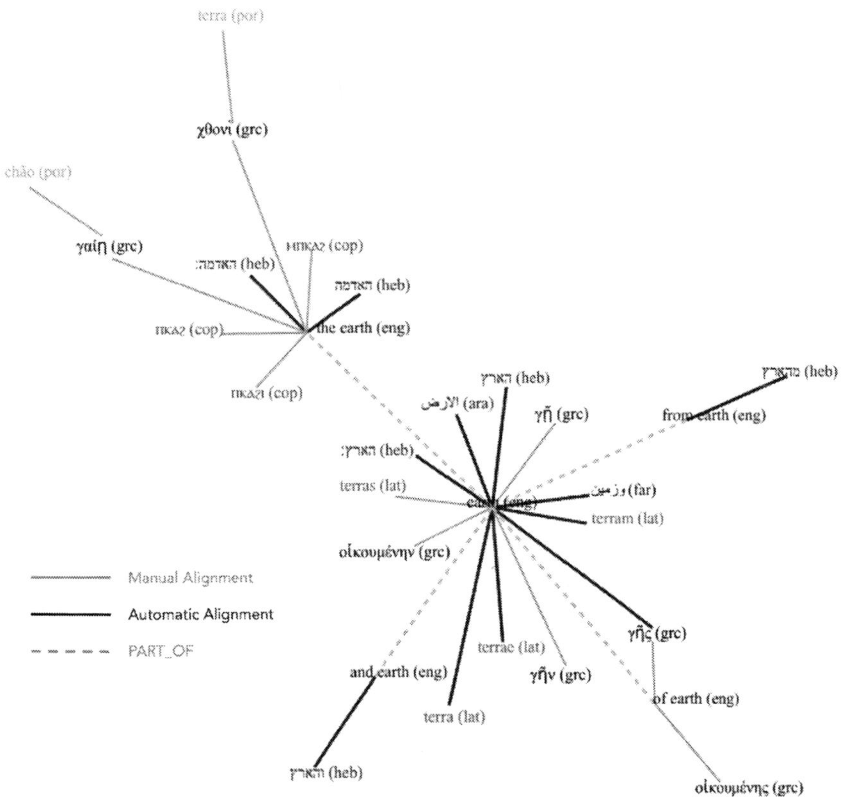

Figure A.4: An example from graph clustering results with extended relations.

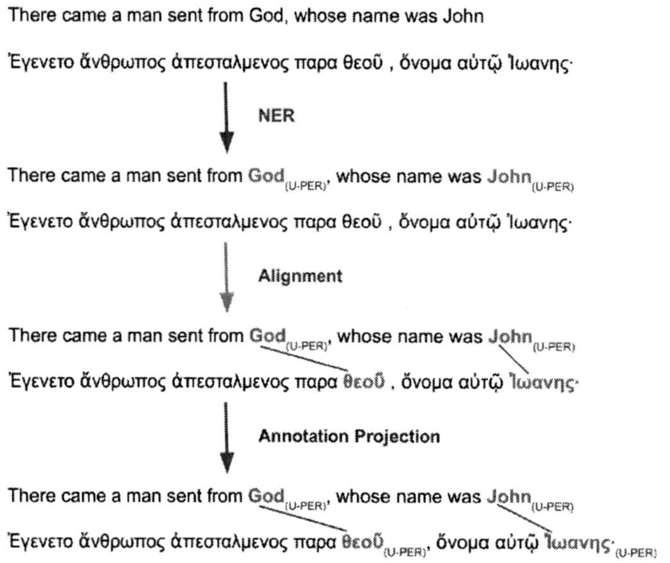

Figure A.5: An example of the annotation projection using the proposed pipeline.

Using Word Embeddings for Identifying Emotions Relating to the Body in a Neo-Assyrian Corpus

Ellie Bennett and **Aleksi Sahala**
University of Helsinki
eleanor.bennett@helsinki.fi
aleksi.sahala@helsinki.fi

Abstract

Research into emotions is a developing field within Assyriology, and NLP tools for Akkadian texts offers new perspectives on the data. We use PMI-based word embeddings to explore the relationship between parts of the body and emotions. Using data downloaded from Oracc, we ask which parts of the body were semantically linked to emotions. We do this through examining which of the top 10 results for a body part could be used to express emotions. After identifying two words for the body that have the most emotion words in their results list (*libbu* and *kabattu*), we then examine whether those emotion words were indeed used in this manner in the Neo-Assyrian textual corpus. The results indicate that of the two body parts, *kabattu* was semantically linked to happiness and joy, and had a secondary emotional field of anger.

1 Introduction

The study of emotions in ancient Near Eastern cultures has grown in the past five years, with two edited volumes covering the topic (Hsu and Llop Raduà, 2021; Sonik and Steinert, 2022). A key question has been how ancient languages used the body to express emotions - or the 'embodiment of emotions'. For Akkadian, this question has been addressed by Ulrike Steinert (Steinert, 2022, 2021). Her work involved the traditional approach of close reading Akkadian texts and close analysis of the most important Akkadian dictionaries to identify words relating to emotions, and how the body was used to express them. She identified 22 Akkadian words that refer to parts of the body that were used to express emotions (Steinert, 2022). As Steinert's results were reflective of Akkadian language as a whole, we were interested in whether her results could be replicated for a textual corpus from a more narrow timespan - namely the Neo-Assyrian period (c. 934-612 BCE).[1]

Neo-Assyria is the best represented time period currently available on the Open Richly Annotated Cuneiform Corpus (Oracc). We can therefore use word embeddings to gather quantitative data of whether the body words identified by Steinert to express emotions were used similarly to emotion words during the Neo-Assyrian period. In addition, word embeddings will allow us to determine whether any of these body words can be considered as part of a semantic field of emotions.

2 Data

The data for this project consists of two sections: the corpus of Neo-Assyrian texts, and the list of Akkadian words that relate to parts of the body.

2.1 Neo-Assyrian corpus

The textual corpus was downloaded from Oracc.[2] The texts were selected according to metadata tags found in the Oracc data. We chose a 'fuzzy' approach to the data, and cast a wide net in order to include as many Neo-Assyrian texts written in Akkadian as possible. We therefore included texts with the following tags for language and time period:

- 'Akkadian'; 'akkadian'; 'Akkadian with Sumerian incipits'; 'Akkadian, Aramaic?'; 'Akkadian, with Aramaic epigraph'; 'Akkadian?'; 'Assyrian'; 'Akkadian, Aramaic'
- 'Neo-Assyrian'; '9th/8th century'; '8th/7th century'; '9th century'; '7th century'; '8th century'

The data is in a word per line format, where every word is represented in the following lemmatised

[1]There is growing research into emotions in Neo-Assyrian material (Valk, 2016; Battini, 2022; Bach, 2022; Nadali, 2022; Schaudig, 2022; Bonatz, 2022; Morello, 2022), but scholarship is still limited with regards to embodied emotions.

[2]This was done through a remix of the following script, which resulted in a lemmatised version of the Oracc dataset in line with Oracc standards: https://github.com/niekveldhuis/compass.

Proceedings of the Ancient Language Processing Workshop associated with RANLP-2023, pages 193–202,
held in Varna Bulgaria, Sept 8, 2023.
https://doi.org/10.26615/978-954-452-087-8_022

form:[3]

lemma[guideword]EPOS[4]

Stop words are given as '<stop>',[5] unlemmatised words as '_',[6] and '#' to indicate the end of a text.

The data underwent a process of minimal cleaning to remove duplicates that appeared due to spelling errors, resulting in a corpus of 7,969 texts, 1,014,890 tokens, and 19,436 unique word forms.[7]

2.2 Word selection

We referred to Ulrike Steinert's work on embodied emotions in Akkadian to select the words that were most likely to be similar to emotion words in the Neo-Assyrian dataset (Steinert, 2021, 2022). We selected 22 words relating to the head (5 words), torso (or the whole body) (3 words), organs (6 words), and limbs (8 words).[8] They can be viewed in Table 1.

3 Word Embeddings

Word embeddings represent words as real-valued vectors in a multi-dimensional vector space. In simple terms, this vector space can be understood as a matrix, where the rows represent each word in the corpus and the columns represent abstractions of their co-occurrences with other words. This property makes word embeddings useful for measuring lexical similarity: if two words A and B are similar to each other in meaning, they likely occur in similar contexts, and thus their vectors should show higher similarity to each other. The most closely related words (often called *nearest neighbors*) can be computed from the vectors by using cosine similarity (Equation 1).

$$\cos(\mathbf{A}, \mathbf{B}) = \frac{\mathbf{A} \cdot \mathbf{B}}{\|\mathbf{A}\| \|\mathbf{B}\|} \tag{1}$$

In word embedding calculations, this metric has a theoretical upper bound of 1 in case the words are perfect synonyms, and a lower bound of 0 in case the semantic relationship between the words is independent.[9]

Some of the better known tools for building word embeddings are Word2vec (Mikolov et al., 2013) and fastText (Bojanowski et al., 2017), which both use shallow neural networks to learn the word embedding space from the corpus. While the neural network based methods are powerful in large datasets, these methods are known to have issues in smaller datasets comprising only a million words (Jungmaier et al., 2020). For low-resource languages and small corpora, word embeddings can be successfully built by using count-based methods, such as word association measures combined with matrix factorization (Levy et al., 2015; Jungmaier et al., 2020). The count-based method used in this paper produces vectors only for words that are documented in the data set. Therefore the similarity between out-of-vocabulary words cannot be measured like in fastText.

PMI-embeddings is a Python script for building count-based word embeddings for low-resource languages.[10] It combines several features from various research papers on count-based word embeddings that utilize Pointwise Mutual Information (PMI) (Church and Hanks, 1990) and Singular Value Decomposition (SVD). Briefly described, PMI-embeddings builds a sparse matrix of the vocabulary that encodes statistical significance of co-occurrences in terms of PMI within a symmetric context window of arbitrary size. This sparse matrix is then truncated into desired dimensionality (typically between 60 and 300) using SVD, yielding the final vector space that can be saved into the standard Word2vec format to be used in various NLP applications.

The script allows tuning several hyperparameters to find optimal settings for the given dataset. These include, but are not limited to, Dirichlet Smoothing

[3]As Akkadian is a highly inflected language, and the research was not focused on syntax or morphology, we worked from the lemmatised version of the dataset. This follows previous Assyriological research projects based on Oracc data (Svärd et al., 2020; Sahala and Svärd, 2021; Bennett, 2023)

[4]This is how the Akkadian words will appear in the tables of this contribution for the ease of non-Assyriological readers, but in the main body we will be using Assyriological standards of italicising the lemma.

[5]A full list of these can be found in the accompanying Zenodo repository, the url of which can be found in Appendix A.

[6]An unlemmatised word in Oracc can be due to many factors, such as a broken text (indicated by 'x' in transliterations), or a word with uncertain meanings.

[7]The dataset is part of the supplementary material, which is described in Appendix A. The corpus can be broken down according to genre in the following manner: letters (33%), royal inscriptions (17%), transactions (15%), scholarly texts (14%), and the remaining 21% was a mix of administrative, religious, legal, political, literaturary, and untagged texts.

[8]We did not include bodily emissions in this research, but could be an interesting future field of emotions research (Sonik, 2022a).

[9]Negative scores up to -1 are also possible depending on how the word embeddings are created, but in this paper discussion on negative values is not necessary.

[10]`https://github.com/asahala/pmi-embeddings/`

Head	Body	Organs	Limbs
īnu[eye]N	pagru[body]N	kabattu[liver]N	ahu[arm]N
pānu[front]N	šīru[flesh]N	kalītu[kidney]N	durā'u[arm]N
pû[mouth]N	zumru[body]N	karšu[stomach]N	idu[arm]N
qaqqadu[head]N		libbu[interior]N	izīru[arm]N
rēšu[head]N		qerbu[centre]N	kirimmu[(crook-of)-arm]N
		ṣurru[interior]N	kittabru[arm]N
			purīdu[leg]N
			zāqu[arm]N

Table 1: The 22 Akkadian words relating to the body selected for this study organised according to whether they refer to the head, the whole body or torso, the organs, or limbs.

(Turney and Pantel, 2010; Jungmaier et al., 2020), several variants of PMI such as shifted and context distribution smoothed PMI (Levy et al., 2015) with various different shifting mechanisms, Dynamic Context Window that gives less significance for co-occurrences that are further apart (Sahlgren, 2006), and Context Similarity Weighting (Sahala and Lindén, 2020) that downsamples noise caused by duplication and repetitiveness in the dataset, which is a problem especially in formulaic Mespotamian royal inscriptions.

If a human-evaluated gold standard for semantic similarity is available, well performing parameters can be searched by using the *hypertune.py* script distributed with PMI-embeddings. Currently the default settings of PMI-embeddings have been defined for the first millennium Akkadian texts using a work-in-progress gold standard based on independent word similarity rankings done by five Assyriologists. This gold standard is distributed as a part of PMI-embeddings.[11]

3.1 Parameters

The default parameters use a vector dimensionality of 300 and the following features for calculating the sparse PMI matrix:

- Shifted PMI with a shift value of 7 using the formula implemented in Jungmaier et al. 2020. This allows some co-occurrences to exist in the sparse matrix even if they are not statistically significant. Typically all statistically independent co-occurrences would be disregarded, which may be harmful in sparse datasets.
- Symmetric dynamic context window of three words, meaning that the co-occurrences are calculated within a span of three preceding and following words to the center word, and that the co-occurrence frequencies are reciprocals of their distance to the center word giving less importance to words that co-occur farther away from each other.
- Context Similarity Weighting with a k-value of 3, meaning that co-occurrences in repetitive or partially repetitive contexts are downsampled with a weight risen to the power of 3. This gives significant penalty to co-occurrences also in partially repetitive contexts.

4 Results

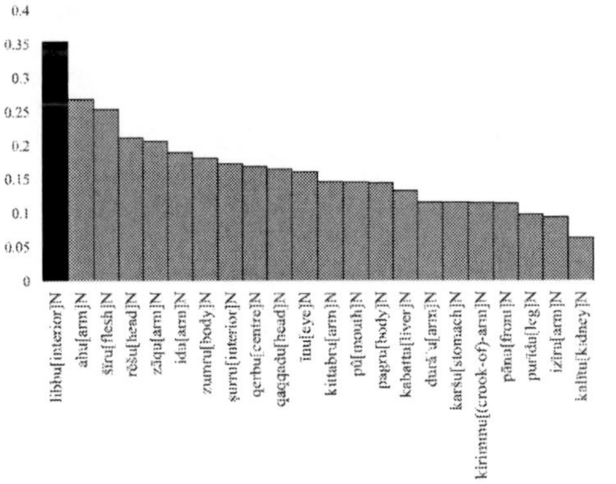

Figure 1: Ranges of the differences between the first and last cosine score in the top ten results for Akkadian body words. *Libbu* is highlighted in black.

We queried the resulting .vec file for each of the 22 Akkadian words relating to the body for the 10 words whose vectors were the most similar to

[11] https://github.com/asahala/pmi-embeddings/tree/main/eval built in cooperation with the University of Helsinki, the LMU Munich and the University of California, Berkeley.

the Akkadian body word, as well as their cosine similarity score.

Libbu had the largest range of cosine similarity scores between the first and tenth result out of all the results lists. *Kalītu* ("kidney") had the smallest difference in cosine score in its top ten results. The mean of the differences in cosine similarity score of the top 10 results was 0.16, and the median was 0.15, indicating most of the body words queried had a similar range of usage in the Neo-Assyrian corpus.

The difference between the body words with the highest (*libbu*) and second highest (*ahu*) range in cosine scores was 0.085 - the largest difference between the cosine ranges (Fig. 1).[12] The large range in cosine score in comparison to the other results lists suggests that *libbu* was used in many different contexts, whereas the smaller difference between *kalītu*'s first and tenth results suggest it had a more specific usage in Neo-Assyrian texts.

The words in the results lists for each body word were then compared to a master Excel file that classified emotions according to 18 different emotion categories: sadness, distress, suffering, anger, happiness, schadenfreude, pleasure, fear, hate, love, desire, disgust, sympathy, envy, pride, surprise, shame, sexual arousal.[13]

If a word in the results lists occurred in this Excel file, the principle emotional field was imported to the results list for analysis. This highlighted the words in the results list that could be used to denote emotions. This was our first indicator of whether a body word was part of an emotional semantic field.

4.1 Words relating to the organs

The group of words referring to organs (column 3 in Table 1) was most likely to have a word in its results list that could express emotions. Of the word relating to organs, *libbu* ("interior") and *kabattu* ("liver") had the highest number of emotion words in their results list (5 and 4 respectively, as seen in Tables 2 and 3).[14]

libbu		
Word	**Score**	**Emotion**
kindu[earth]N	0.786	None
hīpu[break]N	0.525	Sadness
gilittu[terror]N	0.496	Fear
qīlu[burning]N	0.462	None
haluppu[(a-tree)]N	0.458	None
hūṣu[pain]N	0.457	Sadness
hibṣu[swelling]N	0.453	None
terku[blow]N	0.443	Fear
zenûtu[anger]N	0.441	Anger
papānu[(a-kind-of-rush)]N	0.432	None

Table 2: The ten words most similar to *libbu* in the Neo-Assyrian corpus.

kabattu		
Word	**Score**	**Emotion**
teṣû[defecate]V	0.793	None
ṣabru[blinker]AJ	0.788	None
alālu[sing-a-joyful-song]V	0.770	Happiness
elēṣu[swell]V	0.715	Happiness
mussahhiru[turned-to-someone)]AJ	0.701	None
hadû[be(come)-joyful]V	0.697	Happiness
mušnēšu[keeping-alive]AJ	0.683	None
aggu[furious]AJ	0.661	Anger
qurruru[(meaning-unknown)]AJ	0.661	None
epēru[feed]V	0.660	None

Table 3: The ten words most similar to *kabattu* in the Neo-Assyrian corpus.

[12]Removing *libbu* from the results does not change the mean and median of the ranges of cosine scores for the top 10 results of each body word.

[13]The full list of emotional fields can be found in the accompanying Zenodo repository (Appendix A).

[14]Although the guideword translates this as "interior", *libbu* is actually a difficult word to translate. The precise definition is a general sense of "inside", including "inside" a house or the body. The lack of precision for precisely *which* organ inside the human body *libbu* referred to has led to scholars translating the term variously as "heart", "liver", and "mind" (CAD L: 164 *libbu*). We decided to keep the original sense of

The results for *libbu* have a surprising feature. The scores between the first and second results (kindu and *hīpu*, respectively) have the biggest difference of any two scores in the results lists. Kindu, a Sumerian term found in bilingual texts twice, has a score of 0.786, and *hīpu* has a score of 0.525 - a difference of 0.261. As kindu only occurs twice in the corpus, and *libbu* occurs 5,710, this result is either a quirk of the *PMI embeddings* script, or - more likely - is representative of the wide usage range of *libbu* in Neo-Assyrian texts.

The emotion words in the results list of *libbu* are overwhelmingly negative: *hīpu* ("break") and *hūṣu* ("pain") were used in the expression of sadness (Wende, 2022).[15] *Gilittu* ("terror") and *terku* ("blow") were used to express fear, and *zenûtu* ("anger") was used for anger (Wende, 2022; Bach, 2022; Svärd et al., 2020).[16]

In comparison, the emotion words similar to *kabattu* were mostly positive (Table 3). *Alālu* ("sing a joyful song"), *elēṣu* ("swell"), and *hadû* ("be joyful"), were all used to denote happiness (Wende, 2022; Bach, 2022).[17] The only outlier is *aggu* ("furious"), which was used to express anger (Wende, 2022; Bach, 2022).[18]

Of the other words relating to organs, *qerbu* ("centre") had the third highest number of words relating to emotions in its results list, with 2 results.[19] *Zā'eru* ("hostile") was the 4th highest result, with a cosine similarity score of 0.508.[20] It was used in the expression of despisement or hate. The ninth word in the results was *maqtu* ("fallen one"), with a cosine similarity score of 0.471.[21] The principal emotional field of this word is surprise.

Finally, *ṣurru*'s ("interior") results list also featured a word relating to emotions: *rūbu* ("anger"), ranked ninth, with a cosine similarity score of 0.669.[22]

the word, and have simply left it as the guideword "interior". CAD K: 11 *kabattu*.

[15]CAD H: 195 *hīpu*; CAD H: 260 *hūṣu*.

[16]CAD G: 71 *gilittu*.

[17]CAD A1: 331 *alālu*; CAD E: 88 *elēṣu*; CAD H: 25 *hadû*.

[18]CAD A1: 150 *aggu*.

[19]CAD Q: 216 *qerbu*.

[20]CAD Z: 14 *zā'iru*.

[21]CAD M1: 254 *maqtu*.

[22]As with *libbu*, *ṣurru* was also used to denote a general "inside" of the human body, and cannot be connected to any individual (or group of) organs as we understand them today. CAD Ṣ:259 *ṣurru*; CAD R: 400 *rūbu*.

4.2 Words relating to the limbs

Of the eight words relating to the limbs, four had words that could be used to express emotions in their results lists.

Purīdu ("leg") had the highest number of emotion words in its list, with *muštarhu* ("presumptuous one") ranked third (0.543 cosine similarity) and *petû* ("open") ranked fourth (0.519 similarity).[23] *Muštarhu* expresses pride whereas *petû* expressed happiness.

Two of the other words for parts of the arm had positive emotions appear in their results list. *Zāqu* ("arm") saw *ṭābu* ("good") as the most similar word, with a cosine similarity score of 0.751, and was used to express happiness.[24] The ninth result for *kirimmu* ("crook of the arm") was *narāmtu* ("beloved", cosine value 0.508), used to express love.[25]

Lastly, the seventh result for *ahu* ("arm") was *adirtu* ("gloominess") (cosine similarity of 0.546), and was used to express sadness.[26] This was the only result connected to a negative emotion for the words relating to limbs.

4.3 Words relating to the head, torso, and whole body

None of the Akkadian words relating to the head, torso, or the whole body had a word denoting emotions in their results lists.

5 Analysis

The only body words that had more than three results which could be used to express emotions were *libbu* and *kabattu*. Previous scholarship regarding Neo-Assyrian embodied emotions has identified these were often used in phrases to express emotions (Bach, 2022; Luukko, 2021; Morello, 2022; Sonik, 2022b). The results appeared to therefore align with current Assyriological research.

Thus far, we have identified words in results lists that *could* be used to express emotions. Many of these words can be translated in different ways and have alternative usages. This section will assess whether the words in the results lists for *libbu* and *kabattu* were indeed used to convey emotions in the Neo-Assyrian corpus. This will indicate whether

[23]CAD P: 517 *purīdu*; CAD M2: 286 *muštarhu*; CAD P: 338 *petû*.

[24]CAD Z: 64 *zāqu*; CAD Ṭ: 19 *ṭābu*.

[25]CAD K: 406 *kirimmu*; CAD N1: 342 *narāmtu*.

[26]CAD A1: 205 *ahu*; CAD A1: 127 *adirtu*.

emotions in general were part of the semantic field for either *libbu* or *kabattu*. It will also examine whether the emotions conveyed with these words align with current Assyriological research into embodied emotions.

5.1 Emotion words similar to *libbu*

Libbu is consistently identified in Assyriological scholarship as the main seat of emotion, and is described in Akkadian phrases as where anger, fear, and joy were felt (Bach, 2022; Luukko, 2021; Steinert, 2022; Schaudig, 2022).

The first word relating to emotions in *libbu*'s results list was *hīpu* ("break"), which was the second overall result. In the Neo-Assyrian corpus, *hīpu* was attested 72 times, and was used in three ways: to describe a break in a text the scribe was copying;[27] to describe quarrying lapis lazuli;[28] the breakage of physical objects;[29] and to describe the breaking of the *libbu* as an expression of sadness. Only 3 attestations were to express emotion and were only found in the royal inscriptions of Assurbanipal in the construction *hīp libbu* ("broken *libbu*", often translated as "broken heart") (Wende, 2022).[30] Therefore, the primary usage of *hīpu* in the Neo-Assyrian corpus was not to express emotion, but when it was, it was done so only with *libbu*.

The second word on the results list that could express emotion was *gilittu* ("terror"). *Gilittu* occurs most frequently in the Neo-Assyrian corpus in disregard formulae of oracular queries (22 out of 27 attestations) (Svärd et al., 2020; Wende, 2022).[31] In all of the attestations, *gilittu* was used to express fear, and more specifically acute terror. As *gilittu* has a clear semantic field of fear in the Neo-Assyrian corpus, its appearance as third on the results list for *libbu* suggests that of the emotions, *libbu* was connected strongly to fear.

The third emotion word on *libbu*'s results list was *hūṣu* ("pain"). It is ranked sixth in the similarity rankings, and it is unsurprising to see *hūṣu* alongside *hīpu* in the results list for *libbu*, as these words were part of the compound expression *hūṣ hipi libbi* ("an emotional or physical pain within the *libbu*").[32] However, in the Neo-Assyrian corpus this phrase was not used to express an emotion, but in scholarly commentaries to describe an abdominal pain.[33] Thus, in the Neo-Assyrian corpus *hūṣu* connected *libbu* with a medical semantic field.

The fourth word relating to emotions was *terku* ("blow"). *Terku* could be used to describe a throbbing emotional response, but of the 14 Neo-Assyrian attestations this was only found in 1 text. The text was a letter to the Assyrian king and includes a description of someone dying from a throbbing *libbu* due to hearing the speech of the king.[34] The rest of the attestations were in two royal inscriptions and the omen series *Šumma tirku*. In all of these cases, *terku* was used to describe a physical dark spot on either human skin or lambs' wool.[35] Overall, even though *terku* could be used to express a strong emotion or physical response, in the Neo-Assyrian corpus it was used for anatomical descriptions.

The final word used to express emotions in the results list for *libbu* is *zenûtu* ("anger"). It had a clear connection with the emotional field of anger, but was only used in two royal inscriptions from the reign of Esarhaddon in passages explaining the anger of the god Marduk prior to destroying Babylon.[36] It followed the phrase *ēziz libbašu* ("his *libbu* was furious"), which explains it's appearance in the results list, and indicates *libbu*'s connection

[27]In order to aid non-Assyriologists, we refer the reader to the electronic versions of the texts hosted on Oracc. When possible, the urls also link to the exact location of the word under discussion in the text. For examples of *hīpu* used to decribe a break in an original tablet the scribe copied, this can be seen in the first three lines of `http://oracc.org/blms/P394721`, lines rev. ii 8-19 in `http://oracc.org/cams/gkab/P338598`, and four lines in `http://oracc.org/dcclt/nineveh/P386432`.

[28]For example `http://oracc.org/rinap/rinap1/Q003421.4.5`; `http://oracc.org/rinap/rinap4/Q003232.125.4`; and `http://oracc.org/rinap/rinap4/Q003230.308.5`.

[29]For example in a recipe for making glass in line rev. 37 in `http://oracc.org/glass/P394484`.

[30]`http://oracc.org/rinap/rinap5/Q003819.5.2`; `http://oracc.org/rinap/rinap5/Q007602.249.2`; `http://oracc.org/rinap/rinap5/Q003710.875.3`.

[31]For example, in `http://oracc.org/saao/saa04/P238980.29.12`, `http://oracc.org/saao/saa04/P239001.16.1`, and `http://oracc.org/saao/saa04/P238965.22.1`.

[32]CAD H: 260 *hūṣu*.

[33]For example, `http://oracc.org/ccpo/P296515.8.1`, `http://oracc.org/ccpo/Q005179.6.1`, and `http://oracc.org/ccpo/P461217.7.2`.

[34]`http://oracc.org/saao/saa10/P313436.19.2`

[35]For example, `http://oracc.org/cams/gkab/P363488.12.2`, `http://oracc.org/rinap/rinap4/Q003388.5.5`, `http://oracc.org/rinap/rinap4/Q003387.7.7`.

[36]`http://oracc.org/rinap/rinap4/Q003335.18.1`, `http://oracc.org/rinap/rinap4/Q003342.9.7`.

to the semantic field of anger.

Overall, only two of the words that appeared on the results list for *libbu* were used exclusively to express emotions in the Neo-Assyrian corpus: *gilittu* and *zenûtu*. They expressed fear and anger, respectively.

Traditional Assyriological research states *libbu* was the seat of joy based on phrases that locate joy within the *libbu* (Steinert, 2022; Luukko, 2021). Our results diverge from this perspective, and offer an alternative perspective of the emotions associated with *libbu*. Neither *gilittu* nor *zenûtu* were used to express joy, and none of the words in *libbu*'s results list that could be used to express emotions were used to express joy. Interestingly, 27 attestations pair *elēṣu* with *libbu*. *Elēṣu*'s absence on the results list for *libbu* further strengthens the argument that whilst joy might have been connected with *libbu*, *libbu* was not primarily associated with joy or happiness.

Moreover, whilst *libbu* was used in a similar manner to *gilittu* and *zenûtu*, the varied usage of other words in the result list suggests that emotions were not the principle semantic field for *libbu*. This was made even more clear once the results list was expanded to 20 results, as the results pointed to a semantic field more akin to illness and agriculture. These can be found in the supplementary material (Appendix A). These results from close reading also corroborate the suggestion from the ranges in cosine similarity scores (Fig. 1), which suggested *libbu* would have a broader semantic field than other Akkadian body words in this study.

Emotions were therefore not the principle semantic field for *libbu*, and the results list speak to it's diverse usage in the Neo-Assyrian corpus. However, when it was used to express emotions, it was used to express fear and anger.

5.2 Emotion words similar to *kabattu*

In Assyriological scholarship, *kabattu* is consistently identified as an important part of the body where emotions were felt, especially for feeling happiness and joy (Bach, 2022; Sonik, 2022b).

Of the emotion words in the results list for *kabattu*, *alālu* ("to sing a joyful song") was the most similar, and was ranked third in the results list. Of the seven attestations in the Neo-Assyrian corpus, it was used to express the gods' joy five times,[37] and the joy of the king twice.[38] *Alālu* was found in literary texts, royal inscriptions, and a hymn. All of these genres drew upon literary topoi, which suggests *alālu* was imbued with metaphorical meaning (Wende, 2022).

Elēṣu ("to swell")was the second word related to emotions in the results list for *kabattu*, and was ranked fourth. It is mostly attested in Neo-Assyrian royal inscriptions (35 attestations out of 37 in the corpus), and was largely used to describe the happiness and good moods of the gods and the kings (Bach, 2022).[39] In six texts it was paired with *kabattu* (such as *ēteliṣ kabattī*), desribing how joy made the liver swell.[40]

Hadû ("to become joyful") was the third word related to emotions in the results list for *kabattu*, and was ranked sixth. *Elēṣu* and *hadû* were two of four words identified by Mikko Luukko that expressed joy or happiness in Assyrian archival material (Luukko, 2021). *Hadû* specifically related to divine joy and the joy of the king, which aligns with Luukko's view that the happiness and joy of superiors was a concern for subordinates (Luukko, 2021).[41] There is also an interesting usage where *hadû* was used to describe the happiness of fathers in literary texts.[42] This points to a particular type of joy that *hadû* expressed, and *kabattu* could be semantically connected to not just joy, but a specific kind of joy.

The final word relating to emotions that was on the results list for *kabattu* was *aggu* ("furious"),

[37] http://oracc.org/saao/saa03/P334929.85.1, http://oracc.org/rinap/rinap2/Q006494.149.2, http://oracc.museum.org/cams/gkab/P338326.37.2, http://oracc.org/cams/gkab/P363581.33.4, and http://oracc.org/cams/gkab/P338328.30.4.

[38] http://oracc.org/rinap/rinap2/Q006488.194.7, http://oracc.org/rinap/rinap2/Q006483.336.1.

[39] For example http://oracc.org/rinap/rinap2/Q006488.168.9, http://oracc.org/rinap/rinap4/Q003230.496.4, and http://oracc.org/rinap/rinap5/Q007625.37.4.

[40] http://oracc.org/cams/anzu/Q002771.60.5, http://oracc.org/ribo/babylon6/Q006325.77.2, http://oracc.org/rinap/rinap2/Q006596.62.4, http://oracc.org/rinap/rinap2/Q006482.325.2, http://oracc.org/rinap/rinap2/Q006483.189.8, and http://oracc.org/rinap/rinap2/Q006605.77.1.

[41] For example, http://oracc.org/riao/Q004661.10.1, http://oracc.org/saao/saa09/P337163.23.7, http://oracc.org/saao/saa01/P224485.22.1, and http://oracc.org/saao/saa04/P237053.13.8.

[42] http://oracc.org/atae/huzirina/P338675.56.2, http://oracc.org/cams/gkab/P338321.83.3, and http://oracc.org/cams/gkab/P338675.56.2.

which was ranked eighth. It was mostly used in royal inscriptions to describe how the wrath of the gods was not appeased.[43] Even though this was a different emotional field, it ties in to the theme of emotions of gods seen in the usage of the other emotion words similar to *kabattu*.

The findings align with the usage of *kabattu* in similar types of texts. Of the 176 attestations, 120 were in royal inscriptions, which were heavily inspired by literary topoi in order to express emotions as agreed upon by the king and the most senior circle of scribes (Bach, 2022).[44] Most of the attestations of *alālu*, *elēṣu*, *hadû*, and *aggu* were in similarly literary texts. In addition, the results demonstrate an overwhelming concern regarding the happiness of gods and kings, aligning with previous scholarship suggesting happiness was a key aim of Mesopotamian kingship (Morello, 2022; Luukko, 2021).

Overall, the results for *kabattu* included words that were used in texts like royal inscriptions which made extensive use of literary motifs. Of the words that were similar to *kabattu*, and could be used to express emotions, all were indeed used as such in the dataset. Three out of four were used to express happiness or joy. Therefore, *kabattu* was principally part of the semantic field of happiness and joy. The fourth result (*aggu*) suggests a secondary semantic field for *kabattu* was anger, based on these words' usage in royal inscriptions and literary texts.

6 Conclusions

PMI-embeddings has therefore proven to be an important tool to not only identify which areas of the body were most associated with emotions, but to identify which body parts were semantically connected to specific emotional fields in Neo-Assyrian texts.

We highlighted two words that were most similar in usage to words that could be used to express emotions: *libbu* and *kabattu*. Our much more limited list of Akkadian words for body parts that were semantically linked with emotions than Steinert's list suggests the Neo-Assyrian corpus has temporally-specific methods of embodying emotions. Future research could compare our results to datasets built from texts of a different period, such as Middle Assyrian. *Libbu* and *kabattu* were the two Akkadian words relating to the body that were most likely to be part of the semantic field of emotions, aligning with the findings of previous Assyriological research (Sonik, 2022b; Steinert, 2021; Luukko, 2021; Wende, 2022).

We have been able to corroborate results with close readings of texts for *kabattu*, and solidify that in the Neo-Assyrian texts a primary semantic field of the liver was not just emotions generally, but more specifically the semantic fields of happiness and anger.

We have also demonstrated how the results from *PMI-embeddings* can complement and add to close reading approaches in order to provide a more nuanced reading of Neo-Assyrian embodied emotions. We demonstrated that the emotion words most similar to the usage of *libbu* were in the emotional field of fear and anger, which does not align with traditional close reading approaches. Furthermore, our results demonstrate that emotions were only one facet of the many usages of *libbu* in Neo-Assyrian texts.

PMI-embeddings is therefore a tool that can both corroborate results from close-readings, but more importantly has provided new perspectives on how Neo-Assyrian texts embodied emotions. On the basis of this single case study, *PMI-embeddings* will become vital in the suite of tools for digital Assyriology.

Acknowledgements

This research was conducted as part of the project Embodied Emotions: Ancient Mesopotamia and Today, funded by the Finnish Cultural Foundation. The *PMI-embeddings* script was developed with the assistance of the Centre of Excellence Ancient Near Eastern Empires, funded by the Academy of Finland (decision number 352747).

We would like to thank Dr. Ulrike Steinert, who graciously allowed us access to the research of the project "Akkadische und Hethitische Emotionsbegriffe im Kontext" (AHEC).

This research could not have been carried out without the richly annotated dataset on Oracc, almost all of which was manually inputted. We would like to thank the Steering Committee of

[43]This was in eight out of 12 attestations. For example, `http://oracc.org/rinap/rinap5/Q003705.538.3`, `http://oracc.org/rinap/rinap5/Q003703.316.3`, and `http://oracc.org/rinap/rinap5/Q003778.23.3`.

[44]For example, `http://oracc.museum.upenn.edu/rinap/rinap2/Q006596.62.4`, `http://oracc.museum.upenn.edu/rinap/rinap4/Q003286.275.1`, and `http://oracc.museum.upenn.edu/rinap/rinap5/Q007615.16.6`.

Oracc, Jamie Novotny, Eleanor Robson, Steve Tinney, and Niek Veldhuis. We would also like to thank the PIs of the many Oracc sub-projects, and the scores of researchers who were involved in the lemmatisation and digitisation process.

Abbreviations

CAD: The Assyrian Dictionary of the University of Chicago

References

Johannes Bach. 2022. Emotions and Assyrian Kingship. In Karen Sonik and Ulrike Steinert, editors, *The Routledge Handbook of Emotions in the Ancient Near East*, 1 edition, pages 329–358. Routledge, London.

Laura Battini. 2022. Sennacherib's Sieges and Deportations Reliefs: How to Increase Emotions. *Avar: An Interdisciplinary Journal of Life and Society in the Ancient Near East*, 1(2):313–359.

Ellie Bennett. 2023. Age and Masculinities during the Neo-Assyrian Period. *Journal of Cuneiform Studies*, 75:123–154. Publisher: University of Chicago press.

Piotr Bojanowski, Edouard Grave, Armand Joulin, and Tomas Mikolov. 2017. Enriching word vectors with subword information.

Dominik Bonatz. 2022. Fear and Terror in Assyrian Palace Reliefs. In Karen Sonik and Ulrike Steinert, editors, *The Routledge Handbook of Emotions in the Ancient Near East*, 1 edition, pages 525–543. Routledge, London.

Kenneth Ward Church and Patrick Hanks. 1990. Word association norms, mutual information, and lexicography. *Computational Linguistics*, 16(1):22–29.

Shih-Wei Hsu and Jaume Llop Raduà, editors. 2021. *The Expression of Emotions in Ancient Egypt and Mesopotamia*. BRILL.

Jakob Jungmaier, Nora Kassner, and Benjamin Roth. 2020. Dirichlet-smoothed word embeddings for low-resource settings. In *Proceedings of the 12th Language Resources and Evaluation Conference*, pages 3560–3565, Marseille, France. European Language Resources Association.

Omer Levy, Yoav Goldberg, and Ido Dagan. 2015. Improving distributional similarity with lessons learned from word embeddings. *Transactions of the Association for Computational Linguistics*, 3:211–225.

Mikko Luukko. 2021. Expressions of Joy and Happiness in Neo-Assyrian. In Shih-Wei Hsu and Jaume Llop Raduà, editors, *The Expression of Emotions in Ancient Egypt and Mesopotamia*, pages 255–282. BRILL.

Tomas Mikolov, Kai Chen, Greg Corrado, and Jeffrey Dean. 2013. Efficient estimation of word representations in vector space.

Nathan Morello. 2022. Joy and Happiness in Mesopotamian Royal Inscriptions. In Karen Sonik and Ulrike Steinert, editors, *The Routledge Handbook of Emotions in the Ancient Near East*, 1 edition, pages 455–471. Routledge, London.

Davide Nadali. 2022. Shaming the Enemy in Assyrian Palace Reliefs and Royal Inscriptions. In Karen Sonik and Ulrike Steinert, editors, *The Routledge Handbook of Emotions in the Ancient Near East*, 1 edition, pages 614–627. Routledge, London.

Aleksi Sahala and Krister Lindén. 2020. Improving word association measures in repetitive corpora with context similarity weighting. In *Proceedings of the 12th International Joint Conference on Knowledge Discovery, Knowledge Engineering and Knowledge Management, IC3K 2020, Volume 1: KDIR, Budapest, Hungary, November 2-4, 2020*. SCITEPRESS Science And Technology Publications.

Aleksi Sahala and Saana Svärd. 2021. Language technology approach to "seeing" in Akkadian. In *The Routledge Handbook of the Senses in the Ancient Near East*, 1 edition, pages 561–575. Routledge, London.

Magnus Sahlgren. 2006. The word-space model: using distributional analysis to represent syntagmatic and paradigmatic relations between words in high-dimensional vector spaces.

Hanspeter Schaudig. 2022. Anger and Hatred in Neo-Assyrian and Neo-Babylonian Royal Inscriptions. In Karen Sonik and Ulrike Steinert, editors, *The Routledge Handbook of Emotions in the Ancient Near East*, 1 edition, pages 631–647. Routledge, London.

Karen Sonik. 2022a. Emotions and Body Language. The Expression of Emotions in Visual Art. In Karen Sonik and Ulrike Steinert, editors, *The Routledge Handbook of Emotions in the Ancient Near East*, 1 edition, pages 269–325. Routledge, London.

Karen Sonik. 2022b. Emotions and Body Language. The Expression of Emotions in Visual Art. In Karen Sonik and Ulrike Steinert, editors, *The Routledge Handbook of Emotions in the Ancient Near East*, 1 edition, pages 269–325. Routledge, London.

Karen Sonik and Ulrike Steinert, editors. 2022. *The Routledge Handbook of Emotions in the Ancient Near East*, 1 edition. Routledge, London.

Ulrike Steinert. 2021. Pounding Hearts and Burning Livers: The Sentimental Body in Mesopotamian Medicine and Literature. In Shih-Wei Hsu and Jaume Llop Raduà, editors, *The Expression of Emotions in Ancient Egypt and Mesopotamia*, pages 410–469. BRILL, Leiden.

Ulrike Steinert. 2022. Emotion and the Body: Embodiment, Conceptual Metaphor, and Linguistic Encoding of Emotions in Akkadian. In *The Routledge Handbook of Emotions in the Ancient Near East*, 1 edition, pages 51–87. Routledge, London.

Saana Svärd, Tero Alstola, Heidi Jauhiainen, Aleksi Sahala, and Krister Lindén. 2020. Fear in Akkadian Texts: New Digital Perspectives on Lexical Semantics. In S-W Hsu and J. Llop-Raduà, editors, *The Expression of Emotions in Ancient Egypt and Mesopotamia*, number 116 in Culture and History of the Ancient Near East, pages 470–502. Brill, Leiden.

Peter D Turney and Patrick Pantel. 2010. From frequency to meaning: Vector space models of semantics. *Journal of artificial intelligence research*, 37:141–188.

Jonathan Valk. 2016. "They Enjoy Syrup and Ghee at Tables of Silver and Gold": Infant Loss in Ancient Mesopotamia. *Journal of the Economic and Social History of the Orient*, 59(5):695–749.

Janine Wende. 2022. Akkadian Emotion Terms. In Karen Sonik and Ulrike Steinert, editors, *The Routledge Handbook of Emotions in the Ancient Near East*, 1 edition, pages 150–170. Routledge, London.

A Supplementary Data

Supplementary data is available to view for this research. Accompanying files can be found via the following url:

`https://doi.org/10.5281/zenodo.8272738`

The data includes:

- A ReadMe file.
- The Neo-Assyrian corpus downloaded from Oracc.
- A .txt file listing the terms for the body.
- The Excel spreadsheet with the emotion words and their emotional categories.
- The vector files generated by the method outlined in the main text.
- An Excel file with the top 10 results for each word, their cosine similarity score, the frequencies for the words, and their principal emotional fields.
- All images used in this publication.

BabyLemmatizer 2.0 – A Neural Pipeline for POS-tagging and Lemmatizing Cuneiform Languages

A. J. Aleksi Sahala
University of Helsinki, Finland
aleksi.sahala@helsinki.fi

Krister Lindén
University of Helsinki, Finland
krister.linden@helsinki.fi

Abstract

We present BabyLemmatizer 2.0, a linguistic annotation pipeline for POS-tagging and lemmatizing cuneiform languages, as well as pretrained models for a variety of ancient Mesopotamian languages and dialects. We evaluate the system on two dialects of Akkadian: Assyrian and Babylonian, as well as on two genealogically unrelated cuneiform languages: Sumerian and Urartian. We also test our system on Ancient Greek and Latin to experiment with its performance on non-cuneiform languages. Our system achieves a POS-tagging accuracy between 95-98% and a lemmatization accuracy of 94-96% depending on the language or dialect. The system can predict correct POS-tags for 83-91%, and lemmata for 68-84% of out-of-vocabulary word forms depending on the language or dialect.

1 Introduction

Lemmatization is a linguistic annotation task that labels words with their dictionary forms. This is essential for morphologically complex highly inflectional and agglutinative languages, where the relationship between surface forms and their dictionary forms are opaque. In historical languages with less standardized spelling, lemmatization becomes even more crucial because also the relationship between the surface forms and their graphemic representations may be obscure, and make searching attestations of words belonging to highly inflectional part-of-speech classes difficult, or close to impossible, without cumbersome regular expression based search queries.

This issue can be demonstrated with the Akkadian verb *nadānu* "to give", which occurs in 367 different surface forms and in 477 different spellings in the Open Richly Annotated Cuneiform Corpus (Oracc) (Tinney et al., 2006). The simplest finite surface form, the third person singular G-present *inaddin* "he/she gives" is spelled in seven different ways in Oracc: logographically IN.SUM, SUM, SUM{*+in*}, logo-syllabically SUM-*in* and syllabically *i-na-din, i-na-di*$_3$*-in* and *ina-ad-din*. Similarly the third person singular G-preterite and G-perfect forms *iddin* and *ittadin* are spelled in eight and five different ways in Oracc, respectively.

Part-of-speech (POS) tagging is another important concept in the NLP of morphologically complex languages. Besides its obvious use, that is, searching for words that belong to a certain POS-class, POS-tags can be used to some extent to disambiguate lemmatization. For instance, in Akkadian the logogram IGI can denote various concepts depending on its context. If preceded by a preposition, it often denotes being in front of something (e.g. *ina* IGI = *ina pāni*), but in other contexts it can also mean *šību* "witness", *nāmuru* "be(come) visible" or *īnu* "eye", among many other readings and meanings.

Traditionally Akkadian and other cuneiform language lemmatization and POS-tagging has been done with rule-based systems, including a dictionary-based and morphology-based methods. The disadvantage of dictionary-based lemmatizers is that they are unable to provide POS-tagging or lemmatization for previously unseen word forms. Although morphology-based tools can produce annotations for unseen word forms as long as their lemmata and morphology have been defined, they struggle to deal with spelling variation, which is difficult to describe using rules without producing excessive over-generation.

In this paper we present an OpenNMT-based neural lemmatizer and POS-tagger for Akkadian and other cuneiform languages. The presented neural network based approach aims to solve both of the previously mentioned issues. It can learn many-

[0]Aleksi Sahala was responsible for developing the tool, training and evaluating the models and writing the paper. Krister Lindén was the PI of the project and provided feedback for the manuscript. BabyLemmatizer 2.0 is accessible at https://github.com/asahala/BabyLemmatizer

Proceedings of the Ancient Language Processing Workshop associated with RANLP-2023, pages 203–212,
held in Varna Bulgaria, Sept 8, 2023.
https://doi.org/10.26615/978-954-452-087-8_023

to-many relations between all spellings of word forms and their possible lemmata in context, and use these learned mappings to predict annotation for previously unseen word forms, also in previously unseen spellings.

Lemmatization of cuneiform texts opens them to a variety of computational methods, including, but not limited to semantic and network analysis, and enables harmonization of existing resources, which is essential for the digitalization of Assyriological research.

2 Cuneiform and the Cuneiform Languages

The cuneiform writing system was used in ancient Mesopotamia from the middle of the fourth millennium BCE until the first or the second century CE. According to modern understanding, it was first developed by the Sumerians and later adapted by speakers of several other languages such as Akkadian, Elamite, Hittite, Hurrian and Urartian.

Originally cuneiform was a logographic writing system, where all the signs denoted various concepts, such as numbers and commodities that were relevant to trade, taxing and ownership in the early Mesopotamian society. Around 2800 BCE the writing system took its first clear steps toward a more phonetic expression of human language by allowing certain logograms to be used for marking syllabic values (Michalowski, 2008). For example, the sign KA that originally denoted the Sumerian word for mouth /kag/ began also to mark a phonetic syllable /ka/, which allowed ancient scribes to express more abstract ideas such as combinations of grammatical affixes. After the cuneiform writing system had been adopted to the East-Semitic Eblaic and Akkadian languages around the 25th century BCE, the use of syllabic signs became widespread, as logograms alone were too ambiguous for expressing the Semitic stem-internal morphology (Michalowski, 2008).

Cuneiform signs can be used for four distinct purposes. The two basic uses are *logograms* that express ideas such as "king", "wife", "temple" or "to build", and *syllabograms* that express syllable-like sounds like /ma, mu, mi, me/. The remaining uses are *determinatives* and *phonetic complements*. The former were used to classify words into various categories, such as divine names, trees or wooden objects, and places among many others. Phonetic complements, on the other hand, were used sporadically to give hints on how a logogram next to them should be read by repeating some of its sounds syllabically (Jagersma, 2010).

2.1 Transliteration of Cuneiform

Transliteration of cuneiform aims to represent the original text in the Latin alphabet sign by sign. Conventionally, logograms are written in capital letters (except in Sumerian), and the syllabic signs are always written in lowercase. The marking of determinatives and phonetic complements vary. In paper publications they are written in superscript, but in the Oracc notation they are wrapped in curly brackets. Phonetic complements are distinguished from determinatives using a plus sign, as in APIN{*+ru*} for the Akkadian word *ikkaru* "farmer" (Tinney and Robson, 2019).

Another detail relevant to this paper in cuneiform transliteration is indexing that aims to separate cuneiform signs with similar readings from each other. The index of the sign (or its reading) is expressed in subscript numbers. For instance, there are two common cuneiform signs that indicate the syllable /šu/. To keep these two signs separate in transliteration, they are transliterated as *šu* and $šu_2$, allowing the reader to know which sign was used in the original source. This makes the transliteration of cuneiform reversible and more transparent.

2.2 Languages

For this paper, relevant languages are Akkadian, Sumerian and Urartian.

Akkadian is best known as the language of the Babylonians and Assyrians. It belongs to the East-Semitic languages and is documented in writing from the Old Akkadian period ca. 2400 BCE to the first or the second century CE. The Assyrian dialect, once spoken in the northern Mesopotamia, is divided into three chronological variants: Old Assyrian (1950-1500 BCE), Middle Assyrian (1500-1000 BCE), and Neo-Assyrian (1000-612 BCE). The Babylonian dialect is divided into Old Babylonian (2000-1500 BCE), Middle Babylonian (1500-1000 BCE), Neo-Babylonian (1000-626 BCE) and Late Babylonian (626 BCE-100 CE). An artificial language known as Standard Babylonian was also used in literary contexts by Akkadian speaking scholars for over a millennium. Although this language was based on Old Babylonian, the texts written in Standard Babylonian often contain residue from the contemporary spoken Babylonian and Assyrian dialects.

Akkadian features a complex morphology that combines linear (prefixation and suffixation) and nonlinear (root-pattern morphology and infixation) processes (Huehnergard and Woods, 2008). Akkadian is written mostly using syllabic signs, but a selection of logograms is also used. The extent of logogram use varies depending on the time period and genre. Typically, everyday texts, such as letters, do not contain many logograms, but they are abundantly used until the later time periods in scholarly texts.

Sumerian was an isolate language first attested in writing in the middle of the fourth millennium BCE. Sumerian died as an everyday vernacular in the 18th century BCE and transformed into a literary language used by the Babylonian and Assyrian scholars in various contexts until the end of the cuneiform tradition circa the first or the second century CE (Jagersma, 2010). As an agglutinating language with 10 grammatical cases, possessive suffixes and heavy verbal prefixation its morphology is quite rich, not as opaque as that of Akkadian. Although Sumerian is generally written in a logo-syllabic manner, the earliest texts were purely logographic, and some texts written after the second millennium BCE used only syllabic signs. Counter-intuitively, these syllabic, so-called unortographic, texts are often the most difficult ones to understand due to their high ambiguity (Michalowski, 2011).

Urartian was a language spoken in Asia Minor and the northern reaches of Mesopotamia. It belonged to the Hurro-Urartian language family and is attested between the 9th and the 7th century BCE on inscriptions written in the Neo-Assyrian cuneiform script (Wilhelm, 2008). Similarly to Sumerian, Urartian is a heavily agglutinating language with a complex morphology, including nine grammatical cases, Suffixaufnahme (stacking of nominal suffixes in genitive constructions) and rich verb affixation. Due to the relatively low number of surviving inscriptions and their repetitive nature, the Urartian language is far less understood than Akkadian or Sumerian.

3 Digital Resources

The most relevant digital resource to the work presented in this paper is the Open Richly Annotated Cuneiform Corpus, better known as Oracc (Tinney et al., 2006). It contains ca. 112,000 cuneiform texts in various languages, including but not limited to Sumerian, Akkadian and Urartian. Other important digital resources include the Cuneiform Digital Library Initiative (Englund et al., 1998) (ca. 350,000 entries, including texts and metadata), Database of Neo-Sumerian Texts (Molina, 2002) (ca. 105,000 Neo-Sumerian administrative documents), The Electronic Babylonian Library Fragmentarium (Jiménez et al., 2018) (16,000 fragments), Archibab (Charpin, 2009) (10,000 texts), Ebla Digital Archives (Milano and Maiocchi, 2016) (3,000 texts) and Achemenet (Briant and Henkelman, 2009) (4,000 texts). For a more detailed survey on cuneiform language resources, see Charpin (2014).

Oracc contains ca. 2.22 million words of Akkadian as of 2023. As the total number of words in known Akkadian tablets and inscriptions has been estimated to be around 10 million (Streck, 2010), a majority of Akkadian texts remain unannotated to date.[1]

For Sumerian, Oracc hosts texts comprising 4.45 million words and they include the vast majority of the important Sumerian texts and archives. Most of the Sumerian data has already been lemmatized, and therefore the need for Sumerian annotation tools is not as urgent as it is for Akkadian. Nonetheless, many witnesses of Sumerian composite texts still lack lemmatization.

For Urartian, Oracc contains texts comprising 26,000 words, 24,000 of which have already been lemmatized. The total number of non-digitized texts existing outside Oracc is not clear to us.

4 Previous Work

Akkadian lemmatization and POS-tagging have been approached with finite-state morphology on several occasions since the late 1980s. The first attempt to morphologically analyze, lemmatize and POS-tag Akkadian with finite-state transducers was taken by Kataja and Koskenniemi (1988). Barthélemy (1998) and Macks (2002) used Prolog Definite Clause Grammars for parsing Akkadian verbal morphology, and later a procedural approach to Akkadian verb morphology was taken by Sahala (2014). Bamman (2012) built a finite-state model for lemmatizing Old Assyrian letters, and Sahala et al. (2020) published the BabyFST, a finite-state model for Babylonian.

[1]There is no reliable estimate of the total number of Akkadian words in various digital resources, but alongside Oracc, at least 30,000 texts exist in other digital resources with varying accessibility (Charpin, 2014).

For Sumerian, morphological analysis, POS-tagging and lemmatization have been done with the GATE Java Suite (Tablan et al., 2006) and more recently with a dictionary-based approach by Chiarcos et al. (2018).

To date, the most comprehensive lemmatizer for cuneiform languages is L2 (Tinney, 2019), a dictionary and rule-based tool that has been used to annotate Oracc. L2 is also capable of providing morphological analysis for Sumerian.

For a more comprehensive survey on Computational Assyriology see Sahala (2021), and on the use of Machine Learning in ancient language processing Sommerschield et al. (2023).

5 Data

All our cuneiform language data comes from Oracc JSON dumps downloaded in January 2023. For the experiments done in this paper, we extracted all the texts written in Sumerian, Akkadian and Urartian.

We selected the data from Oracc as follows:

- The **Urartian** data set comprised all texts from Oracc labeled as Urartian, the majority of the data coming from the eCUT (Christiansen et al., 2016). In total, this set consisted of 24,000 words.

- The **Neo-Assyrian** data set comprised all texts from Oracc labeled as Neo-Assyrian dialect. In total, this set consisted of 331,000 words. This corpus consists mostly of royal inscriptions and letters that primarily come from SAAo (Radner et al., 2005) and ATAE (Novotny et al., 2017).

- The **First Millennium Babylonian** data set consisted of all Oracc texts labeled as any variant of Babylonian or Akkadian, excluding Neo-Assyrian, in the first millennium BCE, thus containing Standard Babylonian, Neo-Babylonian and Late Babylonian texts. In total, this consisted of 1.33 million words belonging to a wide range of genres. The largest portions of data came from RINAP (Frame et al., 2007), ADSD (Pirngruber et al., 2018), SAAo, RIBO (Frame et al., 2015) and HBTIN (Pearce et al., 2011).

- The **Sumerian (literary)** data set consisted of all Sumerian texts in Oracc's ePSD2/Literary, eSD2/earlylit and ePSD/Praxis* (Tinney et al., 2017). In this data set, the subscript indices were not removed from the Sumerian data as homophones with different indices can belong to different POS-classes and denote completely different lemmata (see section on tokenization). We chose to separate literary texts from administrative texts due to their differing vocabulary and grammar. This data set comprised 268,000 words.

- The **Sumerian (administrative)** data set consisted of all Sumerian Early Dynastic, Old Babylonian, Old Akkadian, Ebla and Lagaš II administrative texts in Oracc's ePSD2 corpus. The Ur III corpus was excluded because it would have completely overwhelmed this data set with its 81,000 texts. As in the data set above, the subscript indices were preserved. This data set consisted of 570,000 words.

To test our system on historical non-cuneiform languages, we used the Latin and Ancient Greek PROIEL treebanks (Haug and Jøhndal, 2008), comprising 205,000 and 210,000 words respectively.

5.1 Training Data Cleanup

All our models are trained by using the Oracc data, but we run it through heuristic cleanup rules to provide more consistent learning results for the models and to minimize the amount of unwanted and meaningless errors in the evaluation, such as $\{d\}$x-x being tagged as a divine name in one place but as an unknown POS-class somewhere else.

For the Akkadian data, we merge some inconsistent lemmatizations with their most common representations in the data (e.g. *aganutillû* vs. *agannutillû*) and correct obvious lemmatization errors such as *bēlēšu*, which is de facto the phonological transcription of the word instead of lemma. We also apply the Helsinki normalizations (Jauhiainen et al., 2019) to all divine names in the corpus to make their lemmatization consistent. Therefore variation such as *Anunnaki, Anunnaku* and *Anunak* is consistently mapped into *Anunnaki*. Unfortunately the normalizations are available only for names that occur in the first millennium Akkadian texts.

For all cuneiform languages, we do the following normalizations:

1. Remove all lacuna indicators such as various brackets, exclamation marks and question marks.

2. Remove all entries that have been transliterated as asterisks. This convention is used in some composite texts where that only exist in phonological transcription, such as *iddinū* for varying spellings in the witnesses like *id-di-nu* and *id-di-nu-u*$_2$.

3. Remove all entries without lemmatization unless they are supposed to be unlemmatized, as is the case of lacunae (breakages in tablets) and numbers.

4. Remove all lemmatizations from numbers and force the POS-tag *n* to them.

5. Force POS-tags for broken personal names, place names and divine names if the determinative is visible but the words have not been POS-tagged in Oracc. This can be done in high confidence for divine names and personal names.

6. Force the POS-tag *u* for broken words in case they do not have a POS-tag.

We did not do any modifications to the Ancient Greek and Latin data. These data sets were used as they are distributed in the Universal Dependencies GitHub repository.

6 Description of the System

Our system first pre-annotates the input text using a encoder-decoder model, and then aims to correct possible errors by using simple post-correction rules. The system is based on the Open Neural Machine Translation Toolkit (OpenNMT) (Klein et al., 2017) and handles the POS-tagging and lemmatization almost completely as a machine translation task. Relying purely on OpenNMT makes the tool easy to setup and allows more flexibility and easier customization. The whole pipeline is written in Python and it comes with an easy-to-use commandline interface and extensive documentation.

As our tool is purely based on Oracc notation, it aims to harmonize various digital resources and to encourage various projects to publish their data openly in Oracc.

6.1 Network Architecture

Our neural network architecture for both, the POS-tagger and the lemmatizer, follows the architecture of the Universal Lemmatizer (Kanerva et al., 2021). We use a deep attentional encoder-decoder network, where the encoder is a two layer BiLSTM that reads the sequence of logo-syllabically tokenized input. The decoder for generating the output character sequences is a two layer unidirectional LSTM with input feeding attention. However, we train the model for a lesser amount of steps relative to the training data size, as it improves the training speed but does not seem to affect the model's performance. We use a batch size of 64 and start the learning rate decay halfway through the training process.

6.2 Tokenization

We tokenize the input sequences in a special way that is particularly suitable for the logo-syllabic cuneiform writing system. From here on, we refer to this as *logo-syllabic* tokenization. In logo-syllabic tokenization, syllabic signs and phonetic complements that represent phonetic sequences are encoded as space-separated character sequences, whereas logograms and determinatives are encoded as indivisible tokens. We retain indices for logograms, because homophonic logograms can refer to different parts-of-speech and lemmata (e.g. in Akkadian DUG$_3$ = *ṭābu* "good" and DUG$_4$ = *qabû* "speak"), but for syllabic signs indexation is removed to bring homophonic readings such as *šu* and *šu*$_2$ closer to each other. Based on our observations, splitting compound logograms such as MA.NA into MA and NA yields better results than handling them as monolithic units.

The tagger is trained with 5-grams of logo-syllabically tokenized word forms and it aims to predict the POS-label for the center word wrapped inside double angle brackets (see Table 1 for tokenization examples). The lemmatizer is trained with tokenized word forms followed by its POS-tag, as well as the word's previous and following POS-tags to provide shallow information about the word's context. This input string sequence is mapped to its lemma on the character level, enabling the system to infer unseen lemmata.

6.3 Lemmatization and POS-tagging Process

The input text is first tokenized logo-syllabically and fed into the tagger. The tagger output is then used as the context information for the lemmatizer, which produces the fully annotated output consisting of the lemma and the POS-tag.

The post-correction comprises two steps. First, we calculate the distribution of lemmata assigned for each word form + POS-tag pair in the training data and in case any single lemma constitutes more

<table>
<tr><td>**Original**</td><td>{*m*}KU$_6$-*li-i-di* *ina* **ŠA$_3$-*bi*** x MA.NA</td></tr>
<tr><td>**Source**
Target</td><td>`{m} KU`$_6$` - l i - i - d i | i n a « ŠA`$_3$` - b i » x | MA . NA`
`N`</td></tr>
<tr><td>**Source**
Target</td><td>`ŠA`$_3$` - b i P0=PRP P1=N P2=u`
`l i b b u`</td></tr>
<tr><td>**Combined**</td><td>`libbu + N`</td></tr>
</table>

Table 1: Example of logo-syllabic tokenization. The upper part shows the tokenization fed into the tagger, the center word wrapped in double angle brackets, and the wanted output **N** (noun). The lower table shows the tokenization fed into the lemmatizer, including the center word and its POS-tag along with the preceding and the following POS-tags, and the wanted output as a sequence of characters.

than 70% of the lemmatizations of the given pair, we replace the predictions made by the neural network with this lemmatization. Next, we repeat the same step but instead of using word forms and their POS-tags, we also use the POS-tags assigned to the preceding and the following words. These steps aim to ensure, that close to unambiguous lemmata are always lemmatized consistently. However, due to the fact that the context information is taken into account already in the neural lemmatization, the post-correction no longer improves the lemmatization results significantly as in the previous version of BabyLemmatizer (Sahala et al., 2022). Therefore the post-correction is now mostly used for assigning lemmatizations with confidence scoring.

Confidence scoring aims to assist humans to manually verify and correct the lemmatization results. This system is mainly designed for detecting out-of-vocabulary (OOV) words, that is, word forms that were not present in the training data, and categorizing these words into different classes based on their spellings. The lowest confidence score of 0 is given to OOV words written logographically as the logogram and its lemma has a suppletive relation. The score of 1 is given for logo-syllabic spellings, which may have partially suppletive relationship to their lemmata. Syllabic OOV spellings are given a confidence score of 2.

Confidence scores between 3 and 5 are assigned for in-vocabulary words. The score of 3 is given to highly ambiguous words, such as polyvalent logograms that exist in contexts that have not been observed in the training data. The score of 4 is given to words that show low or unlikely ambiguity, and the highest score of 5 is given to words that have low ambiguity and exist in a POS-context that has been witnessed in the training data.

The lemmatization process is designed to be iterative. For example, if a batch of 10,000 new texts are to be lemmatized, this data set should be broken into smaller subsets, for example in four batches of 2,500 texts each.

After each lemmatization batch, the tool generates OOV lexicons for all low confidence score classes. These lists are sorted by frequency, allowing maximal number of corrections per each corrected entry. The lemmatizations can be corrected simply entering the corrected lemma and POS-tag for any word form in the OOV list, or accepting the already given lemmatization by removing the symbol # from the beginning of the line. When the lemmatizer is run again, the system appends these changes to the model's lexicon, allowing it to lemmatize them correctly in the future. After the lemmatization results of the current batch are considered to be clean enough, the model can be retrained by using the the data from the current batch appended to the model's existing training data, yielding an updated model augmented with new manual corrections. This approach should significantly reduce the time needed for manual corrections after each batch.

6.4 CoNLL-U+ for Cuneiform

Our tool uses an extended CoNLL-U format for input and output.[2] The first ten columns follow the standard notation, reserving the XPOS field for the Oracc POS-label. In addition to the conventional fields (ID, FORM, LEMMA, UPOS, XPOS, FEATS, HEAD, DEPREL, DEPS, MISC), our CoNLL-U+ format has the following fields: ENG for the English translation, NORM for phonological transcription, LANG for word's language, FORMCTX and XPOSCTX for storing temporary context information for the system, SCORE for the confidence scoring and LOCK for write-protecting the field in

[2]See `https://universaldependencies.org/format.html`

case the file has manual corrections that the system should not overwrite.

The pipeline handles the conversion of CoNLL-U+ into OpenNMT-compatible target and source files and conversion of simple rawtext transliteration into CoNNL-U+.

7 Evaluation

For evaluation, we train ten models for each data set. We use a 80/10/10 train/dev/test split and estimate the model's accuracy, that is, the percentage of correct analyses over all analyses, using 10-fold cross-validation. We measure the accuracy in two categories: first, for all the word forms in the test set, and second for the OOV word forms only to examine the models' ability to predict labels for words that were not present in the training data. The results are summarized in Table 2 and Table 3 respectively. Confidence intervals of the cross-validation are shown in parentheses.

We ignored all fully broken words in the evaluation, as assigning empty labels for completely destroyed words is trivial.

7.1 Results for Cuneiform Languages

With the current data sets, the minimum accuracy scores for POS-tagging and lemmatization of known word forms are 95% and 92%, respectively. For OOV words, the system achieves minimum accuracy of 81% for POS-tagging and 68% for lemmatization. OOV lemmatization accuracy seems to vary greatly depending on the language and the diversity of the data set, the most striking difference being between the first millennium Babylonian (68%) and the Sumerian literary texts (84%). This difference can be explained partly by the diversity of the Babylonian data, and partly by Sumerian morphology, which is significantly more transparent than that of Akkadian. The low performance in the OOV lemmatization in administrative Sumerian can be explained by inconsistencies in the data especially in proper nouns. At times, Oracc renders their lemmata as sequences of signs separated by dots, whereas at times the dots are not used, for instance, **{d}nin-mar{ki}** is lemmatized as *Ninmar*, *Nin.mar*, *Nin.MAR*, which makes it difficult for the model to learn how to generalize. About 18% of OOV lemmatization errors and 13% of all lemmatization errors in this particular data set are caused by such inconsistencies.

7.2 Comparison Against Version 1.0

Compared with the earlier version of BabyLemmatizer, the current tool clearly outperforms its neural network performance, which significantly reduces the improvement gained from post-correction. For comparison, we used the same 500,000 word Babylonian evaluation data set as we used in our earlier report (Sahala et al., 2022). Better performance of the neural network translates directly into a better performance in OOV word lemmatization, improving the prediction accuracy of Lemma+POS labels

Category	Urartian	Neo-Assyrian	Babylonian	Sum. (lit.)	Sum. (adm.)
NN POS-tagger	96.97 (±0.39)	97.67 (±0.17)	96.80 (±0.18)	94.79 (±0.28)	96.32 (±0.08)
NN Lemmatizer	93.45 (±0.66)	95.35 (±0.20)	95.02 (±0.31)	94.67 (±0.25)	95.50 (±0.10)
NN Combined	92.49 (±0.72)	94.48 (±0.26)	93.82 (±0.36)	92.28 (±0.37)	94.57 (±0.09)
PC POS-tagger	96.97 (±0.39)	97.72 (±0.17)	96.80 (±0.18)	94.77 (±0.28)	96.32 (±0.08)
PC Lemmatizer	94.12 (±0.57)	95.47 (±0.21)	95.14 (±0.30)	94.66 (±0.27)	95.53 (±0.08)
PC Combined	93.18 (±0.63)	94.59 (±0.28)	93.94 (±0.34)	92.27 (±0.37)	94.60 (±0.07)
OOV-rate	8.26	9.20	6.06	16.80	5.21

Table 2: Results of the 10-fold cross-validation for the neural net (NN) and the post-corrected (PC) results. Combined represents word forms where both, lemma and POS-tag were predicted correctly. OOV-rate shows the average percentage of OOV words in the test set.

Category	Urartian	Neo-Assyrian	Babylonian	Sum. (lit.)	Sum. (adm.)
POS-tagger	83.00 (±1.96)	90.87 (±0.74)	85.78 (±0.81)	84.39 (±0.84)	81.17 (±0.77)
Lemmatizer	70.10 (±2.16)	71.16 (±1.14)	67.82 (±1.36)	83.93 (±1.00)	70.51 (±1.24)
Combined	65.73 (±2.06)	70.15 (±1.09)	65.52 (±1.31)	76.49 (±1.15)	67.20 (±1.28)

Table 3: Results of the 10-fold cross-validation for OOV words only. This table does not contain separate results for NN and PC, because post-correction does not affect OOV words.

for OOV words on average by 10 percentage points. The performance increase is summarized in Table 4.

Category	All	OOV
NN POS-tagger	+0.14	+4.06
NN Lemmatizer	+8.87	+8.84
NN Combined	+8.91	+10.48
PC POS-tagger	+0.14	+4.06
PC Lemmatizer	+0.35	+8.37
PC Combined	+0.45	+10.01

Table 4: Average improvement in accuracy-% from v1.0 to v2.0, overall and for OOV words (NN for neural net and PC for post-corrected).

7.3 Experiment on Latin and Ancient Greek

To test our system on non-cuneiform languages, we tagged and lemmatized the PROIEL treebanks for Latin and Ancient Greek (Table 5). For these languages, we used character sequences as input format for both the tagger and the lemmatizer with the same context information as in the logo-syllabic tokenization (5-grams for tagger and adjacent POS-context for lemmatizer). We used the training, development and test data provided at the Universal Dependencies GitHub.

Category	Greek	Latin
POS-tagger	96.70	95.31
Lemmatizer	96.70	95.81
Combined	94.96	94.03
OOV POS-tagger	87.54	84.64
OOV Lemmatizer	74.47	75.92
OOV Combined	73.18	74.92
OOV-rate	11.02	10.58

Table 5: Results for the Ancient Greek and Latin data. The upper table shows the overall results and the lower table the results for OOV words only.

8 Conclusions and Future Work

We presented an updated version of BabyLemmatizer, a pipeline for POS-tagging and lemmatizing cuneiform languages and evaluated its performance on Sumerian, first millennium Babylonian, Neo-Assyrian and Urartian texts extracted from Oracc to observe its performance for the first time outside Babylonian texts. The system achieves a POS-tagging accuracy between 95-98% and a lemmatization accuracy of 94-96% depending on the language or dialect. For OOV words only, the current version can predict correct POS-tags for 83-91%, and lemmata for 68-84% of the input word forms from transliteration. Compared with the earlier version, the current one has about 10% higher accuracy in OOV lemmatization and POS-tagging due to better neural network performance. We also tested the system for lemmatizing and POS-tagging the PROIEL Ancient Greek and Latin treebanks, achieving results similar to those with the cuneiform languages.

In the future, we plan to add prediction for UD POS-tags, phonological transcription and morphological labels for Akkadian, Sumerian and Urartian. We also plan on adding full Oracc lemma prediction that includes the English translation of the word following Oracc's *lemma[translation]POS* format, but prior to this more data cleanup is required.

Acknowledgements

We wish to thank the Academy of Finland for funding the Origins of Emesal Project (PI Krister Lindén) and the Centre of Excellence in Ancient Near Eastern Empires (PI Saana Svärd). We also wish to thank Tero Alstola and Jonathan Valk (both at the University of Helsinki) for their valuable feedback on the Akkadian lemmatization results, Niek Veldhuis (UC Berkeley) for the Oracc data acquisition scripts,[3] and Steve Tinney (University of Pennsylvania) for correcting certain broken data sets in Oracc on our request.

References

David Bamman. 2012. *11-712 NLP Lab Report: Akkadian-morph-analyzer.*

François Barthélemy. 1998. A morphological Analyzer for Akkadian Verbal Forms with a Model of Phonetic Transformations. In *Computational Approaches to Semitic Languages*.

Pierre Briant and Wouter Henkelman. 2009. Achemenet.

Dominique Charpin. 2009. Archives Babyloniennes (Archibab).

Dominique Charpin. 2014. Ressources Assyriologiques sur Internet. In *Bibliotheca Orientalis LXXI no. 3-4*.

Christian Chiarcos, Ilya Khait, Émilie Pagé-Perron, Niko Schenk, Jayanth, Christian Fäth, Julius Steuer,

[3]https://github.com/niekveldhuis/compass

William Mcgrath, and Jinyan Wang. 2018. Annotating a low-resource language with LLOD technology: Sumerian morphology and syntax. *Information*, 9(11):290.

Birgit Christiansen, Mirjo Salvini, Dan Roberto, and Stephan Kroll. 2016. Oracc: Electronic Corpus of Urartian Texts (eCUT) Project.

Robert Englund, Jürgen Renn, Jacob L. Dahl, Bertrand Lafont, and Steve Tinney. 1998. Cuneiform Digital Library Initiative (CDLI).

Grant Frame, Jamie Novotny, and Karen Radner. 2015. Oracc: Royal Inscriptions of Babylonia Online.

Grant Frame, Karen Radner, Barry L. Eichler, Erle Leichty, and Steve Tinney. 2007. Oracc: The Royal Inscriptions of the Neo-Assyrian Period.

Dag T. T. Haug and Marius Jøhndal. 2008. Creating a parallel treebank of the old Indo-European Bible translations. In *Proceedings of the second workshop on language technology for cultural heritage data (LaTeCH 2008)*, pages 27–34.

John Huehnergard and Christopher Woods. 2008. Akkadian and eblaite. In R. D. Woodard, editor, *The Ancient Languages of Mesopotamia, Egypt, and Aksum*, pages 83–152. Cambridge University Press.

Bram Jagersma. 2010. *A Descriptive Grammar of Sumerian*. University of Leiden.

Heidi Jauhiainen, Aleksi Sahala, and Tero Alstola. 2019. Oracc in Korp.

Enrique Jiménez, Jussi Laasonen, Aino Hätinen, Zsombor Földi, Adrian Heinrich, Tonio Mitto, Geraldina Rozzi, Ilya Khait, and Fabioan Simonjetz. 2018. The Electronic Babylonian Library (eBL).

Jenna Kanerva, Filip Ginter, and Tapio Salakoski. 2021. Universal lemmatizer: A sequence-to-sequence model for lemmatizing universal dependencies treebanks. *Natural Language Engineering*, 27(5):545–574.

Laura Kataja and Kimmo Koskenniemi. 1988. Finite-state Description of Semitic Morphology: A Case Study of Ancient Accadian. In *Coling Budapest 1988 Volume 1: International Conference on Computational Linguistics*.

Guillaume Klein, Yoon Kim, Yuntian Deng, Jean Senellart, and Alexander Rush. 2017. OpenNMT: Open-source toolkit for neural machine translation. In *Proceedings of ACL 2017, System Demonstrations*, pages 67–72, Vancouver, Canada. Association for Computational Linguistics.

Aaron Macks. 2002. Parsing akkadian verbs with prolog. In *Proceedings of the ACL-02 workshop on Computational approaches to semitic languages*.

Piotr Michalowski. 2008. Sumerian. In R. D. Woodard, editor, *The Ancient Languages of Mesopotamia, Egypt, and Aksum*, pages 19–46. Cambridge University Press.

Piotr Michalowski. 2011. *The Correspondence of the Kings of Ur: An Epistolary History of an Ancient Mesopotamian Kingdom*. Eisenbrauns.

Lucio Milano and Massimo Maiocchi. 2016. Ebla Digital Archives.

Manuel Molina. 2002. The Database of Neo-Sumerian Texts (BDTNS).

Jamie Novotny, Karen Radner, and Poppy Tushingham. 2017. Oracc: Archival Texts of the Assyrian Empire (ATAE).

Laurie Pearce, Stephanie Langin-Hooper, Chris Bravo, Talia Prussin, and Jay Crisostomo. 2011. Oracc: Hellenistic Babylonia: Texts, Images and Names.

Reinhard Pirngruber, Maya Rinderer, and Craig A. Harris. 2018. Oracc: Astronomical Diaries Digital.

Karen Radner, Eleanor Robson, Steve Tinney, and Jamie Novotny. 2005. Oracc: The State Archives of Assyria online.

Aleksi Sahala. 2014. *Babylonian verbimorfologian automaattinen jäsentäminen*. University of Helsinki.

Aleksi Sahala. 2021. *Contributions to Computational Assyriology (PhD Thesis)*. University of Helsinki.

Aleksi Sahala, Tero Alstola, Jonathan Valk, and Krister Linden. 2022. BabyLemmatizer: A Lemmatizer and POS-tagger for Akkadian. In *CLARIN Annual Conference Proceedings, 2022*. CLARIN ERIC.

Aleksi Sahala, Miikka Silfverberg, Antti Arppe, and Krister Lindén. 2020. BabyFST-towards a finite-state based computational model of ancient babylonian. In *Proceedings of the Twelfth Language Resources and Evaluation Conference*, pages 3886–3894.

Thea Sommerschield, Yannis Assael, John Pavlopoulos, Vanessa Stefanak, Andrew Senior, Chris Dyer, John Bodel, Jonathan Prag, Ion Androutsopoulos, and Nando de Freitas. 2023. Machine Learning for Ancient Languages: A Survey. *Computational Linguistics*, pages 1–44.

Michael Streck. 2010. Großes fach altorientalistik: Der umfang des keilschriftlichen textkorpus. In *Mitteilungen der Deutschen Orient-Gesellschaft zu Berlin, 142*.

Valentin Tablan, Wim Peters, Diana Maynard, Hamish Cunningham, and K Bontcheva. 2006. Creating Tools for Morphological Analysis of Sumerian. In *LREC*, pages 1762–1765.

Steve Tinney. 2019. *L2: How it Works*.

Steve Tinney, Phillip Jones, and Niek Veldhuis. 2017. Oracc: The electronic Pennsylvania Sumerian Dictionary 2.7.

Steve Tinney, Jamie Novotny, Eleanor Robson, and Niek Veldhuis. 2006. The Open Richly Annotated Cuneiform Corpus.

Steve Tinney and Eleanor Robson. 2019. Oracc ATF Primer. *Oracc: The Open Richly Annotated Cuneiform Corpus*.

Gernot Wilhelm. 2008. Urartian. In R. D. Woodard, editor, *The Ancient Languages of Asia Minor*, pages 105–123. Cambridge University Press.

Tibetan Dependency Parsing with Graph Convolutional Neural Networks

Bo An
Institute of Ethnology and Anthropology,Chinese Academy of Social Sciences
Building 6, Zhongguancun Nandajie 27, Beijing, China
anbo@cass.org.cn

Abstract

Dependency parsing is a syntactic analysis method to analyze the dependency relationships between words in a sentence. The interconnection between words through dependency relationships is typical graph data. Traditional Tibetan dependency parsing methods typically model dependency analysis as a transition-based or sequence-labeling task, ignoring the graph information between words. We propose a graph neural network (GNN)-based Tibetan dependency parsing method to address this issue. This method treats Tibetan words as nodes and the dependency relationships between words as edges, thereby constructing the graph data of Tibetan sentences. Specifically, we use BiLSTM to learn the word representations of Tibetan, utilize GNN to model the relationships between words, and employ MLP to predict the types of relationships between words. We conduct experiments on a Tibetan dependency database, and the results show that the proposed method can achieve high-quality Tibetan dependency parsing results.

1 Introduction

In recent years, the explosive growth of Tibetan text data, fueled by the popularization of information technology in Tibetan areas, has made the processing and deeper understanding of Tibetan information a hot research topic in Tibetan natural language processing (NLP) (Faggionato and Meelen, 2019). Dependency analysis is an essential task for the semantic modeling of texts, as it provides a basis for deep semantic analysis and has significant research and practical value. The results of dependency analysis can be directly applied to numerous basic natural language processing tasks, such as question answering (Cao et al., 2019), sentiment analysis (Xiaomei et al., 2018), and named entity recognition (Jie et al., 2017).

Traditional Tibetan dependency analysis methods can be mainly classified into two categories: (1) statistical learning-based methods (Hua et al., 2013), which usually require experts to design corresponding rules and features and then use statistical learning models to model and predict dependency syntax. This type of method heavily relies on Tibetan linguistic experts. (2) deep learning-based methods(An and Long, 2021) , which have been widely applied in Tibetan information processing, such as word segmentation, text classification, and dependency analysis, with the rapid development of deep learning. The major advantage of deep learning-based methods is that they do not require expert features. Tibetan dependency analysis can be achieved through a fixed network structure and annotated data.

However, the methods above model Tibetan dependency analysis as a classification or transition problem, ignoring the features of graph data in dependency analysis. Graph data features can better model the relationships between different words and ignore the distance between words in the text, i.e., they can model the dependency information between words that are far apart. They can also model higher-order relationships through indirect relationships between words, which significantly impacts modeling word relationships, such as AMR (Abstract Meaning Representation) (Wang et al., 2020).

This paper presents a method for Tibetan dependency analysis based on graph convolutional neural networks. Tibetan word representations are modeled using Bert (Devlin et al., 2018) and BiLSTM, followed by graph neural networks(GNN) (Zhou et al., 2020) for

Proceedings of the Ancient Language Processing Workshop associated with RANLP-2023, pages 213–221,
held in Varna Bulgaria, Sept 8, 2023.
https://doi.org/10.26615/978-954-452-087-8_024

modeling dependency relationships between words. MLP is then employed for relationship classification and determining the dependency relationship types. The results on Tibetan dependency analysis data indicate that GNN can significantly enhance the performance of Tibetan dependency analysis, thus affirming the value of graph information.

The main contributions of our work are as follows: (1) We propose using graph convolutional neural networks (GCN) to model the dependency relationships in Tibetan sentences. (2) Experimental results show that the proposed method outperforms other methods, such as R-GCN (Schlichtkrull et al., 2018), in Tibetan dependency analysis, which may be due to insufficient training data.

The main contributions are twofold:

- We propose using GCN to model the dependency relationships in Tibetan sentences.
- Experimental results show that the GCN+MLP method outperforms other methods, such as R-GCN, in Tibetan dependency analysis, which may be due to insufficient training data.

The rest of the paper is organized as follows: Section 2 introduces some of the most related work, including Tibetan dependency parsing models and graph neural networks. Our proposed model is detailed described in Section 3. Section 4 shows our experimental results on the introduced Tibetan dependency analysis dataset and presents the effects of different modules. We conclude our work in Section 5.

2 Related Work

This section briefly reviews related work, including Tibetan dependency parsing methods and neural-based methods for dependency parsing.

2.1 Tibetan dependency parsing method

The Tibetan dependency analysis dataset is the foundation for researching dependency analysis methods. Therefore, the existing Tibetan dependency analysis data is introduced first. The current Tibetan dependency analysis dataset includes the following: For instance,Hua et al. 2013 construct a Tibetan dependency tree semi-automatically. It includes a word-pairs dependency classification model, and dependency edges annotation model based on Tibetan language grammar. Tashi and Duo 2015 built a Tibetan dependency treebank of multidimensional windows based on their grammar. Toudan et al. 2018 annotated dependency trees for sentences from Tibetan primary school textbooks. Wu et al. 2019 introduced a Tibetan dependency analysis dataset with 1500 sentences annotated based on complex dependency grammar with 62 types of dependency arcs. (An and Long, 2021) constructs a Tibetan dependency parsing dataset with more than 5000 Tibetan sentences based on an interlinearized annotation dataset.

Currently, most of the Tibetan dependency parsing models are composed of two components: feature extraction and dependency prediction. A discriminant model is proposed to conduct Tibetan dependency parsing based on feature engineering by Tibetan experts (quecai rang and Zhao, 2013). And their model was further utilized for the parsing of Tibetan compound sentences. Xia et al. 2019 extracted unigram, bigram, trigram, and some Tibetan-specific features for each word in the sentence and employed a perceptron classifier to perform Tibetan dependency parsing. All of the above works were based on features designed by Tibetan language experts. Compared with these methods, the main advantage of our method is that our model can extract useful feature vectors automatically.

2.2 Neural-based method for dependency analysis

In recent years, neural-based models have achieved competitive performances in many natural language processing tasks, such as word segmentation, part-of-speech, and semantic parsing. Furthermore, this line of works have two advantages: avoiding complex feature engineering and better generalization. Due to the above advantages, neural-based models are introduced for dependency analysis. There are two main research directions for dependency analysis: translation-based parsers and graph-based parsers.

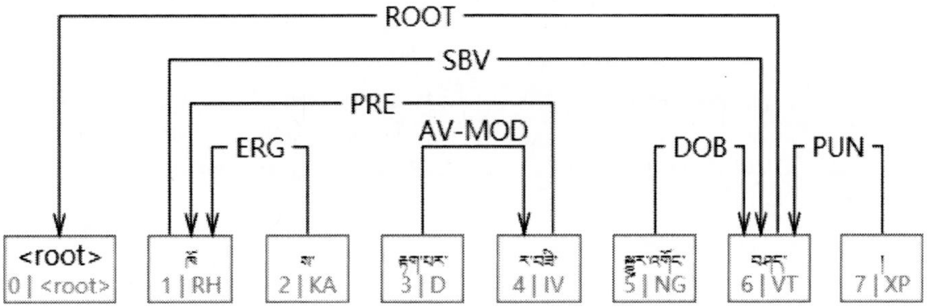

Figure 1: An example of Tibetan dependency tree.

Chen and Manning introduced the first neural translation-based dependency parser (Chen and Manning, 2014), which utilizes a feedforward network to assign a probability to each action the parser. Andor et al. (Andor et al., 2016) augments the above model with a beam search and a conditional random field loss objective for correcting false predictions. The Long-Short-Term Memory (LSTM) model was employed to achieve the state-of-the-art performance (Dyer et al., 2015; Kuncoro et al., 2016).

The first neural graph-based parser 2016 utilizes the attention mechanism from machine translation and LSTM to conduct dependency parsing. Hashimoto et al. 2016 extend the graph-based parser as a multi-task neural model and employ a bilinear MLP label classifier. Furthermore, Cheng et al. 2016 further resolve the limitation of being unable to condition the scores of each possible arc on previous parsing decisions of other graph-based parsers. Dozat et al. 2016 propose bi-affine classifiers to predict arcs and labels for dependency analysis tasks and achieve state-of-the-art performances. Recently, with the wide use of deep contextual embeddings (Peters et al., 2018), Schuster et al. 2019 introduced a multilingual transfer framework that utilizes deep contextual embeddings in an unsupervised fashion.

(An and Long, 2021) proposes a deep learning-based Tibetan dependency parsing method using BiLSTM and multi-layer perceptron. (Duo et al., 2021) models the Tibetan dependency parsing task using deep learning-based transition. Recently, scholars have introduced deep learning methods to the task of Tibetan dependency parsing task, resulting in an improvement in the performance of Tibetan dependency parsing. Despite the potential of graph neural networks, they have not been utilized in Tibetan dependency parsing tasks. Hence, this paper proposes a graph neural network-based Tibetan dependency parsing method to better model the relationships between words.

3 The GCN-based Tibetan Dependency Parsing Method

3.1 Task Definition

Dependency parsing is a natural language processing task that involves analyzing the grammatical structure of a sentence by identifying the relationships between the words in it. Moreover, Figure 1 presents an example of a Tibetan dependency tree.

Specifically, given a sentence S consisting of n words $w_1, w_2, ..., w_n$, dependency parsing aims to construct a directed acyclic graph $G = (V, E)$, where $V = v_1, v_2, ..., v_n$ is the set of vertices representing the words in S, and $E \subseteq V \times V$ is the set of directed edges representing the syntactic dependencies between words.

Each edge $e_{i,j} = (v_i, v_j)$ in E is labeled with a dependency type $r_{i,j} \in R$, where R is the set of all possible dependency types. The dependency tree's root is the vertex with no incoming edges. Thus, the dependency tree $T = (V, E')$ is a tree if it contains $n - 1$ edges and satisfies the constraints mentioned above.

The output of a dependency parser is the dependency tree T that represents the sentence's grammatical structure. This tree can be used for various downstream applications, such as machine translation, information retrieval, and text summarization.

This work employs the dataset introduced by (An and Long, 2021). There are 34 types of dependency arcs in our Tibetan dependency grammar. We present them in Table (1).

3.2 GNN for Tibetan Dependency Parsing

Tibetan dependency parsing includes word segmentation, word relation, and arc label prediction. The framework of Tibetan dependency parsing is presented in Figure 2.

We employ SegT (Huidan Liu and Yeping, 2012) for Tibetan word segmentation in this work. We utilize the Tibetan-Roberta-base to implement the embedding layer, which generates the embedding for each Tibetan syllable. Moreover, we employ BiLSTM (Kiperwasser and Goldberg, 2016) to compose the syllable embeddings into the word embedding h_i.

We employ Graph Convolutional Networks (GCN) to model Tibetan dependency parsing. GCNs can be used to model dependency parsing by constructing a graph representation of the sentence, where the vertices represent the words in the sentence, and the edges represent the syntactic dependencies between them. Each vertex is associated with a word embedding h_i, which captures the semantic information of the word. Formally, let $G = (V, E)$ be the graph representation of the sentence, where $V = v_1, v_2, ..., v_n$ is the set of vertices representing the words in the sentence, and $E \subseteq V \times V$ is the set of directed edges representing the syntactic dependencies between words. Each vertex v_i is associated with a word embedding $h_i \in \mathbb{R}^d$, where d is the dimension of the embedding. To capture the interactions between the vertices in the graph, GCNs perform graph convolution operations on the vertex embeddings. Specifically, the embedding of each vertex is updated by aggregating the embeddings of its neighboring vertices, weighted by an adjacency matrix A that encodes the edge information. The graph convolution operation can be expressed as:

$$h_i^{(l+1)} = \sigma\left(\sum_{j\in\mathcal{N}(i)} \frac{1}{c_{i,j}} W^{(l)} h_j^{(l)}\right)$$

where $h_i^{(l)}$ is the embedding of vertex i at layer l, $\mathcal{N}(i)$ is the set of neighboring vertices of vertex i, $W^{(l)}$ is the weight matrix at layer l, and $c_{i,j}$ is a normalization constant that ensures that the sum of the weights of the neighbors of vertex i is 1. The activation function σ is typically a non-linear function, such as the rectified linear unit (ReLU).

After several graph convolution operations, the final vertex embeddings can be fed into a classifier to predict the syntactic dependency labels between the words.

3.2.1 Arc Prediction Layer

This layer comprises two classifiers; the first predicts the dependency head for each word, while the second classifies the type of dependency arc between the word and its head word.

Head Classifier. The input to this classifier is the feature vectors of each word, and it outputs the index of the word's head. Since the number of words in a sentence is variable, this is a variable-class classification task, making it impossible to utilize a multi-layer perceptron (MLP) typically used for category tasks. We draw inspiration from the biaffine attention model (Dozat and Manning, 2016) to address this challenge and employ two MLP models to build the head classifier. Specifically, we use Equation (1) and (2) to convert the feature vector of each word into two vectors $\vec{f^{head}} \in d^h$ and $\vec{f^{dep}} \in d^h$, respectively, to represent the head and dependent nodes of the dependency arc.

$$\vec{f_i^{head}} = MLP^{head}\vec{f_i} \quad (1)$$

$$f_i^{dep} = MLP^{dep}\vec{f_i} \quad (2)$$

Next, the position of the head node for each word i is calculated using a bilinear attention mechanism as per Equation (3), where $h_i^{arc} \in d^h$ represents the score for the j-th word as the head node of the i-th word. Here, $\mathbf{F^{dep}} \in \mathbf{d^{nh}}$ is a matrix obtained by concatenating the head representation $\vec{f_i^{head}}$ of all words in the sentence, where n is the number of words in the sentence. Additionally, $U \in d^{hh}$ is the parameter matrix, and $\vec{u} \in d^h$ is the parameter vector.

$$h_j^{arc} = \mathbf{F^{dep}}\mathbf{U}\mathbf{f_i^{dep}} + \mathbf{F^{head}}\mathbf{u} \quad (3)$$

Table 1: The types of Tibetan dependency arcs.

Item	Dependency Relationship	Label	Item	Dependency Relationship	Label
1	Subject predicate relationship	SBV	2	Direct object relationship	DOB
3	Indirect object relationship	IOB	4	Subject verb relationship	SBC
5	Predicative verb relationship	CPS	6	Modifier relationship	MOD
7	Apposition relationship	APP	8	Quantitative relationship	QUN
9	Constellation relationship	COO	10	Connection relationship	CON
11	Referential relationship	REF	12	Qualified relationship	DET
13	Negative relationship	NEG	14	Interrogative relationship	ITG
15	Location relationship	LOC	16	Time relationship	TMP
17	Expression relationship	EXP	18	Genitive relationship	GEN
19	Ergative relationship	ERG	20	Dative relationship	DAT
21	Comitative relationship	COG	22	Plural relationship	PLU
23	Honorific relationship	HON	24	Nominalized relationship	NML
25	ROOT relationship	ROOT	26	Tense and aspect relationship	TAM
27	Punctuation relationship	PUN	28	Description relationship	DES
29	Particle relationship	PAR	30	Target relationship	TAR
31	Auxiliary relationship	AUX	32	Manner relationship	MAN
33	Source relationship	SOU	34	Non-predicative verb relationship	PER

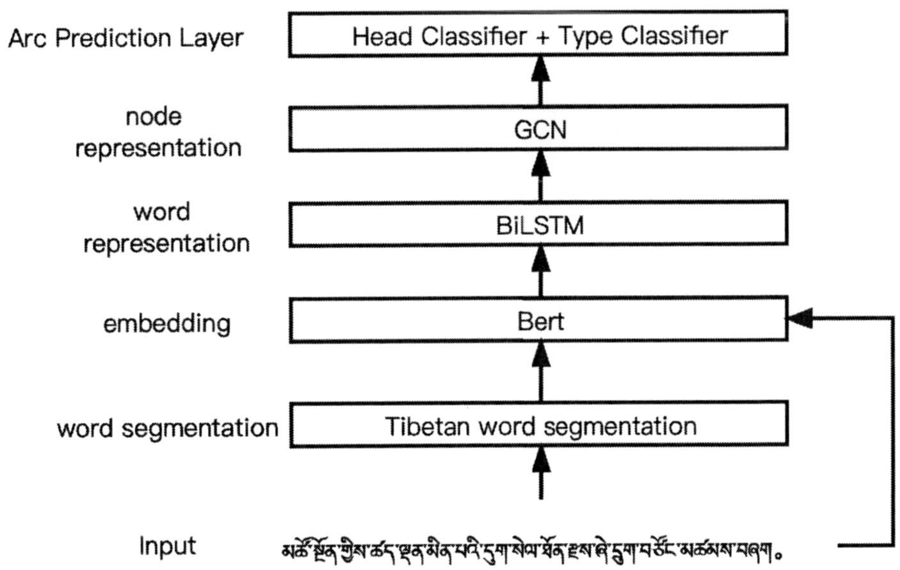

Figure 2: The framework of Tibetan dependency parsing.

Table 2: The statistics of the dataset.

Dataset	#Instances	Average Length
train	4970	6.8
validation	200	6.7
test	400	7.1

Finally, the head node with the highest score is selected as per Equation (4) to correspond to the word.

$$head_i = \max_{0<x<n} h_x \tag{4}$$

Type Classifier. The number of dependencies between head and dependent words is fixed, making this a fixed-class classification problem. To better model the dependency relationship between the head and dependent words, we use both the representations of the head and dependent words to predict the type of dependencies, as shown in Equation (5). Where j is the head word index of word i; $\mathbf{W_1} \in \mathbf{d^{f*m*f}}$ and $\mathbf{W_2} \in \mathbf{d^{2f*m}}$ a parameter matrix; m is the number of types of dependency arcs; $\vec{b} \in d^m$ is a parameter vector.

$$head_i^{label} = \vec{f}_j^T \mathbf{W_1} \vec{\mathbf{r}}_\mathbf{i} + (\vec{\mathbf{r}}_\mathbf{j} \oplus \vec{\mathbf{r}}_\mathbf{i})\mathbf{W_2} + \vec{\mathbf{b}} \tag{5}$$

The type of the dependency arc is predicted using Equation (6).

$$type_i = \max_{0<x<m} head_x^{label} \tag{6}$$

4 Experiments

In this section, we conduct experiments of Tibetan dependency analysis task on the dataset from (An and Long, 2021) .

4.1 Dataset

The dataset is divided into three parts: the training set, validation set, and test set. Table (2) displays the statistics of the dataset.

4.2 Evaluation Metrics

Four evaluation metrics are employed in this paper, as follows.

4.2.1 UAS

The unlabeled attachment score (UAS) is defined as the percentage of all words that have found their correct head word, including the root node. Notably, this metric does not consider the type of dependency arcs. UAS is calculated as per Equation (7), where N_{word}^{head} is the number of words labeled with the correct head word, and N_{word} represents the total number of words in the dataset.

$$UAS = \frac{N_{word}^{head}}{N_{word}} \tag{7}$$

4.2.2 LAS

The labeled attachment score (LAS) is defined as the percentage of all words that have the correct head word and the correct type of dependency arc, including the root node. LAS is calculated as per Equation (8), where N_{word}^{arc} is the number of words with the correct head word and type of dependency arc.

$$LAS = \frac{N_{word}^{arc}}{N_{word}} \tag{8}$$

4.2.3 UEM

The unlabeled exact match score (UEM) is defined as the percentage of sentences in which all the words have the correct head words. UEM is calculated using Equation (9), where $N_{sentence}^{head}$ is the number of sentences with correct head words for all their words, and $N_{sentence}$ is the total number of sentences in the dataset.

$$UEM = \frac{N_{sentence}^{head}}{N_{sentence}} \tag{9}$$

4.2.4 LEM

The labeled exact match score (LEM) is defined as the percentage of sentences in which all the words have the correct head words and type of dependency arcs. LEM is calculated using Equation (10), where $N_{sentence}^{arc}$ is the number of sentences with correct head words and type of dependency arcs for all their words.

$$UEM = \frac{N_{sentence}^{arc}}{N_{sentence}} \tag{10}$$

4.3 Experimental Settings

The validation set is utilized to determine the best hyperparameters for the model. The hyperparameters of the model are then set as follows: Tibetan-Roberta-base[1] is employed to

[1]https://huggingface.co/sangjeedondrub/tibetan-roberta-base

generate the embedding of Tibetan syllables, and the vectors are composed into word embeddings based on BiLSTM. The dimension of the word embedding is set at $d^w = 768$, whereas the dimension of the semantic role label is set at $d^l = 100$.

The dimension of the multi-layer perceptron matrix MLP^{head} is set at $768 * 100$, and the dimension of MLP^{dep} is also set at $768 * 100$. The model's dropout is set at 0.3, and it employs the adadelta optimizer, with the learning rate set at 0.001. All parameters are randomly initialized using a uniform distribution among $[-0.2, 0.2]$.

Moreover, we compare our model with deep learning-based Tibetan dependency parsing models, including word2vec + BiLSTM + MLP (DL-BiLSTM), word2vec + RNN + MLP (DL-RNN), word2vec + GRU + MLP (DL-RNN) and word2vec + Stacked LSTM + MLP (DL-Stacked) from (An and Long, 2021). And the word embedding is trained by fastText (Thavareesan and Mahesan, 2020). In addition, we compare our model with R-GCN (Schlichtkrull et al., 2018) with similar settings.

All experiments were conducted on a GPU server with a CPU configuration of 2* AMD Skyline 7742, 512G DDR4 RAM, and 4* Nvidia A100 40G GPU cards.

4.4 The Overall Experimental Results

The Tibetan dependency parser is designed to predict the head word and type of dependency arc for each word in a sentence. Our framework is implemented using Pytorch, and the overall results are presented in Table (4).

The experimental results demonstrate that the method proposed in this paper achieved the best performance on all four metrics, highlighting the value of graph neural networks in Tibetan dependency analysis. And our proposed method achieves better performances than R-GCN, we speculated that R-GCN requires more data to train the relation representation matrix, whereas our training data is sufficient to train the relation matrix effectively.

4.5 Ablation Study

To better understand the impact of different parts of the model on the experimental results, an ablation study was conducted to analyze the value of pre-trained language models and graph neural networks in Tibetan dependency analysis. The experimental results are presented in Table 3, where "- GCN + LSTM " represents our proposed model replacing GCN with LSTM, "-Bert + GCN" represents our proposed model replacing Bert with word2vec.

From these results, two conclusions can be drawn: (1) Graph neural networks significantly impact the performance of Tibetan dependency analysis, and using word embeddings as the lexical representation method can still improve the performance. (2) Tibetan pre-trained language models also hold value in Tibetan dependency analysis, and the performance of Tibetan dependency analysis declines to some extent when using word embeddings to replace the BERT model.

5 Conclusion

To address the issue of inadequate modeling of dependency graph information in current Tibetan dependency analysis methods, this paper proposes a graph neural network-based approach for Tibetan dependency analysis. Furthermore, a Tibetan pre-trained language model is employed to improve the performance further. The experimental results demonstrate the effectiveness of the graph neural network and the Tibetan pre-trained language model for enhancing Tibetan dependency analysis. Large models such as ChatGPT have recently achieved significant results in natural language processing tasks such as dialogue and knowledge extraction. In the future, we aim to explore large models for low-resource languages and their potential applications in low-resource scenarios.

6 Acknowledgments

This work is supported by the Natural Science Foundation of China (22BTQ010), the National Natural Science Foundation of China (62076233) and the Innovation Project major research of Chinese Academy of Social Sciences (2022MZSQN001).

References

Bo An and Congjun Long. 2021. Neural dependency parser for tibetan sentences. *Transactions*

Table 3: Overall results of various models on Tibetan dependency parsing datasets.

Model	UAS	LAS	UEM	LEM
DL-RNN	0.905	0.851	0.675	0.54
DL-GRU	0.913	0.865	0.677	0.565
DL-LSTM	0.918	0.867	0.687	0.560
DL-Stacked	0.912	0.864	0.680	0.570
R-GCN	0.907	0.852	0.630	0.542
Our model	**0.924**	**0.879**	**0.696**	**0.577**

Table 4: The result of ablation study.

Model	UAS	LAS	UEM	LEM
Our model	**0.924**	**0.879**	**0.696**	**0.577**
- GCN + LSTM	0.913	0.865	0.677	0.565
-Bert + GCN	0.918	0.867	0.687	0.560

on Asian and Low-Resource Language Information Processing, 20(2):1–16.

Daniel Andor, Chris Alberti, David J Weiss, Aliaksei Severyn, Alessandro Presta, Kuzman Ganchev, Slav Petrov, and Michael Collins. 2016. Globally normalized transition-based neural networks. *arXiv: Computation and Language.*

Qingxing Cao, Xiaodan Liang, Bailin Li, and Liang Lin. 2019. Interpretable visual question answering by reasoning on dependency trees. *IEEE Transactions on Pattern Analysis and Machine Intelligence.*

Danqi Chen and Christopher D Manning. 2014. A fast and accurate dependency parser using neural networks. pages 740–750.

Hao Cheng, Hao Fang, Xiaodong He, Jianfeng Gao, and Li Deng. 2016. Bi-directional attention with agreement for dependency parsing. *arXiv: Computation and Language.*

Jacob Devlin, Ming-Wei Chang, Kenton Lee, and Kristina Toutanova. 2018. Bert: Pre-training of deep bidirectional transformers for language understanding. *arXiv preprint arXiv:1810.04805.*

Timothy Dozat and Christopher D Manning. 2016. Deep biaffine attention for neural dependency parsing. *arXiv preprint arXiv:1611.01734.*

Jiecairang Duo, Quecairang Hua, Keyou Huan, and Rangdangzhi Cai. 2021. Transition based neural network dependency parsing of tibetan. In *MATEC Web of Conferences*, volume 336, page 06018. EDP Sciences.

Chris Dyer, Miguel Ballesteros, Wang Ling, Austin Matthews, and Noah A Smith. 2015. Transition-based dependency parsing with stack long short-term memory. *arXiv: Computation and Language.*

Christian Faggionato and Marieke Meelen. 2019. Developing the old Tibetan treebank. In *Proceedings of the International Conference on Recent Advances in Natural Language Processing (RANLP 2019)*, pages 304–312, Varna, Bulgaria. INCOMA Ltd.

Kazuma Hashimoto, Caiming Xiong, Yoshimasa Tsuruoka, and Richard Socher. 2016. A joint many-task model: Growing a neural network for multiple nlp tasks. *arXiv: Computation and Language.*

Quecairang Hua, Wenbing Jiang, Haixing Zhao, and Qun Liu. 2013. Semi-automatic building tibetan treebank based on word-pair dependency classification. *Journal of Chinese Information Processing.*

Weina Zhao Jian Wu Huidan Liu, Minghua Nuo and He Yeping. 2012. Segt:a practical tibetan word segmentation system. *Journal of Chinese information processing.*

Zhanming Jie, Aldrian Obaja Muis, and Wei Lu. 2017. Efficient dependency-guided named entity recognition. In *Thirty-First AAAI Conference on Artificial Intelligence.*

Eliyahu Kiperwasser and Yoav Goldberg. 2016. Simple and accurate dependency parsing using bidirectional lstm feature representations. *arXiv: Computation and Language.*

Adhiguna Kuncoro, Miguel Ballesteros, Lingpeng Kong, Chris Dyer, Graham Neubig, and Noah A Smith. 2016. What do recurrent neural network grammars learn about syntax. *arXiv: Computation and Language.*

Matthew E Peters, Mark Neumann, Mohit Iyyer, Matt Gardner, Christopher Clark, Kenton Lee, and Luke Zettlemoyer. 2018. Deep contextualized word representations. *arXiv: Computation and Language*.

Hua que-cai rang and Hai Xing Zhao. 2013. Tibetan text dependency syntactic analysis based on discriminant. *Computer Engineering*, 39(4):300–304.

Michael Schlichtkrull, Thomas N Kipf, Peter Bloem, Rianne Van Den Berg, Ivan Titov, and Max Welling. 2018. Modeling relational data with graph convolutional networks. In *The Semantic Web: 15th International Conference, ESWC 2018, Heraklion, Crete, Greece, June 3–7, 2018, Proceedings 15*, pages 593–607. Springer.

Tal Schuster, Ori Ram, Regina Barzilay, and Amir Globerson. 2019. Cross-lingual alignment of contextual word embeddings, with applications to zero-shot dependency parsing. *arXiv: Computation and Language*.

Tashi-Gyal and Duo-La. 2015. Theory and method of tibetan dependency treebank construction. *Journal of Tibet University*.

Sajeetha Thavareesan and Sinnathamby Mahesan. 2020. Sentiment lexicon expansion using word2vec and fasttext for sentiment prediction in tamil texts. In *2020 Moratuwa engineering research conference (MERCon)*, pages 272–276. IEEE.

Nima-Zhaxi Toudan Cairang and Wanme Zhaxi. 2018. Study on the technique of tibetan dependence treebank building. *Plateau Science Research*, 2(03):103–109.

Tianming Wang, Xiaojun Wan, and Hanqi Jin. 2020. Amr-to-text generation with graph transformer. *Transactions of the Association for Computational Linguistics*, 8:19–33.

XIA Wuji and HUAQUE Cairang. 2019. Dependency tree based tibetan semantic dependency analysis. *Journal of Tsinghua University (Science and Technology)*, 59(9):750–756.

Zou Xiaomei, Yang Jing, Zhang Jianpei, and Han Hongyu. 2018. Microblog sentiment analysis with weak dependency connections. *Knowledge-Based Systems*, 142:170–180.

Jie Zhou, Ganqu Cui, Shengding Hu, Zhengyan Zhang, Cheng Yang, Zhiyuan Liu, Lifeng Wang, Changcheng Li, and Maosong Sun. 2020. Graph neural networks: A review of methods and applications. *AI open*, 1:57–81.

On the Development of Interlinearized Ancient Literature of Ethnic Minorities: A Case Study of the Interlinearization of Ancient Written Tibetan Literature

Congjun Long and **Bo An**
Institute of Ethnology and Anthropology,Chinese Academy of Social Sciences
Building 6, Zhongguancun Nandajie 27, Beijing, China
{lcj,anbo}@cass.org.cn

Abstract

Ancient ethnic documents are essential to China's ancient literature and an indispensable civilizational achievement of Chinese culture. However, few research teams are involved due to language and script literacy limitations. To address these issues, this paper proposes an interlinearized annotation strategy for ancient ethnic literature. This strategy aims to alleviate text literacy difficulties, encourage interdisciplinary researchers to participate in studying ancient ethnic literature and improve the efficiency of ancient ethnic literature development. The interlinearized annotation consists of original, word segmentation, Latin, annotated, and translation lines. In this paper, we take ancient Tibetan literature as an example to explore the interlinearized annotation strategy. However, manually building a large-scale corpus is challenging. To build a large-scale interlinearized dataset, we propose a multi-task learning-based interlinearized annotation method, which can generate interlinearized annotation lines based on the original line. Experimental results show that after training on about 10,000 sentences (lines) of data, our model achieves 70.9% and 63.2% F1 values on the segmentation lines and annotated lines, respectively, and 18.7% BLEU on the translation lines. It dramatically enhances the efficiency of data annotation, effectively speeds up interlinearized annotation, and reduces the workload of manual annotation.

1 Introduction

The excellent traditional culture of ethnicity is an essential part of Chinese culture, an important cultural heritage of the Chinese nation, and a valuable asset to human civilization. Many excellent traditional cultures have been recorded in ancient ethnic literature (Bender, 2015), some of which record the process of creating the great history of the Chinese nation together and the vivid facts of exchanges and interactions among various ethnic groups. They contain rich national unity and progress ideas and are necessary historical resources for witnessing the Community of the Chinese Nation (Meng et al., 2023). Therefore, the in-depth excavation of ancient ethnic literature is conducive to promoting traditional Chinese culture and showing the historical events of the formation of Sense of Community for the Chinese Nation (Long et al., 2023).

China is rich in ancient ethnic literature, but studying ancient ethnic literature faces many difficulties. First, the degree of digitization is relatively low due to the lack of public resources; second, limited by language and script literacy, the group of ancient ethnic literature research and utilization is small. In exploring the formation of Chinese civilization and promoting Chinese culture, how more disciplines and researchers pay attention to, study, develop, utilize, and popularize the excellent traditional culture contained in ancient ethnic books is an issue worth exploring. The General Office of the CPC Central Committee and the General Office of the State Council issued the Opinions on Promoting the Work of Ancient Books in the New Era, emphasizing the need to encourage interdisciplinary research methods. The 'text structuring', 'knowledge systemization' and 'intelligent utilization' of ancient books are actively carried out (Lei et al., 2022).

The documentary properties and unique cultural attributes of minority antiquarian literature have made it a focus of interdisciplinary experts and a laboratory for interdisciplinary research (Long et al., 2023). However, constructing most ancient ethnic literature re-

Proceedings of the Ancient Language Processing Workshop associated with RANLP-2023, pages 222–231,
held in Varna Bulgaria, Sept 8, 2023.
https://doi.org/10.26615/978-954-452-087-8_025

sources is still difficult to meet the needs of multiple disciplines. For example, experts in computational linguistics focus on the information processing of ancient ethnic documents and need a cooked corpus with information on word segmentation, annotation, entity recognition, and translation, and then carry out deep text mining. Experts in the field of library intelligence explore the collection, collation, cataloging, and citation of multi-language ethnic ancient texts from the perspective of knowledge organization and knowledge management of ancient texts, and build catalog search libraries and full-text search libraries to serve readers better. Linguistics researchers are concerned about the phonology, vocabulary, and grammar of the national languages in the multi-language ancient ethnic document to assist in the construction of the ancient Chinese phonetic system, analysis and comparison of the Chinese and the people's language relations, to explore the language homology differentiation clues, summarize the phonetic, lexical and grammatical type characteristics and the evolutionary path of the language. Researchers in history focus on historical elements such as time, place, people, and events in the ancient texts of multi-language ethnic groups and explore the political systems, economic systems, social histories, and foreign exchanges of different ethnic groups. Scholars in ethnic culture explore the traditional culture, folk customs, cultural heritage, and traditional handicrafts recorded in the ancient texts of multilingual ethnic groups. Experts in religion, philosophy, art, and traditional medicine also hope to obtain the knowledge they need from multilingual ethnic literature.

To better meet the needs of multidisciplinary utilization of ancient ethnic texts, this paper proposes a strategy of interlinearized annotation of ethnic ancient texts, converting the content of ethnic ancient texts into five lines of data, namely, the original line (original line), the line of folk language sub-word (segmentation line), the line of Latin alphabet transcription (transcription line), the line of grammar annotation (annotation line) and the line of Chinese meaning translation (translation line). Researchers from different disciplines can use these annotations to analyze and study the literature content. In conducting interlinearized annotation research, manual annotation was mainly used in the early stage. With the accumulation of annotation data, this paper proposes a multi-tasking framework based on deep learning to automatically generate interlinearized annotation data to assist manual annotation and finally build a large-scale textual structured database of ancient ethnic literature to lay the data foundation for further development and utilization of ancient ethnic documents in multiple disciplines.

2 Related Work

China is a multi-ethnic country, and in the long history of the formation and development of the Chinese nation, people of all ethnic groups have shared honor and disgrace and are closely related to each other, creating Chinese civilization and culture together. The multilingual chapter-aligned, sentence-aligned, and word-aligned historical documents handed down or excavated archaeologically are the best proof of the exchange and intermingling of people from all ethnic groups.

Among the Chinese and Tibetan bilingual aligned historical documents, chapter-aligned documents are the most numerous, followed by sentence-aligned and less word-aligned documents. Chapter-aligned documents are both translated from Chinese into ethnic texts, such as the four ancient Tibetan translations of the Shang Shu Zhou Shu (Wong, 2016) in the first collection of the 1978 Paris photocopy of the Selected Tibetan Documents of the Bibliothèque Nationale de French; there are also translations from ethnic texts into Chinese, such as the oath on the west side of the Tang-Fan Alliance monument, which is a Chinese-Tibetan aligned sentence pair (Li F G, 2007). Most of the materials in the form of word control are found in the dictionary category and word list categories, such as the Great Collection of Translation Nominalities (Z, 2013), the Dunhuang Tibetan texts P.T. 1257 and P.T. 1261 (X, 2014), and the Imperial Five-Style Qing Wenjian (Q, 2000). However, there are not many materials on the full-text word alignment of ancient literature texts. Scholars of linguistics who study ancient ethnic literature often have to translate the documents.

In general, the source and translated texts are still aligned in terms of chapter alignment, such as the translation of Baxie (Supplementary Text) (Ba S N, 1990), the Chinese translation of the History of Buddhism in Buton (Bu D, 2007), and the Tibetan King's Tale (Suo N J Z, 2002), among others. However, some scholars have also adopted the word-alignment model, such as the Study of Tibetan Fatwas in the 8th-9th centuries (Z, 2007), etc. Linguistic researchers have been more rigorous in organizing documentary materials, especially in dialectal and ethnolinguistic materials, and have mostly adopted the word alignment model. This paradigm is used for language text materials in the Chinese Ethnolinguistic Compendium Series, the Newly Discovered Languages of China Series, and the Endangered Languages of China Series. For example, an example of the annotated text for the language of the security language on page 1918 of Languages of China.

The German publishing house Lincom GmbH has been funding the publication of interlinearly annotated corpora and scholarly works in minor languages worldwide for many years. Tikaram Poudel published Rajbanshi Grammar and Interlinearized Text (an Indo-Aryan language of Nepal and Bengal) in 2006 (Poudel, 2006); Karnakhar Khatiwada published A Reference Grammar in 2017 of Dhimal (King, 2008) describing writings and text annotation Interlinearized texts in Dhimal with Grammar notes (Khatiwada, 2017) (interlinearized annotated texts in Dhimal). To date, the publisher has published more than 500 works in small languages. Sino-Tibetan linguists Randy J. LaPolla & Dory Poa also published Rawang Texts grammatically annotated texts at Lincom Europa (LaPolla and Poa, 2001).

Computer experts have developed interlinearized annotation tools to assist linguists in advancing interlinearized annotation successfully. The American Standard Interchange Language (SIL) organization has developed Toolbox [1] annotation tool; British scholars have developed Eudico Linguistic Annotator (ELAN) annotation tool [2], and French scholars adopted the Interlinear Text Editor software (ITE) technology. Chinese scholars have used Toolbox tool to organize and publish the series 'Grammatical Annotated Texts of Chinese Ethnic Languages' (D, 2016), which is a total of 20 books covering 20 languages or dialects of five principal language families or groups in China, namely Tibetan-Burmese, Miao-Yao, Dong-Tai, South Asian and Altaic, with a total word count of about 10 million words. These software tools are widely used in the linguistic community, making it easier and faster for linguists to annotate the corpus and enhancing the standardization of corpus annotation. However, the common drawback is that they mainly rely on manual operations and fail to introduce natural language processing techniques for low-resource languages, especially natural language information techniques.

Interlinearized annotation is similar to the goal of word alignment in machine translation, where the word alignment technique is to obtain word boundaries in sentence pairs and achieve translation alignment based on bilingual pairs, which is a core task in machine translation (Bahdanau et al., 2014). However, the research results devoted to word alignment methods belong to the early stage of statistical machine translation. With the development of ethnolinguistic information processing and the promotion of the 'One Belt, One Road' strategy, machine translation of low-resource languages has become a popular research topic (Ranathunga et al., 2023), and some research results discussing the word alignment between Chinese and Mandarin have appeared. For example, Zhao Yang and Zhou Long discussed the Min-Chinese scarce resource neural machine translation technique (Zhao Yang, 2019); (Su L Y, 2018) discussed the word alignment method in Mongolian-Chinese machine translation; (Liu J M, 2011). Studied the Han-Vi word alignment. However, the current machine translation commonly adopts deep neural network technology, which does not need to discuss word alignment methods separately.

In recent years, the concepts of 'exploring the origin of Chinese civilization' and 'forging a sense of Chinese national community' have been proposed, and interdisciplinary fields have jointly focused on transcribed texts of

[1] https://software.sil.org/software-products/

[2] http://sites.bu.edu/elsa/elan-coding/

ethnic minority oral discourse and ancient ethnic literature. The increasing demand for interlinearized annotation of ethnic texts has made interlinearized annotation a research paradigm. However, it is challenging to meet the needs of multidisciplinary and multilingual interlinearized annotated corpus by manual annotation. This paper combines the linguistic fine-grained annotation paradigm and multi-tasking techniques to conduct automatic interlinearized annotation.

3 Ancient Ethnic Literature Interlinearized Annotation

3.1 The Format of Ancient Literature Interlinearized Annotation

The target of interlinearized annotation is the full text of ancient ethnic literature without explicit markers between words, which need to be divided into 'words' for the full text, and then convert the traditional ethnic script into Latin transcription or international phonetic symbols by word. The words are translated into the other language, and the function words are marked with their grammatical function. The grammatical functions are labeled with English abbreviation tags common to the linguistic community. The final output consists of a line of the original language, a Latin transcription or an International Phonetic Alphabet line corresponding to the line of the minor language, and a line of the translation marker. Under the current technical conditions, meaningful translation lines cannot be obtained automatically and need to be translated manually. Figure 1 takes Tibetan as an example to show an example of interlinearized annotation.

The original line is the original text of the ethnic literature. The segment line is a unit of words (partly morphemes and phrases), a 'word' or 'word suffix' for the input text. However, 'word' is the most basic unit for the machine to understand the text. To satisfy the deep analysis and mining of the text, marking the word boundary is the most basic task. The materials of ancient texts marked with word boundaries help users understand ancient texts. They can be used for training to develop automatic lexical analysis tools for ancient texts, providing resources to support the information processing of ancient literature.

The transcription lines are ethnic texts transcribed in Latin alphabet or the international phonetic alphabet. The aim is to create a cross-reference database of ethnic scripts in syllables. The annotation line: the meaningful words in the annotated lines are translated into Chinese or English. Function words are marked with the abbreviated form of their grammatical function in English, and the abbreviated form often uses a combination of capital letters, which comes from the English word 'AGENT' and semantically indicates the administration of things. This internationally accepted grammatical mark is conducive to the dissemination of national ancient literature materials to the world. The translation line is the Chinese or English translation of the original line.

3.2 The Schema of Ancient Literature Interlinearized Annotation

Designing symbols for interlinearized annotation requires consideration of the usage needs of ancient ethnic literature, which have been discussed earlier. For the same ancient ethnic literature, different researchers have different needs. Such as syllogisms, word segmentation, and named entity recognition are common needs for researchers. Semantic annotation is a common need for linguistics-related disciplines such as syntax and language information services. Named entity annotation (NER) is a common need for history and literature, etc. Chinese translation of meaningful words is closely related to machine translation. This paper focuses on syntactic and semantic annotation and entity annotation, whose annotation materials can meet the needs of most disciplines. Grammatical and semantic annotation can reflect functional words' grammatical meaning and semantic function. Entity annotation includes proper names such as person, place, and time. Labels for function words are generally composed of two or three letters, taking the first three letters of the English word. If repetition is encountered, the abbreviated letters are modified as appropriate. When a grammatical function requires more than one English word to be represented, the appropriate combination of letters from multiple words is selected. The combination of labels also fol-

Type	Content
Origin Line	དེ་བློན་པོས་རྗེའི་སྙན་དུ་གསོལ□
Segment Line	དེ བློན་པོ□/ས རྗེ□/འི སྙན་□ དུ གསོལ་ ས□
Latin Line	de blon po s rje vi snyan du gsol pas
Annotation Line	DEM 大臣 AGE 王 GEN 耳朵 ALL 禀报 CLC
Translated Line	大臣把那（情况）禀报到国王的耳朵里……

Figure 1: The example of Tibetan interlinearized annotation.

lows specific rules, and the linguistic community usually adopts the Leipzig Terminology Rules (The Leipzig Glossing Rules) system [3], which was jointly developed by the Department of Linguistics of the Max Planck Institute for Evolutionary Anthropology and the Department of Linguistics of the University of Leipzig. In our study of interlinearized annotation of ancient civil texts, the Leipzig labeling system was employed as the primary basis, with the addition of some labels. The tagging system includes person and number, grammatical, tense, tone, mood, demonstrative, special word classes, syntax, noun-pronoun correlative markers. The grammatical tags employed for interlinear annotation will vary with the degree of refinement of the corpus, and the tags listed here are only the main ones. Some minority language scripts require an extension of the tagging system according to specific needs but keep the basic system unchanged. The NLP-based NER is adopted.

4 Human-computer Interaction Interlinearized Annotation Platform

Corpus annotation is time-consuming and labor-intensive; however, annotated corpora can provide essential resources for ancient literature research and are indispensable. With enough training corpus, NLP algorithms can assist corpus annotation, such as NER, relation extraction, text classification, and machine translation. The corpus annotation is also a common task in NLP. The interlinearized annotation of ancient ethnic literature is a pioneering work, and by manually annotating a certain scale of training data, the NLP algorithms can assist in data annotation.

To advance the research in this paper, we have developed a semi-automated interlinearized annotation platform. The interlinearized annotation platform mainly has the following modules.

(1) Interlinearized annotation operation module. This module completes the task of interlinear annotation in the original language of ancient ethnic literature and accomplishes four main functions:

(a) Automatic conversion from the original language to the transcription line. The conversion from the original Chinese text to the Latin alphabet depends on the mapping table between the original syllables and the Latin syllables. For example, the Tibetan to-Latin conversion collects about 28,000 syllables, including modern Tibetan, ancient Tibetan, Sanskrit syllables transcribed in Tibetan characters and punctuation marks. Also, it includes syllables that conform to Tibetan spelling rules but do not exist in existing literature.

(b) Automatic word segmentation. The interlinearized annotation is based on the annotation of words (or phrases), and word segmentation is a necessary process.

(c) Annotation line including meaningful word translations and grammatical labels. To be compatible with various text editors and convenient for different researchers, the interlinear annotation results are stored as XML format files, with a set of brackets {} to indicate the four levels of interlinear corresponding lexical entries, which are filled in with the morphological analysis before the split form, Latin transcription, morphological analysis after the Latin transcription and annotation information, respectively.

(d) Manual proofreading. Manual proofreading needs to do three checking aspects: filling in vacant paraphrases, correcting paraphrase errors due to multiple meanings, and annotation errors due to subtext errors.

[3]https://www.eva.mpg.de/lingua/resources/glossing-rules.php

(e) Batch export and import of annotation data: to reduce the workload of manual annotation, the import and export of data are supported after a certain number of interlinear annotation data are completed.

(f) Interlinearized annotation corpus retrieval module. This module supports structured retrieval and can meet the needs of general literature information retrieval, such as the retrieval of Latin transcriptions of ethnic scripts, pairs of translated words and labels; the extraction of cross-referenced word lists, the extraction of named entities, and other functions.

5 Automatic Interlinear Annotation Method based on Multi-task Learning

5.1 Method

In this paper, we propose NLP method to promote the interlinearized annotation of ancient ethnic literature for deep analysis and exploration. In the previous work, we have annotated a dataset of ancient Tibetan interlinearized annotation, so we take ancient Tibetan as an example to introduce the automatic generation method of interlinearized annotation based on deep learning, and the interlinearized annotation of other ethnic ancient literature is similar to ancient Tibetan. The interlinearized annotation dataset of ancient Tibetan includes original, segmentation, Latin, annotated, and translation lines. Among them, the segmentation lines are obtained by automatic word segmentation based on the original lines (Liu H D, 2012), the Latin lines can be transcribed directly by the Tibetan-Latin conversion table, and the annotation lines are generated based on the segmentation lines with corresponding meaningful words and function words annotated. The original line, the syllogism line, and the annotated line are all valuable for generating translation lines. Therefore, the ancient Tibetan interlinearized annotation model is mainly used to generate segmentation, annotated, and translation lines. Translation lines are translations from Tibetan sentences to Chinese sentences, which belong to the research scope of machine translation. Regarding the current research base, the generation of Chinese lines is more complex and requires human intervention. The model's input is the original line, and the output is the content of the segmentation line, the annotation line and the translation line. The information of the annotated line depends on the content of the segmentation line, and the information of the translation line depends on the information of both the segmentation line and the annotated line. Therefore, the pipeline model (Li et al., 2020) is employed in modeling, and its architecture is shown in Figure 4-a. The pipeline approach consists of three models: (1) the word segmentation model: the input of this model is the original line, and the output is the result of the word segmentation line; (2) the annotation model: the input of this model is the information of the original line and the word segmentation line, and the output is the result of the annotation line; (3) the translation model: the input of this model is the original line, the word segmentation line and the annotation line, and the output is the result of the translation line. The pipeline method splices the outputs and inputs of different models, such as using the output of the segmentation line as the input of the annotation line, which facilitates the implementation of the model. However, the pipeline method suffers from problems such as error propagation. For example, the segmentation model can only utilize the information of the original text line, but the information of the annotation line also has important value for the segmentation model, and the error of the segmentation line may cause the obvious error of the annotation line information. However, since the models are independent, the error information cannot be effectively transferred to the segmentation model, and this part of the information cannot be utilized.

Recently, multi-task learning models replaced pipeline-based models in several fields, such as segmentation and annotation models, named entity recognition and entity linking models (Nguyen and Grishman, 2015). The advantage of multi-task learning models is that they can make full use of the correlation between different tasks, e.g., there is a strong correlation between the Tibetan word segmentation and lexical annotation tasks, and the results of word segmentation determine the text block boundaries of linguistic annotation. In contrast, the results of lexical annotation can, in turn, verify whether there are errors in the word segmentation results. Therefore, multi-task learning approaches are widely applied due to the advantages in modeling multiple related tasks. Interlinearized annotation requires the generation of corresponding segmentation lines, annotated lines, and translation lines based on the original text lines, a typical multiple-related task suitable for modeling using a multi-task learning framework.

Based on the above analysis, this paper designs a multi-task model to conduct the word segmentation, annotation, and translation models. The model's input is the original text line, and the shared coding layer encodes the input information. Then, different upper-layer models are used to model the output tasks (word segmentation, annotation, and translation lines). The word segmentation model, the annotation model, and the translation model share the embedding layer (Embedding) (Lai et al., 2016) and the encoding layer (Bi-directional Long Short-Term Memory, BiLSTM) (An et al., 2018; An and Long, 2021), and the word segmentation line is based on the original line, and the words are segmented from each other using spaces. Therefore, in this paper, the word segmentation is modeled as a sequential annotation task, and the task layer uses Conditional Random Field (Sutton et al., 2012). The annotation line contains grammatical annotation information and word translation information for a sequence generation task, which is modeled as an encoder-decoder sequence generation task in this paper. The translation line is the translation of the original line content into Chinese, which is a typical machine translation task, and is also modeled as an encoder-decoder sequence generation task in this paper (Guo et al., 2019).

5.2 Experimental Settings

To verify the effectiveness of the interlinearized annotation model, we completed four interlinearized annotated ancient Tibetan literature, Baxie (Ba S N, 1990), Weixie, Zhumian Shi (Bu D, 2007), and Di Wu Shiji (Schneider, 2002), through the annotation platform. The dataset consists of 12,284 sentences, and we divide it into the training set, development set, and test set according to the scale of 8:1:1.

5.3 Experimental Settings

This section describes the implementation framework and hyperparameters employed in the experiments. We utilize Pytorch to implement a multi-task model. The dimension of Tibetan syllables is 100; the coding layer is BiLSTM. We employ CRF to implement word segmentation tasks. In the annotation task, we decode the sequences using a single-layer BiLSTM to generate grammatical function labels. We use a single-layer BiLSTM to generate the translation line in the translation task. This paper employs the pipeline-based model as the baseline, including the BiLSTM+CRF-based word segmentation model, BiLSTM+BiLSTM-based annotation model, and encoder-decoder-based translation model. These models are trained separately, with input and output data transfer and information interaction. This paper employs Precision, Recall, and F1-value to evaluate the results of the segmentation line and annotation line. We employ BLEU (Papineni et al., 2002) to evaluate the result of the translation line.

5.4 Experimental Result

We conduct three sets of experiments: the first set of experiments adopts a multi-task learning approach, aiming to implement interlinearized annotation of ancient Tibetan literature, generating segmentation lines, annotated lines, and translation lines based on the original lines; the second set of experiments is a stripping experiment, using a multi-task learning approach to model segmentation lines and annotated lines, segmentation lines and translation lines, and annotated lines and translation lines, respectively, to analyze the effect of joint learning of different tasks; the third set of experiments utilizes a pipeline model as a baseline model to compare the performance of proposed models.

5.5 Experimental Results

The input of this experiment is the original text line, and the output includes the segmentation line (Seg), the annotation line (Ann), and the translation line (Tra). The experimental results are shown in Table 1. The experimental results show that the multi-task learning-based model (Multi) proposed in this paper significantly improves all of the three tasks of segmentation lines, annotation lines, and translation lines (6.7%, 15.6% and 32.6%, respectively). The multi-task learning-based model achieved better performance than the pipeline model (Pipe). Therefore, the multi-task-based model can achieve better performance in interlinearized annotation task.

Task	Model	P	R	F	BLEU
Seg	Mult	74.2	67.8	70.9	-
	Pipe	68.2	64.7	66.4	-
Ann	Mult	66.2	60.4	63.2	-
	Pipe	54.1	55.2	54.6	-
Tra	Mult	-	-	-	18.7
	Pipe	-	-	-	14.1

Table 1: The result of multi-task learning model.

5.6 Ablation Study

5.7 Ablation Study

The ablation study aims to analyze the effect of different task combinations. In this experiment, group A (segmentation model + annotation model), group B (segmentation model + translation model), and group C (annotation model + translation model). Table 2 shows the results of the three experimental groups of experiments. Based on the experimental results, we can draw the following conclusions: (a) In both groups of multi-task learning in which the segmentation model participates, the segmentation result improves (F1 value 66.4%), indicating that the results of both the annotated lines and the translation lines can improve the performance of the segmentation model; (b) The segmentation model achieves better results in the results of group A, indicating that the annotation line provides better feedback to the segmentation model than the translation line; (c) In group A, the multi-task model achieves better results than the pipeline model, indicating that the annotation model can give effective feedback to the segmentation model. However, the performance of the annotated rows in group C experiments has a significant decrease, indicating that the information of the segmentation rows has an essential impact on the results of the annotated line; (d) The results of translation lines in both groups B and C decreased compared with the multi-task learning model but better than the pipeline-based model, indicating that the information of both segmentation lines and annotated lines has auxiliary value for the translation model.

Task	Model	P	R	F	BLEU
A	Seg	72.1	66.2	69.0	-
	Ann	60.3	59.4	59.8	-
B	Seg	71.8	66.0	68.8	-
	Tra	-	-	-	15.3
C	Ann	50.3	48.2	49.2	-
	Tra	-	-	-	14.7

Table 2: The result of ablation study.

6 Conclusion

In this paper, we discuss the idea and vision of interlinearized annotation of ancient ethnic literature from the perspective of data resource normalization and sharing. Taking ancient Tibetan literature as an example, we propose accumulating corpus based on manual interlinearized annotation and then using machine learning to conduct automatic annotation. This research provides a new research paradigm for developing and utilizing ancient ethnic literature in China, especially the structured data of interlinearized annotation, which lays a good foundation for ancient literature development and utilization. In the future, we plan to construct ancient language knowledge based on an interlinearized annotation dataset.

7 Acknowledgments

This work is supported by the Natural Science Foundation of China (22BTQ010), the National Natural Science Foundation of China (62076233) and the Innovation Project major research of Chinese Academy of Social Sciences (2022MZSQN001).

References

Bo An, Bo Chen, Xianpei Han, and Le Sun. 2018. Accurate text-enhanced knowledge graph representation learning. In *Proceedings of the 2018 Conference of the North American Chapter of the Association for Computational Linguistics: Human Language Technologies, Volume 1 (Long Papers)*, pages 745–755.

Bo An and Congjun Long. 2021. Neural dependency parser for tibetan sentences. *Transactions on Asian and Low-Resource Language Information Processing*, 20(2):1–16.

Tong J H Ba S N. 1990. *Ba Xie*, volume 10. Sichuan Ethnic Publishing House.

Dzmitry Bahdanau, Kyunghyun Cho, and Yoshua Bengio. 2014. Neural machine translation by jointly learning to align and translate. *arXiv preprint arXiv:1409.0473*.

Mark Bender. 2015. Ethnic minority literature. *A Companion to Modern Chinese Literature*, pages 261–275.

Pi W C Bu D. 2007. *History of Budun Buddhism*, volume 9. Gansu Ethnic Publishing House.

Jiang D. 2016. Chinese national language grammar annotation text series. *(No Title)*.

Wenzhong Guo, Jianwen Wang, and Shiping Wang. 2019. Deep multimodal representation learning: A survey. *Ieee Access*, 7:63373–63394.

Karnakhar Khatiwada. 2017. *Interlinearized Texts in Dhimal with Grammar Notes.* Lincom Europa.

John Timothy King. 2008. *A grammar of Dhimal.* Ph.D. thesis, Leiden University.

Siwei Lai, Kang Liu, Shizhu He, and Jun Zhao. 2016. How to generate a good word embedding. *IEEE Intelligent Systems*, 31(6):5–14.

Randy J LaPolla and Dory Poa. 2001. *Rawang texts*, volume 18. Lincom Europa.

Yuying Lei, Xilong Hou, Xiaoguang Wang, et al. 2022. The logic and approach of digital reconstruction of ancient books in the data intelligence. *Digital Human Research*, 2(2):46.

Jing Li, Aixin Sun, Jianglei Han, and Chenliang Li. 2020. A survey on deep learning for named entity recognition. *IEEE Transactions on Knowledge and Data Engineering*, 34(1):50–70.

Ke W N. W Q L Li F G. 2007. *Study on Ancient Tibet*, volume 1. Beijing Tsinghua University Press.

Zhao W N Liu H D, Nuo M H. 2012. Segt: A practical tibetan word segmentation system. *Journal of Chinese Information Processing*, 26(1):97–103.

Ai S Liu J M, Tu R G. 2011. Research on statistical machine translation-based chinese-uyghur word alignment. *Computer Applications and Software*, 28(4):57–59.

Congjun Long, Bo An, and Shengyan Zhang. 2023. Research on the construction of knowledge graph of old tibetan inscriptions. *Library And Information Service*, 67(8):141.

Linglei Meng, Jingnan Xing, and Mingyan Tan. 2023. Exploration of cultivating a sense of community for the chinese nation in" data structures" course teaching. *International Journal of Education and Humanities*, 7(3):136–139.

Thien Huu Nguyen and Ralph Grishman. 2015. Relation extraction: Perspective from convolutional neural networks. In *Proceedings of the 1st workshop on vector space modeling for natural language processing*, pages 39–48.

Kishore Papineni, Salim Roukos, Todd Ward, and Wei-Jing Zhu. 2002. Bleu: a method for automatic evaluation of machine translation. In *Proceedings of the 40th annual meeting of the Association for Computational Linguistics*, pages 311–318.

Tikaram Poudel. 2006. *Rajbanshi grammar and interlinearized text*, volume 34. Lincom.

Jiang Q. 2000. A textual research on the compilation of qing wenjian in imperial four and five styles.

Surangika Ranathunga, En-Shiun Annie Lee, Marjana Prifti Skenduli, Ravi Shekhar, Mehreen Alam, and Rishemjit Kaur. 2023. Neural machine translation for low-resource languages: A survey. *ACM Computing Surveys*, 55(11):1–37.

Hanna Schneider. 2002. Tibetan legal documents of south-western tibet: structure and style. In *Proceedings of the Ninth Seminar of the IATS, 2000. Volume 1: Tibet, Past and Present*, pages 415–427. Brill.

Niu X H Su L Y, Zhao Y P. 2018. The study on ethnic-to-chinese scare-resource neural machine translation. *Journal of Chinese Information Processing*, 32(6):44–51.

Liu Q L Suo N J Z. 2002. *Tibet Wangtongji*, volume 2. Nationalities Publishing House.

Charles Sutton, Andrew McCallum, et al. 2012. An introduction to conditional random fields. *Foundations and Trends® in Machine Learning*, 4(4):267–373.

Sun-tik Wong. 2016. The critical study of political pbligation in zhou shu of shang shu and liji=" shang shu, zhou shu" ji" li ji"'zheng zhi yi wu'zhi yan jiu. *HKU Theses Online (HKUTO)*.

Dang Z Z X. 2014. Ancient tibetan dictionary.

Huang W Z. 2007. *Research on Tibetan vows in the 8th and 9th centuries*, volume 8. Nationalities Publishing House.

Zhang Y Z. 2013. A collection of translated names – the origin of tibetan bilingual dictionary.

Wang Qian etc Zhao Yang, Zhou Long. 2019. The study on ethnic-to-chinese scare-resource neural machine translation. *Journal of Jiangxi Normal University*, 43(6):630–637.

Author Index

Association for Computational Linguistics
209 N. Eighth Street
Stroudsburg, Pennsylvania 18360

ISBN 978-1-7138-9044-7

CURRAN ASSOCIATES INC.
proceedings.com